Disseminating Jewish Literatures

Disseminating Jewish Literatures

Knowledge, Research, Curricula

Edited by
Susanne Zepp, Ruth Fine, Natasha Gordinsky,
Kader Konuk, Claudia Olk and Galili Shahar

DE GRUYTER

ISBN 978-3-11-061899-0
e-ISBN (PDF) 978-3-11-061900-3
e-ISBN (EPUB) 978-3-11-061907-2

This work is licensed under a Creative Commons Attribution-NonCommercial-NoDerivatives 4.0 License. For details go to https://creativecommons.org/licenses/by-nc-nd/4.0/.

Library of Congress Control Number: 2020908027

Bibliographic information published by the Deutsche Nationalbibliothek
The Deutsche Nationalbibliothek lists this publication in the Deutsche Nationalbibliografie; detailed bibliographic data are available on the Internet at http://dnb.dnb.de.

© 2020 Susanne Zepp, Ruth Fine, Natasha Gordinsky,
Kader Konuk, Claudia Olk and Galili Shahar
published by Walter de Gruyter GmbH, Berlin/Boston
Cover image: FinnBrandt / E+ / Getty Images
Printing and binding: CPI books GmbH, Leck

www.degruyter.com

Introduction

This volume is dedicated to the rich multilingualism and polyphony of Jewish literary writing. It offers an interdisciplinary array of suggestions on issues of research and teaching related to further promoting the integration of modern Jewish literary studies into the different philological disciplines. It collects the proceedings of the Gentner Symposium funded by the Minerva Foundation, which was held at the Freie Universität Berlin from June 27 to 29, 2018. During this three-day symposium at the Max Planck Society's Harnack House, more than fifty scholars from a wide range of disciplines in modern philology discussed the integration of Jewish literature into research and teaching. Among the participants were specialists in American, Arabic, German, Hebrew, Hungarian, Romance and Latin American, Slavic, Turkish, and Yiddish literature as well as comparative literature. The symposium was conceived and carried out in cooperation between the Freie Universität Berlin, the Hebrew University of Jerusalem, Tel Aviv University, the University of Haifa, and the University of Duisburg-Essen.

One point of departure for the joint initiative resulting in the publication of this volume was a conversation about the fact that there is no permanent chair for Hebrew literature in Germany. While Hebrew literature is a subject at universities worldwide, it surprisingly seems to be somewhat neglected in Germany. When we conducted a sample examination of the course catalogues from the last ten semesters at the fifteen largest German universities in German, Slavic, American, Romance, and comparative literary studies, we discovered that Jewish literatures were not adequately represented in academic teaching. As a result, students are neither given the chance to study key texts of world literature nor the literary works in which many of the challenges of our present moment are negotiated. Further discussion with European colleagues made it evident that this is not a phenomenon restricted to Germany: major modern Jewish texts written in Arabic, French, German, Hungarian, Polish, Portuguese, Spanish, Russian, Turkish, and Yiddish do not form an integral part of their respective national philologies in Germany, Europe, Israel, Latin America, or the United States. A third issue under discussion was the state of diasporic literatures in courses on Hebrew literature in Israel. More generally, we observed that in our current BA and MA courses, the focus on teaching the basic gist of relevant understudied texts leaves very little room to introduce our students to a fuller range of world literature. Similarly, our day-to-day teaching routine sometimes neglects more profound methodological reflections. Thus, the editors of this volume have joined forces with scholars from different philological disciplines drawing on different historical focuses and methodological approaches in order to develop concrete proposals on how to address this lacuna, based on case studies from various language cultures.

Despite its inherent transnationality, much of the research into Jewish literatures continues to unfold within a national framework—an approach that is also traceable in hyphenated terms such as "Jewish-American" or "German-Jewish". In addition, the significance of analyzing and comparing what constitutes "Jewishness" in a German or Turkish, Christian or Muslim, literary context must be taken into account. The fact that Islam has now become the second largest religious community in Europe shifts the discourse on Jewish literatures in unprecedented ways. We must react to this. The process of modernization that Judaism has undergone, and which can be traced in its literary history, offers ample opportunity to connect with the challenges that Muslim cultures are facing. Precisely because our students have diverse backgrounds, we need to emphasize the numerous connections in a historicizing perspective rather than essentializing cultural differences.

Seeking to redefine and explore the sociological and cultural conditions of different migrant experiences, diaspora studies has unfolded new perspectives across disciplines in recent decades, and yet, a systematic inclusion into the respective philological disciplines in Germany and Israel remains a *desideratum*. The volume at hand aims to develop ideas and concepts for bringing together different epistemological and textual approaches into the curricula and research programs of the corresponding departments of literary studies in Europe, Israel, and the States. Jewish literatures from their ancient traditions to modernity—from the Bible, Mishna and Talmud, Kabbalah and Hasidism and beyond—challenge our very notion of literature. Even works by authors of Jewish belonging in modernism alone—from Marcel Proust to Osip Mandelstam, from Bruno Schulz to Bernardo Kucinski, from Natalia Ginzburg to Hélène Cixous, from Paul Celan to Dan Pagis—not to mention contemporary Hebrew, Russian, and Palestinian writing in Israel, challenge scholars to transcend the strict confines of national philologies and their respective disciplines.

In his book *From Continuity to Contiguity*, Dan Miron acknowledges the fact that most authors in the history of Jewish literary thinking came from multilingual environments and were deeply immersed in the respective *lingua franca* in the literatures and cultures of their time. Such an observation is not without significance. Miron suggests the mapping of a "modern Jewish literary complex" which is "vast, disorderly, and somewhat diffuse", and which is "characterized by dualities, parallelisms, occasional intersections, marginal overlapping, hybrids, similarities within dissimilarities, mobility, changeability" and more. While we share Miron's poly-perspectival conception of Jewish literatures, which challenges a monolithic, national understanding of what Jewish literature means, we also need to move beyond Eurocentric definitions of what Jewish literatures were and still are. Menachem Brinker's study *Hebrew Literature as European Literature* once again demonstrated the close ties between Hebrew literature and the European literary world. And yet Brinker, like Miron, Gershon Shaked, and many others, considers neither the liturgical traditions of Judaism nor the dialogues of Jewish authors with the traditions of Islam. To address these gaps, the 2018 Gentner Symposium proposed a re-orientation in our fields of studies, acknowledging the multilingual, post-national, ambiguous, and diffuse nature of Jewish literatures, the nature of which also challenges the binaries of Western experience and the conceptions of the East (the Orient), the dichotomies of modernism and tradition, critique and prayer, subjectivity and communal being. Questions of canonisation and curricula need to undergo a renewed discussion, as do our methods and practices of reading.

This volume contains essays with very different approaches. Such a broad conception of Jewish literatures, which is to take into account not only Western European and Latin American literatures, but also the modern Jewish cultural production in the East, in Hebrew as well as in other Jewish and non-Jewish languages (Judeo-Spanish, Judeo-Arabic, Classical Arabic, Turkish, Persian), seems the intellectual alternative that we have to develop against isolating, essentialist perspectives. The volume offers cross-cultural perspectives in a dynamic, multilingual setting, encouraging a post-essentialist engagement with belonging in literary texts, unrestrained by a national canon.

For this reason, we do not consider this volume to be yet another contribution to the definition of what might be understood as Jewish literature; instead, it focuses on the literary representation of different constructions of Jewish belonging. In literary studies, we insist on linking the concept of Jewish belonging to the status of the literary text, not the biography of the author. Nevertheless, we keep witnessing in our respective fields repeated attempts to identify and solidify essentialist understandings of Jewish literature and culture. As recently as 2001, Michael P. Kramer, for example, sought to apply the concept of race to determine what should and should not be regarded as Jewish literatures. The debate that followed is documented in the journal *Prooftexts*. Kramer's polemic criticized pluralist understandings of belonging as an evasive strategy so as to avoid the necessity of facing the consequences of a consistent definition. In contrast, we argue that Jewish belonging as represented and imagined in literary texts is not an *a priori* given, but is instead constructed in and through specific narrative situations. For this very reason, the methodological discussions presented in this book are not intended to establish a canon of Jewish literature.

The Gentner Symposium provided us with an interdisciplinary and collaborative conference setting, which brought together the expertise and the mutually reinforcing perspectives of a variety of literary disciplines in the humanities—such as linguistics and philology, cultural studies, literary hermeneutics, and comparative literature. We would like to express our sincere gratitude to our contributors for their willingness to engage in this unusual format. From our point of view, both the symposium and also the joint efforts to create this volume brought together a group of scholars who recognize that concerted research is indispensable to the future of Jewish studies and the humanities as a whole. We therefore feel that the symposium yielded new approaches for the teaching of diverse Jewish literatures in both Jewish and also non-Jewish languages. The discussions at the symposium offered the opportunity to experiment with different analytical methods, thus encouraging an intensified use of critical and discursive tools of a comparative quality for dealing with the theoretical and practical incorporation of the respective texts of Jewish literatures into the overall framework of literary studies.

As a result, this volume suggests a far-reaching—and not dichotomous—conceptualization of canonical texts of the Jewish literary corpus, which includes writings within Arabic, English, French, German, Hebrew, Hungarian, Italian, Latin-American, Polish, Portuguese-Brazilian, Russian, Spanish, Turkish, and Yiddish studies. Rather than buying into overly enthusiastic concepts of a "transnational space" (assuming that all forms of belonging to a nation state have been dissolved), we suggest a rationale that allows for a historical perspective on experiences related to migration, diaspora, and belonging—in all their variants and concomitant, specific sets of problems.

We proceed from the conviction that philological knowledge is attained by means of a continuous dialogue with the literary text as such. In line therewith, we accentuate literature as determined by language and highlight that historical understanding must be accompanied by an awareness of the inevitable historicity of knowledge. Individual researchers cannot possibly have at their disposal all the tools necessary for comparative research if the literary cultures in question comprise texts in Arabic, French, German, Hebrew, Portuguese, Spanish, Russian, and Yiddish. Consequently, the volume is also meant as an impetus to building networks for future collaboration.

In presenting different case studies, our volume dedicates special attention to the importance of modern Jewish literatures for didactics education within the current parameters of globalization. The case studies assess the potential for moving teacher training further towards a paradigm of transnationalization via the systematic integration of modern Jewish literatures into the curricula of language teaching. The different essays examine these aspects from a wide range of philological perspectives. We have tried to include analyses of different literary genres (poetry, drama, prose) and different literary periods and movements. Our aim is to advance the exploration of key terms and theoretical models that further a complex understanding of Jewish literatures as post-essentialist. We hope to contribute to the development of a high quality interdisciplinary curriculum at both undergraduate and graduate levels. In this way, the volume also intends to promote research on interdisciplinary and integrative methods of teaching and studying modern Jewish literatures and enhancing their visibility.

Our publication in open access format is meant to be an opening towards further cooperation, not an end of it. We hope to enable the construction of a collaborative network based on cross-disciplinary data available to all interested students and teachers of literature. We are very much aware that the plethora of scholarly questions in Jewish literary studies cannot even be approximated by the methods and languages of a single discipline, but instead require a variety of verified approaches and perspectives, enabling the incorporation of concepts and methods from several disciplines simultaneously. We sincerely hope that the case studies collected in this book will stimulate a continued dialogue on the matters we have raised.

The publication of this volume would not have been possible without the continuous commitment from and support of Dr. Lou Bohlen of the Minerva Foundation as well as Dr. Ulrike Krauss, Katja Lehming, and Dr. Christina Lembrecht of De Gruyter Verlag Berlin. We owe them gratitude for enhancing the visibility of this project. A special thanks goes to Dr. Elizabeth Bonapfel for her diligent copy-editing.

We wish to dedicate this book to our students, who rightly expect us to reflect upon post-essentialist approaches to literary studies.

Table of Contents

I Case Studies Spanish and Portuguese Literatures

Or Hasson
On Integrating Jewish Literature(s) into the Teaching of Early Modern Spanish Literature: Preliminary Thoughts —— 3

Einat Davidi
The Jewish Auto-Sacramental Plays as Jewish Baroque Drama —— 9

Ruth Fine
Integrating the Writings of the Western Sephardic Diaspora into the Literature of the Spanish Golden Age —— 17

Susanne Zepp
Post-Essentialist Belonging in Portuguese: Herberto Helder (1930–2015) —— 25

II Case Studies German, Turkish and Arabic Literatures

Laurent Mignon
A Few Remarks about Teaching Jewish Turkish Literature —— 37

Lukas Muehlethaler
Teaching Literatures by Arabized Jews: Medieval and Modern —— 45

Najat Abdulhaq
Dissenting Narratives – The Figure of the 'Arab Jew' in Contemporary Arabic Literature and Film —— 53

Galili Shahar
German-Jewish Literature: An Interruption —— 69

Kader Konuk
Reading Kafka in Turkey —— 81

Shira Miron
Unraveling *Heimat* – Recontextualizing Gertrud Kolmar's *Das preußische Wappenbuch* — 89

III Case Studies American and English Literatures

Claudia Olk
Configurations of Jewishness in Modernism: Woolf and Joyce — 103

Kirstin Gwyer
Planetarity in the Global? Modern Jewish Literature in English — 115

Pascal Fischer
Yiddish in Jewish-American Literature: An Asset to Teaching at German Universities — 127

David Hadar
Affiliated Identities as a Design Tool for a Jewish Literature Course — 135

IV Case Studies French and Italian Literatures

Sara Sohrabi
Case Study: Belonging in Dialogue. How to Integrate Hélène Cixous and Jacques Derrida in French Literary Studies — 143

Stephanie Bung
Teaching Contemporary French Literature: The Case of Cécile Wajsbrot — 153

Nourit Melcer-Padon
Ways to integrate Jewish Literature into the Broader Context of Academic Teaching — 159

Iulia Dondorici
Redefining and Integrating Jewish Writers into the Study of Historical Avant-Garde(s) — 169

Uri S. Cohen
Primo Levi: Between Literature and the World — 183

V Case Studies Latin American Literatures

Verena Dolle
A Case Study in Latin American Literature: Ilan Stavans' *On Borrowed Words* —— 197

Amalia Ran
Jewish Latin American Literary Studies: Between Old Challenges and New Paradigms —— 205

Laura Rivas Gagliardi
An Historical Approach to Contemporary Brazilian Literature: The Example of Bernardo Kucinski —— 213

Saúl Sosnowski
On Integrating Jewish Literatures into Teaching and Research —— 221

VI Case Studies Hebrew and Yiddish Literatures

Allison Schachter
Jewish Writing and Gender between the National and the Transnational —— 229

Hannah Pollin-Galay
Producing Radical Presence: Yiddish Literature in Twenty-first Century Israel —— 235

Iris Milner
The Unhomely In/Of Hebrew Literature —— 243

David Stromberg
The Yiddish Roots of Modern Jewish Writing in Europe and America —— 251

Adriana X. Jacobs
The Place of Hebrew: Maya Arad's *Another Place, a Foreign City* —— 257

VII Case Studies Russian, Eastern European and Hungarian Literatures

Lilla Balint
Traces, Memories: On Péter Nádas —— 269

Natasha Gordinsky
Osip Mandelstam's Postmultilingual Condition —— 281

Klavdia Smola
About the Integration of Jewish Literatures into Slavonic Studies —— 287

Agnieszka Hudzik
Polish Jewish Literature: A Brief History, Theoretical Framework, and a Teaching Example —— 295

I Case Studies Spanish and Portuguese Literatures

Or Hasson
On Integrating Jewish Literature(s) into the Teaching of Early Modern Spanish Literature: Preliminary Thoughts

1 Introductory remarks and rationale

This brief paper focuses on a few methodological and practical challenges one faces when trying to introduce – or integrate – Jewish literature(s) into courses dedicated to modern, and especially early modern, Spanish literature. As a Hispanist, rather than a scholar of Jewish studies, my philological and pedagogic interests in Sephardic Jewry and its literary production are motivated first and foremost by the fact that they are yet another manifestation of Hispanic culture, which, alongside *morisco* culture and colonial culture, reflect on our concept of "Spanishness", and, consequently, on what we consider to be part of the Spanish literary canon.

I deem introductory courses to be the most appropriate context to expose students to the existence of Jewish works and their complex relation to Spanish literature. These courses are often students' first encounter with a literary canon *both* as an abstract – debatable – concept *and* as a corpus of texts, which they are expected to be familiar with by the end of the course. Thus, such courses are an opportunity to think with the students about the major questions and problems that would – hopefully – accompany them through their studies, and sometimes even beyond. At the same time, however, the time constraint imposed by the need to cover a relatively large amount of texts, approaches, and historical contexts, obliges us to modify our syllabi with caution.

My argument is that in order to integrate Jewish literatures into the narrative of courses introducing students with early modern Spanish literature, one does not need to radically change course syllabi nor dismantle the very canon of Golden Age literature. Rather, one needs to introduce minimal changes in the list of works studied – i.e., add one Jewish work, or selections thereof – and gesture, as one teaches other canonical works, towards the story of Hebrew, Jewish, and *converso* literatures – three different concepts with which students must be acquainted. The same holds, of course, for the Muslim cultural and literary heritage of the Iberian Peninsula and for the underrepresented *morisco* literature of the sixteenth century. Given, however, the focus of the present volume on Jewish and modern literatures, I will limit myself to Jewish and *converso* literature.

ᵃ OpenAccess. © 2020 Or Hasson, published by De Gruyter. [CC BY-NC-ND] This work is licensed under the Creative Commons Attribution-NonCommercial-NoDerivatives 4.0 License.
https://doi.org/10.1515/9783110619003-002

Aiming to teach literature in a way that connects it to the historical, social, and political contexts in which it emerges, and upon which it often aims to act, I believe that any introduction to modern Spanish literature needs to address, at least in some capacity, three "big" questions, i.e., (1) what Spain is and how it came to be what it is; (2) who and what is considered Spanish, or what processes of homogenization and exclusion the forging this category entailed; and finally, (3), what geographic, linguistic, religious, and, ultimately, political criteria one uses when defining what Spanish literature is. As a pedagogical tool, I find it useful to briefly discuss in class examples demonstrating the tentative validity of each and every one of these criteria, and show students Hebrew and Arabic *aljamiado* texts – even without reading them, or reading a few lines of each – as a defamiliarizing gesture indicating that Spanish literature can come in different alphabets and render itself legible (or illegible) do different groups.

2 Jewish literature, Spanish literature, Diasporic literature

Let us define "Jewish literature", at least for the sake of this discussion, as the literary production of authors who identify, or whose literary persona is identifiable as Jewish; and/or as a literature written for readers who identify, publically or in private, as Jewish; or, as a literature appropriated by such authors or readers. Let us define "Spanish literature" here, for the sake of the argument, as a literature written by, or for, authors and readers, respectively, who identify as Spanish; or, as a literature appropriated by such authors or readers. Using these narrow, sociological definitions, one could say – with the telling exception, perhaps, of Antonio Enríquez Gómez – that early modern, post-1492 Spanish literature which is also Jewish can be found mostly, if not exclusively, in the Western Sephardic diaspora, particularly in the works of ex-*converso* authors like João Pinto Delgado, Daniel Miguel Leví de Barrios, or Daniel Israel López Laguna, who had all left the Iberian Peninsula and embraced Judaism after spending a significant part of their life in Catholic contexts, and leading, at least publically, Christian lives.

There are, of course, many differences between the genres, topics, and styles that can be found in the heterogeneous corpus I am referring to here as the "Diasporic Spanish-Jewish literature". Yet as it has been shown by scholars who had studied different manifestations of this literary production (some of the most important ones published in this very volume), what is truly remarkable – especially given what we know about and what we expect from Jewish-Iberian literatures –

is that the language, aesthetic models and literary codes employed in this corpus resemble general, i.e., non-Jewish, *Siglo de Oro* literature much more than they resemble the (mostly oral) literary and cultural production of the Jews expulsed from the Iberian Peninsula in 1492. In other words, these are works can be more easily described as "Spanish" than what we usually identify as "Sephardic" or "Judeo-Spanish".

3 Center and periphery, tradition and rupture

From a pedagogical perspective, it makes sense to include one representative work of this diasporic literature in survey course syllabi, as this corpus pushes further the boundaries of Golden Age literature. Just like, in the Muslim/Morisco case, allusions to Garcilaso or Lope de Vega found in an erotological treatise written in Tunisia show us that Spanish classics live beyond the boundaries of Christian Spain and of the Spanish Empire, so does the presence of baroque verse in Liturgical texts written in eighteenth-century Jamaica or dramatic forms such as the *auto sacramental* in the Western Sephardic diaspora helps us to better understand the reach of classical Iberian aesthetics.[1] But like any boundary-pushing phenomenon, this literature – as fascinating and worthy of study as it is – is nevertheless a peripheral one, and should be taught in a manner that accounts for its marginality and reflects about it.

Furthermore, while this literature should be deemed "Jewish" in the aforementioned sense of the term, one must also account for the fact that (perhaps unlike other cases discussed in this volume), early modern Spanish-Jewish literature is not an organic continuation of an Iberian Jewish literary tradition, nor does it draw, at least not significantly, on what is referred to in the study of Hebrew literature as the Golden Age in Spain. Rather, it is a Jewish literature of "New Jews" (a term coined by Kaplan (1989), being a mirror-image of the Iberian concept of "New Christians"), a literature written by authors whose worldview, as shown by historians and literary scholars alike, had been forged in a Christian context, and whose access to the texts, literary forms, and principle language of Jewish creation in the Iberian Peninsula – Hebrew – was limited, to say the least.

---

[1] On the *morisco* case, see López-Baralt 1992 (an abbreviated version of the argument in English can be found in López-Baralt 2018). For Jewish baroque verse and *autos sacramentales*, see, respectively, Fine 2011, and Davidi 2019. Davidi's study will also be of interest to students of comparative literature and Hebrew literature, as it shows the influence of this Golden Age in early modern drama.

In that sense, it is peripheral not only from a Spanish perspective, but also from a Jewish one.

If this Jewish literature is an organic extension or continuation of another literature, it is, as Fine and others has shown in numerous occasions, a continuation of Iberian *converso* literature.² There are two things that I believe are relevant for the framing of *converso* literature than need to be mentioned here. The first is that it cannot be considered "Jewish", certainly not in the strict, sociological sense of the term.³ The second, and this is, of course, relevant for thinking in practical terms of building course syllabi, is that *converso* literature is far from being a marginal phenomenon. One does not need to search in the periphery of Golden Age literature for texts that belong to this critical category. While texts such as *Lazarillo de Tormes* and *Celestina* both reflect an unequivocal consciousness of belonging to a minority (or, to be put in other terms, a sense of not belonging to mainstream, honorable society), these two works, which subvert the very postulates upon which modern Spanishness is premised – lineage, honor, Chrisitian orthodoxy, the ability to make sense of the world and find consolation in religious discourse, veneration for the Church and its institutions – are, at the same time, as canonical as literary works can be.

4 Towards an integrative narrative

What needs to be integrated into the narrative of courses dealing with early modern Spanish literature is not merely the existence of a Jewish literature, in the narrow sense of the term, which is an extension of Spanish Golden Age literature, but rather that this particular Jewish literature reflects, on the one hand, a discontinuity with the long tradition of Hebrew literature in the Iberian Peninsula, and on the other, a continuity with the critical category of *converso* literature, to which various canonical works pertain.⁴

In practical terms, this means that one does not need to make radical changes in the *list* of texts taught in survey courses: by adding one representative work of the diaspora (e. g., López Laguna's *Psalmos* or one of Pinto Delgado's works) and re-contextualizing *Lazarillo* and *Celestina*, one can delineate, through relatively modest gestures, the story of ruptures and continuations between Hebrew literature, *converso* literature, and Jewish literature.

---

2 See, e. g., Fine 2011; Fine 2013.
3 Cf. the tentative, more cautious takes on the topic in Zepp 2014.
4 For a panoramic view and a theorization of this category, see Fine 2013.

In the case of *Lazarillo*, it could be useful to read in class not only the canonical first part of the anonymous novel published in 1554, but also a few chapters from the neglected – and equally anonymous – *Segunda Parte del Lazarillo*, published in Antwerp in 1555. Although it circulated, at least in some editions, together with the first part, this sequel enjoyed very modest scholarly attention, and is rarely included in syllabi of introductory courses. In the sequel, the *pícaro*, under dire circumstances, suffers a metamorphosis from man to tuna fish, and struggles under his new identity to survive among the fish with all the doubts, fears, secrets and complexities such a challenge entails. Without imposing a reading of the *Segunda Parte* as a *roman à clef* depicting exclusively the forced conversion of the Jews, and without resolving the problem of authorship, this small addition to the study of the picaresque novel enables us to reconstruct one reading of the first *Lazarillo*, in which the *pícaro*'s otherness, skepticism, and heterodoxy are tied more explicitly to a forced, traumatic change of identity, secrecy, etc.[5]

In the case of *Celestina*, which, following Gilman's seminal study *The Spain of Fernando de Rojas* (1972) has become a paradigm of Spanish *converso* literature, a relatively modest addition to the curriculum – a reference to the early sixteenth-century Hebrew translation of the work, made by Joseph Tsarfati in Italy – can significantly enrich both the discussion of the *Tragicomedia*'s reception, and the narrative of the course as a whole. While the only extant part of this translation is the prefatory poem (available also in an English translation),[6] the very existence of such a translation, and the stylistic aspects of the prefatory poem, which situate it within the Hebrew literary tradition of late-medieval Spain and Italy, provide grounds for a meaningful discussion in class regarding the unique encounter between (1) the work that marks, for many of us, the beginning of the Spanish Golden Age, (2) the possible appeal of Rojas's masterpiece to Jewish readers – who may or may have not been Sephardic –, and (3) the literary traditions of a Hebrew Golden Age, which, for the most part, are left out of the story.

---

5 For an integrative discussion of the 1554 *Lazarillo vis-à-vis* problem of conversion, see Zepp 2014: 72–92. On the Antwerp sequel and the problem of conversion, see Hasson 2014.
6 For the English translation, see Baron 2012. An edition of the Hebrew poem can be found in Cassuto 1935. For a stylistic analysis of the poem, see Baron & Saguar García 2012.

Bibliography

Anónimo, and Juan de Luna. *Segunda Parte del Lazarillo*. Ed. Pedro M. Piñero. Madrid: Cátedra, 1999.

Baron, Amy, and Amaranta Saguar García. "Historical and literary influences on Tsarfati's *Poem composed by the Poet upon his translation of the tale of Melibea and Calisto*." *Celestinesca*, 36 (2012): 9–34.

Baron, Amy. "English translation of *A Poem Composed by the Poet upon his Translation of the Tale of Melibea and Calisto*, Joseph ben Samuel Tsarfati, 1507." *Celestinesca*, 36 (2012): 35–46.

Cassuto, Moshe David. "Me-Shirei Yosef ben Shmuel Zarfati: Ha-Komedia ha-Rishonah be-'Ivrit [The poetry of Joseph ben Samuel Tsarfati: the first comedy in Hebrew]." *Jewish Studies in Memory of George A. Kohut 1874–1933*. Eds. Salo Wittmayer Baron and Alexander Marx. New York: The Alexander Kohut Memorial Foundation, 1935. 121–128 [in Hebrew].

Davidi, Einat. "The corpus of Hebrew and Jewish *autos sacramentales:* Self-deception and conversion." *European Journal of Jewish Studies* 13 (2019): 182–226.

Fine, Ruth. "De la liturgia al relato testimonial: los *Psalmos de David* de Daniel Israel López Laguna." *Calíope* 17.1 (2011): 177–197.

Fine, Ruth. "La literatura de conversos después de 1492: autores y obras en busca de un discurso crítico." *Lo converso: orden imaginario y realidad en la cultura española*. Eds. Ruth Fine, Michèle Guillemont, and Juan Diego Vila. Madrid: Iberoamericana/Vervuert, 2013. 499–526.

Gilman, Stephen. *The Spain of Fernando de Rojas: The Intellectual and Social Landscape of "La Celestina"*. Princeton: Princeton University Press, 1972.

Hasson, Or. "Hacia una lectura de la conversión en la *Segunda Parte del Lazarillo* (Amberes, 1555)." *eHumanista/Conversos*, 2 (2014): 94–106.

Kaplan, Yosef. *From Christianity to Judaism: The Story of Isaac Orobio de Castro*. Oxford: Oxford University Press, 1989.

López-Baralt, Luce. "A Spanish Kāma Sūtra: The First Erotic Treatise in the Spanish Language." *Eros, Family and Community*. Eds. Ruth Fine, Yosef Kaplan, Shimrit Peled, and Yoav Rinon. Hildsheim: Georg Olms, 2018. 115–129.

López-Baralt, Luce. *Un Kama Sutra español*, Madrid: Siruela, 1992.

Zepp, Susanne. *An Early Self: Jewish Belonging in Romance Literature, 1499–1627*. Stanford: Stanford University Press, 2014.

Einat Davidi
The Jewish Auto-Sacramental Plays as Jewish Baroque Drama

One of the challenges facing Spanish philology in recent years is the study and research of *Converso Literature* as part of the corpus of Spanish Golden-Age literature. But the *converso*-corpus is far from a unified entity. And one of the important distinctions within it, in terms of the literary work's psychological and historical conditioning, is the distinction between *conversos* and *reconversos*. The literature of ex-*conversos* is a rich literature, written mainly in communities that Kaplan has described as "the communities of the western Spanish diaspora", communities that were forged mostly in Protestant cities like Hamburg and Amsterdam and in enclaves of tolerance within Catholic countries, like Bayonne and Livorno. Ex-*conversos* and others persecuted by the inquisition migrated to these communities and were re-educated into Judaism in a community that was strict in its adherence to religious law, on the one hand, but also somewhat open to a Jewish modernity on the other. The epicenter of these communities was the bustling port city and hub of world economy at the time, Amsterdam. The city was the center of colonial trade, the stock market and banking, and home to the West India and East India companies. Due to its prominent status, in the Jewish history of the early modern period it earned the name "Jerusalem of the North" (Kaplan 1992; Israel 1985). This community produced a significant literary oeuvre both in the Iberian tongues (Portuguese and mostly Spanish) and in Hebrew. Every literary text written in the communities of the western Spanish diaspora by former Iberians, including works written in Hebrew that lie beyond the accepted boundaries of conservative philology, belongs to the literature of the Spanish Golden Age and must be studied and taught in the cultural, theological, philosophical and aesthetic contexts of the Spanish Baroque. In 1989, Harm den Boer published a detailed catalogue listing all the Jewish texts printed in Amsterdam, including all works of literature, and this catalogue can be of use to anyone wishing to teach and study this corpus (Boer 1988).

In this paper I wish to address a particular body of work within this rich literature: the group of dramatic works written by Jewish writers from these communities in the dramatic structure of the *auto-sacramental* genre. The genre of the *auto-sacramental* is unique to the Spanish Golden Age of the sixteenth and seventeenth centuries, and over the course of the eighteenth century it shuffled off the stage of history. Despite its resemblance to such medieval dramatic forms as the morality play and the mystery play, it has unique characteristics that connect it more firmly with the early modern period – for instance, expressions of philosophical questions that were discussed intensively at the time (like skepticism and determinism), influences from the Spanish *comedia*, and the influence of Prudentius' "Psychomachia." The backdrop to the emergence of the *auto-sacramental* drama is the atmosphere of the Counter-Reformation. It is a liturgical drama, which in one way or another forms part of the ritual of the Holy Week procession during the Feast of Corpus Christi, a ritual that was imbued with special meaning in the Catholic countries during the Counter-Reformation. The themes expressed in the *auto-sacramental* plays are related, whether implicitly or explicitly, to the Sacrament of the Eucharist, which was known as a central point of contention between Catholic and Reform Christianity, while in the background, of course, lay the clash over Corpus Christi. As a type of agonal liturgical drama which is staged primarily in the springtime and celebrates the world's salvation and the renewal of the cycle of life, this is the closest dramatic genre to the origins of Greek drama in the Eleusinian mysteries. It is an allegorical drama that is centered around a transformation and expresses the main impulse of the mental life of the Christian believer: repentance and conversion. The Eucharistic transformation is the transformation of the bread and wine into the body and blood of Jesus, which occurs as an effect of the word itself, and effect of language.

Its constitutive elements are allegories-prosopopeiaes; the combination of a psychomachic agon and a theomachic agon; a progression from reasonable to bad, to a crisis and from there to salvation, in line with the course of the life of Jesus; concealment and disappearance followed by revelation and a discovery of the truth; transformation and conversion whose deep meaning is sacrifice. Thus, this is a unique genre of Spanish Baroque, and given its close link to the Eucharistic sacrament, a Jewish *auto-sacramental* is, at least on the fact of it, not at all possible. But the period in which the *auto-sacramentales* flourished is also the time when Jewish converts to Christianity were able to emigrate or flee from the Iberian peninsula to northern Europe and convert back to the old-new religion. These Jews were "double" converts, and as a group for whom conversion and transformation was a central tenet of their consciousness as a very real mental and historical event requiring inquiry and interpretation, it is only natural that they should adopt a genre that revolves around conversion and transformation. And indeed, as my research into this subject suggests, a substantial number of the dramatic works produced in the communities of the western Spanish diaspora, as well as works that came under their influence, in Italy and even North Africa, are works with distinctly *auto-sacramental* characteristics. The body of work I have defined – the "corpus of Jewish and Hebrew *auto-sacramentales*" (Davidi 2019) – constitutes an example of a sophisticated, creative and sometimes also subversive appropriation of a genre that is at least apparently tied inextricably to Catholic theology, to the myths that underlie it, and to the ritual of the Sacrament of the Eucharist.

The first *auto-sacramental* play by a Jewish author is the Portuguese play *Dialogo dos Montes*, written by Rehuel Yessurun (Paulo de Pina) in collaboration with Saul Levi Morteira (Polack 1975). It is not a Calderonian *auto*; rather, it conforms to the generic norms of plays by Gil Vicente, that is, to the *auto sacramental* in an early stage of its development, before it was ultimately crystallized by Calderón.

We don't have enough information regarding the performances themselves, but we do know that performing theater pieces in the synagogue was prohibited by the Maamad (the community board of government) in 1632 (and again in 1639). But we know from the records of Miguel de Barrios, who wrote a kind of poetic history of the community, that this play was staged inside the Beit Yaakov synagogue and we know also the identity of the actors in the play, for instance the identity of Moshe Gideon Abudiente, who would go on to assume key roles in the social and religious life of the Sephardi communities of Hamburg and Glückstadt. This fact more than hints at the deep acquaintance of the members of these communities, including their spiritual leaders, with this dramatic structure.

The play's content is agonal: seven anthropomorphized Biblical mountains battle with each other over who deserves to have the Torah given upon it. At the play's core, then, lies a dilemma, a weighing of options, judging, and eventually a decision and a choice. But the most clear-cut Jewish *auto-sacramental* written in an Iberian tongue is the 1665 play "*No hay fuerza contra la verdad*" (Nothing Can Stand Up to the Truth) by Miguel de Barrios.[1] Like part of Calderón's *auto*, the play is based on a particular historical event. Here the event is an *auto-da-fé* in Córdoba in which three Jews were burned at the stake. The historical event undergoes an allegorization designed to emphasize the element of Jewish martyrdom – dying for the sake of "*kidush hashem*," the sanctification of God's Name – and to present it as a theophany. The *auto-sacramental* structure suits this purpose because its characters are all allegorical, and theophanic sacrifice is its central theme. Miguel de Barrios also wrote a string of plays that bear a self-explanatory name: *Mosaic autos*. Through an allegorization of the community's institutions, the poet imbues its history with theophanic depth.[2]

---

[1] Re-edited by Scholberg (1962).
[2] For a detailed discussion of the dramatic development of the plays, see Lieberman 1996, 53–92.

Two plays by Antonio Enríquez Gómez also belong to this corpus, even if only to its outer margins – if the corpus is defined as a corpus of *reconversos* – since Gómez did not convert back to Judaism but rather returned to Spain and there continued to publish under a pseudonym. The first is "*Loa sacramental de los siete planetas*," an opening play that Gómez wrote for Calderón's play "*La cura y la enfermedad*," presented in Seville in 1659 (Enríquez Gómez 1987). The work is a sacramental loa for all intents and purposes, whose manuscript was discovered and author identified thanks to the work of Constance Rose. The second play is "*La culpa del primer peregrino*," printed in Rouen in 1644, an allegorical drama centered on the character of the ambivalent, wavering man, the original sin, and exile and salvation as mental forces (Enríquez Gómez 1735).

The corpus also includes plays in Hebrew. First and foremost is the play "Prisoners of Hope" (*Asirei HaTika*, 1673) by Penso de la Vega, who is known primarily as the author of the first book on the stock market, a book that to this very day receives new translations and appears in new editions while its readers never suspect that its author was an observant Jew. "Prisoners of Hope" deserves to be called "the first Hebrew *auto-sacramental*"; moreover, it marks the first appearance of this genuinely Spanish genre in any non-Iberian tongue. Interestingly, it is also the first Hebrew-language drama to be printed.[3] Thus, significantly, the first Hebrew-language theater piece ever printed is an *auto sacramental*.

In 1771 the play was reprinted in Livorno – not a small feat for a dramatic text. This fact attests to a degree of distribution of the text, which is of a piece with its influence on other Hebrew texts that I will address next. The play "The Celebrating Mass" (*Hamon Hogeg*) by an unknown author exists in manuscript form and was attributed to Moses ben Mordecai Zacuto until Shirman disprove this assumption (Schirmann 1979, 146). This is a "mini" biblical *auto-sacramental* that uses the structure of the genre in a subversive and playful manner such that only identifying the genre makes the comic effect possible: Jacob, the father of the nation, occupies the role typically filled in this genre by the satanic villain, and from this ironic twist we can assume that the contemporary audience was familiar with the *auto-sacramental* structure.

The play "The Eternal Foundation" (*Yesod Olam*) by Moses Zacuto is also a biblical *auto-sacramental* but of greater breadth – it takes the biblical story of the transition from paganism to monotheism, of the young Abraham smashing the idols of his father Terah, and shapes it, in the spirit of the Christian Biblical ex-

---

[3] According to Shirman, the first known Hebrew play is "*Zachut Bedichuta de Kidushin*" (צחות בדיחותא דקידושין), but it was printed only in the twentieth century by Shirman himself. It was not distributed and therefore had no influence on readers of Hebrew. The first Jewish play ever printed was *Esther*, in Venice in 1619.

egesis, as a prefiguration of the seventeenth century conversion from Catholicism (*idolatría*) to Judaism (Zacuto 1874).

Finally, "Praise Be to the Upright" (*LaYesharim Tehilla*) by Rabbi Moshe Chaim Luzzatto (RaMCHaL), from 1743, is the latest play in the corpus (Luzzato 1981).[4] Situating it within this corpus may come as a surprise since in the standard historiography of Hebrew literature this important play is attributed to the Hebrew literature of Italy, a country regarded since Bialik as the cradle of modern Hebrew literature. Yet the RaMCHaL, who famously fled his persecutors who objected to the mysticism of his work, found shelter – lo and behold – in Amsterdam, Jerusalem of the North, and it is there that he wrote and also printed his great allegorical play. If we read the play through literary categories, we can see that it possesses all the essential characteristics of the *auto-sacramental*: it is an agonal play, whose characters are all prosopopeiaes divided into good and evil; in between stands the character of man who bears the burden of choosing, deciding and overcoming temptation; and the play depicts the grappling with deception and the mask, to discover the truth marked by salvation.

Conclusion

The corpus of *auto-sacramentales* is a symptom and an embodiment of the way in which Spanish-Catholic culture seeped into the heart of Jewish culture. But from the perspective of Spanish philology, the corpus is a telling expression of the radiation of Golden-Age Spanish culture beyond the Iberian peninsula, of a migration of literary structures that effectively severed them from the space in which they were organically created and of their subsequent evolution and perhaps universalization. The transformation and transmutation of the *auto-sacramental* genre, which to date has been considered unique to the Spanish Baroque, constitutes but also exemplifies a movement of aesthetic forms and conceptual forms from southern to northern Europe, with Jewish writing and the Jewish realm functioning as transformers and mediators of sorts between Catholic and Protestant countries.

From the point of view of Spanish philology, a discipline in which the study of seventeenth century literature tends to be conservative, the corpus demonstrates that Spanish Golden-Age literature influenced other cultural realms and that the writers of the communities of the western Spanish diaspora served

---

4 An English version: *Moses Haym Luzzatto's Lah-y' Shaw-riem Tehilaw*. Trans. Rabbi Herbert S. Goldstein and Rebecca Fischel. New York: Bloch Pub. Co., 1915.

also as transmitters of this literature, including all the modes of thought that it expresses and carries with it. It is for good reason that this function of the Amsterdam writers as agents of a cultural transfer is not absent from Sullivan's monumental study of Calderón's influence on the German-speaking countries.

The *auto-sacramentales* genre took shape in very particular historical, cultural and theoretical conditions, and there is therefore a tendency to view it as a Spanish genre, local rather than universal. The inclusion of the varied corpus I described here, some of which is written in non-Iberian languages, within the corpus of this genre carries the potential not only to expand the corpus of Spanish Golden-Age literature and to move toward a less conservative and nationalistic and more modern notion of philology (or, indeed, "comparative literature"), but also to influence the controversial theory of the *auto-sacramental* genre. For it is precisely the *auto-sacramental* play, more than any dramatic genre, in Spain and beyond, that is the closest to the dramatic tradition out of which developed theatre in the West, the origins of Greek drama in the Eleusinian mysteries, and the Book of Job, as a paradigm of theatre that grows inexorably out of the question of the existence of evil within the Western understanding of God. If we dare to expand this perspective further and pry open the theory of *auto-sacramentales* (and in this task, identifying the corpus of Jewish and Hebrew *auto-sacramentales* is useful), then we will find that even a whole host of plays written after WWII, including "Waiting for Godot" and some of Grotowsky's works, are types of *auto-sacramentals*.

Bibliography

Boer, Harm den. "Spanish and Portuguese Editions from the northern Netherlands in Madrid and Lisbon public collections: Towards a Bibliography of Spanish and Portugues editions from the Northern Netherlands (1580–1821)." *Studies Rosenthaliana* 22.2 (1988): 97–143.

Davidi, Einat. "The Corpus of the Hebrew and Jewish Autos Sacramentales – Conversion and Selfdeception" *European Journal of Jewish Studies* 13 (2019): 1–45.

Enríquez Gómez, Antonio. *Loa sacramental de los siete planetas: A Critical Edition from the Manuscript*. Eds. Constance Hubbard Rose and Timothy Oelman. Exter: University of Exeter, 1987.

Enríquez Gómez, Antonio. *La Culpa del Primer Peregrino, y El Passagero*. Madrid: Impr. De los herederos de J. García Infanzón, 1735.

Israel, Jonathan Irvine. *European Jewry in the Age of Mercantilism: 1550–1750*. Oxford: Clarendon Press, 1985.

Kaplan, Yosef. "The Sephardic Diaspora in North-Western Europe and the New World." *The Sephardi Legacy Vol. II*. Ed. Haim Beinart. Jerusalem: Magnes Press, 1992. 240–287.

Lieberman, Julia. *The Allegorical Theater of Miguel de Barrios*. Newark: Juan de la Cuesta, 1996.

Luzzato, Moshe Hayyim. *La-yesharim Tehilla* (Hebrew). Ed. Yona David. Jerusalem: Mossad Bialik, 1981; An English version: *Moses Haym Luzzatto's Lah-y' Shaw-riem Tehilaw*. Trans. Rabbi Herbert S. Goldstein and Rebecca Fischel. New York: Bloch Pub. Co., 1915.

Penso de la Vega, Joseph ben Issac. *Pardes Shoshanim. Asirei ha-Tikvah*. Amsterdam: Joseph Athias, 1673.

Polack, Phillip. *Dialogo dos Montes*. Edited with an English Vers translation. London: Tamesis, 1975.

Schirmann, Haim. *Studies in the History of Hebrew Poetry and Drama*. Jerusalem: Mossad Bialik, 1979.

Scholberg, Kenneth R. *La poesía religiosa de Miguel de Barrios*. Madrid: Ed. Edhigar. Columbus: Ohio State UP, 1962.

Zacuto, Moshe, *Yesod Olam*. Berlin: Abraham Berliner, 1874.

Ruth Fine
Integrating the Writings of the Western Sephardic Diaspora into the Literature of the Spanish Golden Age

> The central predicament of early modern Conversos, both inside and outside the Iberian Peninsula, lay in the fact that they inhabited a cultural threshold.
> (Graizbord 2004, 2)

The following reflections briefly address my particular field of research, Spanish Golden Age literature, and in this field, a specific corpus, the literature of the Western Sephardic Diaspora, which I believe presents an illustrative case-study for the purposes of this publication, itself stemming from the International Symposium that preceded it, namely, a reflection on the rich multilingualism and polyphony of Jewish literary writing and the integration of Early Modern and Modern Jewish literary studies into the different philologies.

The students and scholars of Spanish literature, being participants and heirs of a common cultural legacy developed over centuries within the borders of the Iberian Peninsula, inhabit a symbolic universe populated by subtle, invisible, even painful divisions; divisions best expressed in the two separate phrases: the Golden Age *in* Spain and the Golden Age *of* Spain. Two innocent prepositions separate two worlds, which have frequently ignored and even denied each other.

At the beginning of my academic career in Israel, I realized, to my surprise, that when speaking of the Spanish Golden Age before non-Spanish-speaking circles, I had to clarify that I was referring to Spain of the sixteenth and seventeenth centuries, and not Spain of the ninth, tenth, eleventh, and twelfth centuries, the latter being the period that constitutes the centre of interest for the Jewish academic world. And of course, the opposite was equally true – although there is an awareness that during these long ago centuries a Golden Age in Jewish history took place on the Iberian Peninsula, they never acquired a place in the institutionalized body of the Spanish academy and its literary canon. This is evident, for example, when reviewing the official curricula of Spanish schools and academic institutions. Ibn Gabirol, Ibn Ezra, Al Jarizi, Yehuda ha Levi – the latter being in fact the first known author of verse in incipient Castilian, included in his *jarchas* – all these constitute a history of manifest, I would say, shouted silences. Golden centuries erased by other golden ones. Semantic paradoxes and negations, yes, but also appropriations, displacements, and, fundamentally, silent and latent syncretism in what we can consider the in-between, liminal condition of Spanish Jewish literature that is my case study here, the one developed after the expulsion of 1492, and, more specifically, in the seventeenth and eighteenth centuries in northern Europe (Fine 2013).

Seeking to overcome the binomial 'center/periphery' frequently applied to Jewish literature, historian Sander Gilman (1999) replaces it with the notion of a "border space", a place defined neither by the center nor by the periphery but by a constant confrontation located in the margins. Gilman describes this frontier as "terrain-in-the-middle", a "middle ground", a diffuse zone in which different sociocultural entities dialogue, juxtapose, and confront each other. In this dynamic, it is inevitable that each of the agents, voluntarily or involuntarily, will be "contaminated" by the content of the other. The border space is therefore dialogical, plural, conflictive, and, I would say, of an extreme creative richness.

To this intermediate space it is also necessary to add and consider the dynamics of memory and oblivion as constituents of the Jewish experience and identity. Hispanic Jewish and *Converso* writing after the expulsion constantly refers to a paradoxical dynamic of experiences and content from other times, places, and languages; a paradox that was designated by Yosef Haim Yerushalmi (1989) as "the memory of what was already forgotten."

Stemming from these brief conceptual reflections, I choose as a paradigmatic example of the border, in-between, and paradoxical dynamics in Spanish-Jewish literature one that has been the object of my research for the past several years: the literature of the Jewish Iberian *Conversos*, and within it the literature of the so-called "new Jews" (Kaplan 2000) that emerged in northern Europe, especially in Amsterdam and Hamburg, during the seventeenth and eighteenth centuries. These writers of *Converso* origin who embraced Judaism outside of the Peninsula wrote predominantly in Spanish and also, to a lesser extent, in Portuguese. Despite this, most of these writers have been left outside the paradigm of Spanish Golden Age literature (and, evidently, also that of Jewish literature). Let us remember that all these authors returned to Judaism after having lived as Christians for several generations and been nourished by the cultural and religious legacy of Catholicism. Their writings offer, among other levels of interest, the pronounced syncretism already addressed as one of the salient marks of this in-between literature of the border space.

These "new Jews" authors can be considered the last link in a chain of crisis and transformation processes: spanning the first conversion, the expulsion, the second forced conversion of 1497 in Portugal, the inquisitorial persecution, the new and conflictive conversion to Judaism, and, in general, the successive migrations, acculturations, and identity dualities. Daniel Leví de Barrios, João Pinto Delgado, Menasseh Ben Israel are the best-known of these writers, but they are not the only ones: Orobio de Castro, Saúl Leví Mortera, Isaac Cardoso, Samuel Usque, José Penso de la Vega, are some among the many others whose names and texts demand to be integrated into the paradigm of Golden Age studies.

Moreover, this corpus bears witness to a case of cultural mediation, which the literature of the *Conversos* utterly exemplifies in the context of Early Modern Europe. It is a literature that is clearly representative of complex border processes: contamination, elision, recovery of memory. As mentioned, the dozens of works that make up this corpus were written mostly in Spanish by authors of Jewish-convert origin, who adopted Judaism after having lived as Christians for several generations, and who were totally immersed and educated in the Iberian culture. Passionately, these "new Jews" (or should we say renewed Jews) read, translated, interpreted, and, finally, rewrote their Hispanic literary and cultural heritage in a distinct way, and the results permeate the matrix of a deep cultural *mestizaje*. Itinerant writers in a border world (between regions, religions, languages), they not only maintained their ties with Iberian culture through the language in which they continued to communicate orally and to manifest themselves in writing, but also followed with much interest cultural developments on the peninsula, emotionally and intellectually anchored in the Iberian world. Although they had left the peninsula as undesirable inhabitants, they carried with them their cultural knowledge of the region and the past they left behind, especially in their language, their literature, and even their conceptual universe. It was in this way that they thus became, for nearly two centuries, true mediators between apparently divided and conflicted worlds (Fine 2013).

And yet. The literature of the Spanish-Portuguese Jews of the so-called Jerusalem of the North was ignored for centuries by Hispanic scholarship and even today is still perceived by a large swath of the academic milieu as a mere bibliographical curiosity without major impact. It goes unmentioned and unrecognized, for example, in the conferences of the International Association of the Golden Age and of the International Association of Hispanists, where up until the past decade this literature was notable only by its absence. A history and a literature in Spanish silenced and forgotten by Hispanic Studies; and one of many examples of that other broader and silenced literature, the *Conversa*.

In fact, the literature of the Western Sephardic Diaspora has remained almost entirely forgotten as far as the canon of Spanish Golden Age literature is concerned. One interesting exception is Menéndez Pelayo's (1947, 285) brief but caustic judgment in the section of his monumental work in which he includes heterodox writers of Jewish origin: "Poets, novelists and writers of literature for enjoyment. Esteban Rodríguez de Castro. Moshe Pinto Delgado. David Abenatar Melo. Israel López Laguna. Antonio Enríquez Gómez. Miguel Leví de Barrios". He adds, concerning this group of Jewish converted authors:

> It was explained in an earlier chapter why our history should contain, even if only in passing, the Muslims and Jews who, after having received baptism, returned to their former opinions. [...] I will spend a bit more time on the Judaizing writers, because some of them were Jews in race alone and Christians in baptism alone, and ended up as freethinkers, materialists, or Deists, due to which they belong, fully and in their own right, in this book. [...] Certainly it might be said that of the many who have received baptism and dwelt among us, barely a single one of them was a true Christian. But their long residence among us, and the separation in which they lived from rabbinical centres, eventually meant that they were indistinguishable in knowledge, style, language, and artistic forms from other Spanish writers. Moreover, many of these New Christians, though Jewish by lineage, at the bottom of their hearts were not so in belief; indeed, often they barely knew the beliefs of their forefathers. Beyond a few superstitions, they were generally men with no religion or law whatsoever, a fact which explains the philosophical derailing of some Israelite thinkers at the end of the seventeenth century, such as Espinosa, Uriel da Costa, and Prado. (Menéndez Pelayo 1947, 286)

In this passage, typical of Menéndez Pelayo in its derogatory tone and simplistic underlying assumptions, the Spanish scholar nonetheless indicates, presumably without intending to, the complex drives and underlying conflict present in so many manifestations of the bifurcated existential path of both the *Conversos* and their literature. Even so, Menéndez Pelayo insists upon denying nearly all aesthetic value to that literature, as well as any originality, merely highlighting that: "At most the work of certain poets is distinguished by its predilection for Old Testament themes; but the manner of treating them is no different, neither in style nor in rhythmic forms, from the one used by the Christian poets" (Menéndez Pelayo 1947, 308).[1]

Spanish literary scholarship embraced Menéndez Pelayo's perspective with zeal, so much so that even though a reevaluation of research on the expulsion and forced conversion took place by the end of the twentieth century among Spanish historians, there was no such process with respect to literary studies. As Juan Diego Vila points out, even though the centenary of 1992 encouraged an apparent revitalization of approaches to the problems of exile and forced conversions in the Peninsula five centuries earlier, "the process of historical revision did not have projects of equal strength and effective results in the literary field [...] practice that, as you can imagine, led to the progressive isolation of these critical debates as if they were radically different and estranged domains" (Vila 2013, 118–119).[2]

---

[1] My translation.
[2] My translation.

Despite this profound academic silence, the rich corpus of Western Sephardic literature reflects a remarkable and unique literary process in its tenacity, its literary achievements, and its demand to belong: to these writers their Iberian belonging was indisputable.

As an example, I will refer to *Espejo fiel de vidas que contiene los Psalmos de David en verso* – a translation of the Book of Psalms by Israel Daniel López Laguna completed in the second half of the seventeenth century and published in London in 1720. This unique text awakens the critic's interest not only from a literary point of view, but also as a testimonial narrative of persecution and Sephardic exile. It also reflects the complex project of recuperating the Hebrew Bible and its exegesis for those *Conversos* who left the Iberian Peninsula belatedly and had no familiarity with the Jewish versions of this text. Ultimately, López Laguna's book reveals the essentially syncretic character that I believe is attributable to *Converso* literature.

The urge to translate the biblical text, especially the Psalter, was hardly unusual within Sephardic communities. A tradition initiated by the Ferrara Bible, published in 1553, the direct translation of the Bible from Hebrew into Romance languages would continue throughout the centuries. López Laguna belongs squarely to this tradition, participating in the project of translating the Hebrew Bible into Spanish for liturgical purposes (with the Psalter being particularly valorised by the Sephardic communities as a book of prayers) and as a means of reclaiming the Hebrew Bible through textual scholarship.

The work presents not a few compositional and aesthetic merits, while at the same time raising a number of questions. Not only is this a paraphrased translation of the Psalter, but the author is also putting on display his mastery of a wide range of verse forms inspired by the poetic paradigm of the Spanish Baroque, thus configuring a unique syncretic space, in which devotional zeal fuses with both the metric virtuosity of the Baroque and the immediacy of a testimonial narrative, as we will see in a moment.

López Laguna's text also incorporates words 'foreign' to the discursive space of the psalms. A remarkable dialogue takes place between Old Testament idiom and a marked classical and mythological vein. By the same token, in addition to elements of Baroque discourse, those of the social context of the time also filter their way in. As indicated above, one of the work's greatest aspects of interest is its undeniable testimonial value, as much individual as collective. This 'Baroque Psalmist' translates the biblical text into his contemporary context and personal life experience, especially in registering the mark of trauma.

In this oeuvre, López Laguna associatively melds not only the individual with the contemporary collective experience, but also the present trauma with the historical past of the Jewish people, striving to emerge as the voice of a nation and of its history, legitimating the *Converso* experience of expulsion/forced conversion as one more link in the diachronic chain structuring the historical consciousness of the Jews as a people.

The complex rhetorical apparatus of this translation does indeed correspond to such a religious and ideological program. At the lexical-semantic level, López Laguna resorts continuously to amplifications, lexical permutations, interpolations, and associations, inscribed in either the paradigmatic or the syntagmatic axis (i.e. metaphors/similes or metonymies) and reinforced, in turn, by additional rhetorical devices, such as the frequent use of hyperbole. This compositional poetics presents itself as a rewriting of the psalms grounded in the individual and collective experience of a specific historical moment; and this moment is thus reactivated by being inserted into the continuum of the Psalter, whose own cyclical, reiterative structure and rhetoric are concomitant with the memory of Jewish experience perpetuated by and through it.

The work was written for an educated public that was familiar not only with the Spanish language, but also the compositional paradigms of Golden Age poetry; one that was able to appreciate the flexibility of the translator-poet's verse and the scope of his aesthetic achievements. Certainly, for such readers this approach is effective and affective, presenting in an attractive form the biblical/religious contents with which they were to be instructed. Moreover, its inherent syncretism succeeds in harmonizing the classic Hispanic literature of the Christian cultural sphere with Jewish religious and exegetical contents, exalting what could be considered an essential ambition of the Hispano-Hebraic descendants of the *Conversos* and/or expelled: a double belonging in which both traditions are sustained and neither is annulled (Zepp 2014). López Laguna's work constitutes, in this sense, a wide field for the analysis of such a paradoxical dynamic. His creative wager takes poetic nourishment from the vast storehouse of personages, histories, and situations recorded in the Hebrew biblical corpus, interpolating this paradigm into the main corpus of Castilian poetry.

More than a century and a half after the expulsion, the conversions, and the resulting cultural crossings, López Laguna exercises his office of translator using the entire range of voices constituting the Sephardic Diaspora as a multicultural polyphony, more particularly, within the Hispano-Portuguese tradition. The underlying foundation of this Hebrew book translated into Castilian, entails a convergence of multiples lines of influence emanating from the Hispanic cultural legacy. By the same token, the range of addressees the work presupposes, including both Jewish and Christian readers, incorporates the two ethno-religious spheres constituting the humanist landscape of Spain before the expulsion into a concrete situation of literary communication. An active space of 'multiculturalism' is thereby opened up, considering that, in a still Jewish but no longer Iberian context, its sources remain carriers of Spanish and even classical materials. These distinct discourses do not merely coexist within the work as an academic juxtaposition. On the contrary, they develop complex, dynamic interrelations.

In this way, the *Espejo de vidas* is neither the product of a single governing intentionality nor does it present to the reader any unified, univocal signification, or any coherent, uncontaminated form. Rather, López Laguna's translation belongs to an unabashedly 'impure' poetry of *Converso* literature, pointing to various goals and directions, configured according to various codes. This type of 'contamination' is a manifestation of dialogism. The words of those seen as wholly other are modulated in the voice of the lyric subject – at the same time as they shape the word of that subject.

Daniel Israel López Laguna's Psalter can thus be considered a paradigmatic example of *Converso* literature in general and that of the Western Sephardic Diaspora in particular. It is, specifically, a 'mirror', perhaps, of lives, of trajectories, but above all, a space of heterogeneous voices, a space of multiple belongings that recognize and dialogue with one another, creating a scriptural *ethos* open to plurivalent readings.

For all these reasons, I view a critical reconsideration of the literature of the Sephardic Western Diaspora as well as the literary interaction of the Hispanic, Hebrew, Jewish, and *Converso* writings to be imperative. What is required is not only sophisticated analyses of specific works and authors but an inclusive and serious research effort to overcome academic and editorial compartmentation. This is necessary in order to achieve a much needed fertilization of our areas of studies, but also as a long overdue act of literary and historical recognition and repair.

Bibliography

Fine, Ruth. "La literatura de conversos después de 1492: obras y autores en busca de un discurso crítico". *La literatura de conversos después de 1492*. Madrid/Frankfurt a. M.: Iberoamericana/Vervuert. Ed. Ruth Fine/Michele Guillemont et. al. 499–526, Madrid/Frankfurt a. M.: Iberoamericana/Vervuert, 2013.

Fine, Ruth. "*Los Psalmos de David [The Psalms of David]* by Daniel López Laguna, a Wandering Marrano". *The Conversos and Moriscos in Late Medieval Spain and beyond*, vol. III: *Displaced Persons*. Ed. Kevin Ingram / Juan Ignacio Pulido Serrano. Leiden/Boston: Brill, 2016. 45–62.

Gilman, Sander L. "The Frontier as a Model of Jewish History". *Jewries at the Frontier. Accommodation, Identity, Conflict*. Ed. Sander L. Gilman/Milton Shain. Urbana/Chicago: Univ. of Illinois Press, 1999.

Graizbord, David L. *Souls in Dispute: Converso Identities in Iberia and the Jewish Diaspora, 1580–1700*. Philadelphia: Univ. of Pensilvania Press, 2004.
Israel López Laguna, Daniel. *Espejo fiel de vidas que contiene los Psalmos de David en verso, obra devota, útil y deleitable*, London, 5480 [1720] (facsímil edition, Bogotá, 2007, # 163 of 200).
Kaplan, Yosef. *An Alternative Path to Modernity. The Sephardi Diaspora in Western Europe*. Leiden: Brill, 2000.
Menéndez y Pelayo, Marcelino. *Historia de los heterodoxos españoles*, IV. Madrid: Librería Católica de San José, 1947.
Vila, Juan Diego. "La literatura de los conversos españoles: ¿debate crítico o damnatio memoriae?" *eHumanista / Conversos* 1 (2013): 117–131. http://www.ehumanista.ucsb.edu/contact/conversos%201/ehumanconv.Vila.pdf, (24 September 2019).
Yerushalmi, Yosef H. *Zakhor: Jewish History and Jewish Memory*. Seattle: Univ. of Washington Press, 1989.
Zepp, Susanne. *An Early Self. Jewish Belonging in Romance Literature 1499–1627*. Stanford: Stanford Univ. Press, 2014.

Susanne Zepp
Post-Essentialist Belonging in Portuguese: Herberto Helder (1930–2015)

Jewish history, art, and literatures on the Iberian Peninsula constituted for centuries one of the most profound chapters of Jewish history. When Portuguese Jews, however, had to face the prospect of being either baptized or expelled in the winter of 1496–1497, this chapter came to a sudden end. The Inquisition, established under the Portuguese Crown in 1536, continued to harass the recent Christian converts, and during the sixteenth and seventeenth centuries, one can observe their continuous exodus to other countries. With his *A Consolação às Tribulações de Israel*, Samuel Usque wrote one of the most important pieces of Portuguese literature in the sixteenth century (Roani 2011). The book takes the form of a pastoral Renaissance dialogue concerning a concise examination of the history of forced baptism and expulsion in the Iberian Peninsula (Preto-Rodas 1990). The fist edition, which was printed in Ferrara in 1553, was almost entirely destroyed by the Inquisition shortly after its release. The second edition, printed in Amsterdam in 1559, signaled the beginning of Sephardic literature in the Netherlands. Only after the abolition of the Inquisition in 1821 did some descendants of formerly expelled Portuguese families come back to the country. Michaël Studemund-Halévy has drawn attention to the fact that during the nineteenth century, Jews from Gibraltar and Morocco resettled on the Portuguese mainland and on the Atlantic islands of Madeira and the Azores. Between 1850 and 1900, Jews also arrived in the Portuguese colonies of Angola, Mozambique, the Cape Verde Islands, and Madeira. Studemund-Halévy links the limited presence of Jewish remigrants after the abolition of the Inquisition not only to Portugal's peripheral geographical position, but above all else to the fact that the memory of expulsion and forced baptism is still very much alive in the Sephardic diaspora (Studemund-Halévy 1997). To this day, Portugal has one of the most compact Jewish communities in Europe.[1]

So one might ask why students of Portuguese studies should even be concerned with Jewish facets of Portuguese literary history when practiced Judaism hardly determines everyday life in Portugal. One compelling answer to this ques-

---

Note: I would like to thank my co-editors and Professor Antonio Ladeira (Texas Tech University) for their constructive criticism on the manuscript.

[1] See also Mucznik (1995). A three-volume history was published in 2006 by Jorge Martins.

tion can be found in the writings of Herberto Helder, one of Portugal's most eminent poets of the twentieth century. Helder published more than 30 books, most of them poetry, but also books of short stories, essays, and fiction. When Herberto Helder died in March 2015, the Portuguese president Aníbal Cavaco Silva called Helder one of the greatest names in Portuguese culture as a whole. Born in Madeira in 1930, the poet's oeuvre was dedicated to the multiple and continuous processes of transformation of the self and its historical experience that provide modernity with its distinctive plurality.² In a groundbreaking essay on Helder's poetics, Helena Buesco listed the variety of references in a book by Herberto Helder in which he experimented with indirect translations of world poetry:

> The 1966 volume collects materials from Ancient Egypt, the Old Testament, Maya and Nahuatl lore, Ireland, Scotland, Finland, Japan, Indochina, Indonesia, Greece, and Madagascar, together with Zen poems, Arab and Al-Andaluz poems, "Eskimo" and Tartar poems, Haikus, and "Red-Skin" poems. [...] As may well be understood, one of the gestures underlined by the poet is the fact that no national or even regional boundaries make sense in his concept of literature: poetry is understood as a transversal phenomenon which no external boundary may contain or define, not even a language, a literature, or a nationality – there is no mention whatsoever of these categories as being relevant to the choice and the practice of translated poems. (Buescu 2016, 55–56)

Herberto Helder's longing for world culture is reminiscent of Osip Mandelstam's nostalgia, seen also in his attempt to open up Portugal and Portuguese literature and culture to the world. That this gesture is linked to its historical moment – the period in which Salazar's *Estado Novo* propagated the exact opposite, namely a separation from the rest of the world through the preservation of supposed "national values" and Portugal's self-sufficiency – is crucial for the understanding of Helder's writings.³

Even these few general remarks on the oeuvre of the Portuguese author reveal his importance in the context of teaching and research in Portuguese studies, as students can experience in his writings a language-based questioning of nationalistic ideologies that unfortunately also exist in our present moment. Helder's literary procedures sought to de-provincialize the Portuguese language and open it up to global experiences. This includes a resolute decolonization of the language because part of the *Estado Novo*'s character, to which Helder's work

---

2 See also Buescu (2007).
3 For a detailed account of how ideology translated into cultural politics under Salazar, see the first chapter in Diana Gomes Ascenso's book *Poetischer Widerstand im Estado Novo* (Gomes Ascenso 2018, 19–90).

was diametrically opposed, was the claim to consolidate the colonies as Portuguese property in political and ideological terms.

Nevertheless, Herberto Helder's oeuvre also contains texts that transcend essentialist notions of belonging by addressing the question of historical experience. Therefore, discussing his writing in the context of this volume on the diversity of Jewish literatures is by no means an attempt to explain his oeuvre on the backdrop of his own Jewish history. Rather, his writing attempts to resolve essentialist notions of identity. In Salazar's decidedly anti-modern *Estado Novo*, Herberto Helder has created a distinctly modern, if not post-modern, body of work in which symbols of collective identity dissolve – as a universal phenomenon, not as an exclusively Jewish one. For Helder, polyphonic discourse of and about belonging is a universal expression of modernity. In his oeuvre, this also includes – also and not exclusively – Jewish belonging. In addition, in Helder's writings, history in its various languages and cultures provides a path to knowledge, and the engagement with history thus appears as a powerful tool for sharpening one's judgement.

These different aspects can be demonstrated by an exemplary close reading of one of Herberto Hélder's short stories. The story is part of the volume *Os passos em volta*, published in 1963. Portugal's history in the sixties is marked by the colonial wars that began in 1961 and continued until 1974. The title of Helder's 1963 story is "Holanda", meaning "Holland" in English, and this title is already striking: Holland is a region and former province on the western coast of the Netherlands. Although today, the term "Holland" is frequently used informally to refer to the whole country of the Netherlands, this is not a correct designation. From the tenth to the sixteenth century, Holland proper was a unified political region within the Holy Roman Empire as a county ruled by the Counts of Holland. By the seventeenth century, the province of Holland had risen to become a maritime and economic power, dominating the other provinces of the newly independent Dutch Republic. The area of the former County of Holland roughly coincides with the two current Dutch provinces of North Holland and South Holland in which it was divided, that together include the three largest cities in the Netherlands: the *de facto* capital city of Amsterdam; Rotterdam, home of Europe's largest port; and the seat of government in The Hague.

The title of Herberto Helder's short story thus evokes a historical landscape that was crucial in the history of early modern Portuguese Jewry. In the late sixteenth and throughout the seventeenth centuries, many families from Portugal established their homes in Amsterdam. Among them was the prominent writer Menasseh Ben Israel, who was born according to legend on Madeira Island in 1604, with the name Manoel Dias Soeiro, a year after his parents had left mainland Portugal to flee the Inquisition. The family came to Amsterdam in 1610, where Menasseh rose to eminence not only as a rabbi and an author, but also as a printer. He established the first Hebrew press in Holland.[4] Menasseh Ben Israel's and the migrations of many more were made possible by the creation of the Union of Utrecht in 1579. Article 13 stipulated that, "everyone shall remain free in religion and that no one may be persecuted or investigated because of religion."[5] Thus, the Dutch Republic became a haven for men and women, especially of Jewish origin from the Iberian Peninsula, fleeing religious persecution. What they encountered in the Dutch Republic was not absolute religious tolerance, though often local authorities within Amsterdam were rather liberal when it came to the activities of the growing Portuguese Jewish population. However, despite their relative 'freedom' in comparison to their experience in Spain and Portugal, the Portuguese Jewish community acted for over a century in a way that avoided bringing unwanted attention to it. There was a desire to conform more or less to the expectations of the Dutch authorities so that what happened to the Jews in Spain and Portugal would not be repeated in Holland. Often, this meant self-regulation by applying punishments upon those not conforming to the Portuguese congregation, even sometimes resulting in excommunication (Kaplan 1999).

All of these historical contexts are evoked by the title of Herberto Helder's story, with the basic Portuguese word "Holanda". Form and content of the story are extremely condensed: while the protagonist, an unnamed poet, is situated in the spatial context of the historical region of "Holanda", it becomes apparent that the narrative uses almost no time deictics – we find neither adverbs such as "yesterday," "today," and "tomorrow," nor time adverbials such as "last Sunday," "this afternoon," or "next year." An exception is the alternation of day and night, which however cannot be defined more precisely. The narrative is without an event, a traditional plot, and focuses exclusively on the consciousness of a poet without a name who no longer writes poems, but who thinks about (an equally unspecified) tradition, mediated through various narrative procedures. Nor does the poet ask anyone else for their names, but the longer he stays in the country, the story continues, the greater the danger that he will lose his own name. Apart from being located in the historical region of "Holanda", the narrative is otherwise characterized by a great deal of uncertainty as to the time, place, and characters of the storyline. However, the poet's characteri-

---

[4] For a detailed anaylsis of Menasseh Ben Israel's impact on seventeenth-century European cultural history, see Rauschenbach 2019.
[5] Union of Utrecht, 1579, Article 13; A. Th. Van Deursen (1981). The text of the Union of Utrecht is in Kossman and Mellink 1974, 165–173. See also: Boogman (1979).

zation of himself consists almost entirely of time; he describes himself as being nourished by centuries, suffocated by the history of other people:

> Um poeta está sentado na Holanda. Pensa na tradição. Diz para si mesmo: eu sou alimentado pelos séculos, vivo afogado na história de outros homens. E a sua alma é atravessada pelo sopro primordial. Mas tem a alma perdida: é um inocente que maneja o fogo dos infernos. [...] Já não escreve poemas, nem pergunta às pessoas o seu nome. Ele próprio, visto estar destinado à inteira perdição, vai perdendo o nome pelo país adiante. Agora vigia a paz devoradora dos animais, as coisas, a imobilidade. Vou partir – imagina.[6] (Helder 1997 [1963], 15–16)

This aspect of the characterization of the poet is striking: he is made out of time and the history of other human beings, and is thus described as an individual who holds within himself collective history. The primordial breath, it is said, pierces his soul, but he is lost, for he is an innocent man who knows how to deal with the fire of all hells. The poet who carries collective history within himself is also experienced in spiritual matters, here represented through the plural of hell, the otherworldly place of punishment in numerous religions for deeds committed in this world that are considered forbidden by the respective faith. He himself is permeated by a "sopro primordial". This could refer to the breath of life that God breathed into the nose of Adam, his earth-formed creation, thus transforming him into a living being (Genesis 10).

The spatial, temporal and personal deictics of the narrative are consistently indeterminate, even though a lake, cows, and fields are mentioned in the course of the narrative as elements of the region evoked in the title. However, the natural landscape is described in contrast to burning cities; the poet's aimless departure is marked as an imagination of the poet. Just because the poet is a poet, he has to leave, spread out over several places, disperse, divide, and yet, precisely because he is a poet, still be one – even though he sometimes feels like he has been wandering through the desert:

---

[6] In Holland there is a poet. He thinks about tradition. He says to himself: I am being nourished by centuries, living suffocated in the history of other people. And his soul is pierced by a primordial breath. But his soul is lost: he is an innocent man handling the infernal fires. [...] He does not write poetry anymore, nor does he ask people their names. He himself, since he is abandoned to complete doom, will lose his name to the country ahead. Now he watches the devouring peace of the animals, the things, the motionlessness. I am leaving – he thinks. My translation.

> As cidades ardem. Os campos enlouquecem. Um poeta tem de partir, repartir, repartir-se. Um poeta deve ser uno. O inferno não o deixa. Às vezes, lamenta-se: Sinto-me como se tivesse percorrido o deserto; não sei nada.[7] (Helder 1997 [1963], 16)

The close reading of these first few paragraphs of the story reveals the fundamental procedures of the text. The procedures establish and repeat semantic features that might – also, but not exclusively – refer to Jewish history: the title of the historical region of Holland, the theologically versed protagonist who is familiar with all forms of hell, who has wandered the desert, who is permeated by the breath of life fleeing from burning cities. If we just consider the phrase "pelo sopro primordial", for instance, we are reminded not only of the breath of life, but also of the Hebrew "ruach ha-kodesh" that refers to God's power over the universe. Is the desert in which the poet has been wandering the mythical desert of Judaic textual tradition, evoking exodus, divine presence, and sanctity? Is the poet Menasseh Ben Israel, Samuel Usque, or Jacob van Maerlant? All these are possibilities, but it is impossible to determine any of the connotations in this short story as unambiguous. The semantic network in Helder's short story consists exclusively of ambiguous lexemes that do not represent one single story. Different levels of meaning overlap and cannot be separated into binaries. The entire story blends in and out the poet's inner dilemma of experiencing and trying to find words for his experience that appears as particular and universal at the same time.

How can such a difficult mode of representing consciousness help to make students aware of the complexity of Jewish history? Firstly, by reminding them that the meaning of literary texts is greater than the sum of the significations of their components. This short story by Herberto Helder offers numerous interpretations for a process of understanding that leads from the individual textual elements towards a cognitive conception of the meaning of the text as a whole. Depending on the quality of their literature classes at school, university students still need to learn to accept the fact that meanings do not lie waiting in the texts, but are instead generated by the reader. In other words: through the example of Helder's short story, they can experience that linguistic constituents of a text serve as mental impulses for the generation of meaning by the reader. The effortful contextualization of the individual elements of Herberto Helder's text, as exemplified above, opens a multitude of cultural and historical contexts. However, the inherent value of the narrative extends further: the story embodies a pivotal

---

[7] The cities burn, the fields madden. A poet has to leave, to disperse, to split himself up. A poet must be one. Hell will not leave him. He complains now and then: I feel like I have been wandering in the desert. I know nothing. My translation.

insight that can be understood through Jewish history, but reaches far beyond it. Jewish belonging was traditionally negotiated on the basis of religious law and its sacred texts. However, on the path to modernity, traditional characteristics of belonging dissolved. This also holds true for other religious histories faced with secularization. Herberto Helder's story lets its protagonist, the poet, reflect on precisely these questions – which again involves multiple connotations of general and specific contexts of belonging:

> Ou estarei eu marcado por alguma culpa insondável? De onde descendo, que não sou amado dos holandeses nem me acalmo e participo nas tarefas? Mas uma noite recebeu a visitação. O seu espírito iluminou-se: Tu és um homem. Sim, sou um homem – disse – mas não sou holandés. Aliás, não se compreendia bem o que fosse aquilo de ser um homem. – Para onde pensam que vou ou de onde venho? – perguntaria. – Eu aspiro ao amor.[8] (Helder 1997 [1963], 16–17)

The longing for universal belonging expressed here, while at the same time experiencing non-belonging ("Where did I come from, the Hollanders don't like me"), echoes the tension that the historian Dan Diner has identified as inherent to modern diasporic Jewish experience: the tension to transform as individuals into modernity while at the same time exhibiting visible residual features of pre-modernity.[9]

In Herberto Helder's short story, tradition is repeatedly mentioned. However, tradition is not represented as a particular religious or cultural tradition, but rather as a memory, as something that no longer provides any stability:

---

8 Or am I in the end tainted by an indeterminable guilt? Where do I come from, because the Dutch don't like me, nor do I become calm and participate in the work of others. One night, however, he had a vision. His mind was enlightened: You are a human being. Yes, a human being, he said – but not a Hollander. Moreover, it was not quite clear what it meant to be a human being. – What do you think, where am I going or where am I coming from? – he would ask. – I long for love.

9 "Der diasporischen jüdischen Existenz war bereits in der Hochmoderne – wesentlich in der Zeit des ausgehenden langen 19. Jahrhunderts bis weit in das sich als katastrophisch erweisende kurze 20. Jahrhundert – eine Spannung inhärent: die in den jüdischen Individuen angelegte Spannung, sich als Einzelne zu Pionieren der Moderne zu verwandeln und zugleich als Angehörige des jüdischen Kollektivs sichtbar residuelle Merkmale der Vormoderne aufzuweisen. Ein solches Zusammentreffen ungleichzeitiger lebensweltlicher Modi, vielfach in ein und derselben Person, entspricht durchaus den sich durchsetzenden nachmodernen Lagen der Gegenwart. Zugehörigkeit erstreckt sich damit auf verschiedene Lebenswelten, Kulturen und Sprachgemeinschaften. Dabei verweisen die Embleme der Zugehörigkeit auf unterschiedliche Zeitschichten der Erinnerung – eine Konstellation, wie sie von Juden in der Moderne vorweggenommen wurde." (Diner 2011, VIII).

> Pensa furiosamente na tradição, e toda a sua memória está corrompida por uma ardente e desordenada tristeza. O sangue é negro desde a raiz. Porque ninguém sabe onde a corrupção completa a inocência. [...] Tradição, compreende uma: ama-a. Perdeu o nome, essa sabedoria. Beleza, é pouco. Verdade, é muito. Trata-se de um termo subtil que participa de uma e-outra, que se tornou inútil, insensato.[10] (Helder 1997 [1963], 17–18)

The short story's focus on the modes of the inner effects that the transformation of tradition can have for a person allows the reader a glimpse of what it can mean to let go of religious self-understanding and find yourself faced with belonging in post-traditional times. Belonging in Helder's short story occurs only as fractions, fragments, and particles of a unity that no longer exists. The storytelling offers an aesthetic experience of belonging and non-belonging as tense, painful processes of the modern self.

The objective of teaching literature at universities is to enable students to interpret complex linguistic manifestations in terms of their semantic and conceptual contexts: We strive to integrate textual language competence with the students' cognitive ability to mobilize their knowledge of the world and to integrate this into their processes of text comprehension. Herberto Helder's short story represents the search for the self, in particular, the absence of collective belonging, when it traces the disintegration of an essentialist conception of identity. This is not a playful, uncomplicated experience – it can also be potentially disturbing. This is illustrated by the disorientation that the protagonist of the story experiences. Yet essentialist notions of identity present no alternative in Helder's oeuvre.

Our example is not intended to imply that there are no Portuguese literatures in the twentieth and twenty-first centuries that focus explicitly on Jewish history and their environments. There are. Michaël Studemund-Halévy provides numerous examples (Studemund-Halévy 1997, 307),[11] and the oeuvre of Ilse Losa deserves special consideration.[12] The decision to consider Herberto Helder's opus

---

[10] He furiously thinks about the tradition, and all his memory is corrupted by an ardent and disorderly sadness. The blood is black from its roots. For no one knows where the corruption completes the innocence. [...] Tradition, one he understands: he loves it. He has lost the name, this wisdom. Beauty, it is not enough. Truth, it is too much. It is a subtle concept, which is part of both the one and the other and which has become useless, senseless.
[11] See also Garzón (1996).
[12] The Berlin-born Portuguese writer, Ilse Losa (1913–2006), is an eminent figure in twentieth-century history of Portuguese literatures. Ilse Lieblich (as was her maiden name) had fled to Portugal in the 30s, was married in Oporto, and published her first works in the late 1940s. The translingual aesthetics of Losa, a non-native speaker of Portuguese who wrote in Portuguese, negotiate multiple belongings and historical experiences. Losa also made outstanding transla-

as an example in the context of the broader epistemic interest of this volume is not only out of respect for the diversity that characterizes the extensive fields of Jewish literature. It also provides evidence of the theoretical impetus that can be drawn from dealing with diasporic Jewish literatures, as Herberto Helder's oeuvre is dedicated to the entanglements, the spheres in which the particular and the universal interact in human experience. His literary texts and poems are dedicated to the complex mental fabric of an experience of existence that does not dissolve in tradition, be it national or religious. Herberto Helder's work opposed the identitarian ideology of the Salazar regime with a language that did not absorb the national, but into which the most diverse cultural and artistic currents had been integrated. As in the example of his short story, the crass contrast between city and country is a recurring theme throughout his writings. Helder's oeuvre is concerned with historical experiences that are to be understood beyond the national, with inner transformations of belonging that were diametrically opposed to Salazar's essentialist understanding of the Portuguese collective as an *ethnos*. Therefore, it is one of the most important masterpieces in the field of Portuguese studies. At the same time, it allows students to experience aesthetically how vital a reflection of historical experience and belonging can be for present concerns as well. Herbert Helder's texts are not easily comprehensible; they display complex intertextual and historical references that readers first have to grasp in order to access the semantic horizons of his writing. However, this is not a shortcoming, but an important asset. Thus, the post-essentialist impulse of Helder's writing can become a key resource for reflecting on our present – in Portuguese studies and beyond.

Bibliography

Boogman, J.C. "The Union of Utrecht. Its genesis and consequences." *BMGN – Low Countries Historical Review* 94.3 (1979): 377–407.
Buescu, Helena C. "Communicating Voices: Herberto Helder's Experiments in Cross-Cultural Poetry", in: *Forum for Modern Language Studies* 43.2 (2007): 173–186.
Buescu, Helena C. "World Literature in a Poem. The Case of Herberto Helder." *Institutions of World Literature: Writing, Translation, Markets*. Eds. Stefan Helgesson, and Pieter Vermeulen. London: Routledge, 2016. 53–66.
Diner, Dan. "Einführung." *Enzyklopädie jüdischer Geschichte und Kultur (EJGK)*. Ed. Dan Diner. Vol. 1. Stuttgart: J.B. Metzler, 2011. VII–XVIII.

---

tions – she translated Bertolt Brecht and Anna Seghers into Portuguese, for example. None of her texts are translated into English. Including her texts in the modern Jewish literary canon is a necessary, but still pending, step.

Garzón, Jacobo Israel. "Autores judeo-portugueses contemporáneos." *Revista de Estudos Judaicos* 3 (1996): 53–58.

Gomes Ascenso, Diana. *Poetischer Widerstand im Estado Novo. Die Dichtung von Sophia de Mello Breyner Andresen*. Berlin: De Gruyter, 2018.

Helder, Herberto. *Os Passos em Volta*. Assírio & Alvim, 1997 [1963].

Kaplan, Yosef. *Les nouveaux Juifs d'Amsterdam; essai sur l'Histoire sociale et intellectuelle du judaïsme séfarade au XVIIe siècle*. Paris: Chandeigne, 1999.

Kossman, E. H., and A. F. Mellink (Eds.). *Texts Concerning the Revolt of the Netherlands*. Cambridge: Cambridge University Press, 1974.

Martins, Jorge. *Portugal e os Judeus: Volume I – Dos primórdios da nacionalidade à legislação pombalina*. Lisboa: Vega, 2006.

Mucznik, Esther. "Elementos para a Historia da Moderna Comunidade Judaica em Portugal." *Revista de Estudos Judaicos* 2 (1995): 33–35.

Preto-Rodas, Richard A. "Samuel Usque's Consolação às Tribulações de Israel as Pastoral Literature Engagée." *Hispania* 73.1 (1990): 72–76.

Rauschenbach, Sina. *Judaism for Christians: Menasseh Ben Israel (1604–1657)*. Lanham, MD: Lexington Books, 2019.

Roani, Gerson L. "Memória Judaica e Literatura Portuguesa: A Consolação às Tribulações de Israel, de Samuel Usque (1553)." *Arquivo Maaravi: Revista Digital de Estudos Judaicos da UFMG*, 5.9 (2011): 56–63.

Studemund-Halévy, Michaël. "Zwischen Rückkehr und Neuanfang: Juden in Portugal." *Portugal heute. Politik, Wirtschaft, Kultur*. Eds. Dietrich Briesemeister, and Axel Schönberger. Frankfurt/Main: Vervuert, 1997. 299–316.

Van Deursen, A. Th. "Between Unity and Independence: The Application of the Union as a Fundamental Law." *The Low Countries History Yearbook* 14 (1981): 50–65.

II Case Studies German, Turkish and Arabic Literatures

Laurent Mignon
A Few Remarks about Teaching Jewish Turkish Literature

Sometimes news from the publishing world can be a literature professor's best friend. The publication in 2016 of a translation into English of *Kürk Mantolu Madonna* (Madonna in a Fur Coat, 1943) (Ali 2016), a novel by the Turkish socialist writer Sabahattin Ali (1907–1948), allows the lecturer, notwithstanding the authorial intent, to introduce two highly contentious topics to their students. The first one is a variation, with a Turkish twist, on the complex question of the definition of Jewish literature. While Sabahattin Ali is not a Jewish author and Turkish not, strictly speaking, a Jewish language, *Kürk Mantolu Madonna* acquaints the readers with Maria Puder, one of the most fascinating Jewish characters in modern Turkish fiction. If Jewish experiences are to be at the heart of Jewish literature, Puder's predicaments could be considered the epitome of the Jewish bohemian experience in 1920s Berlin, as much as, or as little as, James Joyce's Leopold Blum and George Eliot's Daniel Deronda are representative of Jewish experiences on the British Isles. Ali's novel is not the only literary text in Turkish which explores themes that one might define as Jewish. One of the pioneers of the republican Turkish novel, Yakup Kadri Karaosmanoğlu (1889–1974) made ample use of biblical themes in his works and even wrote a novel entitled *Sodom ve Gomore* (Sodom and Gomorrah, 1928). With righteous prophetic verve the novel condemned the corruption in the Ottoman capital after the end of World War I and its occupation by French and British forces.

In any case, the fact that neither Ali nor Karaosmanoğlu had Jewish ancestry would be considered by most scholars of Jewish literature as an exclusionary factor. Beside the exploration of Jewish themes, in itself a contentious concept, self-identification as Jewish seems to be a *sine qua non* condition for consideration within the field of Jewish literature. Yet, here too, the Turkish literary field provides several examples that question this approach. It is true that there are several authors and poets who wrote or still write in Turkish and claim their Jewishness. Some of them, like the poets İsak Ferera (1883–1933) and Jozef Habib Gerez avoid references to Jewish themes in their verses, while engaging with religious, cultural and historical aspects of Jewishness in their journalistic work, whereas others such as the novelist and short-story writer Mario Levi turn Istanbul's Jewish community into the subject matter of several of their literary works. But where can one situate authors such as Bilge Karasu (1930–1995), Sevim Burak (1931–1983) and Roni Margulies who have or had a complex relationship

OpenAccess. © 2020 Laurent Mignon, published by De Gruyter. This work is licensed under the Creative Commons Attribution-NonCommercial-NoDerivatives 4.0 License.
https://doi.org/10.1515/9783110619003-006

with their Jewish heritage and reject or would have rejected their categorization as Jewish authors and the inclusion of their works into a corpus of Jewish literature?[1] To sum up, the challenges encountered when trying to define Jewish literature within the context of francophone, germanophone or anglophone literatures also exist in the turcophone literary context.

The question of Jewish literature is not the sole problem raised by the publication of the *Madonna in a Fur Coat*. A more general question pertaining to the definition of Turkish literature was being debated in the months Maureen Freely and Alexander Dawe published their translation. Indeed in 2015, the poet Orhan Kahyaoğlu had published his two-volume anthology of modern Turkish poetry with the title *Modern Türkçe Şiir Antolojisi* meaning "anthology of modern poetry in Turkish" which was in clear contradistinction to the usual *Modern Türk Şiiri Antolojisi*, meaning "anthology of modern Turkish poetry". In English, "Turkish poetry" is ambiguous and could signify both "poetry in the Turkish language" and "poetry of the Turks". While "Türk şiiri" (Turkish poetry) and "Türk edebiyatı" (Turkish literature), as commonly used in Turkish, imply that the literary texts in consideration are in Turkish, there is nevertheless the added implication that they, or at least their authors, are also Turkish. In order to avoid this ambiguity, Kahyaoğlu wrote in his introduction that:

> [...] we recognize that poets who write modern poetry are not only Turks. The Kurdish question and the thirty-year-old struggle of this people and their quest for an identity, that developed in parallel to this struggle, has largely contributed to this recognition of ours. Time has come to accept that not every community or group living in Turkey, be it in Rumelia or Anatolia, is Turkish. There are many poets in this anthology who, though their mother-tongue is not Turkish, are or have been writing in Turkish today and in earlier decades as a consequence of the dominant ideology. It is for this reason that we believe that 'poetry in Turkish' [Türkçe şiir] is a meaningful reflection of the respect we show to the communal identity of such poets. (Kahyaoğlu 2015, 16)

Kahyaoğlu's arguments were not new and went back to the controversy around the concept of "Kurdish poets writing in Turkish" that developed after the publication of a special feature on the topic in the literary magazine *Yasakmeyve* (The Forbidden Fruit) in 2004 (Mignon 2014, 196–199). Just like in 2004, Kahyaoğlu's stand led to strong-worded reactions from the religious and secular nationalist establishments. In a comment that he wrote for the secularist nationalist *Aydınlık* (Enlightenment) daily, the poet Özdemir İnce condemned Kahyaoğlu's approach as "absurd, racist and separatist, contrary to universal

---

[1] For a more detailed discussion of the definition of Jewish literature in a Turkish context, see Mignon 2018, 126–130.

uses" (İnce 2016), in terms that were echoing his reaction during the debates in the early 2000s. İnce's approach reflected the Turkish republic's conception of citizenship which, in theory, does not recognize any ethnic, national or linguistic minorities. Hence Kahyaoğlu's use of the concept "Türkçe şiir" was avowedly political and deeply subversive as it aimed to embrace the ethno-religious diversity of the poets who contributed to the history of poetry in the Turkish language over the years.

This is an important issue also in the field of literary historiography, as non-Muslim authors and poets have often been sidelined in the many histories of Turkish literature.[2] Indeed, most historians of Turkish literature seem to be equating Turkishness and "Muslimness" and only include writers of Muslim heritage in their works. Undeniably, approaches such as Kahyaoğlu's create space for the recognition of the specificity of the contributions of Kurdish literati while also integrating non-Muslim authors, such as the Armeno-Turkish pioneers of the novel in Turkish and Greco-Turkish translators of French popular literature into the history of Turkish literature. This discussion is also of relevance in the context of the study of Judeo-Turkish literature (Turkish in the Hebrew script) and of literature in Turkish by authors of Jewish background and should be engaged with in class and lecture rooms when talking about the works of Jewish authors who wrote in Turkish.

However, before moving on to the topic of teaching Jewish literature, it might be necessary to say a word or two about the genesis of Jewish Turkish literature. Some readers may wonder whether there is such a thing as Jewish Turkish literature beyond the works of Mario Levi that have gained international fame –*İstanbul bir Masaldı* (Istanbul was a Fairytale, 1999) having been translated in languages as diverse as Korean, Croatian and even English.

As seen above, the fact that the existence of Jewish Turkish literature is largely unknown even in Turkey is mainly due to an understanding of literary history that has overlooked non-Muslim authors, including Jews. There is however one more issue: Unlike the cases of Armeno-Turkish and Greco-Turkish (also known as Karamanlı) literatures, where native speakers of Turkish, as well as Protestant missionary organizations, were publishing texts in Turkish in communitarian alphabets, Judeo-Turkish printing was mostly the result of decisions taken by religious and secular community leaders who wanted to boost the knowledge and use of Turkish among the mainly Ladino-speaking Jewish community of Ottoman Turkey. Jewish figureheads wanted to promote greater communal empowerment in an age marked by drastic reforms in the Ottoman

---

[2] On the topic see, *i.a.* Mignon 2008, 35–43.

state, the need to confront the rise of Christian antisemitism in Ottoman lands as epitomized by the blood libels in Rhodes and Damascus, new employment opportunities in the public sector for non-Muslims who were fluent in Turkish and the advent of the Alliance israélite universelle schools and their promotion of Enlightenment ideals and French language and culture.³

Though there are a few examples of texts in Turkish in the Rashi script, before the nineteenth century, Judeo-Turkish publications consisted mainly of ephemeral periodicals which were bilingual in Judeo-Spanish and Judeo-Turkish. The only relatively successful publication was *Üstat* (The Master), edited by the educator Moïse Fresko (1859–1912), which was published over two years in Izmir between 1889 to 1891. Its main aim was to promote Turkish and a better knowledge of Ottoman Turkish culture among Jews, while encouraging integration and thus showing the attachment of the Jewish community to the Ottoman state. Publications such as *Üstat* were primarily aimed at creating a Jewish readership for publications in Turkish and paved the way for the emergence of Jewish Turkish literature at a later stage.

From a literary point of view, the turn of the century was also a turning point in the history of Jewish Turkish literature. In 1901, Avram Naon (1878–1947) published a collection of mostly Neo-Parnassian poems entitled *Kalb-i Şikeste* (The Broken Heart, 1901) in Turkish in the Ottoman Turkish script, a version of the Perso-Arabic script used to write Turkish. This collection was followed a few years later by the publication of *Ebr-i Bahar* (Spring Clouds, 1904) and *Aşina Sesler* (Familiar Voices, 1914) –two volumes of poetry by İsak Ferera.⁴ Naon and Ferera were representatives of a new generation of young Jewish intellectuals who had been educated in modern Jewish and Ottoman secular schools, while the Judeo-Spanish press and literature was flourishing. It is notable that this was before Turkish started to be intensively promoted by famous intellectuals and community activists such as Avram Galante (1873–1961) and Moïse Cohen (1883–1961), alias Muhsin Tekinalp. Ferera and Naon would publish *Mirat* (The Mirror), an ephemeral magazine, in the Ottoman Turkish script in 1909. This periodical exclusively published Jewish authors. Unlike other Turkish publications that were published in Turkish by Jewish intellectuals in the few months of great hope after the promulgation of the Second Constitution, such as Nisim Masliyah's *İttihat* (The Union, 1908) and Bohor İsrael's *Ceride-i Felsefiye* (The Philosophical Magazine, 1912), *Mirat* openly embraced an enlightened Jewish-Ottoman identity while addressing Jews and non-Jews alike. Naon wrote in an

---

3 On the genesis of Jewish Turkish literature, see Mignon 2011.
4 For a monograph on Naon and Ferera's poetry, see Karakartal 2006.

editorial that the magazine aimed to be a " show-window for the works of Jewish authors writing in Turkish" and that "no work could be accepted that was from the outside, from a writer who was not Jewish" (Naon 1909, 1). The publication of the magazine was a way to circumvent the discriminatory attitude towards Jews in the literary world. Some articles in the magazine show that despite their commitment to the Turkish language, Naon and Ferera faced adversity because of their Jewishness when trying to publish their work. Regardless of their early efforts to promote literature in Turkish, both poets would hardly be remembered during the republican era, as the alphabet change of 1928 rendered works in the Ottoman Turkish script inaccessible to later generations of readers, unless they had the relevant education. Nonetheless after the establishment of the Republic and the intensification of state-led Turkification policies, Turkish would slowly start to replace Ladino and French as the main language of literary expression for the Jewish community.

So, if something that can be categorized as Jewish Turkish literature exists, how can it be taught? As part of my own teaching practice, I have followed two paths. The first one is the integration of Jewish Turkish literature into a generalist Turkish literature course at both undergraduate and graduate levels. The second path is a graduate course that is focused on Jewish Turkish literature per se. Both approaches present specific challenges.

Teaching the history of Jewish literature in the context of a generalist course on the history of Turkish literature within the framework of a department of Turkish philology introduces the students to the need to deconstruct literary historiography and the canon. This, however, is true when engaging with all minor literatures in the not-unproblematic-sense given to the term by Gilles Deleuze (1925–1995) and Félix Guattari (1930–1992) (Deleuze and Guattari 1976).[5]

Such an approach represents an additional challenge for the lecturer. In a Turkish university context, one can assume that students have a basic understanding of the history of Turkish literature, having been repeatedly faced with a list of great writers and poets, mostly male, who have marked the history of Turkish literature, throughout their school years. Hence students would from early on be very conscious that the evocation of the sixteenth century anonymous *Tarih-i Al-i Osman* (History of the House of Osman) in the Rashi script[6], the reading of a poem by İsak Ferera and the editorial of *Mirat* magazine penned by Avram Naon were a challenge to what they had learned about the history of Turkish literature and the contributions of non-Muslims to that history. Hence

---

5 For a discussion of "minor literature", see, *inter alia*, Bogue 1997 and Klein 2018.
6 For a facsimile, transcription and analysis of this unusual text, see Marazzi 1980.

the teaching of Jewish literature and the critical reflection on history and historiography can progress hand in hand.

Yet, in the context of a Turkish literature course taught to students of Turkish as a foreign language, as it would be taught in universities outside Turkey and northern Cyprus, the lecturer deals with the additional task of having to teach students the canon. This is a necessity if students are to engage critically with the available secondary literature and enter in conversation with their Turkish-speaking peers. Hence while students are taught about the canon they are also learning how to deconstruct it. This provides the lecturer with the opportunity to develop a different and more inclusive history of literature during the teaching process.

Beside a discussion of Jewish literature which is "in conversation" with other aspects of literary history, exploring a variety of issues from the "romantic rebellion" in nineteenth century Turkish literature to the impact of the alphabet reform on literary historiography, there is the option at graduate level of teaching a course focused exclusively on Jewish Turkish literature. Such a course, if it is to include the pre-republican era, will need to embrace a multilingual approach as Judeo-Spanish and French remained the main languages of literary expression for Jewish literati until well into the republican period. Needless to say that the number of potential students with such linguistic skills is limited. The fact that an author such as Avram Galante who advocated the use of Turkish as a literary language within the Jewish community, also published literary works in Judeo-Spanish, while contributing articles to the French-language *Archives israélites* is a reminder of the difficulty of engaging with Jewish authors in only one language. However, there is nothing specifically Jewish about this. Multilingualism was the norm among the Ottoman intelligentsia, hence it was not uncommon for intellectuals to write in more than one language –an important lesson to teach also in a generalist course on Turkish literary history.

In the context of a course on Jewish Turkish literature the discussion of the concept of "Jewish literature" needs to be at the heart of the approach. From biblical themes in Turkish literature to playwright and poet Beki L. Bahar's (1927–2011) Turkish-language works, there is much material that can contribute to a critical engagement with the concept of "Jewish literature". In my own courses, I use a quasi-maximalist definition of Jewish literature, which means that I include any literary work created by a person of Jewish heritage, broadly defined, whether it has a Jewish theme or not. There are some restrictions though: I do not include authors who clearly refuse to be categorized as Jewish authors, unless their works deal with issues that are of relevance within a discussion of Jewish literature, for instance, Bilge Karasu's exploration of the figure of Judas and his writings on minorities and Roni Margulies' theoretical texts about his stance towards Jewishness, such as his essay "Yahudi Olmak Mı Olmamak Mı" (To Be Or Not To Be A Jew, 1997) as I believe that they nourish constructively the debate.

Finally, the discussion of Turkish texts brings in the added benefit of questioning the often very western-centric approaches to Jewish literature. Indeed, there is a need to look beyond New York, Berlin and Jerusalem to the literatures and cultures outside the Americas, Europe and Israel. This leads us back to Sabahattin Ali and his *Madonna in a Fur Coat*. The novel was published in English translation in 2016 to much media interest. Yet it is worthwhile stressing that the first translation of Ali's novel in Vietnamese had already been published thirty years before in 1986 – a reminder that translations of literary works into English are not at all representative of the international reception of literary works. Hence, in conclusion, one could argue that the study of Jewish literature in a Turkish context teaches both teachers and students to be always on the alert and to question the constructedness of history, of the canon and of identities.

Bibliography

Ali, Sabahattin. *Madonna in a Fur Coat*. Transl. Maureen Freely and Alexander Dawe. London: Penguin, 2016.

Bogue, Ronald. "Minor Writing and Minor Literature." *symploke* 5. 1 (1997): 99–118.

Deleuze, Gilles, and Félix Guattari. *Kafka, pour une littérature mineure*. Paris: Minuit, 1975.

İnce, Özdemir. "Türk Şiiri Mi, Türkçe Şiir Mi?" *Aydınlık* (5 July 2016): http://www.aydinlikgazete.com/kultursanat/turk-siiri-mi-turkce-siir-mi-h88162.html.

Kahyaoğlu, Orhan. "Giriş." *Modern Türkçe Şiir Antolojisi*, vol. 1. (2015): 15–36.

Karakartal, Oğuz. *Tevfik Fikret'in izinde iki şair : Avram Naon ve İsak Ferera*. Istanbul: Eren, 2006.

Klein, Rony. "D'une redéfinition de la littérature mineure." *Littérature* 189, no. 1 (2018): 72–88.

Marazzi, Ugo. *Tevarih-i Al-i Osman: Cronaca Anonima Ottomana in Trascrizione Ebraica*. Napoli: Istituto universitario orientale, 1980.

Mignon, Laurent. "Bir Varmış, Bir Yokmuş: Kanon, Edebiyat Tarihi ve Azınlıklar Üzerine Notlar." *Pasaj* 6 (2008): 35–43.

Mignon, Laurent. "Avram, İsak and the Others: Notes on the Genesis of Judeo-Turkish Literature." *Between Religion and Language*. Ed. Evangelia Balta and Mehmet Sönmez. Istanbul: Eren, 2011. 71–83.

Mignon, Laurent. "A Pilgrim's Progress: Armenian and Kurdish Literatures in Turkish and the Rewriting of Literary History." *Patterns of Prejudice* 48.2 (2014): 182–200.

Mignon, Laurent. "Ringen mit Dämonen: Gibt es eine jüdisch-türkische Literatur?" *Ni Kaza en Turkiya: Erzählungen jüdischer Autoren aus Istanbul*. Ed. and transl. Wolfgang Riemann. Engelschoff: Verlag auf dem Ruffel, 2018. 125–144.

Naon, Avram. "Arz-ı Meram." *Mirat* 1 (14 February 1909): 1–2.

Lukas Muehlethaler
Teaching Literatures by Arabized Jews: Medieval and Modern

Many of the courses in Jewish Studies I teach at a German University involve medieval texts written by Arabized Jews.[1] Though these texts seem to lack any relation to modern Arab-Jewish literature, I have come to the conclusion – and this will be my claim – that the challenges one faces when teaching medieval Arab-Jewish literature resemble those one faces when teaching modern literature written by Arabized Jews. In both cases, the challenges derive from the curricular structures, the "Fächerkanon," at German universities and from the background of the students I have the privilege to teach. To substantiate my claim, I outline three curricular challenges which, I think, pertain to the teaching of both medieval and modern Arab-Jewish literature and I present – in the manner of case studies – three courses I have taught on medieval Arab-Jewish literature whose interdisciplinary approach could also be applied to courses on modern literature written by Arabized Jews.

In what context do we read and interpret Arab-Jewish literature?

The first challenge is raised by the cultural narratives which often underlie the perception of and research on works written by Arabized Jews. For the medieval period these are the various generalizing conceptions of Arab-Jewish history, ranging from "Golden Age" depictions to neo-lachrymose conceptions.[2] How one perceives Arabized Jews to have participated in the majority culture, how one conceives of cultural boundaries, and how one gauges the degree of inter-

---

[1] To refer to Arabic-speaking Jews who participate in a culture in which Arabic is the main language I will be using the term 'Arabized Jew' as suggested by Ross Brann (2000) and Moshe Behar (2009) and I will be referring to 'Arab-Jewish' identity or literature following the example of Reuven Snir (2019). An alternative term, 'Arab Jew,' is also used often, but seems less suited because it also forms the center of recent, often vocal, cultural and political debates (Levy 2008, 2017).
[2] Mark R. Cohen (2013) offers a succinct reflection on "golden age" conceptions. The term 'lachrymose' was introduced by Salo W. Baron (1939, 1963; see also Teller 2014) and more recently applied to the context of Arabized Jews by Mark R. Cohen (1991).

ə OpenAccess. © 2020 Lukas Muehlethaler, published by De Gruyter. [CC BY-NC-ND] This work is licensed under the Creative Commons Attribution-NonCommercial-NoDerivatives 4.0 License.
https://doi.org/10.1515/9783110619003-007

communal violence has a strong impact on the approach to Arab-Jewish literature and on its interpretation. The same holds true for the modern period. Though the cultural context of modern Arabized Jews is less remote in time, it has changed dramatically during the second half of the 20th century. Contemporary perceptions and conceptions about relations between "Jews and Arabs" make it often difficult to conceive of the many ways in which Arabized Jews lived as part of the majority culture in different parts of the Arabic-speaking world. The great extent to which the various medieval and modern narratives of Arab-Jewish history are still functional is shown in the contemporary debates on the term 'Arab Jew' (Levy 2017).

Is the literature of Arabized Jews Arabic literature?

At first glance, the question whether the literature of Arabized Jews is Arabic literature appears nonsensical. During most of the medieval period, Arabic served as both the colloquial and the written language for a majority of Arabic Jews and was thus – based on rough demographic estimates – the language used by the vast majority of Jews living at that time. Jews contributed to many genres of Arabic literature. They also applied some of these genres to the Jewish religious tradition. This included both Rabbanite authors who commented on and continued the Rabbinic tradition and Karaite authors who rejected the Rabbinic tradition and aimed at replacing it.[3] Rabbanite and Karaite Jews often wrote Arabic in the script they also used for the Hebrew language. This kind of Arabic writing is often termed Judaeo-Arabic, though scholars disagree on the exact definition and significance of this term (Khan 2017b, 2017a). Despite the central place of Arabic in the literature of Arabized Jews, Arabic (or Judaeo-Arabic) is not the only language they used for literary production. From the 10th to at least the 16th century, Arabized Jews write major works of various genres also in Hebrew. This includes both "Jewish" genres such as halakhic writings as well as more "general" genres such as poetry – both liturgical and "profane" – which was written in Hebrew, though most poets came to use meters and motifs of Arabic poetry.[4] If we were to focus on works written in Arabic, we would miss out on

---

[3] The best monograph on the medieval Jewish literature in the Arabic language is still the pioneering work by Moritz Steinschneider (1902).
[4] Non-Hebraist English speakers can obtain a good "second-hand" impression of this tradition through the superb translations by Peter Cole (2007).

important aspects of the multilingualism and the polyphony in the culture of Arabized Jews.

This requires in some sense a correction of a correction. Initially, the "outside" perspective on the medieval literature of Arabized Jews had focused on works written in Hebrew and on works later translated from Arabic into Hebrew. These works came to find their place on the proverbial Jewish bookshelf while most of the Arabic literary production of Arabized Jews became marginalized during the cultural and societal shifts of the later Middle Ages, which had Arabized Jews lose their former cultural hegemony. Arab-Jewish literature had to be "rediscovered" as part of the broader canon of Jewish literature, a rediscovery to which the proponents and contemporaries of the "Wissenschaft des Judentums" made major contributions.[5] This rediscovery (and necessary correction) put (Judaeo-)Arabic literature at the very center of Arab-Jewish culture and it was their Hebrew prose production which became somewhat marginalized. Yet unless we understand Hebrew works (and in some sense the Hebrew translations of Judaeo-Arabic works) as an integral part of Arab-Jewish literature, we will have only a partial understanding of the culture of Arabized Jews. This is valid even more so because the two languages did not exist side-by-side, but interacted in various interesting ways. Judaeo-Arabic texts, especially texts in traditional genres, often show the impact of the Hebrew language on their vocabulary and syntax; Hebrew texts, in turn, echo Arabic syntax.[6]

Similar effects of multilingualism and polyphony seem to hold true for Arab-Jewish literature written in the Modern period. Arabized Jews write in languages other than Arabic, such as European languages or modern Hebrew and in some cases create works in more than one language. Their choice of language is often not free but determined by (forced) migration and cultural re-orientation.

Three well-known examples should suffice: Jacqueline Shohet Kahanoff (1917–1979) was born in Egypt as the daughter of an Iraqi Jewish father and Tunisian Jewish mother. She received her education in the United States and published in English, but in the mid-1950s immigrated to Israel.[7] Sami Michael (Sāmī Miḫā'īl), born 1926 in Baghdad, wrote in Arabic, had to flee to Iran and in 1949

---

[5] To be sure, these scholars focused on what they considered to be the "classical period" of Judaeo-Arabic literature, as the pioneering monograph by Steinschneider (1902) shows.
[6] Even though Arabic was the literary language of a majority of Jews living in the Islamicate world, they also used (and adapted for their use) languages of other Islamicate cultures, such as Persian and Turkic languages.
[7] In the case of Kahanoff, writing and publishing in English might not have been a choice, because her educational background did not provide her with sufficient knowledge in literary Arabic and Arabic literature (Starr and Somekh 2011).

immigrated to Israel (he still holds Iraqi citizenship). He worked as a hydrologist and at the age of 45 started to publish in Hebrew. Isḥāq Bār-Moshe (1927–2003) was born in Baghdad and immigrated to Israel in the 1950s. He continued to write in Arabic but, he, too, started to publish only in the 1970s. These few examples show that if one were to try to understand the literature of Arabized Jews as a whole based on works written in Arabic alone, one would obtain a lopsided image of that literary production. This is true also with regard to individual writers, especially those who wrote in more than one language.

Is the literature of Arabized Jews "Jewish" literature?

The third curricular challenge relates to the religious identity of the authors and the works they write. To what extent can we consider the literature of Arabized Jews to be "Jewish" literature? In the medieval Christian world, the cultural space of Jews became increasingly circumscribed and was generally limited. Most works written by Jews can be entered in the canon of "Jewish literature" because they are easily identifiable as such. They were either written in Hebrew – which also became the language of most scientific texts written by Jews from the 13th century onward – or they were written for a Jewish audience or on Jewish topics. Though generalizing statements are rarely helpful, much evidence indicates that Jews in the medieval Christian world directly participated in the general culture much less than their Arab-speaking co-religionists in the Islamicate World.[8]

The question is of a much greater import for the social context of medieval Arabized Jews. Lower levels of inter-communal violence (as compared to the contemporaneous Christian West) and a shared language led to more permeable cultural boundaries between various communities and allowed Jews to participate in the general culture. This also meant that Jews contributed to many genres of Arabic literature that lacked denominational markings. One would not identify these works as "Jewish," nor would these works identify their authors as Jews. So much so that a sizeable part of the literature produced during the Middle Ages by Arabized Jews would fall outside of the scope of Jewish studies or related disciplines. The problem with an approach focusing on "Jewish" literature is

---

[8] Gad Freudenthal (2012) provides a helpful discussion of factors contributing to the permeability of inter-communal boundaries in this context.

not so much that it sidelines entire genres, e.g. scientific, philosophical, or medical writings, but that it considers the oeuvre of an author only in part.

If, for example, an author composes two treatises: a treatise on a topic that clearly relates to "Jewish" notions and another treatise that does not even allow the readers to identify the religious affiliation of its author, an approach interested only in Jewish aspects of that author's work would focus on the former treatise and ignore the latter. The image of an author's literary production and interests so obtained would be partial at best.

The same holds true for the modern period. Jewish authors contributed to the *nahḍa*, the "awakening" of Arabic culture during the late 19th and early 20th century (Behar and Ben-Dor Benite 2013; Snir 2006). The Lebanese women's rights activist Esther Moyal (1874–1948), for example, translated Western Literature into Arabic, worked as a journalist, and founded Arabic newspapers (Levy 2013). Focusing on her work as an activist for Jewish women's rights would not give her sufficient credit for her important contributions to Arabic literature. Jewish authors also contributed to new genres in Arabic literature and some of them continued to write in these genres (in both Arabic and Hebrew) after the exodus of Jews from Arab countries led to a decline in the number of Arabic texts written by Jews. The cultural dynamics enabling the participation of Arabized Jews in the renewal of Arabic literature and the change of these dynamics over the course of less than a century has been analyzed by Reuven Snir (2019) using as an example the genre of the Arabic short story.

The above examples and anecdotes are far too few to do justice to the long and rich cultural history of Arabized Jews. It is clear, however, that Arabized Jews participated in the general Arabic culture in different geographical areas during different periods. Some reflected in the works they wrote on their hybrid cultural identity; others did so in some of their works only or not at all. Approaching their literature by asking only questions related to their Jewish identity or to "Jewish topics" would result in a skewed image of Arab-Jewish literature and culture.

To whom can we teach the literature of Arabized Jews?

The curricular challenges mentioned so far suggest that teaching the modern literature of Arabized Jews requires an interdisciplinary effort. However, they also suggest that learning about this literature takes tremendous effort and demands exceptional preparation. For the medieval period, students should combine proficiency in Arabic, proficiency in Hebrew, and a grasp of many historical and cultural contexts with a thorough knowledge of the subject matters of various genres of texts (literature, halakha, exegesis, science, philosophy, etc.). For the modern period one would add to these requirements a knowledge of several western languages, literatures, and cultures. But do such students exist?

I have come to the conclusion that the perfect academic setting for teaching the medieval literature of Arabized Jews does not exist: There are no teachers perfectly qualified to teach all facets of this literature, nor are there students who are perfectly prepared to study this literature. What exists – and this is a source of wonderful surprise and constant encouragement – are the openness and the enthusiasm of students who want to learn about Arab-Jewish literature. All it takes is to choose didactic approaches that allow students from different disciplines and courses of study to collaborate. That these approaches can take very simple forms I would like to illustrate using the example of three courses on medieval Arab-Jewish literature I have taught in recent years.

My colleagues and I have been teaching medieval philosophy in its various languages following an interdisciplinary approach. This approach works particularly well for texts that were translated from Greek into Arabic and then into Latin, and Hebrew. It is less suited for those works by Arabized Jews which were translated neither into medieval Hebrew nor into any modern language. But with some preparation, teaching these texts can be highly rewarding. In a course on the 12th-century Jewish philosopher Abū l-Barakāt al-Baghdādī, for example, half the participants were students of philosophy and the other half students of Arabic and Jewish studies. Some of the students lacked the necessary language skills and others lacked a background in philosophy. To accommodate this heterogeneous group of participants it was sufficient to produce English draft translations of selected chapters and to co-teach the course with a colleague from the philosophy department of Humboldt University.

I experienced how a heterogeneous group of participants enriches the teaching and learning experience also when I taught a course on Aristotle's *Poetics* in Arabic and Hebrew. Among the participants were students from Jewish Studies, Arabic Studies, Islamic Studies, Classical Studies, Byzantine Studies, Religious Studies, and Comparative Literature. They had backgrounds in Greek, Syriac, Arabic, Hebrew, and Latin with all students having reading knowledge of at least one of these languages. We ended up reading selected passages from Aristotle's text, its Syriac and Arabic translations, as well as the Arabic and Hebrew versions of Averroes' commentary in all languages at the same time, so that each student was able to read the text of at least one literary tradition and engage in exchange and discussion with students reading the text in another tradition. Because of the varied background of the students, among them Arab Christians from Iraq and Syria and Arab Israelis, all participants had the opportunity to engage with this complex textual tradition in novel and often unexpected ways.[9]

Several times the initiative for interdisciplinary courses on Arab-Jewish literature has come from students. A few years ago, a group of students from Arabic Studies, Semitic studies and Jewish studies approached me, suggesting I teach an introductory course in Judaeo-Arabic literature. I did so and we had lots of fun. Last semester a different group approached me with the same wish. This time we decided that the only requirement to participate would be a working knowledge of Arabic; all other skills the students would acquire during the course. We decided that we would read both printed texts and texts in manuscript form from the Cairo Geniza, with topics ranging from intellectual history to letters by India traders. Each student contributed according to his or her background and all ended up reading texts in Judaeo-Arabic manuscripts.

The approach illustrated by these "case studies" can be adapted quite easily to the teaching of modern Arab-Jewish literature. All it takes is to allow students of different backgrounds to participate and contribute, to co-teach when appropriate, and to find a suitable blend of texts in the original languages and in translations.[10] The key is, I think, to find the right mixture of didactic courage and academic humility in both teachers and students.

Bibliography

Alcalay, Ammiel. *Keys to the garden: New Israeli writing.* San Francisco: City Lights Books, 1996.
Baron, Salo W. "Emphases in Jewish History." *Jewish Social Studies* 1 (1939): 15–38.
Baron, Salo W. "Newer Emphases in Jewish History." *Jewish Social Studies* 25 (1963): 235–248.
Behar, Moshe. "What's in a Name? Socio-Terminological Formations and the Case for 'Arabized-Jews'." *Social Identities* 15.6 (2009): 747–771.
Behar, Moshe, and Zvi Ben-Dor Benite (Eds.). *Modern Middle Eastern Jewish Thought: Writings on Identity, Politics, and Culture, 1893–1958.* Waltham: Brandeis University Press, 2013.
Brann, Ross. 2000. "The Arabized Jews." *The Cambridge History of Arabic Literature: The Literature of* Al-Andalus. Ed. María Rosa Menocal, Raymond P. Scheindlin and Michael Sells. Cambridge: Cambridge University Press, 2000. 435–454.

---

9 It was this course which motivated me to work toward the English Master's program "Interdisciplinary Studies of the Middle East" which starts at Freie Universität Berlin in the Fall of 2020.
10 There exist sufficient translations to allow opening a course on modern Arab-Jewish literature to non-Arabists. See, for example, Alcalay (1996), Neuwirth and Jamoud (2007), Behar and Ben-Dor Benite (2013), and Snir (2019).

Cohen, Mark R. "The Neo-Lachrymose Conception of Jewish-Arab History." *Tikkun* 6 (1991): 55–60.
Cohen, Mark R. "The 'Golden Age' of Jewish-Muslim Relations: Myth and Reality." *A History of Jewish-Muslim Relations: From the Origins to the Present Day*. Ed. Abdelwahab Meddeb and Benjamin Stora. Princeton and Oxford: Princeton University Press, 2013. 28–38.
Cole, Peter. *The Dream of the Poem: Hebrew Poetry from Muslim and Christian Spain, 950–1492*. Princeton: Princeton University Press, 2007.
Freudenthal, Gad. "Arabic into Hebrew: The Emergence of the Translation Movement in Twelfth-Century Provence and Jewish-Christian Polemic," *Beyond Religious Borders: Interaction and Intellectual Exchange in the Medieval Islamic World*. Ed. David M. Freidenreich and Miriam Goldstein. Philadelphia: University of Pennsylvania Press, 2012. 124–43 (notes 203–209).
Khan, Geoffrey. "Judeo-Arabic." *Handbook of Jewish Languages: Revised and Updated Edition*. Ed. Lily Kahn and Aaron D. Rubin. Leiden and Boston: Brill, 2017a. 22–63.
Khan, Geoffrey. "Orthography and Reading in Medieval Judaeo-Arabic." *Arabic in Context: Celebrating 400 Years of Arabic at Leiden University*. Ed. Ahmad Al-Jallad. Leiden: Brill, 2017b. 395–404.
Levy, Lital. "Historicizing the Concept of Arab Jews in the *Mashriq*." *The Jewish Quarterly Review* 98.4 (2008): 452–469.
Levy, Lital. "Partitioned Pasts: Arab Jewish Intellectuals and the Case of Esther Azharī Moyal (1873–1948)." *The Making of the Arab Intellectual: Empire, Public Sphere and the Colonial Coordinates of Selfhood*. Ed. Dyala Hamzah. Abingdon: Routledge, 2013. 128–163.
Levy, Lital. "The Arab Jew Debates: Media, Culture, Politics, History." *Journal of Levantine Studies* 7.1 (2017): 79–103.
Neuwirth, Angelika and Nesrine Jamoud, editors. *Zieh fort aus deiner Heimat, dem Land deiner Väter... Arabische Kurzprosa irakisch-jüdischer Autoren in Israel*. Berlin: Schiler, 2007.
Snir, Reuven. "Arabic in the Service of Regeneration of Jews. The Participation of Jews in Arabic Press and Journalism in the 19th and 20th Centuries." *Acta Orientalia Academiae Scientiarum Hungaricae* 59.3 (2006): 283–323.
Snir, Reuven. *Arab-Jewish Literature: The Birth and Demise of the Arabic Short Story*. Boston: Brill, 2019.
Starr, Deborah A. and Sasson Somekh. *Mongrels or Marvels: The Levantine Writings of Jacqueline Shohet Kahanoff*. Stanford: Stanford University Press, 2011.
Steinschneider, Moritz. *Die arabische Literatur der Juden. Ein Beitrag zur Literaturgeschichte der Araber, grossenteils aus handschriftlichen Quellen*. Frankfurt a. M.: Verlag von J. Kauffmann, 1902.
Teller, Adam. "Revisiting Baron's 'Lachrymose Conception': The Meanings of Violence in Jewish History." *AJS Review* 38.2 (2014): 431–439.

Najat Abdulhaq
Dissenting Narratives – The Figure of the 'Arab Jew' in Contemporary Arabic Literature and Film

> "I was a Jew in Iraq, and now I am an Iraqi in Israel."
> Samir Naqqash (1938–2004)[1]

Over the last ten years, a topic that had been previously skirted in the public sphere of Arab countries has been broached, namely, the expulsion and departure of the Jewish population from these countries. When writers had addressed this phenomenon in the past, they did so only in the context of the Palestinian/Arab-Israeli conflict. The history of the Jews living in Arab countries (Arab Jews)[2] has been dominated by an official nationalistic discourse that has rarely been questioned (Abdulhaq 2016, 7–48). This discourse consists of two parts, one Arab and the other Zionist. Both reject considering Jews as an organic component of the society in which they live. Arab discourse connects Jewish life to Israel and hence to the Palestinian/Arab-Israeli conflict.

A new generation of authors and film makers is questioning this discourse, through novels mainly and, to a lesser degree, through non-fiction works, with consequences extending beyond the Palestinian/Arab-Israeli conflict. The central figures in these works are the Jew who used to live in Egypt, Iraq, Syria or Tunisia, but had been driven from their countries in the 1950s and 1960s. Only in the last decade a change has taken place, and a heightened interest in Jewish history in Arab countries arose that transcended the official nationalistic thought. This literary trend creates a new space where individual stories about Jews are discussed. This change has not yet brought about a shift in the official line, but literature is clearly questioning its discourse, creating a beginning of the emergence of a post-nationalistic discourse.

This interest in Jewish history is not limited to one Arab country. Between 2004 and the end of 2017, more than 23 novels and works of non-fiction that centered around an Arab Jew were published in Arab countries. These Arab-Jewish figures move beyond the stereotypical disloyal, greedy, selfish Jew so often found in modern Arab literature.

---

[1] Elimelekh (2013).
[2] For discussion of the term "Arab Jew", see Abdulhaq 2016, 31.

As an example, we can take the novels of Ihsan Abdel Quddous (1919–1990). Quddous was a famous Egyptian journalist, an editor of the popular magazine *Rose Al Youssef* and later the editor in chief of the daily newspaper *Al-Ahram*. He wrote sixty novels and collections of short stories, many of which were dramatized and filmed. His works were often described as unconventional and emancipatory but they are faithful to the Arab nationalist discourse. Quddous' novel *Don't Leave Me Alone* employs negative stereotypes of Jews. The figure of the Arab Jew has been at the margin of history, politics, and religion. In the past decade, however, writers and filmmakers have created subversive works that challenge the norms of the previous generation and hegemonic nationalistic discourse. As this essay intends to show, this confrontation – born out of an awareness of liminality and thresholds – evokes a sense of dissent.

This essay analyzes Egyptian films and fictional as well as non-fictional narratives. While circumstances in Arab countries vary, the Egyptian case tells us a great deal about how official nationalistic discourses dominated the scene until a recent change. While about one hundred thousand Jews lived in Egypt by the end of the 1940s, about eight hundred thousand to one million Jews were a major component of the societies from Morocco to Bahrain (Abdulhaq 2016, 82). The war that broke out in Palestine in 1947, followed by the proclamation of Israeli independence in 1948 and the conflicts that arose between Israel and its neighbors, resulted in most of the Jews in Egypt and other Arab nations leaving their countries. In addition, the emergence of nationalism and economic changes had a deep influence on minorities in Arab countries, including the Jews.

In the late 1970s, early 1980s, two discourses started to evolve.[3] While the dominant discourse was nationalistic in character, the other challenges and criticizes a nationalistic framework, and includes works by Western and Egyptian authors who reviewed the social, economic, and political history of Egyptian Jews (Abdulhaq 2016, 36–37).

---

3 For a detailed discussion of these discourses, see Abdulhaq 2016, 7–48.

1 The winds of change

By 2006, a new interest in "Arab Jews" was starting to become evident in literature, in non-fiction,[4] and in a number of translations of books taking up this theme, mainly from English and French.[5]

This new interest in the history of Arab Jews is not limited to writers. Documentary film makers have been in the vanguard in this regard. This trend started with *Forget Baghdad* (2002), a film about Iraqi Jews, in which, Samir Naqqash, among other things, declares that he is an Arab Jew and that he will never write in any other language but Arabic. In the film as well, Ella Shohat talks

---

4 *Exhausted hearts: the Muslim Jew* [qulūb munhaka] (Ruhayyim 2004); *Oh Ali* [yānā ʿAlī] (Alsafar 2006); *The World through the Eyes of Angels* [al-dunyā fī ʾaʿyūn al-malāʾika] (Said 2006); *Diary of a Jew from Damascus* [yaumiyāt yahūdī min Dimashq] (Aljabeen 2007); *The Tobacco Keeper* [ḥaris al-tabgh] (Badr 2008); *The Jews of Bahrain* [yahūd al-baḥrain] (Jallawi 2008); *Days in the Diaspora* [ʾayām al-shatāt] (Ruhayyim 2008); *The last Jews of Alexandria* [ʾākhir yahūd al-ʾiskandariya] (Fatiha 2008); *The Sweet Jew* [al-yahūdī al-ḥālī] (Almaqri 2009); *Abu Jamil Valley* [Wādī abū jamīl] (Abdelsamad 2009); *Widad from Aleppo* [widād min ḥalab] (Muhanna 2010); *The maze of the last one* [matāhat ʾākhīrihim] (Al-Ahmad 2011); *A Jewish woman in my heart* [ʾunthā ʾibriya fī qalbī] (Hamdy 2012); *Dreams of return* [aḥlām al-ʿawda] (Ruhayyim 2012); *The last Jew of Tamentit* [Le dernier Juif de Tamentit] (Zaoui 2012); Mazen Latif, [yahūd al-ʿirāq] (Bagdad: Dar Mesopotamia, 2013); *Book of Ttravel* [ṣifr al-tirḥāl] (Oreid 2013); *The Tattoo* [al-washm] (Adly 2014); *The last Jew* [al-yahūdī al-ʾakhīr] (Nasser 2015); *Migration or expulsion: the circumstances of Jewish migration from Iraq* [hijra ʾaū tahjīr: dhrūf wa mulābasāt hijrat yahūd al-ʿirāq] (Shiblaq, 2015); *The Jews of Alexandria*, [yahūd al-ʾiskandariya] (Nasr 2016); [al-tārīkh al-mansī li- yahūd al-ʿirāq] (Latif 2014); *Samir Naqash: Iraqi cravings for memory* [Samīr Naqqāsh, naqsh ʿ irāqī fil-dhakira] (Latif 2015); *Iraqi intellectuals: Jews in the service of Iraqi journalism*, [muthaqafūn ʿirāqiyūn yahūd fī khidmat ṣaḥibat al-jalāla al-ṣaḥāfa al-ʿirāqiyya] (Latif 2017a); *From the stolen Iraqi archive*, [min ʿarshīf al-ʿ irāq al-manhūb], (Latif 2017b); *Iraqi Jews, poets, and authors with Mesopotamian roots*, [yahūd ʿirāqiyūn, ʾudabāʾ tajrī fī ʿurūqihim miyāh al-rāfidayn] (Latif 2017c).

5 In addition to novels and nonfiction works written by Arabs about Arab Jews, a number of books by Arab Jews themselves or their children enjoyed popularity in Egypt and other Arab countries. The most famous is the autobiography of Lucette Lagnado: *The Man with the White Sharkskin Suit*, an Arabic edition of which was published under the title *Dar al tanani* in Cairo in 2010. Note also the following translations: *Adieu, Babylone* (Qattan 1986), in Arabic: [wadaʿān Bābil]; *Farida*, (Qattan 1991), in Arabic: [farīda]. The Moroccan novelist Edmond Amran el-Maleh also wrote on this theme in three works that were translated into Arabic: *Aïlen, ou, la nuit du récit* (el-Maleh 1983), in Arabic: [Ilān ʾaw layl al-ḥakī]; *Mille ans, un jour* (el-Maleh 1986), in Arabic: [ʾalf ʿām bi -yaum]; *Le retour d'Abou el Haki* (el-Maleh 1990) in Arabic: [ʿawdat abū al-ḥakī]. See also Eli S. Malka's study *Jacob's Children in the Land of the Mahdi: Jews of the Sudan* (Malka 1997), translated into Arabic by Maci Abu Qarja; [al-yahūd fil-sūdān: qirāʾa fī kitāb ilyāhū salamūn malkā : ʾatfāl yaʿqūb fī buqʿat al-mahdī].

about what it means to be an Iraqi Jewish child in Israel, speaking Arabic and living the Iraqi culture at home. The film discusses a question that had not been raised before.[6] *Forget Baghdad* was a film in English, made for the non-Arab audience. Despite being the first of its kind, it did not have much of an impact.

Salata Baladi (2007) is the first documentary of this group, made in Arabic for the Arab audience with English subtitles. The film maker Nadia Kamel documents the story of her mother Mary Rosenthal alias Naila Kamel and her Egyptian Jewish-Catholic-Muslim family. Some family members left the country for Italy and Israel, while Mary Rosenthal stayed in Egypt and participated actively in the political life of the country. Mary was imprisoned for five years for being a communist, during the reign of Gamal Abdel Nasser.[7] She shares her story with her grandson and with the audience that didn't know that the journalist and columnist Naila Kamel is Mary Rosenthal. The film unveils an Egyptian story that had been ignored for decades. A heated debate broke out after screening *Salata Baladi* in Cairo in 2007, not only because the film unfolds a taboo and portrays a part of Egyptian history in a non-conventional way. Nadia faced harsh criticism and was threatened to have her membership in the Cinema Syndicate suspended because the film follows her parents to Israel to visit the mother's relatives whom she had not seen for more than 50 years. This was considered an act of compromise with Israel that did not conform to the official understanding of how to deal with Israel. Rejecting Israel means boycotting it on all levels. Any visit – whatever the reason – is considered as breaking this boycott. The filmmaker and her family stated clearly on different occasions that their visit does not mean that they support Israel. On the contrary, they are loud critics of the Israeli occupation and supporters of the rights of the Palestinian people. Nonetheless, this is part of the family's story that Kamel believed had to be told. The film is still screened worldwide. The last screening took place in Cairo in May 2018.

The debate that was sparked by *Salata Baladi* paved the path that Amir Ramses followed, encountering much less criticism and rejection for his two documentaries titled *Egypt's Jews*.[8] The films are based on interviews with Egyptian Jews in Egypt and France. Despite censorship, Ramses' films reached cinemas in Cairo and Alexandria in 2013 and 2014 and gained much interest and success.[9]

---

[6] *Forget Baghdad*. Dir. Samir (2002).
[7] *Salata Baladi* [The house salad]. Dir. Nadia Kamel. 2007. In 2018, Nadia Kamel published the memoirs of her mother, [al-mawlūda] (Kamel 2018).
[8] *Jews of Egypt*. Dir. Amir Ramses. 2012. *Jews of Egypt: End of a Journey*. Dir. Amir Ramses. 2014.
[9] In 2016 the Arab Film Festival Berlin (ALFILM) dedicated part of its program to the question of Arab Jews in films. The resulting program, *Cousins: Jewish-Arab Identities in Postcolonial Cultural Discourse*, comprised the screening and discussion of ten films, a panel discussion, and a pub-

Other films such as the 2012 documentary *El Gusto* by the Algerian-Irish Safinez Bousbia tell the story of an Algerian music orchestra where Algerian Jews and Muslims sang the popular *chaâbi* music which flourished in the mid-twentieth century, but then faded into the background. Bousbia's film attempts to bring together the members of this orchestra; men who are now in their seventies. Their personal stories paint a picture of the country's turbulent history, with the war of independence proving to be a turning point. Some joined the struggle, while others had to flee after independence to France where there was no warm welcome in store for these *pieds noirs*. Bousbia managed to track down many of the former musicians and bring them together for a reunion concert in Marseilles which forms the stirring climax to this sentimental journey into Algeria's cultural history.[10] The Moroccan-Canadian film maker Kathy Wazana, made the film *They Were Promised the Sea* which tells the story of a people whose identity as Arab Jews challenges the very notion of an enemy. Informed by the director's family history, the film investigates the exodus that virtually emptied Morocco of its Jewish population, many believing they were no longer safe in their Arab homeland. Intimate interviews, poetry, recordings of Judeo-Andalusian music performed in Arabic, Hebrew, and Ladino thread the subjects' storylines and reveal a little-known history of a land and a people that resisted the separation of Arabs and Jews and a country that sees itself as reincarnating the spirit of Andalusia.[11] The two latest films of this group are *From Brooklyn to Beirut* (2016) and *At Titi's Balcony* (2017). *From Brooklyn to Beirut* by the Lebanese filmmaker Rola Khayyat tells the story of Lebanese Jews who left Beirut to New York and are returning to visit their home city and to renovate one of the old synagogues.[12] *At Titi's Balcony* by the French Egyptian film maker Yasmina Benari deals with the life of the Egyptian Communist Jew Albert Arie.[13]

The above-mentioned films subversively challenge the official nationalistic discourse. Documentary films and novels shifted the whole discussion forward and opened a new space that enables to rethink the concept of the nation and facilitates a more critical and differentiated discussion in the public sphere. Here, I argue, we are observing the emergence of a new, post-nationalistic dis-

---

lication. See http://www.alfilm.de/2016/spotlight-cousinscousinen/ (14 January 2018), see also *Cousins: Jewish-Arab Identities in Postcolonial Cultural Discourses*. Berlin: Makan 2016.
10 *El Gusto*. Dir. Safinez Bousbia. 2011. https://www.idfa.nl/en/film/aad6988b-0964-47e0-968c-39459dc0ad4a/el-gusto (6 February 2020).
11 *They Were Promised the Sea*. Dir. Kathy Wazan. 2013. https://www.imdb.com/title/tt1965232/ (6 February 2020).
12 *From Brooklyn to Beirut*. Dir. Rola Khayyat. 2018.
13 *At Titi's Balcony*. Dir. Yasmina Benari. 2017.

course. This rethinking did not find a broad acceptance in the academia in the Arab world, despite the work of a few historians and social scientists who work on this topic.[14]

2 Beyond stereotyping

In the literary discourse two novels *The Tobacco Keeper* by the Iraqi writer Ali Badr[15], *The Book of Travel* by the Egyptian writer Fatma Oreid[16], and the non-fiction work of Ali Jallawi on the Jews of Bahrain.[17] These literary works are exceptional in that they were not written by the Jews who lived in these countries and left them in the last decades, their children, or even those who have known Jews living among them. The writers represent a new generation of authors, the majority of them in their thirties, a cohort without the experience of encountering Jews in their daily life. Theses, novels, and non-fictional works share common aspects, despite differences in details. All of them try to reconstruct the lives of Jews, whether historical or contemporary. Most of the fictional accounts are based on real biographies, or real stories, that have been changed for literary purposes.

Badr is an Iraqi author who published more than 14 novels and plays some of which were translated into several languages. His novel *The Tobacco Keeper* was nominated for the Arab Bookers Prize in 2009. The novel tells the story of the musician Yousef Saleh, an Iraqi Jew who was forced to leave Baghdad for Israel in the 1950s. Determined to return to his home country, he succeeded only after assuming the identity of Kamal Midhat, an Iranian-Iraqi. He gained fame as a concert violinist while hiding his real personality and background. His wife and son, whom he left behind in Israel, learned the details of his life through letters that reached Jerusalem by way of Prague and Moscow. All did not end well. Saleh was kidnapped and killed in Baghdad in 2006 after a visit from an American marine. That marine, it turns out, was his son, who had migrated to the United States at an early age and had decided to visit him. The price of this fateful visit is his father's life. *The Tobacco Keeper* hence explores the com-

---

14 Aomar Boum is a Moroccan socio-anthropologist who works on the Jews of Morocco at the University of California, Los Angeles. Among his publications: *Memories of Absence: How Muslims Remember Jews in Morocco.* (Boum 2013) and "Partners Against Anti-Semitism: Muslims and Jews Respond to Nazism in French North African Colonies, 1936–1940" (Boum 2014).
15 Badr, *ḥaris al-tabgh* (Badr 2008).
16 Oreid, *ṣifr al-tirḥāl* (Oreid 2013).
17 Jallawi, *yahūd al-Baḥrain* (Jallawi 2008).

plexity of the refusal of displacement and uprooting and deals with the psychological impact of arriving in an alien land.

In her first novel, *The Book of Travel* (2013), the Egyptian short story writer, novelist and lawyer Fatma Oreid tells the story of an old woman named Sarah who travels for medical treatment from Cairo to Paris where her granddaughter Amina lives. Sarah's illness brings them both closer, as Amina learns something of the life of her grandmother, who is one of the last Jews living in Egypt. Stories of Sarah's love for her Muslim husband unveil a world of which Amina knew nothing. The novel is structured as an intergenerational dialogue where family secrets are brought to light. The reader is led through the streets of cosmopolitan Alexandria, passing the shops, the apartment towers, and the synagogues. The joy of the Jewish high holidays fades as the city loses its faithfuls, and Sarah grows accustomed to a unique loneliness. Like Badr, Oreid relegates the Palestinian-Israeli conflict to the margins of her novel. The story is not about the national cause, or the political enemy. Hence, *The Book of Travel* offers a dissenting discourse.

The Jews of Bahrain, published in 2008, is a study by the Bahraini Ali Jallawi. The study documents the social and economic history of Bahrain's Jews. Prior to the book's appearance this history had been ignored. Jallawi is a writer, poet, artist, and dissident who sought asylum in Germany in 2011. With his work he hoped to fill a gap in Bahrain's history. Writing and publishing the book was subversive, a refusal to be complicit with the official discourse.

These three books are representatives of the numerous works on Arab Jews published over the course of the last decade. These works leave the narrow circle of nationalistic narratives, deconstructing it to understand the story of the individuals behind historical events.[18] This is the beginning of a discourse that is at odds with the official one. The films and literary works discussed here moved the debate forward and opened a new space that enables a rethinking and a more critical and differentiated discussion.

In the Arab context, literature and documentary films are spheres in which unconventional questions can be raised and discussed. This rethinking is taking place in distinct intellectual spheres that allow free expression of thought. The rise of this new discourse is part of a wider process of questioning the official discourse of Arab states on the history of the Jews in Arab countries and implies questioning authoritarian regimes. It is part of a broad emancipation process, reflected in the Arab Spring that filled the streets of Tunis, Cairo, Damascus, and Sana'a, culminating in the eighteen days of protests in Cairo's Midan al-Tahrir.

---

[18] There is an exception to this generalization: Moustafa Nasr's *The Jews of Alexandria* remained faithful to the nationalistic discourse.

These processes are not unconnected. A vivid example is the change that took place in Tunis, celebrating the *al-Ghariba* feast, a Tunisian-Jewish feast on Jerba island. Prior to 2012, this feast was not public and took place secretly. After 2012 it returned to be a public event in which Tunisians, Jewish and non-Jewish, participate. The government adopted this celebration and its representatives attend the official part of it.[19] Keenly aware that questioning the history of the Jews was a threat, other states imposed systematic censorship, banning any publication that might raise questions about and challenge them. The novel by the Syrian author Ibrahim Aljabeen titled *Diary of a Jew from Damascus* (2006) was censored and banned.[20]

3 A step forward, a step backward: the role of television and mass culture

In Egypt, television drama series, known as *musalsalat*, have their share in this phenomenon. The first to present an Arab Jew in a sympathetic light was a 2009 Egyptian series, *'Anā qalbī dalīlī* (My heart is my guide).[21] It portrays the life of the famous Egyptian Jewish singer Laila Murad. Since the series was broadcast during Ramadan via satellite TV, it reached an audience beyond Egypt in all Arab countries. Laila Murad's Jewishness was a topic but not the focus of the show.

The question of Egypt's Jews started to gain public attention after decades of being neglected. At the end of 2012, during an interview, Issam al-Aryan, a leader of the Muslim Brotherhood, offered displaced Egyptian Jews an invitation to return.[22] This invitation boosted a public debate taking place mainly on television and in social media. On 4 January 2013, for the first time an Egyptian Jew, Magda Haroun,[23] was interviewed on television by the famous moderator Hafiz Almira-

---

19 The author attended this feast on 2–3 May 2017 and 2–3 May 2018.
20 Aljabeen, yaumiyāt yahūdī min Dimashq.
21 *'Anā qalbī dalīlī*. Dir. Mohamed Zuhair Rajab. 2009.
22 Bi-tawqīt al-qāhira (Cairo Time), talk show of Hafiz al-Mirazi on the Egyptian Channel Dream, on 28.12.2012. https://www.youtube.com/watch?v=rnAW47yVPf4 (14 January 2018).
23 Magda Haroun is the daughter of the famous lawyer Shehata Haroun (1920–2001). A Jewish communist, he refused to leave and emigrate from Egypt. He later published memoirs entitled *A Jew from Cairo*. Magda Haroun grew up in Cairo. On March 2013 she was chosen by the Jews who still live in the country to be the head of the Egyptian Jewish Community. The Egyptian Jewish community represents the 10 Jews who still live in Egypt and is responsible for the Synagogues and other community ownership in the country.

zi.²⁴ Besides Haroun, who subsequently became the head of the Egyptian Jewish community, other Jews were interviewed by telephone during the program, including Albert Arie and Nadia Haroun. Other interviews followed, one of the most famous being Professor Khaled Fahmy's conversation with Liliane Dawood on 14 January 2013.²⁵

Since these individuals were getting the chance for the first time to speak for themselves about their own history, this marked a turning point. Other television and newspaper interviews followed. One of these was the appearance of Magda Haroun on one of Egypt's most popular television shows *sāhibat al-sa'āda* (Her Excellency), which is a hybrid between a talk show and an interview in which the famous Egyptian actress Isaad Younis interviews prominent figures of cinema, art and society.²⁶ They featured Magda Haroun on 16 September 2014²⁷, the BBC broadcasted an interview with Giselle Khoury on 14.09.2015.²⁸ Television programmers and journalists hence ended years of complicity with the official narrative, offering a competing version of events.

In 2015, however, the official discourse regained ground. During Ramadan, at prime time, the Egyptian satellite channel CBC broadcast a drama entitled

---

24 Bi-tawqīt al-qāhira (Cairo Time), talk show of Hafiz al-Mirazi on the Egyptian Channel Dream, on 04.01.2013, see: https://www.youtube.com/watch?v=WOrf35rPJbs (14 January 2018). This video does not exist online any more due to the changes in the media system in Egypt and the security service taking over media houses. As a result of this, the open online archives have been deleted. I did not mange to find any downloads. More on the Egyptian State taking over media production, please see: https://madamasr.com/en/2017/12/21/feature/politics/looking-into-the-latest-acquisition-of-egyptian-media-companies-by-general-intelligence/ (05 July 2020) and https://madamasr.com/en/2017/04/12/feature/politics/egypts-media-in-a-state-of-emergency/ (05 July 2020).

25 Interview with Professor Khaled Fahmy by Liliane Dawood in her talk show al-sūra al-kāmila (Full Picture) on the Egyptian ON-TV channel, on 13.01.2013, see: https://www.youtube.com/watch?v=Bgquuxr1brY (1 January 2018). The historian Prof. Khaled Fahmy and the presenter Lilain Dawood have been banned from the TV. See: https://madamasr.com/en/2016/06/27/news/u/update-tv-host-liliane-daoud-deported-to-beirut/ (05 July 2020) and https://www.bbc.com/news/world-middle-east-36649781 (05 July 2020). Notice that the Egyptian authorities banned the talk show of Liliane Dawood and she was deported from Egypt. All her shows are banned from youtube since March 2018.

26 Her Excellency [sāhibat al-sa'āda], talk show by Isaad Younis, on the Egyptian CBC channel, interview with Magda Haroun on 16.09.2014, https://www.youtube.com/watch?v=oNm9ZFRgVgk (14 January 2018).

27 Her Excellency [sāhibat al-sa'āda], talk show by Isaad Younis, on the Egyptian CBC channel, interview with Magda Haroun on 16.09.2014, https://www.youtube.com/watch?v=oNm9ZFRgVgk (14 January 2018).

28 The Scene [al-mashhad], long interview format -mainly political- by Gisele Khoury BBC Arabic, on 14.09.2015, see: https://www.youtube.com/watch?v=gnEuIKYvLjA (14 January 2018).

Haret al-Yahud (The Jewish Quarter), about the Jewish quarter in Cairo. Not only were Egyptians watching; millions in other Arab countries swelled the broadcast audience. This television drama consolidated the nationalist discourse tremendously due to the very high number of viewers throughout the Arab world and beyond. In her study, *Dramas of Nationhood*, Lila Abu-Lughod analyzed the politics of television in Egypt. Reaching all social strata, television and other mass media in Egypt have enormous power: "Television drama is a key institution for the production of national culture in Egypt."[29]

Going beyond Abu-Lughod's contention that television drama produced cliched versions of Egyptian personalities, the concept of a "culture industry" developed by Max Horkheimer and Theodor Adorno is a model that can shed light on the role of TV Series and soap operas in influencing public awareness. Along with "mass culture," this term was fundamental to the *Dialectic of Enlightenment* (1944). According to Horkheimer and Adorno, a cultural industry exists when culture and art become functional instruments (technologies) to create a mass culture that aims to shape popular awareness (Horkheimer and Adorno 1979, 161). "Criticism and respect," they explained, "disappear in the cultural industry; the former becomes a mechanical expertise, the latter is succeeded by a shallow cult of leading personalities." (Horkheimer and Adorno 1979, 161)

Besides the technical aspect of the culture industry,[30] the production company Al-Adl group is one of the most powerful production companies in Egypt and they are allies of the political system in Egypt. The images of the Jewish quarter in *Haret al-Yahud*, with its expensive apartments, fancy clothing, and snatches of French conversation reflect the lives of the middle and upper middle class. Contradicting reality, one never catches a glimpse of the narrow alleys of the quarter that was inhabited by the Jewish and non-Jewish Egyptian working class. Most of the Jews depicted in the show are either Zionists who want to emigrate to Israel or followers of the king who dislike the Free Officers. If one had to assign a cause for Jewish emigration, based on the show, one would point to the Muslim Brotherhood, whose faithful are shown burning the stores of good Jewish neighbors and undermining any harmony between Muslims, Christians, and Jews. Neither the title of the soap opera nor the story itself reflects the reality of the quarter as it existed in the second half of the 1940s. One could say, in an Adorno/ Horkheimerian mode, that the show becomes a "technology" to manifest the official and

---

[29] Lila Abu-Lughod, *Dramas of Nationhood: The Politics of Television in Egypt*, The Lewis Henry Morgan Lecture series (Chicago: University of Chicago Press, 2004), 8.

[30] Max Horkheimer and Theodor Adorno. The Culture Industry: Enlightenment as Mass Deception, in: Meenakshi Gigi Durham and Douglas Kellner (eds.), Media and Cultural Studies: keyworks. Oxford: Blackwell Publishing 2006. 41–73.

nationalist narrative about Egyptian Jews which brought success to the production company. Departing from Abu-Lughod's statement and Horkheimer and Adorno's notion of cultural industry, the series presents normative images of good and bad along the lines of religious affiliations.

Haret al-Yahud received significant media attention. Over seventy articles and reports discussed the series, among them the main media outlets of the Arab world and foreign newspapers and television channels.[31] Most of the coverage was positive, though some accused General Sisi of flirting with Israel and

---

31 Al-hayat newspaper. *The Jewish Quarter and it's Tails* [ḥārit al-yahūd wa ḥikāyatuha] 25.09. 2015, http://www.alhayat.com/Articles/11351227/.

al-jazeera: *The Jewish Quarter, a drama controversial in Egypt and Israel* [ḥārit al-yahūd, drāmā tuthīr al-jadal bi-misr wa 'isrāīl], 22.06.2015- link al-jazeera. *The Jewish Quarter, gains back the normalization between Cairo and Tel Aviv,* [ḥārit al-yahūd, yu'īd ṭarīq al-taṭbī' bayn al-qāhira wa tal abīb] 22.06.2015, http://www.aljazeera.net/news/reportsandinterviews; al-jazeera English. *Ramadan soap rediscovers Egypt's Jews* http://www.aljazeera.com/indepth/opinion/2015/06/ramadan-soap-rediscovers-egypt-jews-150625094603247.html;

Rowan El Shimi. *Ramadan series 'The Jewish Alley' to show birth of sectarianism in Egypt* (Mada Masr, 18.06.2015) https://www.madamasr.com/en/2015/06/18/feature/culture/ramadan-series-the-jewish-alley-to-show-birth-of-sectarianism-in-egypt/;

Hala Moustafa. *The Jewish Quarter,* [ḥārit al-yahūd], (al-Ahram, 18.07.2015), http://www.ahram.org.eg/NewsQ/415047.aspx; English Ahram, *The Jewish Quarter* Wins Best TV Series Award at Bahraini Festival, (Ahram Online, 20.03.2016) http://english.ahram.org.eg/News/19340

Yousef al-Qaeed, *Scenes, Shihata Haroun* [mashāhid- Shiḥāta Hārūn] http://m.alraimedia.com/Home/Details?Id=d3d09bad-f5c7-4d99-ac67-31b6de1f70b5 (Al-Rai, 15.09.2015); Saleh al-Nuami. *Sisi's Egypt speakes Hebew* [Miṣr al-Sīsī tatakalam al-'ibrīya], https://www.alaraby.co.uk/opinion/2015/6/30 David K. Kirkpatrick. For Egypt, TV Show's Shocking Twist Is Its Sympathetic Jews, (New York Times, 23.06. 2015), https://www.nytimes.com/2015/06/24/world/middleeast/for-egypt-tv-shows-shocking-twist-is-its-sympathetic-jews.html; Josef Joffe, *Soap* miracle [Seifenoper Wunder] http://www.zeit.de/2015/32/tv-serie-aegypten-juden-muslime, (Zeit Online, 06.08.2015); Ronen Steinke. Forbidden Love [Verbotene Liebe], http://www.sueddeutsche.de/medien/israel-in-arabischen-fernsehserien-verbotene-liebe-1.2550722, (Süddeutsche Zeitung, 05.07.2015); Julia Nikschick. *The invisible Jews on the Nile* [Die unsichtbaren Juden vom Nil], http://www.juedische-allgemeine.de/article/view/id/23179, (Jüdische Allgemeine, 27.08.2015); Willliam Booth and Sufian Taha. *The Jewish Quarter:* New Egyptian TV Program is Promoting Peace in the West Bank, http://www.independent.co.uk/arts-entertainment/tv/features/the-jewish-quarter-new-egyptian-tv-programme-is-promoting-peace-in-the-west-bank-10403053.html; (The Independent 20.07. 2015); Eyal Sagui Bizawe, *How The Jewish Quarter Became the Talk of Cairo,* https://www.haaretz.com/israel-news/culture/television/.premium-1.664402, (Haaretz, 5.07.2015); Alawa Mizyani. *The Jewish quarter series is controversial in Egypt and creates anger in Israel* [musalsal ḥārit al-yahūd yuthīr jadalan fī-misr wa ġaḍaban fī 'isrāīl], http://www.france24.com/ar/20150625; n.tv, *Egypt loves and hates this series,* [Ägypten liebt und hasst diese Serie] https://www.n-tv.de/leute/Wenn-ein-Araber-mit-einer-Juedin-geht-article15381056.html, (n.tv, 26.06.2015).

others criticized the show's lack of historical accuracy. At no point, however, the narrative departs from the official nationalistic discourse on Egypt's Jews. Despite the fact that such a broadcasting event was unimaginable a decade ago, the series constitutes a step backward because it reinforced the official nationalistic discourse. The producers hijacked the figure of the Arab Jew and the Jewish quarter, putting them to the use the cultural industry mandated, in an act of complicity with the official nationalist discourse. The contrast between the depiction of Jews in *Haret al-Yahud* and the work of young authors and filmmakers highlights the zone of dissent opened by the latter.

This essay argues that despite setbacks a post-nationalistic discourse is being born. This post-nationalistic discourse may not yet be systematically implemented across the range of genres in the culture industry of Egypt. However, it occupies a narrow margin that rejects any form of complicity with the official narrative and a represents a movement toward dissent, to a more differentiated and a more critical perception of history.

Bibliography

Abdel Quddous, Ihsan. *Don't Leave Me Alone* [Lā tatrikūnī hunā waḥdī]. Cairo: Rose al Yusuf, 1979.

Abdelsamad, Nada. *Abu Jamil Valley* [Wādī abū jamīl]. Beirut: Dar Alnahar, 2009.

Abdu, Ali Ibrahim and Khayriyya Qasimiyya. *The Jews of Arab Countries* [Yahūd al-bilād al-ʿarabīyya]. Beirut: Markaz al-Abhath al-Filistiniyya, 1971.

Abdulhaq, Najat. *Jewish and Greek Communities in Egypt: Entrepreneurship and Business before Nasser.* London: I. B. Tauris, 2016.

Abu-Lughod, Lila. *Dramas of Nationhood: The Politics of Television in Egypt.* The Lewis Henry Morgan Lecture series. Chicago: University of Chicago Press, 2004.

Adly, Rasha. *The Tattoo,* [al-washm]. Cairo: Dar al-nahda, 2014.

Al-Ahmad, Mohamed. *The maze of the last one* [matāhat ʿākhīrihim]. Diyali: Diyali University, 2011.

al-hayat newspaper. "The Jewish Quarter and it's Tails." [ḥārit al-yahūd wa ḥikāyatuha]. (25. 09. 2015): http://www.alhayat.com/Articles/11351227/.

Aljabeen, Ibrahim. *Diary of a Jew from Damascus* [yaumiyāt yahūdī min Dimashq]. Damascus: Dar Khutuwar lil-nashr wal tawzi' 2007.

Al-Jazeera. "The Jewish Quarter, gains back the normalization between Cairo and Tel Aviv." [ḥārit al-yahūd, yuʿīd ṭarīq al-taṭbīʿ bayn al-qāhira wa tal abīb]. (22. 06. 2015): http://www.aljazeera.net/news/reportsandinterviews/2015/6/22/.

Almaqri, Ali. *The Sweet Jew* [al-yahūdī al-ḥālī]. Beirut: Dar Alsaqi, 2009.

Al-Nuami, Saleh. "Sisi's Egypt speakes Hebew." [Miṣr al-Sīsī tatakalam al-ʿibrīya]. *Al-Araby.* (30. 06. 2015): https://www.alaraby.co.uk/opinion/2015/6/30/

Al-Qaeed, Yousef. "Scenes, Shihata Haroun." [mashāhid- Shiḥāta Hārūn]. *Al-Rai* (15. 09. 2015): http://m.alraimedia.com/Home/Details?Id=d3d09bad-f5c74d99-ac631b6de1f70b5.

Alsafar, Mohamed: Oh Ali [yānā ʿAlī] (Cairo: Dar Libya lil-nashr, 2006).
At Titi's Balcony. Dir. Yasmina Benari. 2017.
Badr, Ali. *The Tobacco Keeper* [ḥaris al-tabgh]. Beirut: al-muʾasassa al-ʿarabiya lil-nashr, 2008. English publication by Bloomsbury Qatar Foundation. Doha: Bloomsbury Qatar Foundation, 2012.
Bi-tawqīt al-qāhira [Cairo Time]. Talk show of Hafiz al-Mirazi on the Egyptian Channel *Dream*. (28.12.2012): https://www.youtube.com/watch?v=rnAW47yVPf4 and (04.01.2013): https://www.youtube.com/watch?v=WOrf35rPJbs. (14 January 2018).
Bizawe, Eyal Sagui: "How The Jewish Quarter Became the Talk of Cairo." *Haaretz* (5.07.2015): https://www.haaretz.com/israel-news/culture/television/.premium-1.664402. (6 February 2020).
Booth ,William and Sufian Taha. "The Jewish Quarter: New Egyptian TV Program is Promoting Peace in the West Bank." *The Independent* (20.07.2015): http://www.independent.co.uk/arts-entertainment/tv/features/the-jewish-quarter-new-egyptian-tv-programme-is-promoting-peace-in-the-west-bank-10403053.html. (6 February 2020).
Boum, Aomar. *Memories of Absence: How Muslims Remember Jews in Morocco.* Stanford, CA: Stanford University Press, 2013.
Boum, Aomar. "Partners Against Anti-Semitism: Muslims and Jews Respond to Nazism in French North African Colonies, 1936–1940." *The Journal of North African Studies* 19.4 (2014): 550–570.
Diab, Khaled. "Ramadan soap rediscovers Egypt's Jews." *Al-jazeera English* http://www.aljazeera.com/indepth/opinion/2015/06/ramadan-soap-rediscovers-egypt--jews-150625094603247.html. (23 July 2020).
El Gusto. Dir. Safinez Bousbia. 2011. https://www.idfa.nl/en/film/aad6988b-0964-47e0-968c-39459dc0ad4a/el-gusto. (6 February 2020).
El Shimi, Rowan. "Ramadan series 'The Jewish Alley' to show birth of sectarianism in Egypt." *Mada Masr* (18.06.2015): https://www.madamasr.com/en/2015/06/18/feature/culture/ramadan-series-the-jewish-alley-to-show-birth-of-sectarianism-in-egypt/. (6 February 2020).
Elimelekh, Geula. "The Search for Identity in the Works of Samīr Naqqāsh." *Middle Eastern Studies* 49.1 (2013), 63–75.
El-Maleh, Edmond Amran. *Aïlen, ou, la nuit du récit.* Paris: François Maspero, 1983. In Arabic: [Ilān ʿaw layl al-ḥakī]. Casablanca: Dar Alkalil, 1987.
El-Maleh, Edmond Amran. *Mille ans, un jour.* Grenoble: La pensée sauvage, 1986. In Arabic: [ʾalf ʿām bi -yaum]. Casablanca: al-Najah, 1991.
El-Maleh, Edmond Amran. *Le retour d'Abou el Haki.* Grenoble: La pensée sauvage, 1990. In Arabic: [ʿawdat abū al-ḥakī]. Casablanca: Iriqya al-sharq lil-nashr, 2000.
English Ahram. "The Jewish Quarter Wins Best TV Series Award at Bahraini Festival." *Ahram Online* (20.03.2016) http://english.ahram.org.eg/NewsContent/5/159/193408/Arts--Culture/Entertainment/The-Jewish-Quarter-wins-Best-TV-Series-award-at-Ba.aspx. (23 July 2020).
Fatiha, Mutaz. *The last Jews of Alexandria* [ʾākhir yahūd al-ʾiskandariya]. Cairo: Dar Oktob lil-nashr wal tawzi', 2008.
Fatma Oreid. *The Book of Ttravel* [ṣifr al-tirḥāl]. Cairo: Dar al tanani lil nashr, 2013.
Forget Baghdad. Dir. Samir. 2002.
From Brooklyn to Beirut. Dir. Rola Khayyat. 2018.

Hamdy, Khawla. *A Jewish woman in my heart* ['unthā 'ibriya fī qalbī]. Cairo: Dar Kayan lil-nashr wal tawzi', 2012.

Her Excellency [sāhibat al-sa'āda]. Talk show by Isaad Younis, on the Egyptian CBC channel, interview with Magda Haroun. *CBC* (16.09.2014): https://www.youtube.com/watch?v=oNm9ZFRgVgk. (14 January 2018).

Horkheimer, Max and Theodor Adorno. *Dialectic of Enlightenment*. Transl. John Cumming. London: Verso 1979.

Horkheimer, Max and Theodor Adorno. "The Culture Industry: Enlightenment as Mass Deception." *Media and Cultural Studies: keyworks*. Eds. Meenakshi Gigi Durham and Douglas Kellner. Oxford: Blackwell Publishing, 2006. 41–73.

Jallawi, Ali. *The Jews of Bahrain* [yahūd al-baḥrain]. Manama: Dar Fradis lil-nashr wal tawzi' 2008.

Jews of Egypt. Dir. Amir Ramses. 2012.

Jews of Egypt: End of a Journey. Dir. Amir Ramses. 2014.

Joffe, Josef. "Soap opera miracle" [Seifenoper Wunder]. *Zeit Online* (06.08.2015): http://www.zeit.de/2015/32/tv-serie-aegypten-juden-muslime. (6 February 2020).

Jubeh, Claudia (Ed.): *Cousins: Jewish-Arab Identities in Postcolonial Cultural Discourses*. Berlin: Makan, 2016.

Kamel, Anas Mustafa. *Jewish Capitalism in Egypt* [al-ra'smāliyya al-yahūdiyya fī Miṣr]. Cairo: Mirit, 1999.

Kamel, Nadia. *The Born* [al-mawlūda]. Cairo: alkarma, 2018.

Khoury, Yacoub. *The Jews in Arab Countries* [al-yahūd fi al-buldān al-'arabiyya]. Beirut: Dar al-Nahar lil-nashr, 1970.

Kirkpatrick, David D. "For Egypt, TV Show's Shocking Twist Is Its Sympathetic Jews." *New York Times* (23.06.2015): https://www.nytimes.com/2015/06/24/world/middleeast/for-egypt-tv-shows-shocking-twist-is-its-sympathetic-jews.html. (23 July 2020).

Lagnado, Lucette. *The Man with the White Sharkskin Suit.* New York: Ecco/HarperCollins, 2007.

Latif, Mazen. *The Jews of Iraq* [yahūd al-'irāq]. Bagdad: Dar Mesopotamia, 2013.

Latif, Mazen. *The forgotten History of Iraqi Jews* [al-tārīkh al-mansī li- yahūd al-'irāq]. Baghdad: Dar Mesopotamia, 2014.

Latif, Mazen. *Samir Naqash: Iraqi cravings for memory* [Samīr Naqqāsh, naqsh ' irāqī fil-dhakira]. Baghdad: Dar Mesopotamia, 2015.

Latif, Mazen. *From the stolen Iraqi archive* [min 'arshīf al-' irāq al-manhūb]. Baghdad: Dar Mesopotamia, 2017a.

Latif, Mazen. *Iraqi intellectuals: Jews in the service of Iraqi journalism* [muthaqafūn 'irāqiyūn yahūd fī khidmat ṣaḥibat al-jalāla al-ṣaḥāfa al-'irāqiyya]. Baghdad: Dar Mesopotamia, 2017b.

Latif, Mazen. *Iraqi Jews, poets, and authors with Mesopotamian roots* [yahūd 'irāqiyūn, 'udabā' tajrī fī 'urūqihim miyāh al-rāfidayn]. Baghdad: Dar Mesopotamia, 2017c.

Malka, Eli S. *Jacob's Children in the Land of the Mahdi: Jews of the Sudan*. Syracuse, NY: Syracuse University Press, 1997. Transl. into Arabic by Maci Abu Qarja: [al-yahūd fil-sūdān: qirā'a fī kitāb ilyāhū salamūn malkā: 'atfāl ya'qūb fī buq'at al-mahdī]. Abu Dhabi: Althufra lil tiba'a wal nashr 2004.

Mizyani, Alawa. "The Jewish quarter series is controversial in Egypt and creates anger in Israel." [musalsal ḥārit al-yahūd yuthīr jadalan fī-misr wa ġaḍaban fī ʾisrāīl]. *France24:* http://www.france24.com/ar/20150625.
Moustafa, Hala. "The Jewish Quarter." [ḥārit al-yahūd]. Al-Ahram (18.07.2015): http://www.ahram.org.eg/NewsQ/415047.aspx.
Muhanna, Qahtan. *Widad from Aleppo* [widād min ḥalab]. Damascus: Dar Mamduh Edwan lil nashr 2010.
My heart is my guide [ʾanā qalbī dalīlī]. Dir. Mohamed Zuhair Rajab. 2009.
Nasr, Moustafa. *The Jews of Alexandria* [yahūd al-ʾiskandariya]. Cairo: Maktabat al dar alarabiyya lil kitab, 2016.
Nassar, Siham. *Egyptian Jews between Egyptianism and Zionism* [Al-yahūd al-misriyūn bayn al-miṣriya wal ṣuhyūniyya]. Cairo: al-Arabi, 1980.
Nasser, Abduljabbar. The last Jew [al-yahūdī al-ʾakhīr]. Cairo: Al Dar Almisriyya Allibnaniyya, 2015.
Nikschick, Julia. "The invisible Jews on the Nile" [Die unsichtbaren Juden vom Nil]. *Jüdische Allgemeine* (27.08.2015): http://www.juedische-allgemeine.de/article/view/id/23179. (23 July 2020).
Oreid, Fatma. *The Book of Ttravel* [ṣifr al-tirḥāl]. Cairo: Dar al tanani lil nashr, 2013).
Qattan, Naim. *Adieu, Babylone*. Montréal: Leméac Éditeur, 1986. In Arabic: [wadaʿān Bābil]. Beirut: Dar Aljamal, 2000.
Qattan, Naim. *Farida*. Montréal: Hurtubise,1991. In Arabic: [farīda]. Beirut: Dar Aljamal, 2006.
Ruhayyim, Kamal. *Days in the Diaspora* [ʾayām al-shatāt]. Cairo: Sphinx Agency, 2008.
Ruhayyim, Kamal. *Exhausted hearts: the Muslim Jew* [qulūb munhaka]. Cairo: Sphinx Agency, 2004. Trans. Sarah Enany (*Diary of a Jewish Muslim*). Cairo: American University in Cairo Press, 2014.
Ruhayyim, Kamal. *Dreams of return* [aḥlām al-ʿawda]. Cairo: Sphinx Agency, 2012. Trans. Sarah Enany (*Menorahs and Minarets*). Cairo: American University in Cairo Press, 2017.
Said, Mahmud. *The World through the Eyes of Angels* [al-dunyā fī ʾaʿyūn al-malāʾika]. Cairo: Mirit, 2006. Trans. Samuel Salter, Zahra Jishi, and Rafah Abu Innab. New York: Syracuse University Press, 2011.
Salata Baladi [The house salad]. Dir. Nadia Kamel. 2007.
Sami, Rashad. *The Jewish Figure in the Novels of Ihsan Abdel Quddus* [al-shakhsiya al-yahūdiya fī riwāyāt iḥsān abd-al-qaddūs]. Cairo: Dar Alhilal, 1992.
Schwinghammer, Benno. "Egypt loves and hates this series" [Ägypten liebt und hasst diese Serie]. *n.tv* (26.06.2015): https://www.n-tv.de/leute/Wenn-ein-Araber-mit-einer-Juedin-geht-article15381056.html (6 February 2020).
Shiblaq, Abbas. *Migration or expulsion: the circumstances of Jewish migration from Iraq* [hijra ʾaū tahjīr: dhrūf wa mulābasāt hijrat yahūd al-ʿirāq]. Beirut: Institute for Palestine Studies, 2015.
Steinke, Ronen. "Forbidden Love" [Verbotene Liebe]. *Süddeutsche Zeitung* (05.07.2015): http://www.sueddeutsche.de/medien/israel-in-arabischen-fernsehserien-verbotene-liebe-1.2550722. (23 July 2020).
The Scene [al-mashhad]. Interview format by Gisele Khoury. *BBC Arabic* (14.09.2015): https://www.youtube.com/watch?v=gnEuIKYvLjA, broadcast on 14.01.2018. (23 July 2020).
They Were Promised the Sea. Dir. Kathy Wazan. 2013.
Zaoui, Amin. *The last Jew of Tamentit* [Le dernier Juif de Tamentit]. Algiers: Barzakh, 2012.

Galili Shahar
German-Jewish Literature: An Interruption

1 An Interruption

The question under consideration is the following: What and how the study of Jewish literature in its German contexts can contribute to the research and teaching frameworks of general and comparative literature. When inquiring into the contributions of German-Jewish literature, we tend to stress its interruptive implications and problematize its values as acts of intervention. Not integration but rather estrangement is the measure of its contribution. Indeed, from its emergence during the eighteenth century, German-Jewish writing was regarded as an interference in the major realms of German letters, evoking resistance and reactions. Understanding Jewish literature as an act of interruption in the major courses of the European project of modernity is therefore the point of departure, the *Ansatzpunkt*, of this short essay.

The question how to study, how to read, how to teach German-Jewish literature begins with a reflection on its interruptive value. This is not to argue that every contribution by Jewish authorship was or should be understood as a "break," an "accident," or a "crisis" in the course of German literary affairs. The significant contributions that German-Jewish authors have made in both literary and scholarly writings attest also to the integrative dimension of the German-Jewish cultural enterprises. Here, however, the argument is different: the very question of how German-Jewish writing should be introduced into the field of general and comparative literary studies, which texts should be included in our courses, what methods of reading should be applied in our seminars, implies an act of intervention. According to this view, Jewish writing is defined by its acts of discontinuity, rupturing the canonical frames of European literature.

The nature of this interruption, however, is not arbitrary. The disruptive actions of Jewish writing, its "noises," the ways in which it challenges the history of the European novel, modern drama, and lyrics and interferes in the history of literary criticism itself, were and still are associated with its traditions, and first and foremost – the liturgical. What German-Jewish writing brought about in the last two centuries (1800–2000) – its interventions – was also based on the remnants of Jewish liturgical tradition.

Although this argument may be too strong, it implies that in order to properly engage the question regarding the German-Jewish contribution to literary study it first requires acknowledging its interruptive course, understanding the values of its *Gegenwort*, its counter-word, that acted within and against the major frames of modern literature. These acts, however, were grounded in a certain tradition that was translated, adapted, reinterpreted (often also misinterpreted), and ironized in Jewish literary works. The work of prayer, the Talmudic Midrash, the Kabbalistic writings, and the remnants of the *piyut* (the Hebrew liturgical poem) were among the major sources of this tradition. In modernist contexts, this tradition was transformed into discourses of justice, claims for radical correction (*tikkun*), acts of responsibility (*teshuva*), and communion – a theo-political assembly. These adaptations, both playful and creative, challenged the courses of European literature and offered a different understanding of the Western literary enterprise. Among the major agents of this German-Jewish writing, to mention a few, were Heinrich Heine, Franz Kafka, Walter Benjamin, Franz Werfel, Else Lasker-Schüler, and Paul Celan. In their works we find the echo of a lost liturgical poem that becomes a source for a radical interpretation of literature, to quote Kafka (1994c, 171), as a "form of prayer."

2 Listening

My reflections began with the claim that German-Jewish writing should be understood as an act of intervention in the realm of European literature after 1800. I also argued that German-Jewish writing challenges the very idea of literature by its commitments to the Jewish liturgical tradition. This was not to assert the "religious values" of modern Jewish writing but rather to point to the remnants of tradition, not its Halachic (legal) precepts. It was not the prayer itself but rather its echoes, its sounds, its acoustic figurations that remained as a resonance in the modernist writings of German-Jewish authors.

German-Jewish writing in the twentieth century and its contribution to the European literary heritage should be understood along these lines as "deconstructive" – but how precisely? It was only through acts of "self-destruction" (fragmentation, translation, over-interpretation, irony, silencing) that the Jewish liturgical tradition turned into a source of interruption in modern European literary contexts. The Hebrew prayer, when it was forgotten and denied by its own publics and left as a remnant, turned into a distortive element in modernist writing, interrupting major schemes of European literature. Arnold Schönberg's musical project, the atonal figuration of the European canonical musical sound, can be seen as a radical manifestation of this phenomenon, as is well demonstrated by his opera *Moses und Aron* (1932), in which the atonal elements are associated with the tradition of Hebrew prophecy, especially through its broken speech-acts, the "stuttering" of its main protagonist – Moses.

German-Jewish writing, alongside its acts of interruption, also involves attempts at new beginnings. It was not characterized by crisis and distortion alone but also by the quest for reorientation, searching different directions in the worlds of modernity. An inquiry into its contribution to the realm of literary study must also take into consideration its futuristic dimensions, its revolutionary commitments (as in the works of Gustav Landauer, Walter Benjamin and Rosa Luxemburg, among others). Any reading of German-Jewish literature, the efforts to introduce it anew in comparative contexts, thus begins by listening to the sounds (the noises) of its interventions.

3 A Step Back

This argument requires, however, a "step back."[1] A first example can be found in the case of Moses Mendelssohn. Mendelssohn's writings – his essays on aesthetics and articles on the idea of Enlightenment and *Bildung*, alongside his Bible translations and works of exegesis (*bi'ur*) – were conceived already by his contemporaries not only as examples of the integrative aspects of German-Jewish writing, but also as an interruption of major developments in the age of Enlightenment. Mendelssohn's Hebrew writings, his significant contributions to the corpus of the Hebrew *Haskala* (Enlightenment), and his theological reformational texts attested both to his scholarly, critical efforts and also to the liturgical commitments of his enterprise. These residues – the remnants of the Jewish liturgical tradition, the prayer, the blessing, the *piyut* – were perceived, however, as obstacles, as the remains of an archaic religious heritage that challenged the modern, secularist vision of European literature around 1800. Although some thinkers and authors of the Enlightenment and the Romantic era quite often engaged Christian liturgical traditions, alongside ancient Hebrew (to recall Herder's and Goethe's engagement with *Song of Songs*), transforming them into modern forms of representation, Jewish authors who dealt with traditional Hebrew sources were regarded as foreign, isolated from the main trends of European writing. German-Jewish writing, in engaging the leftovers of Jewish/Hebrew liturgy, challenged the conformist visions of European literature by alluding to different forms of knowledge, different forms of life. According to Franz Rosenzweig (1998, 335–337), this was precisely the Jewish contribution to the literature of the world: estranging the secularist world-view of the major European enter-

---

[1] On the implications of a "step back" as an interruption in the history of Western metaphysics, see Heidegger 1986.

prise. Once we ask about the interruptive act of German-Jewish literary writing, we have to consider its challenge to the modern, secularist perception of literature.

Even the writings of Heinrich Heine are not only an exception, but also an example of a German-Jewish author who reflected – with a fine irony, not without joy – his own conditions, his foreignness, his states of denial and cultural amnesia. Heine, a converted Jew, a poet of the free spirit, an exiled German author, conducted literary journeys in his works, notably in his *Deutschland. Ein Wintermärchen*, that ostensibly paid little attention to the Jews of his homeland, whom he presented from a somewhat cynical perspective. The jokes, the parodies that Heine recounts in his writings, his critical engagement with German political culture and his attack on its false literary heritage, while celebrating (again, not without irony) his own "homecoming," are associated, we recall, with a "falscher Stimme" (false voice) (Heine 1995, 397). However, alongside these "comic effects" in Heine's works, the key message of his writing was a claim for justice. While *Deutschland. Ein Winterreise* provides a critical perspective on Germany's future and should be understood as a political poem (Grab, 1992), its own discordant voices, its wounded sounds, are heard as an echo of a (desperate) Jewish prayer (Adorno 1998).

4 Judgment

Understanding German-Jewish literary works in their modernist contexts as an echo of a Jewish prayer, namely, as a remnant of a liturgical poem, is not self-evident. Occasional references to the tradition of Jewish prayer and its modernist interpretation can be found in the writings of Walter Benjamin, himself a German-Jewish author and one of the critical speakers of this enterprise in the realm of German literature. One of these references appears in his short essay of 1928, titled first "Eine neue Kraus-Notiz" (Benjamin [1928] 1991), in which he discusses the "Jewish portrait" of the Austrian critic Karl Kraus. Being-Jewish, in Benjamin's view, was not an essence, but rather an allusion to a certain constellation of tradition, in which remnants of the Jewish liturgical work were still in act. According to Benjamin, "Jewish" was the name for a tradition that suffered crisis, inversions, and demonic adaptations, yet preserved its liturgical intentions. Let us recall the opening sentence of his note on Kraus:

> In [Kraus] ereignet sich der großartige Durchbruch des halachischen Schrifttums mitten das Massiv der deutschen Sprache. Man versteht nichts von diesem Mann, solange man nicht

erkennt, daß mit Notwendigkeit alles, ausnahmslos Alles, Sprache und Sache, für ihn sich in der Sphäre des Rechtes abspielt. (624)

Benjamin argues that the writings of Kraus should be read as texts intended "before the law," written as documents to be submitted to the court, for everything in Kraus's world belongs without exception (*ausnahmslos*) to the realm of the law. However, Kraus's own act of writing should be understood as a breaking-through, an act of eruption, *Durchbruch*, as an intervention (perhaps, an inversion) of the Jewish *Halacha*. Kraus's work should thus be read as a Talmudic interference in the realm of German court language. What can that mean?

Halacha, implying in Hebrew "a way-of-life," a guide, a path of being in the world, is first and foremost an act of study. It refers to a scholarly debate regarding the implications of the law. In the Talmudic corpus *Halacha* is interwoven with (over)interpretations (and often interruptions) of the *Mishna* (the ancient Hebrew codex), alongside the *Aggadah* (tales) – stories and anecdotes about scholars, rabbis, and disciples of *Torah*, among them great teachers but also laymen and fools. What *Halacha* implies in this context is not so much an ancient version of a Jewish theological seminar, but rather forms of writings based on radical interventions in the realm of the law. *Halacha* is a method of studying in which storytelling (*Aggadah*) interferes in the procedures of judgment, creating detours, suspensions, and corrective acts. When Benjamin compares Kraus's writing to Halachic texts and asserts its "breaking-through" into the realm of German letters, he implies a comparison with a Jewish literary corpus, in which the producers of the law are interrupted by the cause of literature (the *Aggadah*). Furthermore, when Benjamin writes about the *Durchbruch des halachischen Schriftums*, he refers also to a certain dimension of resistance that Hebrew/Aramaic – the liturgical languages – represents in the realm of German language. What *Halacha* means here is not only an act of resistance in the realm of the law, but also an interruptive movement in the world of the German language, based on the historical work of the forgotten Semitic languages.

Kraus wrote his essays and literary criticism, as well as his dramas, in German. The Talmudic associations of his writings were ironic, or as Benjamin himself hinted – "demonic." In his writings, Kraus expresses the destructive element of judgment. However, his work, according to Benjamin, also implies a move from the realm of judgment into the space of justice. Benjamin writes:

Der sprachliche und sittliche Siblenstecherei dieses Mannes meint nicht Rechthaberei, sie gehört zu der wahrhaft verzweifelten Gerechtigkeit einer Verhandlung, in der die Worte und Dinge, um ihren Kopf zu retten, das verlogenste Alibi sich ersinnen und unaufhörlich durch

> den Augenschein oder die nackte Rechnung widerlegt werden müßen. (Benjamin [1928] 1991, 625)

Kraus's work mainly performs the tasks of *ein Ankläger*, a prosecutor and a critic. His major writings should be read as acts of judgment as well as interventions in the realm of German law. The secret of Kraus's work, we read further, its hidden core, is liturgical: "Ein Dasein, das, eben hierin, das heißeste Gebet um Erlösung ist, das heute über jüdische Lippen kommt" (Benjamin [1928] 1991, 625).

Benjamin listens to the hidden voice of Kraus – to the remnants of a (Jewish) prayer that is concealed in his demonic acts of judgment. Not prayer itself, but its intentions, not Hebrew but rather its German echo, not the liturgical work of angels, but the devilish work of a critic, are the modernist manifestations of Kraus's writings.

5 Noise

More should be said on the work of prayer, the act with which Benjamin concluded his short note on Kraus. The liturgical task Benjamin relates to Kraus is of a Talmudic meaning. In the final section of his 1931 essay on Kraus, Benjamin invokes this liturgical act, referring to the *Unmensch*, the inhuman, as a "new angel":

> Ein neuer Engel. Vielleicht von jenen einer, welche, nach dem Talmud, neue jeden Augenblick in unzähligen Scharen, geschaffen werden, um, nachdem sie vor Gott ihre Stimme erhoben haben, aufzuhören und Nichts zu vergehen. Klagend, bezichtigend oder jubelnd? Gleichviel – dieser schnell verfliegenden Stimme ist das ephemere Werk von Kraus nachgebildet. Angelus – das ist der Bote der alten Stiche. (Benjamin [1931] 1991, 367)

The new angel is a modernist figuration of a liturgical body that was created for singing the hymn before God's throne. These angels are mentioned in the Talmudic tractate of *Hagigah* (Festival Offering), which recounts how the angels were born from God's breath for singing the song of glory. However, how should this angelic prayer sound? According to Jewish traditions (such as the *Zohar* and the *Hekhalot* literature), the songs of the angels are so mighty that no human ear can bear them. The voices of the heavenly creatures are beyond all measure, dissolving the structure of the world itself. In a few sources, following the Prophetic scriptures, the sound of the angelic prayer is heard as a "great noise" (in Hebrew: *rahash gadol*). In other sources, it is compared to a whisper or the sound of breathing.

Benjamin's note, which inquires about the implications of Kraus's work as an intervention in the realm of German letters, leads us to the question regarding Jewish prayer and its voices, its noise. In his infamous essay on *Das Judentum in der Musik* (1850), Richard Wagner identifies "with horror" the voice of Jewish prayer and the poems recited in the synagogue as "gurgle, yodel and cackle." (Wagner, 1911 [1850]). He hears the Jewish song of prayer as a disharmonic vocal texture, a noise, and thus as evidence of the Jews' unmusical character, itself an outcome of their exilic being. Nonetheless, Wagner's statement, anti-Semitic of its kind, corresponds with the traditional depiction of the creaturely, ear-splitting nature of the angelic prayer. This should not surprise us. The Jewish prayer, because of its unfamiliar, disharmonic sound, ruptures and disrupts the harmonies of European music. Wagner, who denied the radical implications of the Jewish voice, rejected its traditions altogether, failing to understand its depth: the cry, the shout, the twittering and whispering are significant signs of its liturgical task.

6 Twittering

The study of German-Jewish literature within the comparative frameworks of European languages and literatures begins with interventions. Hence, the introduction of German-Jewish writings into larger contexts of literary studies challenges the core concepts of study (theory and method) and draws new attention to the forgotten liturgical aspects of the literary enterprise. What we call, following Kafka, "Schreiben als Form des Gebetes" (1994c, 171), writing as a form of prayer, demands listening to its remnants. The noise, the whispering, the twittering – the distressing voices being related to German-Jewish writing, are also residues of the Hebrew/Aramaic prayer.

Another hint at this interruptive value of German-Jewish writing is found in Kafka's own prose, in his stories on neglected, forgotten creatures. One of these stories, "Josefine die Sängerin, oder das Volk der Mäuse" (1994b),[2] can be considered as a testimony of the German-Jewish vocal heritage. Josephine is a musician, her singing, however, we are told, is dubious. Her voice is a whistle – a "quite ordinary piping" (1983a, 361). The whistle, the story tells, is an expression of a collective form of life: piping is "the real artistic accomplishment of our people, or rather no mere accomplishment, but rather a characteristic expression of our life" (361). Piping, the lowest, weakest, minor form of the musical expres-

---

[2] In the following, I will quote from the English translation (Kafka 1983a).

sion, is a manifestation of the being of the people, for whom "every day brings surprises, apprehensions, hopes, and terrors" (363). We are told of a certain commitment of the mouse people to Josephine's art. However, "unconditional devotion is hardly known among us" (365). This source of conflict leads to Josephine's downfall. Neglected, forgotten by her own people, wounded and tired, Josephine ceases to sing. According to the latest news, "she disappeared." "The time will soon come," we are told, "when her last notes sound and die into silence" (375).

Josephine, one can argue, with her poor singing, attests to the leftovers of a Jewish prayer, a piping, a noise that interferes with the harmonious textures of European literature. Her whistles belong to the realm of the minor voices in Kafka's work, the esoteric, distorted voices – the piping, the cries, the twittering, and the stuttering (Deleuze 1994). An echo of these voices can be heard in the chapter the "Nature Theater of Oklahoma," one of the final fragments of Kafka's unfinished novel *Der Verschollene (Amerika), The Man Who Disappeared*. A young immigrant, Karl Roßmann, wanders through the lands of the new country and finally arrives at the theater of Oklahoma, where "everyone is welcome." At the entrance, he hears a band of hundreds of women dressed as angels, playing trumpets. Their playing, however, is distorted and sounds like a "big noise" (Kafka 1994a, 296–297). Kafka's protagonist does not seem to be troubled by this fact, but rather appears astonished and amused by it. For what matters is not the bad music but the gathering itself – the liturgical congregation of immigrants, wanderers and refugees, celebrating their being-together. These distorted voices, alongside their modernist implications, are evidences (again: remnants) of a lost communion. What we hear in these stories by Kafka are the echoes of a forgotten Jewish hymn.

7 Mauscheln

Kafka's story on the singing of Josefina, her piping and whistles as well as her silences, can be read as modernist figurations of the work of prayer. The unmusical nature of the mouse people hints, however, at another relic of a Jewish dialect – the *Mauscheln*. It is a pejorative title given to the German-Jewish idiom, understood as a 'jargon,' similar to Yiddish. Kafka referred to it in a short note, included in a letter to Max Brod in June 1921, written while he was staying at a sanitarium in Matilary, Slovakia (Kafka 1995, 334–338). After reporting on his health, he turned to the issue of German-Jewish literature and to Karl Kraus's satirical operetta "Literatur. Oder Man wird doch Da sehn." Kafka defines the nature of Kraus's work as an expression of this improper Jewish idiom of the German language. In this context, *Mauscheln* should be understood as the name given to the voice of a creature (*ein Maus*), which has, however, certain Hebrew liturgical connotations, associated with the name of Moses, the ancient Hebrew prophet, a lawgiver himself and a stutterer, an unmusical body. Kafka, however, provides this "Jewish dialect" with a comic interpretation: "Der Witz ist hauptsächlich das Mauscheln, so mauscheln wie Kraus kann niemand, trotzdem doch in dieser deutsch-jüdischen Welt kaum jemand etwas anderes als mauscheln kann" (Kafka 1995, 336). *Mauscheln* is a form of "Jewish language" that interrupts the German language, transforms it into a creaturely sound. In the hands of Jewish writers, German becomes *ein fremder Besitz* (Kafka 1995, 336). The Jewish way of handling the German language is one of estrangement.

Kraus's contribution to the world of German letters, defined by Benjamin as *Halachic* intervention, is characterized by Kafka as a *Mauscheln*. Both interpretations are rather comic, referring to the interruptive value of his writing and hinting at its association with traditions such as the songs of (fallen) angels, the language of (false) prophesy. In Kafka's view, *Mauscheln* also has certain cultural and social connotations: "(das) Verhältnis der jungen Juden zu ihrem Judentum" (Kafka 1995, 337). The complex relations of young Jewish writers (mainly young males) to Judaism (more precisely: to the Judaism of their fathers) is the condition that finds its voice in Kraus's work. The Jewish voice, however, is also a voice of lament, which is manifested in Kraus's operetta in the cry "oi." This short, minor speech-act is the last gesture of the grandfather, who, at the end of the operetta, reveals what *Mauscheln* is: a yell that bears the remnant of a Jewish prayer.

In Kafka's view, the essential element in Kraus's work is the creation of poetical textures that express the Jewish condition – the foreignness, rootlessness, and anxiety of being a Jew. These poetical textures are of dramaturgical nature: they are written as gestures and are based on intensive acts of body language. *Mauscheln* is the language of a dramaturgical body – a body of exaggerated gestures and foreign sounds. This body, however, is of a creaturely nature. In his letter, Kafka describes this corpus associated with the being of the Jewish authors as follows:

> Weg vom Judentum, meist mit unklarer Zustimmung der Väter (diese Unklarheit war das Empörende), wollten die meisten, die deutsch zu schreiben anfingen, sie wollten es, aber mit den Hinterbeinchen klebten sie noch am Judentum des Vaters und mit den Vorderbeinchen fanden sie keinen neuen Boden. Die Verzweiflung darüber war ihre Inspiration. (Kafka 1995, 337)

The image of this creaturely body, the body of a young Jewish writer, desperately searching for "einen neuen Boden," a new ground, while turning away from Judaism, is the image of *Mauscheln*. In this context, Kafka notes the "three impossibilities" of Jewish literary writing: "(Die) Unmöglichkeit, nicht zu scheiben, (die) Unmöglichkeit, deutsch zu schreiben, (die) Unmöglichkeit, anders zu schreiben" (the impossibility of not writing, the impossibility of writing in German, the impossibility of writing differently) (Kafka 1995, 337–338). These impossibilities, or paradoxes, of German-Jewish writing derive from the rootlessness and anxieties of a collective literary body that has already lost its base in tradition, yet has found no new land in which to take root.

Mauscheln, to follow Kafka's comments, is the name for the poetics of anxiety arising from certain historical, sociological, and psychological contexts of Jewish life and letters around 1900. *Mauscheln*, however, can also be understood as the expression of what literature is. What Kafka sees as the essential element in Kraus's work – a poetical texture of anxiety and despair – also hints at the foundational tensions of modernist literature. *Mauscheln* expresses an impossible possibility of literary production. This too can be considered as a contribution of German-Jewish writers to world literature: the attempt to escape the world of (patriarchal) tradition and to enter the world of German letters brought about a poetic texture of crisis, expressing the fragility of universal writing.

Kafka's remarks on Kraus, *Mauscheln*, and German-Jewish literature, I argue, are comic, reflecting the Jewish literary enterprise through an ironic perspective. However, Kafka's notes can also be considered as reflections on his own project of writing, while his comments on *Mauscheln* can be applied to his story *Die Verwandlung* (Kafka 1983), which recounts the misfortunes of Gregor Samsa – a human body, a creature, a Jew?

8 Jewish, too-much

What Kafka calls *Mauscheln* – a sort of German-Jewish dialect that becomes a resource for interference in the realm of German letters – was echoed forty years later by the poet Paul Celan in his notes on the future of poetry after 1945 by means of the term *Verjudung*. In his drafts to the *Meridian-Rede* (1960), Celan writes:

> Verjudung: Es ist das Anderswerden. Zum-anderen-und-dessen-Geheimnis-stehn […]
> Umkehr – dazu scheint es ja nun doch zuviel Einbahnstraßen zu geben. Gegenverkehr und Umkehr, das ist zweierlei aber auch auf den Feldwegen scheint es, ach, wenig Gelegenheit dazu zu geben. (Celan 1991, 131)

Verjudung, Judaization, (making too-Jewish), implies a poetical writing that demands deconstruction of the conventional syntax of the German poem, causing a distortion within its inner structure. In so doing, the poem attests to a certain historical experience, associated with "what is Jewish," namely with the deformations of being, with an experience of foreignness and being-other.[3] This, to follow Celan, is the path of the poem, a return (*Umkehr*), moving against (*Gegenverkehr*) the major stream of language. The poem, in turning back, moves again toward the (forgotten) other, signifying a future – the dimension of an encounter, a belated one. The poem, when distorted by "Jewish" vocal textures, does not serve the false harmonious plan of European lyrics. The poem thus turns into an act of witnessing, which implies not only a tale about the past, but also an openness, a movement towards the other, attesting to, saving his/her secret. Yet, Celan too was aware that this movement (the opening towards the other) is a movement towards the unknown. The path of the poem is not so much a return as a path of departure and of loss. The poem signifies "nowhere," giving a desperate sign for "where to?"

What we call "the future" contains tensions of this kind: it is shaped by the unfolding of tradition, the reinterpretation of past forms, which then produce a vortex in literary studies. The engagement of German-Jewish writers with traditions involves endless attempts at reorientation. Reading Celan today takes us *anderswo*, to other places. This too belongs to our experience of literary studies.

Epilogue

Our point of departure was the question: how can the study of German-Jewish literature contribute to the research and teaching in frameworks of general and comparative literature? Beginning with a reflection on acts of intervention and acknowledging the interruptive values of German-Jewish literature, I argued that German-Jewish writing should be understood as an interference in the major, canonical corpus of European literature. In order to study the nature of German-Jewish literary interventions, we should listen to its sounds – the noises of its *Durchbruch*, its "breaking through." Among our case studies were Walter Benjamin's and Franz Kafka's remarks on Karl Kraus, followed by a short comment on Paul Celan's poetics of intervention. These cases offer vocal interpretations of the German-Jewish contribution, stressing not only its materialistic implications – body language, gestures, vocal failures (stuttering, twittering, whispering), as exemplified in Franz Kafka's prose, but also its radical adaptation of liturgical traditions – the prayer and the "angelic" songs. What Ger-

---

3 For further reading, see Mosès (1987); Eshel (2004); and Liska (2013).

man-Jewish literature offers to the general field of literary studies is a modernist interpretation of tradition, which does not relinquish its messianic power, but instead provides it with a double irony. The "comic" interpretation of the German-Jewish literary project suggests, however, to cite Kafka's remark on Kraus, not only a joke (*ein Witz*), but a short moment of relief in the course of our studies.

Bibliography

Adorno, Theodor. "Die Wunde Heine." *Noten zur Literatur*. Frankfurt am Main: Suhrkamp Verlag, 1998. 95–100.
Benjamin, Walter. "Eine neue Kraus-Notiz" [1928]. *Gesammelte Werke*, Vol. II.2. Frankfurt am Main: Suhrkamp Verlag, 1991. 624–625.
Benjamin, Walter. "Karl Kraus" [1931]. *Gesammelte Werke*, Vol. II.1. Frankfurt am Main: Suhrkamp Verlag, 1991. 334–367.
Celan, Paul. *Der Meridian: Endfassung, Vorstufen, Materialen*. Tübinger Ausgabe. Frankfurt am Main: Suhrkamp, 1999.
Deleuze, Gilles. "He Stuttered." *Gilles Deleuze and the Theater of Philosophy*. Ed. Constantin v. Boundas and Dorothea Olkowski. New York and London: Routledge, 1994. 23–29
Eshel, Amir. "Paul Celan's Other: History, Poetics, and Ethics." *New German Critique* 91 (2004): 55–77.
Grab, Walter. *Heinrich Heine als politischer Dichter*. Büchergilde Gutenberg, 1992.
Heidegger, Martin. "Der Satz der Identität." *Identität und Differenz*. Pfullingen: Verlag Günther Neska, 1986. 9–30.
Heine, Heinrich. *Deutschland: Ein Windermärchen. Werke*, Vol. I. Köln: Könemann Verlag, 1995.
Kafka, Franz. "Josephine the Singer, or the Mouse Folk." *The Complete Stories*. Trans. Willa and Edwin Muir. New York: Schocken, 1983a. 360–376.
Kafka, Franz. "The Metamorphosis." *The Complete Stories*. Trans. Willa and Edwin Muir. New York: Schocken Books, 1983b. 89–139.
Kafka, Franz. *Der Verschollene*. Frankfurt am Main: Fischer Taschenbuch Verlag, 1994a. 296–297.
Kafka, Franz. "Josefine die Sängerin, oder das Volk der Mäuse." *Gesammelte Werke*. Frankfurt am Main: Fischer Taschenbuch Verlag, 1994b.
Kafka, Franz. *Zur Frage der Gesetze*. Frankfurt am Main: Fischer Taschenbuch Verlag, 1994c.
Kafka, Franz. *Briefe 1902–1924*. Frankfurt am Main: Fischer Tachenbuch Verlag, 1995.
Liska, Vivian. "'Man kann verjuden': Paradoxes of Exemplarity." *Against the Grain: Jewish Intellectuals in Hard Times*. Ed. Ezra Mendelsohn, Stefani Hoffman et al. New York: Berghahn, 2013. 198–212.
Moses, Stéphane. "'Wege auf denen die Sprache stimmhaft wird': Paul Celans 'Gespräch im Gebirg.'" *Argumentum e Silentio*. Ed. Amy Diana Colin. Tübingen: de Gruyter, 1987.
Rosenzweig, Franz. *Der Stern der Erlösung*. Frankfurt am Main: Suhrkamp Verlag, 1998.
Wagner, Richard. "Das Judentum in der Musik." *Schriften*, Vol. 13. Leipzig: Hesse Verlag, 1911. 7–29.

Kader Konuk
Reading Kafka in Turkey

An investigation of the reception and appropriation of Kafka in Turkey reveals the ongoing effort to secure freedom of speech in a country that is marked by a long history of Turkification and Islamisation. The strong tradition of Kafka reception in Turkey has sensitised readers to the kinds of literary allusions and rhetorical flourishes that are associated with the Prague author. Characters such as Herr K. and Gregor Samsa, labyrinthine narratives and the motif of estrangement left a lasting imprint on literary texts that openly challenge or circumvent censorship.

The Turkish reception of Kafka is also instructive for research in the field of Turkish-German Studies. There is a long-standing relationship between Turks and Germans dating back to Ottoman times that is marked by imperial and national interests, intellectual exchange, exile, labour migration and economic interests. A dynamic market for Turkish literature has evolved in Germany since the 1980s and vice versa. Since Kafka's work explores ethnic, national, imperial or religious categories, it continues to provoke debate about what it means to belong. The work of the most prominent German authors of Turkish descent, such as Emine Sevgi Özdamar and Zafer Şenocak, applies Kafka in new ways. Şenocak's most recent work, *In deinen Worten: Mutmaßungen über den Glauben meines Vaters* (2016), echoes Kafka's *Brief an den Vater* (*Letter to His Father*), in which the son discusses his father's transmission of religious tradition.[1] Albeit in different fashions, both texts address the transformation of minority religions in the context of migration and assimilation.

This article focuses on the reception of Kafka as a diagnostic means for assessing the status and treatment of ethnic and religious minorities in Turkey. For scholars and writers alike, Kafka remains a dominant figure, one who signifies the possibility of moving beyond nationally defined literary fields. Nurdan Gürbilek, for example, adopts a comparative approach in her analysis titled *Benden Önce Bir Başkası* (*Somebody Else Before Me*), in which she reads literary texts

---

[1] This essay is a shorter version of the article published in "Kafka is among us: Turkey's Transnational and Interlingual Literatures," *Diyâr: Zeitschrift für Osmanistik, Türkei- und Nahostforschung*, Jg.1 (2020): 153–174. The author would like to thank the editors of *Diyâr* for granting permission to reprint a section of the article.
    For a forthcoming article, see Konuk, Kader. 'Kritikfähigkeit und Zweifel in Zafer Şenocaks Werk'. In Gutjahr, Ortrud (ed.). *WORT.BRÜCHE: Fragmente einer Sprache des Vertrauens im Werk Zafer Şenocaks*. Bielefeld: transcript.

against each other ('çapraz okuma').[2] She analyses the evolution of the motif of the monstrous vermin from Dostoevsky to Kafka, arguing that readers' ability to appreciate the significance of Kafka's vermin depends on the literary groundwork laid by Dostoevsky. Likewise, intertextual links between Kafka's *Letter to His Father* and Oğuz Atay's (1934–1977) *Babama Mektup* (*Letter to My Father*) are explored in a manner that transcends the conventional styles in which Turkish writers' engagement with European literature has been analysed. The strength of Gürbilek's work lies in her comprehensive approach, an approach that moves away from the East-West paradigm. It is perhaps owing to the assertion that progress and the future lie in the West that a sense of belatedness and inadequacy has tended to infuse early Turkish literature. Gürbilek proposes the term 'criticism of lack' to capture the sense of insufficiency, deprivation, and shortage that pervades Turkish literature, which she attempts to overcome in her analysis of intertextual relations.[3] An approach that merely conceptualises European literature as a medium of empowerment for Middle Eastern societies would be equally misleading. To invoke the title of Azar Nafisi's 2003 memoir, I am not proposing a 'Reading *The Trial* in Istanbul'. In *Reading Lolita in Tehran*, the author, an Iranian professor of English literature, captures the liberating potential of reading Western literature in Tehran. Nafisi's memoir portrays Iranian women's engagement with Western literature as an act of intellectual freedom and feminist resistance to the theocracy that rules their lives. Although I have strong reservations about this perspective, it is worth noting that Nafisi also shows 'how *Lolita* gave a different color to Tehran and how Tehran helped redefine Nabokov's novel, turning it into this *Lolita*, our *Lolita*'.[4] Similarly the intention here is not merely to elaborate how Kafka's work plays out in Turkish literature as a way of articulating cultural critique and political resistance, but rather to ask whether Kafka's Turkish reception provides new angles to Kafka criticism generally. By following the traces of Kafka in Turkish literature since the 1950s, this approach provides a model for the study of Turkish literature and culture within a global context.

While only a small circle of writers and critics was aware of Kafka's writing during his lifetime, there are a number of decisive moments that mark the history of the reception of his work. Although his books fell victim to the infamous book burnings perpetrated by the National Socialists, Kafka came to be recognised after the war as one of the most significant authors of European modernism.

---

[2] Gürbilek 2011.
[3] Gürbilek 2003, 600.
[4] Nafisi 2003, 6.

The reception of his work, however, was divided along strictly ideological lines. With the relaxing of Cold War ideologies, Kafka came to be seen as a transnational writer par excellence and a cornerstone of world literature. Literary critics would henceforth identify the roots of his work at the intersection of the Habsburg monarchy, Jewish identity and European modernism. Today, Kafka's oeuvre is seen to uniquely demonstrate the interrelatedness of ethnic, religious, linguistic, imperial and national affiliations.[5]

Parallels may be drawn between Prague and Istanbul as sites of literary production – both cities underwent fundamental changes during the transition from empire to nation state. In *Prague Territories* Scott Spector argues that in the peripheral spheres of declining German power, language became the most politically charged issue.[6] The language politics of Prague at the turn of the century and the *Tschechisierung* (Czechisation) of the city finds a parallel in the Turkification of Istanbul in the early 20th century, and both may be understood as a consequence of the kinds of assimilation processes that accompany modernisation. This prompts one to question whether there is a figure like Kafka in the Turkish literary context – an author who is a member of a minority group, writes in Turkish, develops a unique style, and "deterritorialises" the Turkish literary landscape. Is there, in other words, a Kafkaesque author who subverts Turkish national and ethno-religious boundaries? How is the isomorphism between national territory, language and literature that was created in the transition from the Ottoman Empire to the Turkish Republic challenged through literature?

Following Laurent Mignon, Murat Cankara, Hülya Adak, Etienne Charrière and others by expanding research to include the diverse literatures of the Ottoman Empire and Turkey, we can resist the homogenisation enforced by the Turkish state. The language and cultural reforms of the early Republican period suppressed the diversity of Ottoman literatures and territorialised the newly emerging literary narratives. A Turkish Renaissance was invoked as a means to create a homogenous Turkish identity. Comparisons with other countries suggest themselves. Whereas the elevation of the vernacular to a literary language is usually thought to have catalysed the European Renaissance and the Enlightenment, and hence it is mostly regarded in positive terms, in the Ottoman Empire the valence is more ambivalent. On the one hand, elevating the vernacular had a democratising effect during the early decades of the Turkish Republic. The genre *köy edebiyatı* (village literature), for example, provided the means for a literary imagination in Turkish. On the other hand, elevating and standardising vernacular

---

[5] David Suchoff 2007 gives a comprehensive overview of the changing modes in Kafka criticism.
[6] Spector 2000, 68–82.

Turkish came at the price of minoritising and suppressing literatures in Ottoman, Armenian, Greek and Kurdish.

Because Turkishness is defined along religious lines (with the Sunni male constituting the norm for Turkishness), non-Muslim writers have historically occupied a precarious position within society. Since articulating affiliation to a religious minority constrains broader recognition as a writer, Turkish authors have developed a variety of strategies in the publishing world. These strategies range from those practiced by atheist poet and essayist Roni Margulies (b. 1955), who writes about Jewish life but prefers not to be referred to as a Jewish writer, to that of novelist Vivet Kanetti (b. 1956), who published her first books under the pseudonym E. Emine, a quintessentially Turkish name. While Margulies keeps the memory of Turkey's diverse past alive, he does not mourn the loss of Ladino, nor does he want to be referred to as a Jewish poet or a representative of a minority literature. Nonetheless, Margulies was invested in making Yehuda Amichai's Hebrew poetry available in Turkish. Other writers have resisted pressure – like that faced by Kanetti – to conceal their Jewish background, turning it instead into a wellspring of creativity. Mario Levi, one of the most important contemporary Turkish writers, for example, has written a number of books explicitly dealing with Jewish life in Turkey. Given both their shared minority status and identification with Jewish heritage, it should come as no surprise that Kafka's literary influence is recognised in Levi's work.[7]

Bilge Karasu (1930–1995), a renowned author of Jewish and Greek Orthodox heritage, engaged even more directly with Kafka's work and developed a narrative style that for many resonates with Kafka's nightmarish plots. *Gece* – translated by Güneli Gün as *Night* – is a lengthy novel in which the author conceives of a society governed exclusively by fear and suspicion. There is no divine revelation, no security, and no coherence that might give meaning to human existence in the fear-driven world of the novel. Owing to the similarities between Karasu's and Kafka's narrative styles, Karasu is often referred to as the Turkish Kafka – an attribution that he himself strongly opposed.[8] Establishing literary correlations between authors on the basis of their religious and ethnoreligious affiliations is a temptation that ought to be resisted. Rather, it might be asked how Kafka has had a direct impact on literary imagination since the first Turkish translations of his work in the 1950s.[9] Süreyya İlkılıç provides a comprehensive

---

[7] Levi 2005.
[8] Karasu 2007.
[9] Within this context it is interesting to see that a Kurdish translation project, which started after the liberalisation of laws related to the Kurdish language, made translating *Die Verwandlung* into Kurmanji Kurdish a priority; Kafka 2010.

account and analysis of the translations and their reception in Turkey, detecting a correlation between them and the political upheaval caused by the military coups.[10] One of the first scholars to recognise the significance of Kafka's reception outside of Western Europe and the United States, however, was Atef Botros. In *Kafka: Ein jüdischer Schriftsteller aus arabischer Sicht* (2010), Botros examines the Arab reception of Kafka, arguing that the question of Kafka's contested Zionist leanings became central to Arab intellectuals after the Six-Day War of 1967. Looking at the Turkish context, there is little evidence that Kafka's stance towards Zionism was central to his popularity in Turkey. For obvious reasons, the Israeli-Palestinian conflict has not had comparable political ramifications in Turkey and hence never provoked debate about Kafka's ideological position.

This article argues instead that Kafka became a seminal figure for writers in Turkey whose investment was not necessarily in Kafka's Jewishness but in specific narrative techniques, the adaptation of which allowed them to develop their own literature of resistance. This can be traced in works written from the late 1970s onwards, works that experiment with literary styles from realism to existentialism and postmodernism. Of particular interest to writers, artists and intellectuals are those themes that are readily identified with Kafka's work – alienation in the modern age, proto-existentialism, polyglottism and social subversiveness – themes that reveal society's ills. Kafka was not, as might be assumed, mobilised in Turkey primarily as a representative of Western literature or Jewishness. Rather, he has been received as an exemplar of resistance and alienation. By reflecting on the ways in which Kafka has been received in the Turkish literary landscape, it becomes possible to unravel various discursive threads that undermine the state's homogenising project. Four novels stand out in this regard: Ferit Edgü's *Hakkâri'de bir Mevsim* (1977), Erhan Bener's *Böcek* (1982), Bilge Karasu's *Gece* (1985) and Orhan Pamuk's *Kar* (2004). Reading Turkish literature through the lens of Kafka – be it in terms of reenactment, intertextuality, interlingual relations or reassemblage – yields new insights. Ferit Edgü's reimagination of K.'s arrival in a strange village provides a powerful subtext in a climate of censorship, heightening the awareness that Assyrian and Kurdish were subjugated and forced into oblivion. Erhan Bener, on the other hand, was fascinated by the absurd and the monstrous in Kafka's works, qualities he employed in *Böcek* to portray the fascist mentality of a particular generation. Bilge Karasu's almost puristic, technical approach to language in *Gece* and *Göçmüş Kediler Bahçesi* is reminiscent of Kafka's linguistic style. Karasu articulates the consequences of linguistic assimilationism in subtle ways. Pamuk, on the other hand,

---

10 İlkılıç 2016, 276.

adopts K. as a figure of exile, creating a narrative that functions like a spectre of the destroyed multilingual and multireligious worlds of the Ottoman Empire.

Reading Turkish literature through Kafka delivers several insights: running the risk of stating the obvious, it is a reminder that there is nothing essentially Turkish about Turkish literature. Turkish literature is inherently transnational not only by virtue of its history of encounters and exchange with European literatures, but also because of its interaction with the indigenous languages and literatures of the Ottoman Empire. Second, there is a strong correlation between sociopolitical conditions and aesthetic developments – including those brought into being by existentialism and postmodernism – that mark the evolution of Turkish literature. In addition to the aesthetic transformations traced in this article, we can observe how Kafka is repeatedly deployed as a figure of resistance against the suppression of free speech and processes of enforced linguistic assimilation. Edgü and Karasu in particular serve as examples of the ways in which Kafka's style evolves into new forms.

The interlingual literature that negotiates and sometimes resists linguistic assimilationism in Turkey sheds new light on the linguistic consciousness triggered by Kafka's oeuvre. Acknowledging and illuminating Turkish literary history from the point of view of minoritised communities does not mean distinguishing authors according to fixed ethnoreligious rubrics and constructing parallel, neatly segregated literary histories, something Mario Levi succinctly referred to as *ada edebiyatı*, 'island literature'.[11] It is the diverse, intertwined, and at times interlingual nature of these literary histories that are slowly coming to the fore.[12] Etienne Charrière, Will Stroebel and Laurent Mignon have contributed to the reconceptualisation of literatures in the Ottoman Empire and Turkey, perhaps most notably in Mignon's article on the use of Kurdish expressions in Turkish texts that have the effect of transcending national and linguistic borders.[13] Reconnecting modern Turkish to its Ottoman heritage while illuminating its continuing exchange with Armenian, Jewish, Greek, Persian, Ladino, Arabic and Kurdish literatures will allow us to transnationalise Turkish Studies from within and construct a more comprehensive picture of Turkey's multicultural and polyglot heritage. This is all the more important at a moment when such plurality is being disavowed and Ottoman history is being co-opted for nationalist and neo-imperialist ends.

---

[11] Sayın 1999, 195.
[12] Roni Margulies' critique and Mehmet Yaşın's intervention in his *Poeturka* – a collection of essays published in the mid-1990s – are early landmarks in this direction; Yaşın 1995.
[13] Mignon 2014, 199.

Bibliography

Bener, Erhan. 2000. *Böcek* [Vermin]. İstanbul: Remzi Kitapevi.
Cankara, Murat. 2015. 'Rethinking Ottoman Cross-Cultural Encounters. Turks and the Armenian Alphabet'. *Middle Eastern Studies*. 51.1. 1–16.
Charrière, Etienne. Forthcoming. 'Translating Communities. Novel Translation as a Trans-Communal Practice in the Tanzimat Period'. In Charrière, Etienne and Ringer, Monica (eds.). *Modernity in Ottoman Culture. Reform and the Tanzimat Novel*. London: I.B. Tauris.
Edgü, Ferit. 1976. 'Varoluşçuluğun Türk edebiyatına etkisi [The Impact of Existentialism on Turkish Literature]'. *Milliyet Sanat*. 202. 10–29.
Edgü, Ferit. 2009. *Hakkâri'de Bir Mevsim* [A Season in Hakkari]. İstanbul: Sel Yayıncılık.
Gürbilek, Nurdan. 2003. 'Dandies and Originals. Authenticity, Belatedness, and the Turkish Novel'. *South Atlantic Quarterly*. 102.2. 599–628.
Gürbilek, Nurdan. 2011. *Benden Önce Bir Başkası* [Somebody Else Before Me]. İstanbul: Metis.
İlkılıç, Süreyya. 2016. *Kafka in der Türkei. Rezeption von Kafkas Werken in der Türkei und ihre Einflüsse auf die moderne türkische Literatur*. Würzburg: Königshausen und Neumann.
Kafka, Franz. 2006. *Der Prozeß*. Frankfurt am Main: Fischer Taschenbuch Verlag.
Kafka, Franz. 2010. *Veguherîn* [Metamorphosis]. Translated by Ferhat Aydın. Diyarbakır: Weşanên Lîs. http://www.wesanenlis.com/Detay.aspx?ID=90 (accessed 20.09.2015).
Karasu, Bilge. 1994. *Night*. Translated by Güneli Gün. Baton Rouge: Louisiana State University Press.
Karasu, Bilge. 2007. 'Türk Kafka'sı değilim [I am not Turkey's Kafka]'. *KAOSGL*. 12.07.2007. http://www.kaosgl.com/sayfa.php?id=1270 (accessed 09.03.2013).
Karasu, Bilge. 2013. *Gece* [Night]. İstanbul: Metis.
Konuk, Kader. Forthcoming. 'Kritikfähigkeit und Zweifel in Zafer Şenocaks Werk'. In Gutjahr, Ortrud (ed.). *WORT.BRÜCHE. Fragmente einer Sprache des Vertrauens im Werk Zafer Şenocaks*. Bielefeld: transcript
Levi, Mario. 2005. 'Kafka'nın *Değişim*'i. Hangi Değerler Hangi Ahlâk Kuralları [Kafka's Metamorphosis. Which Values, Which Ethical Principles]'. In Levi, Mario. *Bir Yaz Yağmuruydu* [It was a Summer Rain]. İstanbul: Doğan Kitap.
Mignon, Laurent. 2014. 'A Pilgrim's Progress. Armenian and Kurdish Literatures in Turkish and Rewriting of Literary History'. *Patterns of Prejudice*. 48.2. 182–200.
Mignon, Laurent. 2018. 'Ringen mit Dämonen. Gibt es eine jüdisch-türkische Literatur?'. In Riemann, Wolfgang (ed.). *Ni kaza en Turkiya. Erzählungen jüdischer Autoren aus Istanbul*. Engelschoff: Auf dem Ruffel. 125–144.
Nafisi, Azar. 2003. *Reading Lolita in Tehran. A Memoir in Books*. New York: Random House.
Pamuk, Orhan. 2004. *Snow*. New York: Alfred A. Knopf.
Sayın, Şârâ. 1999. 'Çokkültürlü İstanbul'u "Okumak" ["Reading" Multicultural Istanbul]'. In Sayın, Şârâ. *Metinlerle Söyleşi* [Conversation with Texts]. İstanbul: Multilingual. 191–204.
Şenocak, Zafer. 2006. 'Modernität ohne Mythos. Der Mangel der Türkei'. *Die Welt*. 09.06.2006. http://www.welt.de/print-welt/article701243/Modernitaet-ohne-Mythos-Der-Mangel-der-Tuerkei.html (accessed 07.03.2013).

Spector, Scott. 2000. *Prague Territories. National Conflict and Cultural Innovation in Franz Kakfa's Fin de Siècle*. Berkeley: University of California Press.
Stroebel, William. Forthcoming. 'Longhand Lines of Flight. Cataloguing Displacement in a Karamanli Refugee's Commonplace Book'. *PMLA*.
Suchoff, David. 2007. 'Kafka's Jewish Languages. The Hidden Openness of Tradition'. *The Journal of Jewish Thought and Philosophy*. 15.2. 65–132.
Yaşın, Mehmet. 1995. *Poeturka. Deneme* [Poeturca. Essay]. İstanbul: Adam.

Shira Miron

Unraveling *Heimat* – Recontextualizing Gertrud Kolmar's *Das preußische Wappenbuch*

1 Introduction: difference and belonging

The call to "disseminate Jewish literatures" posits a challenge rooted in the double belonging of the matter in question. While such an attempt seeks to remedy the dearth of scholarly work on "Jewish literatures" from a separation from literary studies, it nevertheless continues to perceive them as marked by a significant difference. However, the nature of this difference varies from case to case and affects each particular attempt at dissemination–both in regard to the discussed literary text as well as its place within the wider discourse. Hence, in order to disseminate Jewish literatures, one should first carefully consider both the initial separating factors as well as the possibility of a dual belonging. This should be done while remaining aware of the presumptions in play, which often serve as the origin and perpetuating force of the ghettoization of the so-called Jewish literatures.

In the case of the German-Jewish poet Gertrud Kolmar, her decades-long exclusion from the corpus of German poetry brings together matters of historical circumstances, reception history, and literary traditions germane both to her own oeuvre as well as to the literary discourse from which it was excluded. Her life as a Jew in Germany under the Nazi regime, her deportation from Germany, and murder in Auschwitz in 1943 seemed until not too long ago to be the main lens for the interpretation of her works.[1] This biographical mode of interpretation is a direct consequence of the fact that Kolmar's works were almost entirely posthumously published, a process that started with the first publication of her last poetry cycle *Welten* ("Worlds") in 1947, a decade after it was written, and ended with the publication of the critical edition of her collected poetry in

---

[1] The first major study of Gertrud Kolmar's work which was since often described as a dominant influence on the research dedicated to the poet written since then is Johanna Woltmann's biographical monograph (1995; cf. Heimann 2012, 3, 10–11). A recent example to the biographical tendency is Friederike Heimann's monograph, which despite a recognition of the problematic nature of such an approach (2012, 5–31) cannot fully unchain itself from it.

ᴆ OpenAccess. © 2020 Shira Miron, published by De Gruyter. [CC BY-NC-ND] This work is licensed under the Creative Commons Attribution-NonCommercial-NoDerivatives 4.0 License.
https://doi.org/10.1515/9783110619003-011

2003.² The belated publication was a result of the fact that Kolmar, whose first poems were published in 1917, did not enter her main productive writing phase until 1927. Although the official ban of publications by Jewish writers was not issued by the Reich Chamber of Literature (Reichsschrifttumskammer, RSK) until 1935 (Barbian 2013, 153–154, 194–196), the political events and atmosphere complicated the publication situation, as noted by Kolmar herself in a letter to her cousin Walter Benjamin (2014, 208/2004, 159). From 1935 onwards, the few poems published during Kolmar's lifetime were printed only in Jewish newspapers and appeared under her birth name Gertrud Chodziesner (a paragraph in the 1935 RSK orders prohibited Jewish authors from using a penname). In the years following the war, the publication of her work was inevitably marked by this historical segregation, which further framed her work as Jewish and prevented its integration into the wider context of German poetry and prose.³ So influential was this initial segregation of Kolmar's work that it was not until the late 1990's that the predominantly German language scholarship on Kolmar's poetry began to slowly turn away from this biographical framework in favor of a wider contextualized reading.⁴

The contributing factors that led to the scholarly emphasis on Kolmar's difference in the German literary landscape and consequently to her exclusion from the canon cannot be simply dismissed as irrelevant. Nevertheless, the first step in the establishment of an organic relation to the wider literary discourse should be a careful consideration and less immediate application of this difference when approaching Kolmar's work. The following contribution suggests a reading

---

2 For a detailed and most updated discussion of Kolmar's posthumous publications see Nörtemann (2005).
3 An early example is the first publication of the 1939 written novella *Susanna* in an anthology of prose by Jewish writers (Otten 1959). To that kind of publications joins the later discussion of works written by German-Jewish authors under the Nazi regime, which was often founded on an implicit premise that perceived the historical circumstances as the key to the understanding and appreciation of such works. An explicit stance of such a perception that calls for a different mode of apprehension of works by German-Jewish authors that were written under the Nazi regime could be found in Henry Wassermann's introduction to the bibliography of Jewish literature written under the third Reich: "Es [the creation under the totalitarian regime and amongst it the Jewish literature under the Nazis] kann nur gewertet werden auf dem Hintergrund der politischen, sozialen, wirtschaftlichen und religiösen Umstände in Nazi Deutschland." (Wassermann 1989, xii, and cf. Schoor 2010, 11–36).
4 A first example of an attempt at a wider contextualization of Kolmar's poetry was offered by Birgit R. Erdle's monograph *Antlitz – Mord – Gesetz: Figuren des Anderen bei Gertrud Kolmar und Emanuel Lévinas* (1994). A more recent example which traces in Kolmar's poetry a line of poetic development rather than an autobiographical mirroring sequence is Silke Nowak's monograph *Sprechende Bilder: Zur Lyrik und Poetik Gertrud Kolmars* (2007).

of Gertrud Kolmar's 1927 opening poem of the collection *Das preußische Wappenbuch* that will seek to defer this difference, thus allowing for a consideration of an active dialogue from within the wider literary discourse unrestricted to the realm of "Jewish literature." Hence, the differentiating, utterly biographical elements will not be read as the foundation of the understanding of a text unless the reading proves them to be so. In other words, the dissemination will be prior to the separation. Such an approach enables the disclosure of mutual affinities that challenges the categorical separation of "Jewish literature" from "German literature."

2 First hindrances on the way to an interpretation of *Das preußische Wappenbuch*

In the winter of 1927/1928, Kolmar wrote her first major poetic work, a collection of 53 poems titled *Das preußische Wappenbuch* [The Book of Prussian Coats of Arms]. Each of the poems, arranged in thirteen groups named after Prussian provinces, carries the name of a coat of arms of a Prussian city or village. Kolmar's immediate, seemingly prosaic source of inspiration for this collection was a stamp booklet distributed as an advertisement by the German coffee brand *Kaffee Haag*, in which customers collected small stamps featuring illustrations of Prussian coats of arms drawn by the German artist Otto Hupp. One of the booklets, which were widely popular in Germany between the wars, belonged to Georg Chodziesner, Komlar's younger brother (Woltmann 1993, 67–78; Kolmar 2003, III. 134–136).

Each poem opens with a motto-like description of the coat of arms that appears to be a distilled version of Hupp's own descriptions that were printed on the backside of the stamp (Woltmann 1993, 72; Sauder 1996, 45–46). Thus, Kolmar further plays off of the expectations of the reader, who, after reading the collection title, the poem title and the short description, anticipates a poem that will verbally capture the mute emblem. Such a presupposition of the poem as offering a mode of deciphering in the form of "art writing" is grounded in the widespread understanding of the reciprocal relations between picture and language, which had a deep influence on European pictorial aesthetics (Mitchell 1986, 116–121). In the words of Simonides of Ceos, "a poem is a painting that speaks, and a painting is a mute poem." This intimate relation between word and image serves as the core of heraldic poetry (in the *Wappendichtung* and in some instances of the *Blason*) developed in medieval Europe (Fürbeth 2007). However, as was already pointed out in the few previous discussions of the collection, the poems deviate from the heraldic literary tradition, as each of them abandons, ignores, or further develops the visual elements appearing on the coat of arms to such a degree that they no longer serve as mere poetic descriptions (Erdle 1994, 185; Sauder 1996, 53).

While such a deviation appears to be a conspicuous dimension of the collection, it would be wrong to reduce Kolmar's interest in the coats of arms to a mere aesthetic fascination (Sauder 1996, 52). Such a claim empties the *Wappenbuch* of its historical, local, and traditional meanings, reducing Kolmar's notion of the coat of arms to a reference to her brother's booklet, devoid of any connection to the heraldic tradition. Yet, it is Kolmar's words themselves that contradict this position. In a letter written in December 1940 to her sister Hilde Wenzel, who since 1938 had lived in exile in Switzerland, Kolmar refers directly to her own idea of the coat of arms by quoting a letter of Rainer Maria Rilke.[5] In a letter to Baron Rolf von Ungern-Sternberg written in 1922 at the Château de Muzot,[6] Rilke admires the Baron's family coat of arms appearing on the seal of the letter he received from him, remarking that "mir sagen Wappen außerordentlich viel, es ließe sich aus ihnen viel mehr schließen und wahr-sagen, als je versucht worden ist" [coats of arms are extraordinarily expressive to me, one could draw much from them and tell the truth much better than has been attempted]) Rilke 2002, 96; Kolmar 2004, 64). To this, Kolmar adds "Ich hab' es versucht und diese Worte gar nicht gekannt " [I have tried it without even knowing these words] (2014, 102/2004, 64). Her notion of the coat of arms is by no means purely technical or simply aesthetic. Rather, it stands in a close affinity to Rilke's image of coat of arms,[7] while continuously alluding to the old tradition of heraldic poetry. Thus, a new relation between the pictorial source and the poem is created.

An additional noteworthy obstacle for the reception and interpretation of the collection has to do with its relation to the German regional traditions of *Heimatkunst* and *Heimatlyrik*, which are often associated with jingoistic, nationalist,

---

[5] Although Kolmar's poetry was often compared to Rilke's (Kolmar 2003, III. 346; Nowak 2007, 279), the affinity to Rilke was not the result of influence. As she herself declared, she came to know his poetry "too late" and only after her own poetic voice was already formed (2014, 88/2004, 53).

[6] In a letter from July 1940 Kolmar shares with Hilde her fascination from Rilke's *Briefe aus Muzot* which she came to know through an acquaintance. In this later letter from 15th December 1940, five days after her 46th birthday, Kolmar tells her sister that she asked and received a copy of Rilke's *Briefe aus Muzot* as a birthday present from her father and that she finds it to be "eine wahre Schatzkammer" [a true treasure] (2014, 77–78, 87/2004, 64).

[7] Rilke poetically expressed this idea earlier in his 1907 poem "Das Wappen" (2006, 533).

and anti-Semitic elements.[8] Studies of the collection tend to avoid addressing the relation between the *preußisches Wappenbuch* and the tradition of *Heimatliteratur*, assuming the collection could not be connected to a literary movement that expresses a sense of rootedness and belonging. This exclusion stems from the positioning of Kolmar's work within the context of German-Jewish literature, a perception that does not allow a German-Jewish poet to speak of a German *Heimat*.

It is again Kolmar's own words that render the dismissal of the role of this tradition in *das preußische Wappenbuch* impossible. In 1934, shortly after the publication of a selection of twenty poems from the collection, Kolmar stated in the aforementioned letter to Walter Benjamin that she had insisted on including the date of origin on one of the first pages of the book and explains: "I wanted to make clear that I composed the 'Wappen' at a time when regional poetry [*Heimatlyrik*] was not yet all the rage" (2014, 208/ 2004, 153). This comment, which was previously dismissed by scholars as an expression of involuntary sarcasm (Erdle 1994, 185) or as a reference to the historical expulsion of Kolmar and her father from the family house deserves closer attention.[9] By suspending this biographical covering-law and instead reading Kolmar's poems in a wider literary context, the following discussion of the opening poem of the collection will uncover a less unequivocal idea of *Heimat* in Kolmar's *Das preußische Wappenbuch*.

3 *Heimat* reconsidered

Wappen von Allenburg

Ein rotes Elchhaupt auf Silbergrund, aus grünem Röhricht steigend.

Ich geh' durch Erde, die schon nicht mehr ist;
Denn meine Erde ist nur Teil von mir,
Wie ich mit Schaufel, Haupt und Widerrist
Ein blödes, graues, ungeschlachtes Tier.

[Coat of Arms of] *Allenburg*

On a silver ground, a red elk's head emerges from green reeds.

I tread forgotten earth now long deceased;
For this lost land is but a part of me,
A shy and clumsy, terrifying beast,
With haunches, head, and shovel-antlered tree.

---

8 On *Heimatkunst* and the anti-Semite context see Kilcher (2012), XI-XIII, for the recent discussion on *Heimatliteratur* in Europe based on a comparatist approach see Van Uffelen (2009).
9 Sauder draws a connection between the absence of home in the collection and the historical homelessness Kolmar and her father were forced into in 1938 ("Sie waren mitten in Berlin schon heimatlos"), thus imposing later biographical facts on previously written works (1996, 52).

Sie klatscht um meine Kniee als ein Sumpf,	It laps about my knees, a murky swamp,
Hängt von der trägen Lippe als ein Schlamm,	Hangs from my sluggish lips like dripping phlegm,
Hockt, Nebelschlange, feucht am roten Rumpf,	Wraps 'round red flanks a snake of fog and damp,
Schiebt unters Maul den flechtenblassen Stamm.	And feeds my mouth the lichen crusted stem
Ich bin, die war, die ferngestorbne Zeit,	I am what was, the far departed age
Die wüst im großen Wäldermoor gehaust,	That, wild, in giant wooded moors once housed,
In tiefe Flocken Wölfe hingeschneit,	That blew the wolves along when blizzards raged,
Mit dunklem Sturm den Uhu hergebraust.	And, dark with storms, the sleeping owls once roused.
Ich bin das Wilde, Dumpfe, das man schlug,	I am the dumb, the wild, the things now dead
Das man erschlagen, weil es fremd und stumm;	That men have killed for being mute and strange,
Was schlau und müde Karren schleppt und Pflug,	That dragged the heavy plough and spurred the sled,
Dem legt der Mörder bunten Halsschmuck um.	Adorned by murderers with charming chains.
Mir ward, die ihre Öde klagt und schnarrt,	And when the barren darkness wailed and moaned,
Die Nacht des Raben freundlich zugesellt,	I was the friend of ravens in the night,
Die im Geröhre ächzt, in Birken knarrt	Who rasped in reeds and in the birches groaned,
Und vor dem Licht der warmen Dörfer hält.	And halted at the villages' warm light.
Mir ward ein Regenhimmel, graulich schwer,	For me the rainy sky, whose heavy gray
Der zäh und stickig niederplumpt ins Luch,	Fell thick and stifling down upon the fen,
Das Fell am Leib, an meinem Hirn die Wehr,	Became my fur, my antlers' stiff array –
Nicht Hand noch Peitsche, Stall und Trog und Tuch.	Not hand, not whip, nor stall, nor trough, nor pen.
Das tierisch Mächtige hat sie entsetzt,	The mighty beasts struck terror into man.
Das arglos Fromme meuchelt ihre List:	With cunning tricks he hunted innocence,
Daß es verende, wund und tot gehetzt,	And wounded it, and slew it as it ran:
Die Erdenkindheit. Die doch nicht mehr ist.	In earthly childhood. That has passed long since.
(2003, II. 9–10)	(1975, 168–171)

With the opening pronoun, the subject of the poem becomes the speaker. The elk, bursting out of the coat of arms, negates its very existence as it describes itself walking through a land that has ceased to exist ("die schon nicht mehr ist"). Time and space, which are frozen together in the two-dimensional coat of arms, are torn apart in the poem, whose mixture of past and present sets the image in motion.[10] The harmonious, almost organic relation to the land captured in the coat of arms and its opening description ("Ein rotes Elchhaupt auf Silbergrund, aus grünem Röhricht steigend") is undermined as the speaker declares the land to be a part of its body while at the same time recognizing it as contributing to its designation as "blödes, graues, ungeschlachtes Tier" [A shy and clumsy, terrifying beast]. As in many of Kolmar's poems written in first person, it is unclear whether the elk describes his own self-perception or whether it observes itself from the outside.[11] This divergent perception is further deepened in the fourth stanza, which shifts from the "ich"[I] to the self-description from the outside as "es" [it]—"Ich bin das Wilde, Dumpfe, das man schlug, Das man erschalgen, weil es fremd und stumm."

In the second stanza, the extinct land is evoked through the bodily presence of the subject. The depiction of earth, the supposed *Heimat*, merges with the negative self-image of the elk in the closing lines of the first stanza and turns into a "Sumpf", a swamp that strangles its inhabitant, and "Schlamm" [sludge]. Though it is negatively expressed, the interdependence between the elk and the land is deepened; it is not only the elk who emerges from the green reeds, but also the earth that grips its body.

The belonging of the elk to the land in the form of a *Heimat* is further complicated by its forced domestication, described in the first stanza and carried out by new inhabitants who no longer speak the language of "die ferngestorbne Zeit" [the far departed age]. The image of the unified unanimous men who exploit the elk challenges the relation between the symbolic elk on the coat of arms and the people who use it as their identifying mark. The rupture between the lyrical I and the crowd is thematized, as in other works by Kolmar, by the impossibility of communication, which renders the elk, the carrier of the poetic voice, mute and strange in the eyes of the others.[12]

Only in the fifth and sixth stanzas does the elk find rest, as sky falls and mixes with earth in the form of a storm that transforms the land back into the primal world before God separated earth from sky as in Genesis 1,1. This is a

---

10 About the unique temporal structure in *Das preußische Wappenbuch* cf. Hausmann (2012).
11 As for example in the poem *Die Kröte* from the year 1933 (2003, II. 358–359).
12 This theme serves as the core of Kolmar's late work with the prominent example of the 1937 poem *Kunst* that seals the cycle *Welten* (2003, II. 545) and the 1939 novella *Susanna* (1993).

world untouched by the men who appeared in the last stanza and whose absence is encapsulated here by the lack of their means of control over the land (the hand, the whip, the stall, the trough, and the pen). Only then do sky and land merge into the elk's own body and shelter him as a true *Heimat* ("Mir ward ein Regenhimmel [...] Das Fell am Leib, an meinem Hirn die Wehr").

The struggle ends with the disappearance of the speaker in the last stanza and the description of its death in the third person. The closing line ("Die Erdenkindheit. Die doch nicht mehr ist") undermines the existence of the elk and the poem itself, while at the same time evoking it once again. The *Heimat*, then, is present and absent at the same time, while being experienced by the speaker as well as by the voice of the others who wish to *house* it and consequently disinherit it. Thus, the *Heimat* turns from a stable image in the form of the coats of arms into a relative term. So are also foreignness and belonging, two poles which throughout Kolmar's work are constantly challenged.

The opening poem of Kolmar's collection reveals the *Wappenbuch* as a proof of the belonging of the depicted and as a remainder from times long gone that challenges the present. Just like the figure of loyal Mortimer in Friedrich Schiller's drama *Maria Stuart*, who seeks proof of the identity of the true queen by consulting many old heraldry books ("Viel alte Wappenbücher schlug ich nach"; Schiller 2008, 27), here as well the poet turns to the *Wappenbuch* as a source establishing identity, belonging, and proof of origin from ancient times. These, as it becomes clear in the opening poem, are never absolute and get refracted through the voices claiming them as their own.

Perplexed by Kolmar's choice of title and source of inspiration which did not seem to befit the grand narrative of the connection between Kolmar's work and life, previous interpretations tried to sand down the contradiction between *Das preußische Wappenbuch* and the European and German tradition of *Heimatkunst* in different ways. Some interpretations have offered a compromise by focusing on the *Zivilisations-* and *Modernekritik* expressed in some of the collection's poems, a critical view that served as one of the foundations of the literary instantiations of *Heimatkunst* (Erdle 1994, 185; Schumann 2002, 21; Hausmann 2012, 248). This critical standpoint towards modernity appears in *Wappen von Allenburg* in the form of the struggle between mankind and nature, yet it does not seem to replace the dimension of *Heimat* and belonging as its core. Other readings tend to solve what they recognize as a conflict between Jewish and German literatures, defining Kolmar's poems as a "countermovement to the logic of the national-anti-Semitic construction of identity" (Nowak 2007, 30, my translation). An additional interpretation of the poem suggests that the "elk" is "the Jew," thus defining it as the ultimate representative of the Other and overlooking the interrelation of otherness and belonging within the poem (Schumann 2002, 184–193).¹³

It is again Kolmar's words that turn us in a different direction and lead us back to the poem itself. In a second letter to Walter Benjamin Kolmar reveals the source of inspiration for the poetic figure of the elk as "a natural offspring of Leconote de Lisle's mighty bird in 'Le Sommeil du Condor'" (2014, 210/ 2004, 155; 2003, II. 138; Sauder 1996, 50). In de Lisle's poem, the great bird is depicted soaring above the south American continent in a grand gesture that allows the bird to grasp it in its whole ("Le vaste Oiseau [...] Regarde l'Amérique et l'espace en silence." 1976, 166–167). Like de Lisle's condor, Kolmar's elk is part of the landscape in a way that makes it irreducible to a mere oppressed Other. Kolmar's notion of land and *Heimat* is a broad and nonlocal one; thus, her collection gathering together all the Prussian provinces and cities is an attempt to look upon the Prussian landscape and more broadly on the idea of *Heimat* from above, as one turning pages in a Wappenbuch o ras Lencote de Lisle's condor. Kolmar's *Heimatlyrik* is indeed not the traditional *Heimatlyrik* to which Robert Musil refers as "local" and recognizes its blossom as symptomatic of the decay of literature (1974, 133). Kolmar's poetry, which emphasizes the fragility and ephemerality of *Heimat* both as an idea and a state of mind, suggests a *Heimatliteratur* of a different kind. A reading of Kolmar's *Wappenbuch* based on her later biographical homelessness, or, more generally, on the premise of the lack of belonging as characteristic of "Jewish literatures" will not be able to uncover Kolmar's unique approach to this themes and results in a simplistic, inflexible understating of *Heimat* that the collection itself negates.

---

13 Schuman concludes her reading proclaiming that: "Durch die Austauschbarkeit von Elch und Jude impliziert das Gedicht *Wappen von Allenburg* einen Zusammenhang zwischen der Jahrhunderte währenden Geschichte der Verfolgung (und Vernichtung) der Juden und einer Zivilisation, die auf dem gewalttätigen Ausschluß des fremden basiert." The poem's retrospective understanding, which is symptomatic of the research on Kolmar until recently (see fn. 1 and 9), is marked by the shade of the Holocaust which leads Schumann to her problematic interpretation of a poem, written on 1927, as one that deals with the extermination of the Jews, an event Kolmar could not possibly imagine at the time. A similar, albeit more carefully formulated stance, appears in Erdle's interpretation of the poem as centered around the oppression and murder of the elk, which is finally connected by Erdle to the persecution of the Jews (1994, 192–193), cf. Sauder's rejection of Erdle's position (1996, 52).

4 Conclusion

In the case of the poetic work of the German-Jewish poet Gertrud Kolmar, the act of dissemination turns out to be a recontextualization back into the wider discourse her work originates from. Such an approach not only renders a more comprehensive understanding of the poetic text but also provides a wider definition of the literary sources that influence it. By considering the *Wappenbuch* in light of the tradition of *Heimatliteratur* and in the broader context of German and European literary traditions, as suggested by Kolmar herself, rather than thinking of such attribution as a conflict that should be resolved, both sides of the equation – the idea of "Jewish" literature and the wider literary discourse of *Heimat* – are unraveled. Kolmar's relativized yet overarching notion of *Heimat* embodied in the poem *Wappen von Allenburg* gives rise to a less rigid idea of Heimat and consequently a less conservative and naïve definition of *Heimatkunst* than the one Robert Musil encapsulates in the term *Lokaldichtung*. As a result, the effort towards dissemination takes shape as a double-ended process that finally turns the initial separating discursive difference into a reciprocal connecting force.

Bibliography

Barbian, Jan-Pieter. *The Politics of Literature in Nazi Germany. Books in the Media Dictatorship*. New York and London: Bloomsbury Academics, 2013.

Erdle, Birgit R. *Antlitz – Mord – Gesetz: Figuren des Anderen bei Gertrud Kolmar und Emanuel Lévinas*. Wien: Passagen, 1994.

Fürbeth, Frank. "Heraldische Dichtung." *Metzler Lexikon Literatur. Begriffe und Definitionen*. Ed. Günther Schweikle and Dieter Burdorf. Stuttgart: Metzler, 2007. 312.

Hausmann, Sibylla. "Vergangenheit und Gegenwart 'im Buch und Bilde': Zeitstrukturen und Bildbezüge in *Das Preußische Wappenbuch* von Gertrud Kolmar." *Sand in den Schuhen Kommender: Gertrud Kolmar Werk im Dialog*. Ed. Chryssoula Kambas and Marion Brandt. Göttingen: Wallstein, 2012. 239–250.

Heimann, Friederike. *Beziehung und Bruch in der Poetik Gertrud Kolmars: verborgene deutsch-jüdische Diskurse im Gedicht*. Berlin: De Gruyter, 2012.

Kilcher, Andreas B. "Einleitung." *Metzler Lexikon der deutsch-jüdischen Literatur*. Stuttgart: Metzler, 2012. VI–XXVII.

Kolmar, Gertrud. *Briefe*. Ed. Johanna Woltmann. Göttingen: Wallstein, 2014.

Kolmar, Gertrud. *Dark Soliloquy. The Selected Poems of Gertrud Kolmar*. Trans. Henry A. Smith. New York: Seabury, 1975.

Kolmar, Gertrud. *Das lyrische Werk*. Ed. Regina Nörtemann. Göttingen: Wallstein, 2003. 3 Volumes.

Kolmar, Gertrud. *My Gaze is Turned Inward. Letters, 1934–1943*. Trans. Brigitte M. Goldstein. Evanston: Northwestern, 2004.
Kolmar, Gertrud. *Susanna*. Frankfurt am Main: Jüdischer Verlag im Suhrkamp Verlag, 1993.
Leconte de Lisle. *Œuvres*. Ed. Edgard Pich. Vol. 2 *Poèmes barbares*, Paris: Belle lettres, 1976.
Mitchell, W. J. T. *Iconology: Image, Text, Ideology*. Chicago: University of Chicago Press, 1986.
Musil, Robert. *Drei Frauen*. Rowohlt: Hamburg, 1974.
Nörtemann, Regina. "Zur Wiederentdeckung und Rezeption des Werks von Gertrud Kolmar in der BRD und DDR." *Fremdes Heimatland. Remigration und literarisches Leben nach 1945*. Ed. Irmela von der Lühe and Claus-Dieter Krohn. Göttingen: Wallstein, 2005. 199–215.
Nowak, Silke. *Sprechende Bilder: Zur Lyrik und Poetik Gertrud Kolmars*. Göttingen: Wallstein, 2007.
Otten, Karl (ed.). *Das leere Haus. Prosa jüdischer Dichter*. Stuttgart: Cotta, 1959.
Rilke, Rainer Maria. *Die Gedichte*. Frankfurt am Main: Insel, 2006.
Rilke, Rainer Maria. *Briefwechsel mit Rolf von Ungern-Sternberg und weitere Dokumente*. Ed. Konrad Kratzsch. Frankfurt am Main: Insel, 2002.
Sauder, Gerhard. "Gertrud Kolmars Wappengedichte." *Widerstehen im Wort. Studien zu den Dichtungen Gertrud Kolmars*. Ed. Karin Lorenz-Lindemann. Göttingen: Wallstein, 1996.
Schoor, Kerstin. *Vom literarischen Zentrum zum literarischen Ghetto*. Göttingen: Wallstein, 2010.
Schumann, Annegret. *‚Bilderrätsel' statt Heimatlyrik,*. München: Iudicium, 2002.
Van Uffelen, Herbert et al. *Heimatliteratur 1900–1950, regional, national, international*. Wien: Praesens, 2009.
Wassermann, Henry (ed.). *Bibliographie des Jüdischen Schrifttums in Deutschland 1933–1943*. Munich: K.G. Saur, 1989.
Woltmann, Johanna (ed.) "Getud Kolmar 1894–1943." *Marbacher Magazin* 63, (1993).
Woltmann, Johanna (ed.). *Gertrud Kolmar: Leben und Werk*. Göttingen: Wallstein, 1995.

III **Case Studies American and English Literatures**

Claudia Olk
Configurations of Jewishness in Modernism: Woolf and Joyce

In May 1935, Virginia and Leonard Woolf drove from London via the Netherlands and Germany to take a vacation in Italy. In the car with them was their little pet marmoset by the name of Mitzi. At the Dutch border to Germany, as Virginia Woolf notes in her diary, they felt enormous relief, when the German custom officers let them pass and when "the officers smile[d] at Mitzi" (Woolf 1982, 311). She then describes the scene in which they, on their way to a hotel on the Rhein near Bonn, were inadvertently driven through a welcome reception arranged for the Minister President Goering: "We were chased across the river by Hitler (or Goering) had to pass through ranks of children with red flags. They cheered Mitzi. I raised my hand. People gathering in the sunshine – rather forced like school sports. Banners stretched across the street 'The Jew is our enemy' [...] Our obsequiousness gradually turning to anger" (Woolf 1982, 311).

This bizarre but dangerous first-hand experience for the accomplished writer and her Jewish husband, in which the couple was perhaps saved by their exotic pet, further increased Woolf's disdain of fascism, war and imperialism that she poignantly combines with her feminist stance in works like *Three Guineas* (1938) in the form of three imaginary letters to a poet.

Yet, Virginia Woolf's works, as many critics have noted, present an ambivalent example, when it comes to representations of Jewishness. In her novels and stories, Jewish stereotyping occurs frequently, but so do her increasing attacks on fascism in the 1930s (Simpson 2016, 32). Early on, both Leonard and Virginia Woolf were acutely aware of the dangers of rising fascism in Europe. They looked to Germany, Spain and Italy with concern but were also alarmed by the activities of Oswald Mosley's "British Union of Fascists" that had gained much popularity in the mid-1930s and in 1934 ironically set up its headquarters at Hogarth House, Richmond, which had been Virginia and Leonard Woolf's residence from 1915 to 1924. In 1935, Leonard Woolf remembers "people were just beginning to understand" the menace that Hitler and the Nazis presented (L. Woolf 1967, 192). He also recalls feeling shocked and helpless to see how "a powerful nation completely subservient to a gang of squalid, murderous hooligans" destroyed civilisation (L. Woolf 1967, 248).

The Woolfs were at the centre of many modernist literary circles. Both Leonard and Virginia were part of the Bloomsbury Group, both actively engaged in journalism and literary criticism and both established their own Publishing

ᵈ OpenAccess. © 2020 Claudia Olk, published by De Gruyter. [CC BY-NC-ND] This work is licensed under the Creative Commons Attribution-NonCommercial-NoDerivatives 4.0 License.
https://doi.org/10.1515/9783110619003-012

House, The Hogarth Press, in 1917 which became an important agent in the dissemination of Jewish literature. Woolf had met Sigmund Freud, who after his emigration was living in Hampstead with his daughter Anna Freud, and the Press published the *Standard Edition* of his Complete Psychological Works in James Strachey's translation. The Press also contracted and printed the only novel *The Refugees* (1938) by Jewish American author Libby Benedict, which is set in Berlin, Paris and London after the *Reichstagsbrand* in 1933 and records the fate of several people who chose to stay in Germany or decided to leave (Gillespie 2016, 18).

In the same year, the Hogarth Press published Woolf's *Three Guineas* in which she famously describes herself as an outsider: "as a woman, I have no country. As a woman I want no country. As a woman my country is the whole world" (Woolf 2001, 99). With the Second World War entering into more devastating phases, the Woolfs sensed the growing and imminent danger. They were on the Nazis' death list, and living close to the Sussex coast planned suicide in the event of a German invasion.

The wealth of Virginia Woolf's essays, diaries and criticism defined the critical historical moment in which she lived. Woolf and her circle were deeply involved in literary debates but her diaries, letters and her critical works of the 1930s also reflect on politics and feminism, and are above all fraught with the anxiety of yet another war rising.

In Anglo-American Modernism, apart from Woolf, also the works of T.S. Eliot, Ezra Pound, Amy Levy or James Joyce offer a complex and at times contradictory range of approaches that reflect upon, reify or resist national or religious stereotypes, and more generally, literary Modernism in England significantly engages with representations of Jewishness. In modernist texts, disturbing anti-Semitic stances sometimes coexist with more differentiated and positive depictions of Jewish characters and culture. In some accounts, Jewishness as such is regarded as a defining element of modernism. As Maren Tova Linett suggests: "Jews were often viewed as moderns *par excellence*. Like modernity itself, they were seen as cosmopolitan, rootless, and urban" (Linett 2007, 80).

Approaches to teaching modernist literature with regard to representations of Jewishness need to be aware of these ambivalences. They need to contextualise their object of study in a dialogue with cultural history, rather than isolate statements and take them as representative of an entire work, or fall into the trap of an intentional fallacy in believing literary works to truthfully represent the stance and opinion of their author. Incongruences such as Woolf's anti-Jewish remarks and her being married to Leonard Woolf cannot and should neither be overlooked nor be explained away. As Linett explains, many modernist writers "found in the fictional Jew a floating signifier she could use to define the contours of her literary endeavors" (Linett 2007, 188).

In order to gain insights into the discursive constructions of religion and ethnic belonging identity in modernism, it is necessary that conceptions of 'race' in England during the Victorian era and the early twentieth century be addressed. This also involves looking at the ideological framework of the British Empire, at its colonising policies and political movements such as Irish Home Rule.

Issues of empire and imperial dominance also reveal strategies of constructing the other, in which racial and imperial attitudes often mutually reinforce one another. As Edward Said has shown, 'othering' and ostracising others relies on establishing binaries and constructing the other as a stable, essentialised stereotype (Said 2003, 206). Understanding the ideologies that drive cultural master narratives including those of ethnocentrism as well as teleological and hierarchical interpretations of cultural development also involves looking at newspapers, magazines and popular media in general, in which strategies of placing the other close to savagery, infantilising, or downright de-humanising them can be insidious.

Apart from a thorough knowledge of the historical and cultural realm in which literary texts were written and with which they interacted, for any student or reader of literature, it is vital to analyse the intrinsic and immanent poetic strategies of the texts themselves.

Many of the mechanisms of creating images and narratives of the self and the other are evinced, targeted and undermined by modernist works such as James Joyce's *Ulysses* (Cheng 1995, 15), sometimes from the oblique angle of allegory or within the dense intertextual network that creates national and religious identities as discursive configurations.

Famously, *Ulysses* was rejected by the Hogarth Press and prompted Joyce's friend Sylvia Beach to eventually publish the novel with her own press: "Shakespeare and Company" in Paris in 1922. Modelled on Homer's *Odyssey*, Joyce's novel is set in Dublin on a single day, June 16th, 1904. The Joyce-congregation had later dubbed this day 'Bloomsday', after Joyce's protagonist, the Jewish Leopold Bloom, whose adventures during that day, among a plethora of other things, the novel records. The character of Leopold Bloom caused much controversy. On one occasion, while attending the Dublin symposium on the centennial of Joyce's birth, for instance, Gershom Scholem recalled "a conversation [...] in which David Ben-Gurion said, 'Well, the rabbis might not say that Bloom was a Jew, but I do'" (Epstein 1982, 221).

Jewish literature, religion and culture clearly fascinated Joyce. Hardly any author engaged with Jewish literature and conceptions of Jewishness in quite the way Joyce did. Neil Davison argues that "'Jewishness' [...] becom[es] pivotal to the representational, narratological, and even historiographical aspects of the novel" (Davison 1996, 1). Part of the reason why Joyce created Leopold Bloom, the convert and peripatetic, marginal figure in a Christian nationalistic culture, as his Ulysses-figure was his interest in the exiled status of the Jewish people and their close family ties which were perhaps the result of it.

At the same time, Joyce portrays the paralysis of Western institutions such as the church, excessive nationalism, sentimental patriotism as well as emotional deprivation and the wilful embrace of a self-deluding stasis. Early on, in his collection of Short Stories *Dubliners* (1914) he portrayed the petty hypocrisy governing personal relationships along with the pathos of sentimental patriotism in characters that were alienated from social and religious institutions but cannot escape from them.

Joyce had been struggling with his publisher Grant Richards over the publication of *Dubliners* for seven years, almost as long as it took him to write *Ulysses*, and during this time, the printer for his Dublin publisher destroyed "the unpatriotic" proofs for the book (Ellmann 1982, 335).

The difficulties Joyce encountered in bringing *Dubliners* to the public provide a record of late-Victorian prejudice and prudery, with the objections of the various printers and publishers. Joyce, however, albeit being close to despair on several occasions, fought in defence of the placing of every word, and on other occasions he was by no means bashful when he stated his intention to write *Dubliners*. In his letters we find statements such as: "My intention was to write a chapter of the moral history of my country" or "I have taken the first step towards the spiritual liberation of my country" (*Letters II*, 134); (*Letters I*, 62–63). In a letter to Grant Richards, Joyce described the harm his reluctant publisher would cause if he continued to refuse to print *Dubliners*:

> It is not my fault that the odour of ashpits and old weeds and offal hangs round my stories. I seriously believe that you will retard the course of civilisation in Ireland by preventing the Irish people from having one good look at themselves in my nicely polished looking-glass. (Letter to Grant Richards, 23 June, 1906 (*Letters I*, 63–64))

Joyce's lofty remark about helping along "civilization" and his belief that his stories would liberate the spirits of his countrymen was accompanied by the sentiment that Ireland appeared to him as hostile and stifling to any sort of artistic freedom. Although this cannot be taken as an authorial guarantee to interpret his short stories, he called Dublin the "centre of paralysis" ((*Letters II*, 134) Grant Richards May 5, 1906).

Joyce, who targeted paralysed institutions, and in *A Portrait of the Artist as a Young Man* (1916) considers the Irish "a priestridden race" (Joyce 2003 [1916], 37) was acutely aware of the growing prejudice and propaganda against Jews on the European continent that also infiltrated Ireland. Wilhelm Marr's pamphlet *Der Sieg des Judenthums über das Germanenthum* from 1879 was, as Jacob Katz notes, the first "anti-semitic best-seller", and on September 3rd, 1881, the London paper *The Atheneum* records that "Anti-Semitic literature is very prosperous in Germany".

In both cases, Semitic is conceived as a racial stereotype that relies on the assumption of innate, essentialist characteristics that inform a racial inferiority. During Joyce's lifetime, Jews in many parts of Europe were stereotyped in such ways. They underwent oppression in Russia in the aftermath of Czar Alexander II's assassination in 1881, and German propaganda inundated further parts of Europe. While in Paris, Joyce became familiar with the upheavals around the Dreyfus affair, which had reached one of its crises in September 1902 just before he arrived there (Davison 1996, 61–73).

In England, the Victorian discourse on Jewishness had been influenced by Matthew Arnold's polemics and his schematic observation in *Culture and Anarchy* where he suggests that Western culture is driven by the contrary yet ideally complementary impulses of the Hebraic (i.e. 'energy driving at practice' with an attendant 'obligation of duty, self-control, and work') and the Hellenic ('the indomitable impulse to know' to see things as the really are...in their essence and beauty') (Davison 1996, 106–111).

Thus, when Stephen Dedalus at the beginning of the novel is urged by Buck Mulligan to be of service to his country and "Hellenise it" (*U* 1, 6, 158) this becomes synonymous with the mission to bring cultural and aesthetic superiority to Ireland as opposed to what by some parts of society was perceived as the culturally inferior Hebraic element. Stephen's response is insubordinate and seeks to overcome this dichotomy: "To ourselves ... new paganism ... omphalos" (*U* 1, 7, 176).

In the first scene of *Ulysses*, Buck Mulligan's boisterous incantation "*Introibo ad altare Dei*" (*U* 1, 3, 5) not only denotes the beginning of the Latin Mass, but also refers to Psalm 43 composed by the Hebrews in Babylonian exile. From the beginning, the themes of occupation and exile are woven into the text with reference to the history of Jewish displacement which is often seen in analogy to the Irish concern for Home Rule (Cheng 1995, 151).

Throughout its eighteen chapters, *Ulysses* presents a number of characters who voice scathing anti-Jewish sentiments. In the first chapter (Telemachus) the Englishman Haines, whose family had profited from fraudulent colonial trade, and whose name contains the French word for hate 'la haine', proposes a stereotyped nationalist and economic doctrine that draws on the widespread assumption of a Jewish domination of the financial sector: "Of course I'm a Britisher, Haines's voice said, and I feel as one. I don't want to see my country fall into the hands of German jews either. That's our national problem, I'm afraid, just now" (*U* 1, 18, 666–668).

Parochial nationalism also pervades the second chapter (Nestor) where the history curriculum at the school in which Stephen Dedalus teaches consists of Roman history and versions of hegemonic histories of imperial power. To Stephen such "History [...] is a nightmare from which I am trying to awake" (*U* 2, 28, 377). His criticism of imperialist practices and beliefs, however, is countered by the sinister headmaster Mr. Deasy, who confronts Stephen Dedalus with his self-righteous and chauvinistic version of Jewish-Irish history: "I just wanted to say, he said. Ireland, they say, has the honour of being the only country which never persecuted the jews. Do you know that? No. And do you know why? [...] Because she never let them in, Mr Deasy said solemnly" (*U* 2, 30, 437–442). Mr Deasy's statement is yet another misconstrued view of Jewish history in Ireland, where Jews were expelled in the late thirteenth century and resettled in the 1650s in both England and Ireland under Cromwell. (Davison 1996, 195; Reizbaum 1999, 35–38).

Ulysses is written against these anti-Jewish sentiments that Joyce witnessed on the continent and in Ireland. In 1938 he, for instance, helped Hermann Broch leave Vienna and reach England. During the war, he was himself listed as a Jew by the Swiss *Fremdenpolizei* when he applied for visas and for permissions to stay in Zurich and when his application was rejected on these grounds to be eventually reconsidered in the light of further evidence. As Richard Ellmann points out: "The subject of the Jews had seized upon Joyce's attention as he began to recognize his place in Europe to be as ambiguous as theirs" (Ellmann 1982, 230).

Yet, Joyce in *Ulysses* does not only engage in a dialogue with Jewishness in biographical and historical terms. Jewishness rather provides an angle from which to portray and to reflect on contemporary politics and culture. In *Ulysses*, as I would like to argue, Jewishness becomes both a poetic and a performative stance in which the text presents notions of exile, wandering, hybridity, and otherness in its theme and structure.

To some extent, Leopold Bloom epitomises some characteristics of Joyce's poetic model of Jewishness. As Ben-Gurion is reported to have said, Bloom is not a Jew in the halalic sense of the word. He is a fictional character whose mother was a gentile and he was not circumcised. To a degree, he became familiar with Jewish customs and religious traditions, and yet, time and again, he tried to be part of Irish, and Dublin society in particular. He was baptised a Protestant and then a Catholic. Some critics read him as an Everyman-character, but other than Everyman, Bloom verges more towards the Homeric 'Nobody' and remains a marginal figure, a drifter, both an insider and an outsider.

The Dublin of *Ulysses* that structures Bloom's wanderings is permeated by tokens of imperial ideologies of domination and nationalist rebellion against them. Time and again, his fellow Dubliners make it clear to him that he is not one of them and never will be. When he is attacked by the xenophobic Citizen in the Cyclops-episode, which also represents the myopia of Irish nationalism, he defends himself saying: "Christ was a Jew like me" (*U* 12, 280, 1808–1809), only to be attacked even further for his blasphemy. In episodes like these, Bloom exposes the intentional one-sidedness of hegemonic claims to religious, nationalist and cultural superiority.

Leopold Bloom enters the world of *Ulysses* in the fourth chapter, Calypso, which is set in the home of Leopold and Molly Bloom, where he goes about his domestic routines and can be compared to Odysseus who is held in thrall by the nymph Calypso on her enchanted island. As opposed to Stephen Dedalus, who contemplates the ineluctable modalities of the visible and the signatures of all things in the preceding Proteus-chapter, Jeri Johnson calls Calypso "a bodied text [–] a corpus" (Joyce 1998 [1922], 793). And indeed, the chapter begins and ends with descriptions of somatic processes, and is interspersed with moments in which the characters both conceal and reveal their physical needs. Molly, like Calypso the concealer, hides a letter from her lover Blazes Boylan, and Bloom likewise more or less secretly indulges in fantasies about other women.

The processes of incorporation and metabolic exchange are treated in highly ambivalent ways that invoke a number of discourses on Jewishness. The chapter starts with the sentence: "Mr Leopold Bloom ate with relish the inner organs of beasts and fowls" (*U* 4, 45, 1–2). He decides to go on his first errand and buy a pork kidney for breakfast at Dlugacz, a polish-Jewish butcher. Similar to the processes of filtration and absorption accomplished by the human kidney, Bloom becomes a hybrid somatic entity. He absorbs some parts alluding to his Jewish identity, rejects others, and transforms them into new combinations: "Kidneys were in his mind" (*U* 4, 45, 6) as he serves milk to his cat.

This entirely unkosher constellation of food is even further elaborated on when Bloom enters the butcher's shop and inhales the smell of blood: "[he] breathed in tranquilly the lukewarm breath of cooked spicy pigs' blood" (*U* 4, 48, 143–144). Sensual impressions guide Bloom's meandering thoughts in a way in which he transports images from one context into another and synthesises, even conflates them. He finally sees the object of his desire, the kidney, and is enthralled by it: "A kidney oozed bloodgouts on the willowpatterned dish: the last" (*U* 4, 48, 145). The sight of the different meats on display leads his thoughts to wander further and from there to contemplate the body of a female customer in unorthodox ways. He wonders whether he should follow her: "To catch up and walk behind her if she went slowly, behind her moving hams. Pleasant to see first thing in the morning" (*U* 4, 49, 171–173). Bloom's craving for pork and his erotic appetites merge until the former prevails and Bloom decides to return home.

Bloom remains an observer who is interested in the materiality of words and things. He contemplates the Eucharist: "*Corpus:* body. Corpse. Good idea the Latin. [...] They don't seem to chew it: only swallow it down. Rum idea: eating bits of a corpse. Why the cannibals cotton to it. [...] Something like those mazzoth: it's that sort of bread: unleavened shewbread. Look at them. Now I bet it makes them feel happy" (*U* 5, 66, 350–359). His empirical, non-judgmental view makes it possible to relate the incongruous as he recognises cultural similarities between Christians, cannibals, and Jews.

Jewishness furthermore becomes a discursive framework in which images of the body and of land become mutually pervasive. The notion of the body, particularly the female body, for Bloom, is tied to the notion of space and place. On his way home, he passes an advertisement for a Zionist colony by the Agendath Netaim, the "company of planters", to develop land for prospective settlers, and his imagination wanders to erotically charged images of orange groves and melon fields.

Analogous to bodily processes of exchange and transformation that are carried out by the kidney as the organ the chapter consistently returns to, Bloom ponders the dynamics of financial exchange: "You pay eighty marks and they plant a dunam of land for you [...]. Every year you get a sending of the crop. Your name entered for life as owner in the book of the union. [...] Bleibtreustrasse 34, Berlin, W 15" (*U* 4, 49, 194–199).

The lure that homecoming presents to the exile and the appeal of possessing, of owning a piece of land for life, is, however, linked to a moral obligation: to remain true. "Bleibtreustrasse" alludes to Molly's and Bloom's infidelity in religious, cultural and sexual terms, which not only render them outcasts from the eternal homeland envisioned by the Zionist project, but also from the mythological Ithaca with Molly conforming not exactly to the model of the chaste Penelope.

Bloom associates fruitfulness and fecundity with his wife Molly when he thinks about olives and relates oranges and citrons to both Jaffa and Gibraltar (*U* 4, 49, 211), the place where Molly was born. However, similarly to the loss of his homeland, he realises that he will never exclusively or entirely possess Molly. The chain of associations about fertile arable land released by his contemplation of Molly, however, is abruptly contrasted by the sight of an old woman carrying a wine bottle, which leads him to think about barrenness, and old age: "The oldest people. Wandered far away over all the earth, captivity to captivity, multiplying, dying, being born everywhere. It lay there now. Now it could bear no more. Dead" (*U* 4, 50, 225–227). Horrified at his vision, he resumes his senses and hurries home to "[b]e near her ample bedwarmed flesh. Yes, yes" (*U* 4, 50, 238–239) – anticipating Molly's final yesses that will conclude the novel (Olk 2013, 333).

In Bloom's imagination his home-land and his wife become a point of departure and return. Both, however, have become highly ambivalent and offer no stable epistemological ground to find comfort on. Rather the notion of home and the Homeland itself becomes an imaginary utopia, a no-place that challenges nationalist ideas of origin and teleological models of history. Hence at the end of this passage, Bloom realises the loss of land, the partial loss of his wife, and above all the loss of Rudy, his son, which makes it impossible for Bloom to continue any patrilineal aspirations.

Next to 'Calypso', the chapter that most explicitly deals with multiple perspectives on Jewishness, is 'Circe', another female enchantress living on an island. Role-play, concealing and revealing of diverse identities are at play in the Circe-chapter of *Ulysses* that is set in the Dublin underworld. In Circe, the novel itself undergoes a change of generic identity and becomes a play. The chapter, part theatre part courtroom, consists of carnivalesque as well as nightmarish scenes in which Bloom undergoes a number of trials and is confronted with the psychopathologies of his past. Figures from his past such as his father Rudolph appear in the fashion of Hamlet's father's ghost to chide him "not [to] go with drunken goy ever" (*U* 15, 357, 253–254) and reprimand him for his guilt of apostasy in a paraphrase of Genesis 12:1: "Are you not my son Leopold, the grandson of Leopold? Are you not my dear son Leopold who left the house of his father and left the god of his fathers Abraham and Jacob?" (*U* 15, 357, 260–262)

The chapter also recapitulates the more immediate past of the novel when e. g. the polish-Hungarian butcher Moses Dlugacz appears as a mock allegory of Justitia, "holding in each hand an orange citron and a pork kidney" (*U* 15, 379, 988–989) and announces: "Bleibtreustrasse, Berlin, W. 13" (*U* 15, 379, 991).

From rituals of punishment and scapegoating, Bloom emerges as a Messianic figure, who announces the coming of a new era: "I, Bloom, tell you verily [...] ye shall ere long enter into the golden city which is to be, the new Bloomusalem in the Nova Hibernia of the future" (*U* 15, 395, 1542–1545). The motif of the Promised Land here includes both Israel and Ireland, "green Erin, the promised land of our common ancestors" (*U* 15, 394, 1517–1518), and points to both the Irish and the Jews struggling for their homeland.

Bloom pronounces his aims and ambitions as leader of this "[n]ew worlds for old" in a mock-biblical, prophetic style:

> Union of all, jew, moslem and gentile. Three acres and a cow for all children of nature. Saloon motor hearses. Compulsory manual labour for all. [...] Electric dishscrubbers. Tuberculosis, lunacy, war and mendicancy must now cease. [...] weekly carnival with masked licence, bonuses for all, esperanto the universal language with universal brotherhood. No more patriotism of barspongers and dropsical impostors. Free money, free rent, free love and a free lay church in a free lay state. [...] Mixed races and mixed marriage (*U* 15, 399–400, 1686–1699).

Bloom's bold parodic vision of a free, Esperanto-speaking universal interfaith brotherhood that indulges in the amenities of modern life responds to patriotism as well as exclusive notions of race, religion and marriage. Once again, his promotion of motored hearses, electric dish-scrubbers and the end of tuberculosis reveal his interest in everyday life as well as a practical and unsentimental attitude to the benefits of modern machinery and medicine.

After the chapter fantastically stages the second coming (and going) of Elija, Bloom and Stephen eventually get together: "Woman's reason. Jewgreek is greekjew. Extremes meet" (*U* 15, 411, 2097–2098). Derrida in *Writing and Difference*, comments on Ulysses: "Are we Jews? Are we Greeks? We live in the difference between the Jew and the Greek, which is perhaps the unity of what is called history [...] What is the legitimacy, what is the meaning of [...] [Joyce's] proposition [...] 'Jewgreek is Greekjew. Extremes meet?'" (Derrida 1978 [1967], 151).

Derrida is referring to the Arnoldian division of modern Western civilisation, and on the surface, Stephen Dedalus and Leopold Bloom could be seen as manifestations of both principles: Greek metaphysics represented by the Aristotelian Stephen, and Biblical Messianism represented by the prophetic Bloom. In Derrida's view, both cultures have remained dualistically opposed in Western history to the extent that they offered rival 'logocentric' systems. In the Circe-chapter, however, Bloom and Stephen also assume character attributes of one another. Bloom, after having met Stephen, becomes more rational and self-contained whereas Stephen acts increasingly unreasonable and impulsively destroys a chandelier. The chiastic constellation is further complemented by the idea that Bloom the Hebraic father has reunited with Stephen the (lost) Hellenic son.

Ulysses, in the character of Leopold Bloom, throughout the novel rehearses topoi and discourses related to ideas of Jewishness. He contemplates their practical as well as somatic effects, interacts with stereotypical conceptions, and undergoes many conversions himself. Bloom, his physical wanderings, his transformative imagination and the performative bodily transformations that he undergoes, figure a kind of Jewishness in which opposites are no longer dualistically opposed, as in the paternal code, but are subversively played off against one another until the opposition is undone. In this vein, the novel also presents Molly Bloom as a third element between the extremes. Notwithstanding the many ambivalences that govern the representation of Jewish characters and the engagement with Jewishness in Modernist fiction, in major works such as *Ulysses*, the negotiation of multiple perspectives leads to new imaginative syntheses that configure Jewishness as a product and effect of the text.

Bibliography

Cheng, Vincent J. *James Joyce, Race, and Empire*. Cambridge: Cambridge University Press, 1995.
Davison, Neil R. *James Joyce, Ulysses and the Construction of Jewish Identity*. Cambridge: Cambridge University Press, 1996.
Derrida, Jacques. *Writing and Difference*. Trans. Alan Bass. Chicago: The University of Chicago Press, 1978.
Ellmann, Richard. *James Joyce*. Oxford: Oxford University Press, 1982.
Epstein, Edmund L. "Joyce and Judaism." *The Seventh of Joyce*. Ed. Bernard Benstock. Harvester: Indiana University Press, 1982. 221–224.
Letters of James Joyce. Vol. I. Ed. Stuart Gilbert. New York: Viking Press, 1957; reissued with corrections (1966); vols. II and III. Ed. Richard Ellmann. New York: Viking Press, 1966.
Gillespie, Diane F. "Publishing on the Brink of World War II: The Woolfs, the Hogarth Press and The Refugees." *South Carolina Review* 48.2 (2016): 14–30.
Joyce, James. *Dubliners*. Ed. Terence Brown. London: Penguin, 1992.
Joyce, James. *A Portrait of the Artist as a Young Man*. Ed. Seamus Deane. London: Penguin, 2003.
Joyce, James. *Ulysses*. Ed. Jeri Johnson. Oxford: Oxford University Press, 1998.
Joyce, James. *Ulysses*. Ed. Hans Walter Gabler. London: Bodley Head, 1986.
Linett, Maren Tova. *Modernism, Feminism and Jewishness*. Cambridge: Cambridge University Press, 2007.
Nadel, Ira. *Joyce and the Jews: Culture and Texts*. Houndmills: Palgrave Macmillan, 1989.
Olk, Claudia. "Why say Yes in Joyce? Molly Bloom's Yes Because in the 'Penelope'-Episode of Ulysses". *Interfaces of Morphology: A Festschrift for Susan Olsen*. Ed. Holden Härtl. Berlin: Akademie, 2013. 323–334.
Said, Edward W. *Orientalism*. London: Penguin, 2003.
Simpson, Kathryn. *Woolf. A Guide for the Perplexed*. London: Bloomsbury Publishing, 2016.
Reizbaum, Marilyn. *James Joyce's Judaic Other*. Stanford: Stanford University Press, 1999.
Woolf, Leonard. *Downhill All the Way: An Autobiography of the Years 1919–1939*. New York: Harcourt Brace Jovanovich, 1967.
Woolf, Virginia. *Three Guineas*. Ed. Naomi Black. London: Shakespeare Head, 2001.
Woolf, Virginia. *The Diary of Virginia Woolf* IV. Ed. Anne Olivier Bell, and Andrew McNeillie. London: The Hogarth Press, 1982.

Kirstin Gwyer
Planetarity in the Global? Modern Jewish Literature in English

The questions raised by the present volume – including questions of how to acknowledge and emphasize the diversity and particularity of Jewish literatures while at the same time promoting their inclusion in, and recognizing their contribution to, other philologies – are relevant and timely in ways that far exceed the specific context of literature in Jewish languages or by authors identified as Jewish. Arising during a cultural moment when literary studies more broadly, and indeed the humanities and social sciences in general, are grappling with the need for fundamental reorientation and reorganization, they are questions that go right to the heart of how we see the world.

Against a backdrop in which the political and cultural upheavals and realignments of the past three decades have prompted literary studies to turn with increased urgency to questions of globalization, cosmopolitanism and transnationalism, "the decentered case of multilingual Jewish writing" has persuasively been put forward as a "counterpoint to available World Literature models" (Levy and Schachter 2017, 3). Two decades into the twenty-first century, the need for such a model appears more pressing than ever in light of the fact that theoretical shifts towards an idiom of hybridity, fluidity and deterritorialization are considerably further removed from being reflected in a corresponding shift in real-world thought and practice than developments at the end of the twentieth century might have given cause to hope for (see e.g. Appadurai 1996).

Embedded in a transnational, yet locally particular, multilingual and polyphonic network of linguistic and cultural exchange, Jewish writing across the world stands as a "non-universal global" model of a diasporic or deterritorialized configuration at once cosmopolitan and peripheral (Levy and Schachter 2017). Resistant to efforts to distil from it a unifying common denominator or view it as part of a historical continuum, it is a literary complex whose components are connected by "contiguity" rather than "continuity" (Miron 2010). In this, it gestures towards a "planetary" relational system, to borrow Gayatri Spivak's term, as a multi-centric, pluralizing and deterritorializing alternative to "the center-periphery model of global literary circulation" (Spivak 2003, 73; Levy and Schachter 2015, 93; see also Gilroy 2005, 70).

In this "non-universal global" reading, the term Jewish literature is naturally understood as emerging from "the circuit of modern Jewish languages composed of multiple centers in Asia, Africa, Europe, and North America" (Levy and

∂ OpenAccess. © 2020 Kirstin Gwyer, published by De Gruyter. This work is licensed under the Creative Commons Attribution-NonCommercial-NoDerivatives 4.0 License.
https://doi.org/10.1515/9783110619003-013

Schachter 2015, 93). However, what happens when the Jewish literature in question was written in global English by an author whose work is accepted and acclaimed as part of the Western literary establishment? Can Jewish literature in such an overtly monolingual and apparently non-peripheral form still be considered part of a non-universal-global paradigm? Can it still be taught in a way that offers access to the relationality of collective diversity that marks the transdisciplinary configurations of Jewish literatures in other languages, or taken together? Is it even still Jewish? Or has its Jewishness been subsumed, and any diasporic origin or planetary aspiration erased and displaced, by it being re-embedded in a centre-periphery view that can only stress either a work's global-English majority status or its Jewish minority one, but which struggles to engage with any intersection between the two?

My contribution to this volume will take the form of a short case study to propose that a text's planetary outlook is not insurmountably tethered to what language it was, or was not, written in, or where in the world it was published. Nor is its Jewishness, however we may choose to qualify or quantify this. I shall suggest that the transnational networks of linguistic and cultural exchange that inform the "circuit" of Jewish literatures as a multilingual, polyphonic collective can be identified even in a single work in global English, where the use of global English has been combined with a self-consciously Jewish awareness of its own planetarity, if we learn to adapt our reading practices. A text need not be diasporic or deterritorialized in a physical sense to be able to forge – or for us to be able to read it as forging – "a counter-discourse challenging the temporal and spatial trajectories operative in Eurocentric theorizations of world literature and its history" (Frydman 2014 [2011], 232).

This is emphatically not to suggest that access to Jewish literature should be circumscribed by what is available of it in Anglophone writing. On the contrary, it remains a vital priority to resist the displacement of (not only) Jewish minority languages by the spread of global English. Nor should it be interpreted as an attempt to bestow minority status on what most would take to be an author with mainstream privileges. Rather, it should be taken as an effort to show how even a supposedly mainstream text can be written to unsettle, or can be read as unsettling, the very distinction between majority and minority, centre and periphery, or origin and derivation, and with it any sense of national or cultural hierarchy, and any straightforward understanding of literary roots and "belonging".

The approach I am promoting in this is not at all without precedent. In his thought-provoking piece on the "diaspora" diaspora, Rogers Brubaker, for instance, argues for a de-substantialization of the notion of diaspora, to theorize it not as "a bounded group" but as "a category of practice, project, claim and stance" (Brubaker 2005, 13). There is a risk in adopting the term "diasporic" for such a category of practice, not least in that the already watered-down concept of diaspora can end up losing all conceptual coherence and become meaningless as an analytical tool (see also Alexander 2017). However, the distinction between "entity" and "stance" deployed by Brubaker, or, more precisely, his expansion of the notion of the diasporic to encompass not just condition but performance, is a useful one (Brubaker 2005, 10).

By analogy with Brubaker, but substituting the concept of "planetarity" for that of diaspora, the following short reading is designed to show that, even when operating in global English, we can learn to identify and adopt a planetary stance. Planetarity, in Spivak's loose definition, resists the homogenizing logic of globalization, as defined by its imposition of "the same system of exchange everywhere" (Spivak 2003, 72). Informed by a methodology of relationality based on "universal alterity" and an "ethics of difference", planetary thinking "privileges a relational ethos of *cultural* debt", rather than financial, and so, as Joseph Keith puts it citing Christian Moraru, a debt that "'worlds' us by making visible our physical and nonphysical 'proximity', our 'cross-cultural, cross-geographical, indeed, world-scale contacts, juxtapositions, borrowings, and barterings'", in recognition of the fact that: "'Whatever I am or become, comes about under the impact of remote, heterogeneous sources, places, and styles'" (Keith 2018, 271–272. Original emphasis.).

In the process, planetarity asks us to question both our territorial preconceptions and our temporal ones: the spaces we think we inhabit and our (literary) roots and sources, but also the timelines that inform our thinking in the West and which are determined by the "teleological time of Western modernity's universal narrative of progress, colonial violence, and the linear time of capitalist exploitation" (Cheah 2016, 12). Thus foregrounding heterospatiality and heterotemporality, and identifying the linguistic and cultural plurality that underlies even the seemingly universal and unified global, a planetary approach makes it possible for authors such as the one under discussion here to write back to the imperializing forces of monolingualism, and of a World Literature studies still largely indebted to a nation-state model, apparently from within both.

Crucially, engaging with a text on such planetary terms calls for a way of reading that is not intrinsic but which can be learnt and taught: a form of reading that destabilizes, dislocates and defamiliarizes and which, more than any explicit theme or content, can identify even a text written in universalizing global English as a work of non-universal-global literature.

"Franz Kafka is Dead"

My little case study is built on a very short short story. It is a Jewish story by a Jewish writer. And what makes it a Jewish story by a Jewish writer is not least the fact that it grapples with, and troubles, both components of the statement I just used to describe it. The story is called "Franz Kafka is Dead":

> He died in a tree from which he wouldn't come down. 'Come down!' they cried to him. 'Come down! Come down!' Silence filled the night, and the night filled the silence, while they waited for Kafka to speak. 'I can't,' he finally said, with a note of wistfulness. 'Why?' they cried. Stars spilled across the black sky. 'Because then you'll stop asking for me.' The people whispered and nodded among themselves. They put their arms around each other, and touched their children's hair. [...] Then they turned and started for home under the canopy of leaves. Children were carried on their fathers' shoulders, sleepy from having been taken to see the man who wrote his books on pieces of bark he tore off the tree from which he refused to come down. [...] And they admired those books, and they admired his will and stamina. [...] Doors closed to warm houses. Candles were lit in windows. Far off, in his perch in the trees, Kafka listened to it all: the rustle of clothes being dropped to the floor, of lips fluttering along naked shoulders, beds creaking under the weight of tenderness. It all caught in the delicate pointed shells of his ears and rolled like pinballs through the great hall of his mind.

> That night, a freezing wind blew in. When the children woke up, they went to the windows and found the world encased in ice. One child, the smallest, shrieked out in delight and her cry tore through the silence and exploded the ice of a giant oak tree. The world shone.

> They found him frozen on the ground like a bird. It's said that when they put their ears to the shell of his ears, they could hear themselves.

Those are 23 sentences of English-language text. Just under 300 words. Since their initial publication, this story, and the book in which it appears, have been translated into 35 further languages. But this global reach obscures the extent to which, even in their present form here, these 300 words of English text are already a profoundly polyglot and polyvocal product of multiple acts of transmission, translation, reading and re-reading. Weaving together at least eight source texts from seven different countries, in English, German, Greek, Hebrew, Polish and Spanish, with Aramaic and Czech hovering in the background, these 300 words of text construct an intertextual network with roots that can be traced back to fourth-century Egypt, and forward to twenty-first-century Brooklyn, New York. It is an intertextual network that engineers a correspondence between two contemporary American-Jewish authors, but it does so via the New Testament, Lurianic Kabbalah, a German philosopher, a Polish modernist, an Argentinian proto-postmodernist, and of course the famous German-speaking Bohemian from the story's title. In 300 words.

The text in which this passage appears is the 2005 novel *The History of Love* by Nicole Krauss (Krauss 2006 [2005], 116–117). *The History of Love* is a book that summons ghosts. This particular passage, which is presented in the text as an obituary, is at once conjuring and apparently attempting to exorcise Kafka. And it is doing so through a narrator who is meant to channel Polish-Jewish interwar modernist Bruno Schulz.

Thematically, the passage is referencing Kafka's short story "A Hunger Artist" (Kafka 2012 [1922], 56–63). Parents take their children to see Krauss's Kafka up on his perch, admiring "his will and stamina", and his life-as-performance derives its justification from their presence as his audience, but the demand to see him is waning; the audience is growing tired (Krauss 2006 [2005], 117). Like Kafka's hunger artist, he cannot stop performing, even in their absence, yet in their absence, his performance, and his life, cease to be. The form of the passage – the circularity of its reasoning, its parody of the parabolic genre, creating the expectation of a parable but frustrating exegesis – is also one familiar from Kafka's own writing.

Stylistically, the passage recalls Schulz. The imagery – the personification of night, the spilling stars and canopy of leaves, fathers carrying their half-asleep children, the descriptions of touch, tenderness and intimacy – all of this is Schulzian, not Kafkaesque. The man-as-bird perched on high may be evoking Kafka's self-stylization, via Czech, as a bird, and the element of metamorphosis, but it is also a trope familiar from Schulz stories (Schulz 2008 [1934 / 1937]).

The references to shattering and the extraction of light from the material world, meanwhile – evoked in the image of the child exploding the ice of the oak tree and causing the world to shine – are references that derive neither from Schulz nor from Kafka directly but from Jewish mysticism, if again through a reading of Schulz, as well as of Jorge Luis Borges, and via an intertextual route that also takes in Friedrich Nietzsche and more Kafka, before ending up at Philip Roth.

Let me just unravel that a bit: According to kabbalistic cosmology, the universe came about because God drew in his divine light to leave a void for the creation of the world, but the vessels God formed to hold his light were unable to contain it and shattered, dispersing sparks of divine light, trapped in shards of broken vessels, across the world. By releasing the scattered sparks from their imprisonment, humanity may participate in the repair and redemption of the world.

In Schulz's fiction, this cosmological myth is an important recurring trope, but he secularizes and refigures it – as indeed does Borges – so that it reads as an illustration of intertextuality: Schulz envisages the origin of creation as an absent source text from which all meaning emanates, known simply as The

Book with a capital "B". The original Book having long since disintegrated and been dispersed – in a process analogous to the shattering of the vessels – all that is left behind are disseminated text fragments or palimpsests. Any books written since the dispersal of The Book are, according to Schulz, exilic and can only ever hope to be a pale imitation of this original source text, but, as pale imitations, they may nevertheless be animated by sparks of divine inspiration.

In Krauss's refiguration of Schulz's refiguration, this connection to intertextuality is left implicit. It is only suggested, fittingly enough, through intertextual allusion, in the evocation of Schulz, but also, as we shall see, in a connection to Borges, and by means of a passing nod to Nietzsche.

The act of shattering, followed by an emanation of light, is an act performed in this passage by the voice of a female child, a young female who, in the process, takes over from the famous author whose light and voice have been extinguished. Read through Schulz's reimagining of the creation myth as a process of intertextuality, and reinforced by the Nietzschean echo of the obituary's title – "Franz Kafka is Dead" – "Gott ist tot" –, which also underlines the New Testament association of Christ being called down, in vain, from the cross, or tree, to prove his divinity – this might suggest a reading in which Kafka has withdrawn himself to make space for the younger female's act of re-creation, leaving sparks of his former light behind as glimpses of his original inspiration. On this analogy, Kafka, in his quasi-divinity, may have written The Book, but Krauss can write a book in his image, animated by sparks of his inspiration. She may even write a book to act as "the axe for the frozen sea inside us", as, in a further intertextual nod to Kafka, the image of shattered ice might also be taken to suggest (Kafka 1977 [1904], 16).

But the analogy does not end there. In the story, the act of shattering is attributed not to the divine light itself but to the girl's response to it – to her delight – and her linguistic enactment of that delight. Read in conjunction with the implicit ambition of writing a book to shatter Kafka's ice for him, this suggests that the dividing line between the divine and the mere mortal, between precursor and successor, or inspiration and derivation, is being blurred. And the pressure of following in the footsteps of the "divine" – of being worthy of hearing herself in "the delicate pointed shell of his ears" – this pressure is underlined intertextually by the question that follows from Nietzsche's madman's pronouncement about God being dead and us having killed him: the question of whether the "greatness of this deed" may be such that we "murderers of all murderers" must "ourselves [...] become gods simply to appear worthy of it" (Nietzsche 1974 [1882], 181–182 (sec. 125)).

So from the outset, from its very title, this passage seems to resonate with an anxiety of influence: a tension between exorcising and summoning, or toppling (from the perch) and self-investiture. This is a tension that we encounter in much contemporary Jewish writing conscious of the weight of its heritage in a historical, a familial and a literary sense, where more general fears of not living up to the authors of one's past are coupled with more specific anxieties relating to what it means to live and write as contemporary Jews, and contemporary post-Holocaust Jews, and, in the case of Krauss, as a contemporary female American-Jewish author.

Indeed, Krauss's piece also reads as a response to a canonical contemporary American Jew and to *his* intertextual engagement with Kafka: to Philip Roth and particularly to his response to Kafka's "Hunger Artist" story, a response titled "'I Always Wanted You to Admire My Fasting'; or, Looking at Kafka", from 1973 (Roth 2001 [1973]). As with Krauss's other intertextual connections, this one too appears marked by an interplay between affirmation and disavowal. Roth's Hunger Artist piece also reads as an obituary of sorts and imagines Kafka in 1924, the year of his death, and in his relationship with Dora Dymant, a young Jewish woman of nineteen in whose company Roth pictures Kafka, for a brief while, at peace and almost liberated, writing, and learning Hebrew from Dymant, and encouraging her to pursue a career as an actress. One strand of Roth's piece ends with Kafka's death and with Dymant inconsolably lamenting his loss.

By creating her own version of Roth's story, Krauss could be seen to be attempting to legitimize herself as a modern American-Jewish author, shoring up her own credentials by aligning herself with a canonical contemporary, and in doing so also attempting to step out from under the shadow of the mighty canon of seemingly more "authentic" old-world Jewish writing, to claim a place for herself among the cosmopolitan contemporary (Jewish-)American mainstream. Roth offers a template for a redemptive, mutually inspiring relationship between Kafka and a younger female, a relationship in which he fosters her creative impulses and she liberates his creative drive, which sanctions the blurred precursor-successor model Krauss seems to be hinting at in her piece. However, the blurring of precursor and successor is not just adapted from Roth but also applied to him, which becomes visible when we read it across the eighth strand in Krauss's intertextual warp and weft, the strand in which she summons Borges.

Borges is in the background of a great deal of what Krauss has written, and there is much triangulated contact between her, Borges and Schulz, arising, as has already become apparent, from a kabbalistically inspired reading of the universe as intertext, or hypertext, which in all three authors gives rise to a wealth of imagery relating to infinite books, infinite libraries, and other textualized multiverses. Indeed, *The History of Love* as a whole reads like an attempted approximation of Borges's "Book of Sand", a theoretically infinite book with no beginning and no end (Borges 2001 [1975], 89–93).

But there is also a great deal of confluence between Krauss, Borges and Kafka, and I use the term confluence, rather than influence, consciously here, since it is particularly relevant to how Krauss deploys Borges against Roth in the passage we are looking at. What Borges has perhaps most crucially supplied Krauss with in this context are the reflections that underpin his 1951 piece titled, fittingly, "Kafka and his Precursors", an essay in which Borges has, as it were, "written the book" on anxiety of influence, or intertextuality, and which famously contains the lines: "In the critics' vocabulary, the word 'precursor' is indispensable, but it should be cleansed of all connotation of polemics or rivalry. The fact is that every writer *creates* his own precursors" (Borges 2000 [1962], 236).

Over a decade earlier, in 1939, Borges had already given literary form to aspects of this idea in his short story "Pierre Menard, Author of the *Quixote*", another fictitious obituary (Borges 2000 [1962], 62–71). In "Pierre Menard", the eponymous protagonist is an author who has recreated, line for line, Cervantes's famous *Don Quixote*, but despite the fact that his version is therefore identical, it is deemed, by the narrator, to be the much richer work for having been written in the twentieth century, since this means that it has to be read against the backdrop of everything that has happened since the seventeenth century of its original creation. And the logical and temporal inversion implicit in the idea of "creating one's own precursors" is taken further still in both Borges's Kafka essay and in Krauss's Kafka obituary, to suggest a more general destabilization of literary influence, where the precursor is shaped by the successor, in the act of being read.

Therein also lies Krauss's response to Roth, a response that sees her rewrite a crucial aspect of his story and, in the process, differentiate herself from both him and Kafka: in Roth's version, it is Kafka who encourages his female companion to be creative, and his formative influence turns her into who she will become. In Krauss, it is the younger female's creative response to his influence that allows him to become who he was meant to be: his light shines because of her delight.

In her most recent publication, the 2017 novel *Forest Dark*, Krauss turns this whispered intertextual response to Roth into a book-length text that sees her emphatically distance herself from any sense of unidirectional influence and passive inheritance (Krauss 2017). In it, she takes up the other strand of Roth's Kafka essay, which raises the question of what might have happened to Kafka had he not died in 1924, and she projects a version of events in which Kafka escapes to Mandatory Palestine, thus putting him in a position where he will have a transmigrational encounter with one version of a fictionalized Krauss herself in twenty-first-century Israel. This ultimately allows Krauss to go some way towards putting the spectre of both Kafka and Roth to rest and distinguish herself both within and from what in the novel is referred to as "the great machine of Jewish literature", while at the same time firmly emphasizing the connections between this great machine and non-Jewish world literature by cross-reading Kafka against Dante, and vice versa, displacing both from their familiar contexts in the process (Krauss 2017, 125).

Of the two of Krauss's works referenced here, *Forest Dark* may be the more intentionally planetary for being consciously conceived as a multiverse constructed on, and out of, "juxtapositions, borrowings, and barterings" across time and space, and languages, cultures and creeds (in Keith 2018, 272; for a more in-depth reading of *Forest Dark* see Gwyer 2018). However, the planetary scope and movement of Krauss's writing are already clearly evident in "Franz Kafka is Dead". In 300 words of a tightly constructed intertextual network, Krauss is not just writing a fictitious obituary to help her manage an anxiety of influence; she is (de-)situating herself as a modern female Jewish author in relation to both "old-world", and contemporary American, Jewish writing, against a backdrop of diaspora and persecution, and a foreground of a cosmopolitan (and male-centric) mainstream represented by Philip Roth whom at least one obituary has labelled "the great novelist of modern America" (Freeman 2018). And while all these contexts and influences have come together to determine who Krauss is, or how she may be perceived, she at the same time finds herself peripheral to, or displaces herself from, all of them. So her alignment with each of these precursor authors is always also a form of differentiation: a de-essentializing process of locating the self by decentring and deterritorializing it, and a nomadic process of dislocating borders and boundaries, both in and through her writing, boundaries between cultures, between languages, even while writing in global English, between canons, between dominant Judaeo-Christian Western culture and diaspora, but also between diaspora and Israel, to find a home in the interstitial, and the intertextual, but a home that is forever in flux–or planetary.

At the same time, hers is a process that also de-essentializes and dislocates her precursor figures, in a dynamic that is reinforced by the fact that it is achieved through the medium of postcolonial Borges, an author who occupies a similarly marginal position to the literary canon he inherits as many Jewish writers do to theirs. Far beyond simply being a way of managing an anxiety of influence, Krauss's 300 words bring out the planetary potential of modern Jewish writing in and for a world-literary context. In its extended illustration of intertextuality, her piece urges a fluidly comparative reading in which each of her multiple contexts and "sources" is repeatedly decontextualized and decentred by being read against all the others, thus disrupting any sense of unidirectional linearity or hierarchy in any sense, historical, geographical or influential.

So what do we stand to gain from separating the planetary stance of a text from its genetic context and its thematic content? Jewish writing has recently received a fair amount of critical attention on a global stage, particularly in postcolonial studies, where there has been a push by scholars such as Paul Gilroy, Aamir Mufti or Bryan Cheyette to bridge disciplinary segregation by conceptualizing both Jewish and postcolonial studies as representatives of a greater "transcultural diasporic imagination" (Cheyette, 2013, xii; see also Gilroy 1993 or Mufti 2007). However, while we are, in the wake of this Holocaust turn in postcolonial studies, now witnessing a significantly increased focus on what Mufti has called the "metaphorical possibilities of Jewishness for contemporary postcolonial culture" (Mufti 2007, 25), this focus has predominantly been on the content and context of Jewish writing and culture, rather than its forms. Within these parameters, it is difficult to see beyond the Jewish model as one of a history of suffering and instead think of it as partaking of a "multidirectionality" of memory (Rothberg 2009), let alone recognize it as a constituent of a present-day mode of planetary thinking and writing. Yet it is the planetary as stance and methodology that holds the key to truly multidirectional thought and practice.

To conclude, by illustrating a mode of thought that allows parallels, cross-connections and contact zones to emerge – without eliding difference – both across the transnational, transcultural, translingual networks of Jewish literature's own field, and as a potential protean template for boundary-troubling thought and literature more globally, the miniature case study presented here operates as a plea for a reading of Jewish literature as planetary and for a planetary reading of (Jewish) literature. Rather than merely ask how we can make Jewish studies a more integral component of other disciplines, we should perhaps at the same time be exploring how to foreground the extent to which Jewish studies are already integral to, or certainly indicative of, what it might mean to think comparatively on a global scale, as planetary subjects. Because 300 words of text can be a multilingual, polyphonic world in a grain of sand. But they can also be a microcosm pointing to a way of seeing a planet beyond.

Bibliography

Alexander, Claire. "Beyond the 'The "diaspora" diaspora': a response to Rogers Brubaker." *Ethnic and Racial Studies* 40 (2017): 1544–1555.

Appadurai, Arjun. *Modernity at Large: Cultural Dimensions of Globalization.* Minneapolis, MN: University of Minnesota Press, 1996.

Borges, Jorge Luis. *Labyrinths*. Trans. Donald Yates and James Irby. Harmondsworth: Penguin, 2000 [1962].

Borges, Jorge Luis. *The Book of Sand* and *Shakespeare's Memory*. Trans. Andrew Hurley. London: Penguin, 2001 [1975].

Brubaker, Rogers. "The 'diaspora' diaspora." *Ethnic and Racial Studies* 28 (2005): 1–19.

Cheah, Pheng. *What is a World: On Postcolonial Literature as World Literature*. Durham, NC: Duke University Press, 2016.

Cheyette, Bryan. *Diasporas of the Mind: Jewish and Postcolonial Writing and the Nightmare of History*. New Haven and London: Yale University Press, 2013.

Freeman, Hadley. "On *American Pastoral* (1997)." In "'Savagely funny and bitingly honest' – 14 Writers on their Favourite Philip Roth Novels." *The Guardian*. 23 May 2018 https://www.theguardian.com/books/2018/may/23/savagely-funny-and-bitingly-honest-10-writers-on-their-favourite-philip-roth-novels (30 September 2019).

Frydman, Jason. "World Literature and Diaspora Studies." *The Routledge Companion to World Literature*. Ed. Theo D'haen, David Damrosch and Djelal Kadir. London and New York: Routledge, 2014 [2011]. 232–241.

Gilroy, Paul. *The Black Atlantic: Modernity and Double Consciousness*. London and New York: Verso, 1993.

Gilroy, Paul. *Postcolonial Melancholia*. New York: Columbia University Press, 2005.

Gwyer, Kirstin. "'You think your writing belongs to you?': Intertextuality in Contemporary Jewish Post-Holocaust Literature." *Humanities* 20 (2018): 1–18.

Kafka, Franz. *A Hunger Artist and Other Stories*. Trans. Joyce Crick. Oxford: Oxford University Press, 2012 [1922].

Kafka, Franz. *Letters to Friends, Family, and Editors*. Trans. Richard and Clara Winston. New York: Schocken Books, 1977.

Krauss, Nicole. *Forest Dark*. London: Bloomsbury Publishing, 2017.

Krauss, Nicole. *The History of Love*. London: Penguin, 2006 [2005].

Levy, Lital, and Allison Schachter. "A Non-Universal Global: On Jewish Writing and World Literature." *Prooftexts* 36 (2017): 1–26.

Levy, Lital, and Allison Schachter. "Jewish Literature / World Literature: Between the Local and the Transnational." *PMLA* 130 (2015): 92–109.

Miron, Dan. *From Continuity to Contiguity: Toward a New Jewish Literary Thinking* (Stanford, CA: Stanford University Press, 2010).

Mufti, Aamir. *Enlightenment in the Colony: The Jewish Question and the Crisis of Postcolonial Culture*. Princeton, NJ: Princeton University Press, 2007.

Nietzsche, Friedrich. *The Gay Science*. Trans. Walter Kaufmann. New York: Vintage Books, 1974 [1882].

Roth, Philip. "I Always Wanted You to Admire My Fasting"; or, Looking at Kafka." In *Reading Myself and Others*. New York: Vintage Books, 2001 [1973]. 281–302.

Rothberg, Michael. *Multidirectional Memory: Remembering the Holocaust in the Age of Decolonization*. Stanford, CA: Stanford University Press, 2009.

Schulz, Bruno. *The Street of Crocodiles and Other Stories*. Trans. Celina Wieniewska. New York and London: Penguin Classics, 2008 [1934 / 1937].

Spivak, Gayatri Chakravorty. *Death of a Discipline*. New York: Columbia University Press, 2003.

Pascal Fischer
Yiddish in Jewish-American Literature: An Asset to Teaching at German Universities

There are many good reasons to teach Jewish-American literature at German universities. An obvious motivation, which hardly applies to the German context alone, is that many novels and short stories of Jewish writers undoubtedly constitute an important part of the canon of American fiction in general. At the same time, this literature falls into the category of minority writing and thus negotiates identities distinct from the American mainstream. Several theoretical concepts of postcolonial studies, 'race,' 'alterity,' and 'hybridity' among them, should be part of a teaching unit on Jewish writing, particularly if it deals with the immigrant experience. The contested idea of the American Melting Pot, popularized by the Jewish-British author Israel Zangwill, may be discussed in conjunction with Jewish-American landmark texts addressing the issue of assimilation. In this essay, I will focus primarily on arguments that are of particular relevance to German higher education: the linguistic particularities of Jewish-American literature by authors of Eastern European descent and the cultural proximity of parts of American Jewry to German students. Apart from my principal aim of facilitating a deeper understanding of Jewish-American literature for them, I also want to bring to mind that Jewish history does not consist of the Holocaust only. Frequently, Jewish history is exclusively equated with the Holocaust, which may preclude an appreciation of existing Jewish life-worlds. I want to counterbalance this tendency by offering students the opportunity to go through complex processes of identification, empathy and understanding.

I have been teaching Jewish-American literature and culture for many years at several universities in Germany and I am now part of the Jewish Studies program at the University of Bamberg, which includes modules on literature, the arts and other aspects of culture. The number of students in this program being modest, most of the participants in the lectures and seminars I teach on this topic are regular students of English and American Studies.

The starting point for my reflections on teaching Jewish literature in this context may sound a bit sobering: Most of the students have very little previous knowledge of Jewish history and culture and – for that matter – languages. Without these insights, clearly, it is hard to understand many of the central concerns, conflicts and stylistic characteristics of Jewish-American fiction.

Our students have certainly learnt a few things about the Jewish faith at school, and one can also rely on reasonable knowledge of the history of anti-Se-

∂ OpenAccess. © 2020 Pascal Fischer, published by De Gruyter. This work is licensed under the Creative Commons Attribution-NonCommercial-NoDerivatives 4.0 License.
https://doi.org/10.1515/9783110619003-014

mitic persecution in general and the Holocaust in particular. When it comes to Jewish culture beyond that, specific religious tenets, customs, holidays, and aspects of identity – in short – Jewish life, the situation appears to be somewhat disheartening. The German federal state governments put much effort into educating students about the Holocaust, but they are less successful when it comes to educating them about the breadth of Jewish realities – nonwithstanding the fact that many students show a great interest in Jewish topics. To provide an example: As part of my seminar on Jewish-American literature and culture, I ask my students the following question: "What language was spoken by the majority of Jews in Eastern Europe at the end of the nineteenth century?" In a class of more than 20 students, the reaction is generally – silence. Someone may say: "Probably Russian or Polish." "Hebrew" is another answer I have received. If I am very lucky, there may be a student who reluctantly suggests "Yiddish?" When I then tell them that in the Russian census of 1897, almost 98 percent of all Jews living in the Russian Empire claimed Yiddish as their mother tongue (Harshav 1990, 87; Fishman 1991:86), the reaction is surprise – if not incomprehension. Our students do not know that the vast majority of Jews murdered during the Holocaust spoke Yiddish, in fact at least five out of six million (Birnbaum 1988, 3). If I ask the students what kind of language Yiddish is, the reactions are hardly more encouraging. Only few students know that Yiddish is predominantly a Germanic language with Middle High German providing the lion's share of its grammar and lexicon.

The most important Anglophone Jewish-American writers have been of Ashkenazic Eastern European descent and those who wrote fiction in the first decades of the twentieth century regularly depicted processes of integration and assimilation. Since linguistic assimilation is at the center of that, Yiddish and a mixture between Yiddish and English (sometimes referred to as Yinglish) play an eminent role in their novels and short stories. A tutor thus has to provide some information on the cultural and linguistic background of the Jewish immigrants who came to the shores of America around 1900. At the same time, one has to introduce the students to the literary techniques applied by authors to convey something of the character and flavor of their mother tongues, commonly subsumed under the term "literary dialect". (see e.g. Cole 1986; Rothman 1993)

When studying Jewish-American novels with my students, I emphasize the points of similarity between their own culture and Jewish culture without downplaying the differences. This can quite effectively be done by highlighting the connections between German and Yiddish. German-speaking students have the great advantage of understanding most of the Yiddish expressions that appear in the Jewish-American novels I discuss in class. The problems that Jewish literary characters face in learning English are similar to the problems of German learners.

At the beginning of my teaching unit on immigrant writing, I thus devote some time to Yiddish. I talk about the history and composition of the language, about regional variants and about the functional diglossia of the *mameloshn* (mother tongue) Yiddish and the *losh koydesh* (holy tongue) Hebrew in Eastern Europe (Fishman 1972, 137–140; see Glinert 1987 for a modified view). When I play them a recording of Yiddish, students are confronted with something that sounds familiar and alien at the same time. The last recording I chose was a short contribution from the *Forverts* Sound Archive about the Yiddish writer Sholem Aleichem (1859–1916). My students enjoy recognizing phrases and frown when they do not. I also show them some written Yiddish in the original – with Hebrew letters – and provided them with a schema to transliterate the characters. Since we have talked about Sholem Aleichem anyway, I ask them to read the title of his story די שטאט פון די קליינע מענטשעלעך / *The Town of the Small People* in the Yiddish original with the help of the alphabet (שלום עליכם 1918, 9). I may have to help them a little bit, but in the end we come up with: *Di Shtot fun die kleyne mentshelekh*. Of course, I hope for the epiphanic moment when they suddenly recognize words behind something that looked so utterly strange and opaque to them at the beginning. As the modern German words sound very similar to this, no student has problems understanding the Yiddish title.

Having equipped them with some Hebrew characters, I then present to them Yiddish writing related to the immigrant experience. Yiddish was, after all, the language spoken on the streets of Jewish immigrant neighborhoods in America, of which the Lower East Side of Manhattan was by far the largest. As an example of the identification of many Jewish immigrants with America, I show them the sheet music cover of the song לעבען זאל אמעריקא / *Leben zol Amerika*. In my explanations of the role of journalism for the integration of Jewish immigrants, I introduce them to the most important Yiddish newspaper, the פֿאָרווערטס / *Forverts*. It certainly helps that my students understand *Leben zol Amerika* and *Forverts* as 'Long live America' and 'Forward,' because these are the same words in German.

When reading excerpts of Jewish novels of the late nineteenth and early twentieth centuries with my students, I also emphasize the significance of language in the immigrant experience. The linguistic dimension of that literature cannot only illustrate the hybrid and transcultural nature of immigrant identities (Fischer 2009), it can also open up interesting perspectives for German students.

On the first pages of Elias Tobenkin's 1916 novel *Witte Arrives*, Masha and her children have just set foot on American soil in the harbor of New York in 1890 and are about to board a train to the Midwest:

> Then came the train with a welcome surprise – a conductor who greeted them in German. There was a difference of centuries between the German which the American conductor spoke and the ghetto Yiddish of Masha Witkowski and her children. Nevertheless she and her children were cheered to the marrow. With a man who spoke German they felt kinship. Masha even took it as a good omen. She put her questions in the most cosmopolitan Yiddish she could summon to her command. (Tobenkin 1916, 2–3)

This is a good opportunity to reflect upon the role of language for our sense of belonging and how the kinship of languages may contribute to a feeling of communality. In view of the Holocaust, reading about the feeling of friendship a Yiddish speaker expresses towards a German speaker may also arouse embarrassment and shame on the part of German students. Around 1900, when anti-Semitic writers in Germany increasingly portrayed Jews as the antagonists of the German *Volk* – Wilhelm Marr and Houston Stewart Chamberlain come to mind – these literary characters take it for granted that Germans and Eastern European Jews are closely related.

Tobenkin's novel can furthermore illustrate that even for Yiddish speakers their language (which some pejoratively called "jargon") had a low prestige in comparison to German (Harshav 1990, 28) and that some speakers tried to elevate their language by bringing it closer to German. In this passage, Germanizing the language primarily fulfils a communicative function – Masha later addresses a policeman with the question "Sprechen Sie Deitsch?" – 'Do you speak German?' (Tobenkin 1916, 7), but in other Jewish-American novels of the period דײַטשמעריש / *daytshmerish*, Yiddish heavily influenced by modern German, is sometimes used by characters who want to flaunt their sophistication and cosmopolitanism. In Abraham Cahan's novella *Yekl. A Tale of the New York Ghetto* (1896), the narrator points out that the proud immigrant "lady" Mamie has recourse to an "affectedly Germanized" Yiddish (Cahan 1896, 49).

Students may want to speculate why some Jewish-American immigrant novels present bits of transliterated Yiddish – as in the case of Masha's question to the police officer – even though American readers would understand little of it. Most likely, authors like Tobenkin wanted these readers to experience something of the tone of Yiddish. Or maybe, the intended readership was Jewish anyway? In a scene at the immigration office of Ellis Island in Henry Roth's *Call it Sleep* (1934), the newly arrived Genya asks her husband Albert, who has already spent some time in America, shortly after their reunion:

> "Gehen vir voinen du? In Nev York?"
> "Nein. Bronzeville. Ich hud dir schoin geschriben." (Roth 1934, 12)

This may sound a bit strange to them, but most German students will be able to figure out the meaning of these words:[1] 'Are we going to live / dwell in New York? No. Brownsville. I have already written you.'

In the following example from Cahan's *Yekl* the recently arrived immigrant woman Gitl does not speak English yet. While most of her Yiddish is rendered as perfect English, the novel also provides a line of transliterated Yiddish, but a Yiddish that has been influenced by English. Gitl's husband Yekl has just criticized his wife for still using the Yiddish word "fentzter" instead of the word "window", which has entered the Yiddish lexicon in America. Gitl apologizes and promptly inserts the English word "window": "Es is of'n veenda mein ich." (Cahan 1896, 41) – 'It is on the window, I mean'. My German students, of course, recognize the German *Fenster* behind the unusual spelling of the Yiddish word.

Jewish-American novels of that period repeatedly illustrate the problems immigrants face in learning English. Roth's *Call it Sleep*, a novel that focuses on the experience of a little boy of six to eight years, presents us with a scene in the *Cheder*, the Jewish primary school. While the pupils are required to speak Yiddish with the Rabbi and have to learn Hebrew in their lessons, they speak an English immigrant dialect among themselves and proudly show off their vocabulary. But when a kid substitutes the Yiddish word "blitz" for the English word "lightening," he is taunted by his classmate:

"I seen a blitz just w'en I commed in."
"A blitz, yuh dope!"
"So hoddy you say blitz wise guy?"
"A lighten', yuh dope. A blitz! Kent'cha tuck Englitch? Ha! Ha!" (Roth 1934, 309)

The shaky pronunciation of English and the many grammatical mistakes are less important than the use of the right vocabulary. The little boy is still later derided as a "greenhorn" for his use of "blitz".

It should be explained to the students that in the case of such a great author as Henry Roth, the play with languages is more than an attempt at realism, as Hana Wirth-Nesher superbly explains in her reading of the novel. There is, for instance, a very subtle form of humor in the interlinguistic pun contained in *Englitch* (Wirth-Nesher 2006, 3; 78) The word appears to be a composite of *English* and the Yiddish word גליטש / *glitsh* 'slip', which German students will also recognize from the verb *glitschig* 'slippery' in their language. Remarkably, the Yiddish word has entered the English lexicon as *glitch* – 'malfunction'. Wirth-Nesher also

---

[1] The correct Yiddish form should be "ich hob" איך האָב rather than "ich hud".

points to the subversive tendency of this use of language. The development of the word *glitch* may also be a good opportunity to recapitulate the students' insights into contact linguistics.

Yiddish expressions still play a role in post-war Jewish-American literature. In Bernard Malamud's *The Assistant* (1957), the Jewish character Breitbart answers the question "How is it going?" with "Schwer." (Malamud 1957, 245) The word means 'hard' or 'difficult' in Yiddish as well as in German. Some students realize that Breitbart, who speaks English fluently, could have used an English expression, but prefers the Yiddish word, as it more adequately seems to encapsulate his notion of Jewish suffering. After the Holocaust, Yiddish is not the language of the "greenhorn" in the first place, but the language of the victims.

In most of the texts I discuss in class, the Yiddish words facilitate identification with the Jewish characters. The shared heritage of Yiddish and German may lead to a feeling of communality and thus enhance understanding. At the same time, I do not want to create the impression that the relationship between Eastern European speakers of Yiddish and central European speakers of German has ever been easy. Jewish-American novels by authors of Eastern European descent regularly address the conflicts between their own history of immigration and the one experienced by German Jews, who had come to America before them, chiefly in the middle decades of the nineteenth century, and had achieved some prosperity there. These conflicts have been an important part of the Jewish-American narrative ever since.

Talking about the success stories of German Jewry in America is not hard in Bamberg, as many prominent German Jews emigrated from that region – Franconia – to America (Wilhelm 2012). In order to render this part of Jewish-American history tangible, I try to anchor the individual life stories of some noteworthy immigrants into the local geography my students are familiar with. I talk about the Gebrüder Lehmann from Rimpar near Würzburg, who called themselves the "Lehman Brothers" in America (Flade 1999). I mention Mark Goldmann from Trappstadt and his son-in-law Samuel Sachs, the son of his friend Joseph Sachs, whom Goldmann had met in the religious school in Würzburg (Caplan 2012). Of course, students are familiar with the investment bank Goldman Sachs. I furthermore point out that the upscale department store chain Bloomingdale's was founded by immigrants from Gunzenhausen (Barkai 1994, 82). Most of my students are aware of the fact that Löb Strauß, or Levi Strauss, the founder of Levi's Jeans, was born in Buttenheim, just fifteen minutes south of Bamberg. In the house where he was born, there is now a small museum that brings to life his Jewish-Franconian heritage, the history of his emigration and his career in America. To set a counterpoint to these business people, I also mention that important American rabbis had come from Franconia, among them

Abraham Reiss/Rice, who was born in Gochsheim and became the first rabbi in the United States; Leo Merzbacher from Fürth, first rabbi of Temple Emanu-El in New York City; and Kaufmann Kohler, the famous reform rabbi of Cincinnati, who was born in Fürth as well. I have the impression that some of my Franconian students are not only surprised to learn about this part of the history of their native region, but also take pride in it.

German Jews are generally viewed with awe by the Yiddish-speaking immigrants in Jewish-American fiction of the early 1900s, but they also excite their envy or even incur their wrath. Philip, a Yiddish-speaking character in Samuel Ornitz' *Allrightniks Row "Haunch, Paunch and Jowl"* (1923) primarily sees German Jews as exploiters of Eastern European immigrants and gets all worked up about "these damned nice, superior people, the German Jews: so good, so respectable, so proud: with their vaunted charities and rich temples which make you worms grovel before them. They are the ones who have been grinding you." (Ornitz 1923, 102) Similarly, in Abraham Cahan's *The Rise of David Levinsky* (1917) the German Jew Jeff Manheimer is presented as a relentless boss in the garment industry who looks down upon his coreligionists from Russia: "Altogether he treated us as an inferior race, often lecturing us upon our lack of manners." (Cahan 1917, 187)

I find it particularly productive to encourage students to assume different perspectives in these intra-Jewish confrontations. On the one hand, they may find it easier to relate to the culturally closer German Jews, on the other, these narratives are designed to channel sympathy to the Yiddish-speaking victims of exploitation. This leads to interesting processes of reflection, loyalty and empathy, which may, hopefully, contribute to my overall learning objective, namely to arrive at a better understanding of the complexity of Jewish existence. If I am lucky, my students more fully appreciate Jews in their multifaceted existence – involved in conflicts, struggling to get by in the world; some successful, some not; some happy, some sad; some hopeful, some frightened – just like the rest of humankind.

Bibliography

Barkai, Avraham. *Branching Out. German-Jewish Immigration to the United States, 1820–1914*. New York: Holmes & Meier, 1994.

Birnbaum, Salomo A. *Grammatik der Jiddischen Sprache. Mit einem Wörterbuch und Lesestücken*. Hamburg: Helmut Buske, ^{5}1988.

Caplan, Sheri J. "Marcus Goldman". *Immigrant Entrepreneurship: German-American Business Biographies, 1720 to the Present*, vol. 2. Ed. William J. Hausman. German Historical Institute. https://www.immigrantentrepreneurship.org/entry.php?rec=100

Cahan, Abraham. *Yekl and The Imported Bridegroom. And Other Stories of Yiddish New York.* New York: Dover Publications, 1970 [¹1896 *Yekl. A Tale of the New York Ghetto*].

Cahan, Abraham. *The Rise of David Levinsky. With an Introduction and Notes by Jules Chametzky.* New York: Penguin Books, 1993 [¹1917].

Cole, Roger W. "Literary Representations of Dialect: A Theoretical Approach to the Artistic Problem." *The USF Language Quarterly* 24.3+4 (1986): 3–8.

Fischer, Pascal. "Linguistic Dimensions of Jewish-American Literature." *Transcultural English Studies: Theories, Fictions, Realities.* Ed. Frank Schulze-Engler; Sissy Helff. Amsterdam/New York: Rodopi, 2009. 169–185.

Fishman, Joshua. *Language in Sociocultural Change.* Stanford: Stanford University Press, 1972.

Fishman, Joshua. *Yiddish: Turning to Life.* Amsterdam: Benjamins, 1991.

Flade, Roland. *The Lehmans: From Rimpar to the New World. A Family History.* Würzburg: Königshausen u. Neumann, 1999 [¹1996].

Glinert, Lewis. "Hebrew-Yiddish Diglossia: Type and Stereotype Implications of the Language of Ganzfried's *Kitzur.*" *International Journal of the Sociology of Language* 67 (1987): 39–56.

Harshav, Benjamin. *The Meaning of Yiddish.* Berkeley: University of California Press, 1990.

Malamud, Bernard. *The Assistant.* New York: Farrar, Straus & Company, 1963 [¹1957].

Ornitz, Samuel. *Allrightniks Row "Haunch, Paunch and Jowl": The Making of a Professional Jew*, New York: Markus Wiener Publishing, 1986 [¹1923].

Roth, Henry. *Call it Sleep.* New York: Cooper Square Publishers, 1970 [¹1934].

Rothman, David J. "Notes toward a Theory of Literary Dialect." *Hellas. A Journal of Poetry and the Humanities* 4.2 (1993):123–35.

די שטאט פֿון די קליינע מענטשעלעך. שלום עליכם *Ale Verk fun Sholem Alechem*, Bd. 3: קליינע מענטשעלעך מיט קליינע השגות. New York, 1918. 9–17.

Tobenkin, Elias. *Witte Arrives.* New York: The Gregg Press, 1968 [¹1916].

Wilhelm, Cornelia. "Die Emigration der Fränkischen Juden im 19. Jahrhundert nach Amerika." *Die Juden in Franken.* Ed. Michael Brenner; Daniela F. Eisenstein. München: Oldenbourg, 2012. 169–180.

Wirth-Nesher, Hana. *Call it English: The Languages of Jewish American Literature.* Princeton: Princeton University Press, 2006.

David Hadar
Affiliated Identities as a Design Tool for a Jewish Literature Course

My book *Affiliated Identities in Jewish American Literature* suggests a framework for understanding writers' Jewish identity.[1] The basic argument of *Affiliated Identities* is that Jewish writers often build, shape, and maintain their public identities as Jews by way of exhibiting ties with other Jewish writers. Much of this networking takes place as part of works of literature. I believe that this framework is highly pertinent for the pedagogy of Jewish literature in higher education, especially Jewish literature as a transnational multi-lingual phenomenon. In this short paper, I will suggest that instructors can use this idea as tool for designing courses or segments of courses. Thus, the teaching of Jewish literature can be planned around a certain author's network of literary affiliations. At least in the American case, which was my focus, these ties are often international rather than restricted to a national canon (or even to a linguistic one). Thus, designing courses around the concept of Jewish literary networking will also establish Jewish literature's multi-lingual and border-crossing nature in a way that is more organic than simply deploying a survey of "the best of" Jewish writing in a plethora of languages. Furthermore, Jewish writers also connect themselves to non-Jewish writers. Following these links can help show how Jewish writing is embedded in non-Jewish national and linguistic traditions.

Let me give two American examples for what I mean. The idea of the course is to have an author or a text as the central node of a literary network and then explore (or let students explore) the other texts or authors that are once or twice removed from this central node. In the first example the center is an author, while in the second example it is a novel that works to connect its authors to other writers.

Emma Lazarus is often credited as the founding mother of Jewish American literature. She is hardly a household name, but three lines she wrote are some of the most well-known lines in American poetry. They come from "The New Colossus," a poem dedicated to The Statue of Liberty: "Give me your tired, your poor,/ Your huddled masses yearning to breathe free,/The wretched refuse of your teeming shore" (Lazarus 2005, 48–9). Lazarus comes from a German Jewish and Sephardi heritage. Both sides of her family have lived in America before she was born and were largely assimilated. At the beginning of her career she

---

[1] Bloomsbury Academic, 2020.

OpenAccess. © 2020 David Hadar, published by De Gruyter. This work is licensed under the Creative Commons Attribution-NonCommercial-NoDerivatives 4.0 License.
https://doi.org/10.1515/9783110619003-015

was deeply influenced by the American philosopher-poet Ralph Waldo Emerson and corresponded with him. This connection is an opportunity to show a Jewish writer embedding herself within a national tradition – Emerson being one of the central figures in the American canon (See Levinson 2008, 18 ff.). Later in her life, partly due to the anti-Semitic violence in Russia and the wave of poor Jewish immigrants that hit American shores in the early 1880s, she reconnected to her Jewish identity and supported relief efforts and an early version of Zionism. This change was also marked in her poetry. One important poem for this shift is "In the Jewish Synagogue at Newport." This poem is clearly an answer to Henry Wadsworth Longfellow's well known poem "The Jewish Cemetery at Newport." However, whereas Longfellow puts Jews squarely as a dead nation that belongs to the past, Lazarus shows that Jews are part of the present and future of America (Wolosky 1996, 117). This is an example of a Jewish writer rewriting a non-Jewish writer in a way that defangs some anti-Semitic notions. In this case, Lazarus deflects the idea that Jews belong to the past and should remain outside of the modern nation.

Lazarus also engages with Jewish writers. Her association with Jewish themes began with a translation of "Donna Clara," a poem about Jewish history written by Heinrich Heine, the Jewish German poet, two years before his conversion to Christianity. Lazarus not only translated the poem Heine wrote but also used a letter detailing two poems that were to complete a trilogy, to write her own, thus "entering modern Jewish literature via Heine's abandoned project" (Levinson 2008, 28). Lazarus forms her Jewish identity in correlation with rewriting Heine, who despite his conversion is usually considered important for Jewish literature.

Furthermore, Lazarus could also provide examples of how Jewish writers utilize biblical texts and connections to biblical authors in particularly Jewish ways. In "The New Ezekiel," Lazarus associates herself with a biblical prophet, one who is said to have written the book that caries his name. Ezekiel is thus also a figure of literary strength. The poem opens: "What, can these dead bones live, whose sap is dried/ By twenty scorching centuries of wrong?" bringing to mind Ezekiel's Vision of the Valley of Dry Bones (Ch. 37), an image that functions as a national allegory for the return of the exiled to the Land of Israel. The line also places us at a certain moment in history, "twenty scorching centuries" placing the speaker of the poem at least two-thousand years after the original Ezekiel and close to the historical Emma Lazarus. The second stanza promises: "I ope your graves, my people, saith the Lord/ And I shall place you living in your land" (Lazarus 2005, 85). This poem offers renewal of prophecy along with the renewal of Israel. It thus renders the poet as a new literary prophet, specifically a new Ezekiel. In writing this poem of national revival, Lazarus places herself in

Ezekiel's sandals, creating a literary affiliation that sustains her role as a Jewish writer and one of prophet-like importance and resonance. Scholars also found biblical resonance in "The New Colossus." Daniel Marom argued that the Statue is the biblical matriarch Rachel, while Shira Wolosky identifies the Statue with Deborah of the Book of Judges (Marom 2000; Wolosky 1996). The association with Deborah is especially significant for our purposes because Deborah was a prophet and a poet, producing the victory hymn known as "The Song of Deborah" (Judges 5:2–31).

"The New Colossus" offers an opportunity for showing how others connect to the author under discussion (or at least her best known texts). The lines inscribed on the Statue of Liberty's pedestal have become a motto that the emblemized the United States' acceptance of immigrants, especially Jewish immigrants fleeing European anti-Semitism. As such it was a target of various kinds of citations and revisions. For example rock singer Lou Reed protest song "Dirty Blvd." includes a line that suggests that "The Statue of Bigotry" says she will "piss on" the huddled masses and then "club 'em to death" (1989). More recently, Donald Trump's adviser Stephen Miller downplayed the poem in a press conference as part of defending draconian immigration policies. This downplaying of a central American symbol was received with much chagrin on many quarters. Both Reed and Miller are Jewish – what my readers do with this fact is up to them. You could certainly challenge students to find other moments when "The New Colossus" is referenced in literary, popular culture, or political texts.

Another path is to focus on a certain text that does an extensive job of affiliating its author with other writers.[2] Philip Roth's *The Ghost Writer* is a good example. In this short novel (and I think it is important to choose a relatively short text in this kind of course as to leave time for other texts) a young writer named Nathan Zuckerman visits a more experienced author E. I. Lonoff in his secluded New England home. Lonoff is easily associated with Bernard Malamud, but has also reminded some readers of I. B. Singer. Much of the first part is dedicated to discussing other writers, fictional and real, most of them Jewish. The main fictional writer they talk about is the hugely successful, somewhat pompous Felix Abravanel, who may lead to reading Norman Mailer and Saul Bellow. Zuckerman describes both Lonoff and Abravanel as related, thematically and stylistically to the Russian-Jewish Isaac Babel: "It's as though, as I see it, you are Babel's American cousin – and Felix Abravanel is the other" (Roth 1995, 47). Later

---

[2] The inspiration for a course that orbits around one relatively short text comes from a wonderful graduate seminar I took with Prof. Shuli Barzilai at the Hebrew University – the central text was Freud's Wolf Man case history.

on in the novel, much attention is given to a story by Henry James, so students can be reminded that Jewish writers have association with non-Jewish ones as well.

However, the most radical association created by the novel is with the person it describes as the most "famous" Jewish writer: Anne Frank (Roth 1995, 152). In one chapter of the novel, Zuckerman imagined that Anne Frank survived the Holocaust and is now living under a false name in the US, carrying out an affair with Lonoff. She cannot assume her true identity because she believes that the value of her diary would evaporate if the world knew she was alive. Later on, Zuckerman, who has been accused of Jewish self-hatred because of a story he is about to publish, imagines marrying Anne Frank as a kind of protection against such accusations. The Anne Frank connection should lead the class to read the *Dairy* as a nonfictional literary text. You could also examine its fascinating reception and adaptation history (see Spargo 2001). Thus, in this one novel, readers are sent to Russian, Yiddish, Dutch, and American texts, many of which but not all of which are Jewish.

I gave examples from American authors, but my readers may choose other starting points. A scholar of Polish literature might begin with Bruno Schulz, the short story writer and painter, who was murdered by a Nazi officer. One may explore Schulz's connection with Kafka and earlier Polish or Yiddish writers, but continue to the various Eastern European, American, and Israeli engagements with his literary legacy and tragic death.[3] Other likely starting points from a variety of literatures could be King David as the Psalmist, Rabbi Yehuda HaLevi, Heine, Sholem Aleichem, Kafka, Anne Frank, or Yoram Kanyok (though, his best most networked novel, *The Last Jew*, is probably too long for this purpose). My readers would surely have their own candidates based on their own field and personal preferences.

Affiliated identities could be a covert principle behind the course's design at first. You could set up a course about Jewish poetry, but make sure that many of the writers Lazarus is connected to appear. Let students slowly discover the connections. Perhaps they will find some connections that you did not know about. Conversely, you can make affiliations, canon building, or intertextuality the main theme of the course. A novel like *The Ghost Writer*, where characters are preoccupied with these themes, is a perfect candidate for such an explicit concentration on how Jewish authors and texts are tied together. For the more direct approach add your favorite theoreticians of intertextuality: Bakhtin, Kristeva, and Harold Bloom come to mind.

---

[3] For some of the American and Israeli engagements see Budick 2015, 127–145.

Unfortunately, I have never deployed this approach as principle behind a whole course. However, I did have the chance to utilize this approach in sections of a Jewish American Literature course I taught to MA students at the John F. Kennedy Institute for North American Studies, Free University Berlin. This was a group of German and international students with a strong grasp of American culture, but (with some exceptions) little knowledge about Judaism or Jewish literature (American or otherwise). I deployed the affiliated identities approach on several occasions. I let students compare Lazarus's and Longfellow's Newport poems and made sure to connect *The Ghost Writer* to Bellow and Malamud, which they already read. To introduce a new example, I assigned Singer's "Gimpel, The Fool" (translated by Bellow); on the same week I assigned "Envy, or Yiddish in America" by Cynthia Ozick, a story that engages with Singer's success in creating a name for himself outside of Yiddish circles as well as the failure of most other Yiddish writers to do the same. Thus, even though the focus of the course was squarely on English language texts, we could not ignore a Yiddish context for Jewish literature.[4]

To conclude, it has often been argued that professors should narrow the gap between our teaching and our research. This paper offered an example how my research shapes the way I think about course design and individual lesson plans. I do not presume that many of my readers will now hurry to plan their next semester in accordance with the suggestions here. I do want to ask you to examine your own research and look for the places that show Jewish literature at its most international, trans-lingual, and intertextual, along with the places where your texts connect to Hebrew, Yiddish, Ladino, Jewish-Arabic and similar Jewish linguistic traditions. These angles from which you do your research might hold the keys for disseminating Jewish literature, broadly defined, in whichever tradition you teach and to whatever kind of students you have.

Bibliography

Budick, Emily Miller. *The Subject of Holocaust Fiction*. Bloomington: Indiana UP, 2015.
Lazarus, Emma. *Selected Poems*. Ed. John Hollander. New York: The Library of America, 2005.
Levinson, Julian. *Exiles on Main Street: Jewish American Writers and American Literary Culture*. Bloomington: Indiana UP, 2008.

---

[4] Students also had an earful of some Modern Hebrew when my partner called me in the middle of class with a child related emergency. Everything's fine now.

Marom, Daniel. "Who Is the 'Mother of Exiles'? An Inquiry into Jewish Aspects of Emma Lazarus's 'The New Colossus.'" *Prooftexts* 20.3 (Sept. 2000): 231–61. *Project MUSE*, doi:10.1353/ptx.2000.0020.

Reed, Lou. "Dirty Blvd." *New York*. New York: Sire Records, 1989.

Roth, Philip. *The Ghost Writer*. New York: Vintage, 1995.

Spargo, R. Clifton. "To Invent as Presumptuously as Real Life: Parody and the Cultural Memory of Anne Frank in Roth's 'The Ghost Writer.'" *Representations* 76 (Autumn 2001): 88–119.

Wolosky, Shira. "An American-Jewish Typology: Emma Lazarus and the Figure of Christ." *Prooftexts* 16.2 (1996): 113–125.

IV Case Studies French and Italian Literatures

Sara Sohrabi
Case Study: Belonging in Dialogue. How to Integrate Hélène Cixous and Jacques Derrida in French Literary Studies

It is uncontested that Hélène Cixous and Jacques Derrida are among the most important thinkers of French expression in the twentieth century. Due to the complexity and vast scope of their writings, it is, however, rare to find their texts in French Studies curricula in German universites.

Nonetheless, these oeuvres contain texts that, due to their brevity and composition, are not only highly suitable for academic education, but also address fundamental issues of our time such as displacement, migration and belonging and their representation in language.

This contribution aims to illustrate this by means of two essays. First, *Mon Algériance* by Hélène Cixous, a short essay that was first published 1997 in *Les Inrockuptibles*, a journal explicitly dedicated to participating in the public sphere.[1] The second text is *L'anti-Macias : Moi, l'Algérien* by Jacques Derrida, published in 2003 in *Le Matin*.[2]

---

[1] This essay by Cixous was first published as a contribution in the *parlement international des écrivains* of the series *littérature déplacée* in the cultural magazine *Les Inrockuptibles* 115 (1997): 71–74; the English revised translation first appeared in the literary magazine TriQuarterly of Northwestern University, Evanston: *TriQuarterly* 100 (1997): 259–279. Later it was published as one of ten essays in: Cixous, Hélène, "My Algeriance. In other words: to depart not to arrive" (Cixous 1998, 203–231). This revised translation comprises an additional paragraph entitled "Shoeshine": 221–3. The paragraph entitled "The Name of Cixous" is extended by further considerations: "My house is encircled", "Do you remember Cinna the poet?", "The illegitimate" and "'The legitimate'" (My Algeriance: 211–218, cf. Mon Algériance: 72–73). The chapter "Impressions, im-prints, mirrors" comprises considerations to binary thought in "my aunts shop Aux deux mondes, The Two Worlds", (My Algeriance: 219–21, cf. Mon Algériance: 73–74). These additional elements can also be found in *Pieds nus* (Cixous 1997b: 60).

[2] In a first part, the essay is structured by three starting points of reflections and marked by the colons after them, "Mes héritages :" , "L'arabe, langue interdite :" and "Foi et savoir :". In a kind of second part, separated from the first part by two asterisks, there is a further development of the reflection on religion and faith: a *foi universelle* as the basis of every ‚adresse de parole' as a common place of people and as an opportunity for social questions concerning secularity and religion in France. This version appeared posthumously in the newspaper Le Matin. Derrida, Jacques. "L'Anti-Macias : Moi, l'Algérien de Jacques Derrida", *Le Matin*, 21.11.2007. Hereinafter: "Moi, l'Algérien". The essay comprises selected extracts from a conversation between Mustapha Chérif and Jacques Derrida as closing talk "Algérie-France, Hommage aux grandes figures du

---

∂ OpenAccess. © 2020 Sara Sohrabi, published by De Gruyter. [CC BY-NC-ND] This work is licensed under the Creative Commons Attribution-NonCommercial-NoDerivatives 4.0 License.
https://doi.org/10.1515/9783110619003-016

Both texts reflect Jewish historical experiences of the twentieth century in a post-essentialist perspective that can prove extremely fruitful in the context of traditional French philology. They also pursue their reflections in the French language itself, thus performing a de-nationalization of the French language.

At the same time, the integration of Jewish historical experience is epistemologically universalized, and addresses the colonial remnants engraved in the French language, amongst other essentialisms.

Marked by the dialogical profile of the respective mode of thinking and writing, both essays deal with historical experiences in a specific way. My thesis is that Derrida's and Cixous' philosophical approaches to historical experiences through language can be described as a hinge position between different memories, one which makes the tectonic layers visible that compose French-Algerian memory.³ Through this linguistic-philosophical procedure, it becomes evident how historical experiences were an impetus for their writing.⁴ It is in this sense that these aesthetic, literary and philosophical texts became modes of universal critique.⁵

The different oeuvres of Cixous and Derrida converge in their questioning of identitarian assumptions about language, literature, and historical experiences. It is against this backdrop that the connections between these two eminent figures of French intellectual history, whose writings are mostly affiliated with the categories of poststructuralism, French feminism and psychoanalysis, are to be understood.⁶ However, if we contextualize their works historically, they appear closely linked to historical events in and beyond Europe since the nineteenth century, to the Algerian experience, and their collective memories:

> Ma pensée est née avec la pensée que j'aurais pu naître ailleurs, dans un des vingt pays où avait atterri un éclat vivant de ma famille maternelle qui avait sauté sur le champ de mines nazi. Avec la pensée du hasard, de l'accident, de la chute. La pluie d'atomes de Lucrèce, en

---

dialogue des civilisations" on the occasion of a conference colloquium organised by Chérif in 2003 as part of the series "Dialogue des civilisations". The closing talk took place on 27 Mai 2003 at the Institut du monde arabe, Paris. As far as the rhetorical dressing of the text is concerned, the "vous" addresses the interlocutor Chérif, (Chérif 2006). An English (Chicago: University of Chicago Press, 2008) and a German Version were published subsequently (Paderborn: Fink, 2009).

3 Cf. (Diner 2007, 64–67).
4 Cf. (Zepp and Gordinsky 2009, 102–103).
5 Cf. (Stevens 2002, 77–79).
6 For a critical summary of research on and reviews of the oeuvres of Cixous and Derrida in research cf. (Christopher 2001, 79–84).

pleuvant l'atome de ma mère avait rencontré l'atome de mon père. La molécule étrange détachée de la nue noire de Nord avait atterri en Afrique. (Cixous 1997a, 71)[7]

For the speaker in the text *Mon Algériance*, the Algerian experience, broadly described as exile, does not assume the role of a rupture requiring substitution or replacement. She represents her own experience of leaving and the related questions that she associates with places in general and Algeria in particular, not as a "lack of" or as a "less". From the speaker's perspective, such negative connotations are redundant; she intends to free herself from a premise of national belonging and to open a much broader space. She speaks of the experience of belonging to the world, in which national ideas and constructs and thus also essentialist ideas of identities dissolve, that before had set her in a "double bind" (Cixous 1997a, 72).[8] She therefore perceives her existence as one of a *passante de l'histoire:*

> Mon histoire est prise entre une double mémoire contradictoire :
>
> – d'un côté ma famille allemande installée à Strasbourg au début du XXᵉ siècle s'est vu octroyer par la France victorieuse de 1918 une nationalité française qui alors ne la retint pas de rentrer précipitamment "chez elle" en Allemagne et qui par la suite s'avéra salutaire pour ma mère et ma grand-mère, lorsque la mort devint le maître de l'Allemagne comme dit Celan :
> – de l'autre côté la même France si c'est la même – dont le geste de 1918 sauvait in extremis ma grand-mère en 1938 – nous jetait en 1940 hors de la citoyenneté française et nous privait de tous les droits civils, à commencer pour moi par celui d'aller à l'école, et pour mon père celui d'exercer la médecine qu'il venait pourtant en 1939 d'exercer sur le front tunisien dans l'armée française.
>
> Ni la France, ni l'Allemagne, ni l'Algérie. Pas de regret. C'est une chance. Une liberté, une liberté incommode, intenable, une liberté qui oblige à lâcher prise, à s'élever, à battre des ailes. A tisser un tapis volant. *Je ne me suis trouvée bien nulle part.* (Cixous 1997a, 72)[9]

---

[7] "My way of thinking was born with the thought that I could have been born elsewhere, in one of the twenty countries where a living fragment of my maternal family had landed after it blew up on the Nazi minefield. With the thought of the chanciness, of the accidence, of the fall. Lucretius's Rain of atoms, in raining, the atom of my mother had met the atom of my father. The strange molecule detached from the black skies of the north had landed in Africa." (Cixous 1998, 126)

[8] "les paradoxes de ce passeport [...]: l'avoir m'enferma toujours dans un double bind" (Cixous 1997a, 72).

[9] "My history is held between a double contradictory memory: – on one hand my German family which moved to German Strasbourg at the beginning of the twentieth century was granted French nationality by a France victorious in 1918, yet this did not keep the family from returning

It is striking how Cixous de-nationalizes here the iconic French concept of liberty. To not belong to either France, Germany or Algeria is described as a liberty that is profound and full of opportunity.

Derrida's parallel reflection is marked as well by an awareness of the specific scope and existence of the categorical constraint that emanates from a binary thought system:[10]

> L'héritage que j'ai reçu de l'Algérie est quelque chose qui a probablement inspiré mon travail philosophique. Tout le travail que j'ai poursuivi, à l'égard de la pensée philosophique européenne, occidentale, comme on dit, gréco-européenne, les questions que j'ai été amené à lui poser depuis une certaine marge, une certaine extériorité, n'auraient certainement pas été possibles si, dans mon histoire personnelle, je n'avais pas été une sorte d'enfant de la marge de l'Europe, un enfant de la Méditerranée, qui n'était ni simplement français ni simplement africain, et qui a passé son temps à voyager d'une culture à l'autre et à nourrir les questions qu'il se posait à partir de cette instabilité. (Derrida 2007)[11]

The text stresses the important cognitive value of being "in-between": being neither one nor the other. From this only seemingly unstable situation can emerge epistemological questions that mark Derrida's philosophical work as a whole:

> Tout ce qui m'a intéressé depuis longtemps, au titre de l'écriture, de la trace, de la déconstruction de la métaphysique occidentale – que je n'ai jamais quoi qu'on en ait répété, identifiée comme une chose homogène ou définie au singulier, tout cela n'a pas pu ne pas pro-

---

hastily 'home' to Germany and it subsequently turned out to be salutary for my mother and my grandmother, when death became the master of Germany, as Celan says. – on the other hand the same France, if it is the same – which saved my German grandmother at the last minute in 1938 by its gesture of 1918 – threw us out of French citizenship in 1940 in Algeria and deprived us of all civil rights, beginning for my brother and me with the right to go to school, and for my father to practice medicine which he had just practiced in 1939 as a lieutenant on the Tunisian front in the French Army. Neither France, nor Germany nor Algeria. No regrets. It is good fortune. Freedom, an inconvenient, intolerable freedom, a freedom that obliges one to let go, to rise above, to beat one's wings. To weave a flying carpet. *I felt perfectly at home, nowhere*" (Cixous 1998, 127–128).

10 Amongst many, I here recommend the encyclopedic entry "Deconstruction" by Eric Prenowitz in *Encyclopedia of Jewish History and Culture* (Prenowitz 2018, 81–87).

11 "The cultural heritage I received from Algeria is something that probably inspired my philosophical work. All the work I have pursued, with regard to European, Western, so-called Greco-European philosophical thought, the questions I have been led to ask from some distance, a certain exteriority, would certainly not have been possible if, in my personal history, I had not been a sort of child in the margins of Europe, a child of the Mediterranean, who was not simply French nor simply African, and who had passed his time traveling between one culture and the other feeding questions he asked himself out of that instability" (Chérif 2006, 31–33).

céder de cette référence à un ailleurs dont le lieu et la langue m'étaient pourtant inconnus ou interdits. (Derrida 2007)[12]

Describing his own writing as "la trace, la déconstruction de la métaphysique occidentale" is also an answer to critique: from the position of the in-between, it is quite logical that the field of interest is not homogeneous.[13]

In a similar move, Cixous further describes the experience of *partir* as crucial for these epistemological constellations:

> Quand j'ai eus 3 ans, l'âge des expériences décisives et de l'analyse, je sus que j'étais destinée de partir. Certes ce serait plus tard, mais ce serait au plus tôt. Cette destination, destinalité, décision était si forte que j'ai pu dire : quand j'avais 3 ans je suis partie. C'était un pur partir. Je n'avais pas de visée ou de vision d'arrivée, de but, pas de pays désiré, j'étais en sursis et en survol. En détachement quasi originel. (Cixous 1997a, 73)[14]

The essay is emphasizing the experience of leaving without a goal or the need to arrive – "partir (pour) ne pas arriver d'Algérie" (Cixous 1997, 74). In this way, the speaker establishes a perspective that cannot be reduced to a binary logic. Such a conception of belonging surpasses any state of exile:

> Ma propre famille maternelle, l'allemande, s'était déjà détachée de ses sols (Strasbourg, Budapest, Osnabrück, Bratislava, etc.). La possibilité de vivre sans enracinement m'était familière. Je n'appelle jamais cela exil. Certains réagissent à l'expulsion par le besoin d'appartenir. Pour moi, comme pour ma mère, le monde me suffisait, je n'eus jamais besoin d'un pays terrestre, localisé. (Il reste dans le mode d'habitation familiale une sorte de dépouillement de nomade : jamais de meubles. Toujours le sac à dos.) (Cixous 1997a, 73)[15]

---

12 "Everything that has interested me for a long time, regarding writing, the trace, the deconstruction of Western metaphysics – which, despite what has been said, I have never identified as something homogeneous or defined in the singular (I have so often explicitly said the contrary)- all of that had to have come out of a reference to an elsewhere whose place and language were unknown or forbidden to me" (Chérif 2006, 33–35).
13 On the concept of trace in Derrida's thinking cf. Bennington 1994, 229–230.
14 "When I was three, the age of decisive experiences and of analysis, I knew that I was destined to leave. Of course it would be later on, but it would be as soon as possible. That destination, destinality, decision, was so strong that I have been able to say: when I was three I left. It was pure departure. I had no aim or vision of an arrival, no goal, no desired country, I was in deferment and flight. In quasi-original detachment" (Cixous 1998, 137).
15 "My own maternal family, the German one, had already detached itself from its earth (Strasbourg, Budapest, Osnabrück, Bratislava, etc.). The possibility of living without taking root was familiar to me. I never call that exile. Some people react to expulsion with the need to belong. For me, as for my mother, the world sufficed, I never needed a terrestrial, localized country. (In the family mode of dwelling there remained a nomad's simplicity: never any furniture. Always the backpack.)" (Cixous 1998, 137).

In Cixous essay, all elements of thought attest to a reflection or a course of argumentation that are derived from engagement with the French language itself, the neologism in the title *Mon Algériance* being the first of many linguistic subversions of standard French.

In both essays, historical references open up multiple levels of meaning, multifold linguistic experiments and their implications. Thus, language is being performed as the subject: through double, multiple, and even contradictory linguistic meanings, thoughts can be presented that dismantle and rebuild meaning, to emphasize what proves to be a fundamental intellectual challenge:

> J'avais la langue et ses sousterrains.
> Ou plutôt j'avais: *Mes langues.*
> Je l'ai souvent raconté, on jouait aux langues chez nous, mes parents passant avec plaisir et adresse d'une langue à l'autre tous les deux, l'un depuis le francais l'autre depuis l'allemand, en sautant par l'espagnol et l'anglais, l'un avec un peu d'arabe et l'autre avec un peu d'hébreu. (Cixous 1997a, 73)[16]

The contact with many different languages has had an effect on the French language that is valued very highly. The speaker denies that there exists one privileged relationship to one language, a so-called mother tongue: She never submitted herself to such notions of obedience and obligation of a single language. For Cixous, German, French, English, Spanish, Arabic and Hebrew were not only the languages in which she grew up:

> Cette agilité, ce sport translinguistique et amoureux m'abrita de toute obligation ou velléité d'obédience (Je ne pensai pas que le français fût ma langue maternelle, c'était une langue dans laquelle mon père m'apprenait) à une langue materpaternelle. (Cixous 1997a, 73)[17]

Cixous also distinguishes between her mother's several languages and those of her father to highlight the dialectics of historical experience in her family. During the colonial period in Algeria, the Arabic and Hebrew languages stood for historically marginalized and antagonized communities. The Arabic language in par-

---

[16] "I had the language and its subterranean passages. Or rather I had: My languages. We played at languages in our house, my parents passed with pleasure and deftness from one language to the other, the two of them, one from French the other from German, jumping through Spanish and English, one with a bit of Arabic and the other with a bit of Hebrew. When I was ten years old my father gave me at the same time an Arabic teacher and a Hebrew teacher" (Cixous 1998, 137).

[17] "That translinguistic and loving sport sheltered me from all obligation or vague desire of obedience (I did not think that French was my mother tongue, it was a language in which my father taught me) to one mother-father tongue" (Cixous 1998, 138).

ticular was violently suppressed by the colonial powers in Algeria's administration and public life:

> Nous vécûmes toujours dans les épisodes d'une Algériade brutale, jetés dès la naissance dans un des camps grossièrement façonnés par le démon de la Colonialité. On disait : "les Arabes", "les Français". Et on était joués de force dans la pièce, sous une fausse identité [...] Mes langues glissaient l'une dans l'autre oreille d'un continent à l'autre. Longtemps j'assurai – mais je n'y croyais pas – que ma langue maternelle était l'allemand – mais c'était pour conjurer le primat de la langue française, et parce que l'allemand à jamais éloigné de la bouche de ma conscience par l'épisode nazi, était devenue la langue idéalisable de ma parenté morte. Ces circonstances excluantes firent que la française comme l'allemande me parurent toujours venues à moi charmantes comme la fiancée étrangère. Mais à l'école je voulus toujours être la meilleure "en français" comme on disait pour honorer mon père, le chassé. (Cixous 1997a, 72–73)[18]

In Derrida's essay, the Arabic language and the history of Algeria before 1830 in the context of the colonial system are used to address the violence of oppression against Algerian cultures. Derrida emphasizes that the Arabic language had assumed an existential significance for him. It had become a counterpoint, an alternative with regard to French humiliations. The memory of this language evokes Derrida's childhood and youth in Algeria. Arabic was not allowed to be spoken in schools:

> L'arabe, langue interdite : la langue arabe, cet ailleurs, m'était comme inconnue ou interdite par l'ordre établi. Un interdit s'exerçait sur la langue arabe. Il prit bien des formes culturelles et sociales pour quelqu'un de ma génération. Mais ce fut d'abord une chose scolaire, un dispositif pédagogique. L'interdit procédait d'un "système éducatif", comme on dit en France. Vu les censures coloniales et les cloisons sociales, les racines, étant donné la disparition de l'arabe comme langue officielle, quotidienne et administrative, le seul recours pour l'apprentissage de l'arabe était l'école, mais au titre de langue étrangère ; de

---

[18] "We always lived in the episodes of a brutal Algeriad, thrown from birth into one of the camps crudely fashioned by the demon of Coloniality. One said: 'the Arabs'; 'the French.' And one was forcibly played in the play, with a false identity. [...] My languages slid into each other's ear from one continent to another. For a long time I asserted – but I did not believe it – that my mother tongue was German – but it was to ward off the primacy of French, and because German, forever distanced from the mouth of my conscience by the Nazi episode, had become the idealizable language of my dead kin. These excluding circumstances made French and German always seem to be coming to me charming like the foreign fiancée. But at school I always wanted to beat the French in French, to be the best 'in French' as they said, to honor my father, who had been driven out." (Cixous 1998, 128 and 138)

cette étrange sorte de langue étrangère comme langue de l'autre, certes, quoique, voilà l'étrange et l'inquiétude, de l'autre comme le prochain le plus proche. (Derrida 2007)[19]

Derrida describes the historical experiences of the Algerian-Jewish community as a position between contested memories:

> Mes héritages : je voudrais parler comme Algérien, né juif d'Algérie, de cette partie de la communauté qui avait reçu en 1870, du décret Crémieux, la nationalité française et l'avait perdue en 1940. Quand j'avais 10 ans, j'ai perdu la citoyenneté française au moment du régime de Vichy et pendant quelques années, exclu de l'école française, j'ai fait partie de ce qu'on appelait, à ce moment-là, les juifs indigènes, qui ont rencontré parmi les Algériens de l'époque plus de solidarité que de la part de ce qu'on appelait les Français d'Algérie. C'est l'un des tremblements de terre de mon existence. Il y en a eu d'autres. (Derrida 2007)[20]

Derrida's essay does not want to be understood as a definition of colonial structures. Rather, the text is an example of what it means to write philosophically about the consequences of colonial experience. These perspectives are all the more important because the social and cultural consequences of the historical experiences and wars of the twentieth century so plainly mark today's time and today's Europe.

In this respect, both essays share a common political claim, realized in the demand for the right not to belong in an identitarian thought system. Hélène Cixous and Jacques Derridas' writings elude the logic of binary systems and orders. The experience of non- or multiple affiliations opens up perspectives that, in

---

19 "The Arab language, that other, was unknown or forbidden to me by the established order. A ban was placed on the Arab language. The ban took on many cultural and social forms for someone of my generation. But it was above all a school issue, something that happened at school, a pedagogical matter. The ban came out of an 'educational system', as we say in France. Given the colonial censures and the social barriers, the various forms of racism, given the disappearance of Arabic as a daily, official, and administrative language, the only way to learn Arabic was at school, but as a foreign language; as that strange sort of foreign language that is the language of the other, although – and this is what is strange and disturbing – of another who was the closest of the close." (Chérif 2006, 33–35)

20 "My heritages: I would like to speak today as an Algerian. I was born a Jew in Algeria, from that part of the community which in 1870 had obtained nationality through the Cremieux Decree, and then lost it in 1940. When I was ten years old, during the Vichy regime, I lost my French citizenship, and for a few years, unable to attend the French school, I was a member of what at the time was called the native Jews, who during those times experienced more support from the Algerians than from what were known as the Algerian French. That was one of the earth-shattering experiences of my existence, one of the earth-shattering Algerian experiences of my existence. There have been others" (Chérif 2006, 29).

times of new nationalisms, are worth turning to – also for matters beyond literary questions.

Thus, the integration of these two texts into the corpus of French Studies allows not exclusively conveying Jewish historical experience. The two texts also offer a variety of opportunities for critical reflection on French colonial history between language policy, citizenship and violence. Moreover, the texts can also enable a discussion of the transformations of the key concepts of the French Revolution (freedom, equality, fraternity) in the light of France's history in the twentieth century.

Bibliography

Bennington, Geoffrey. *Legislations: The Politics of Decontruction*, London: Verso, 1994.
Chérif, Mustapha. *L'Islam et l'Occident. Rencontre avec Jacques Derrida*, Paris: Odile Jacob, 2006.
Churchill, Christopher. *L'Algérie en 'je': Remembering Colonial Algeria in the Works of Hélène Cixous and Jacques Derrida*. Ontario: Queens University, 2001.
Cixous, Hélène. "Mon Algériance." *Les Inrockuptibles* 115 (1997): 70–74.
Cixous, Hélène. "My Algeriance." *Stigmata. Escaping Texts*. Oxfordshire: Routledge, 1998. 203–231.
Cixous, Hélène. "Pieds nus" *Une enfance algérienne. Textes inédits recueillis par Leïla Sebbar.* Ed. Leila Sebbar. Paris: Gallimard, 1997. 57–77.
Derrida, Jacques. "L'Anti-Macias : Moi, l'Algérien de Jacques Derrida." http://www.lematindz.net/news/373-lanti-macias-moi-lalgerien-de-jacques-derrida.html. Le Matin d'Algérie, 21.11.2007 (18 December 2019).
Diner, Dan. *Gegenläufige Gedächtnisse. Zur Geltung und Wirkung des Holocaust*. Göttingen: Vandenhoeck & Ruprecht, 2007.
Diner, Dan (ed.). *Enzyklopädie jüdischer Geschichte und Kultur*. Stuttgart: Metzler, 2011.
Prenowitz, Eric. "Deconstruction." https://brill.com/view/package/ejhb Encyclopedia of Jewish History and Culture Online. Ed. Dan Diner. 2018 (18 December 2019).
Rimmon-Kenan, Shlomith. *Narrative Fiction. Contemporary Poetics*. New York: Routledge, 2005.
Stevens, Christia. "Hélène Cixous, auteur en 'algériance'." *Expressions maghrébines* 1 (2002): 77–91.
Zepp, Susanne, and Natasha Gordinsky. *Kanon und Diskurs: Über Literarisierung jüdischer Erfahrungswelten*. Göttingen: Vandenhoeck & Ruprecht, 2009.

Stephanie Bung
Teaching Contemporary French Literature: The Case of Cécile Wajsbrot

While research on contemporary French literature, the literature of the so called "extrême contemporain"[1] becomes more and more accepted, teaching it remains a challenge. When you have not much time on your hand, because your students have only to attend a limited number of major courses on literature, what would you rather do? Introduce them to Molière, Balzac and Proust or discuss a novel written by Cécile Wajsbrot, a contemporary French writer whose name, however, sounds not exclusively French? From a distance, this seems like an unfair competition. However, if you dare to take a closer look, this is not a question of evaluation. Teaching means taking choices and whether we choose Wajsbrot over Proust does not affect the value neither of their work nor (necessarily) of our teaching. Still, the decision to teach a class on Cécile Wajsbrot may have an impact on the awareness of these choices, since we have to explain carefully why we think that the discussion of Wajsbrot's work might help us to understand more about French literature. We have to show explicitly that her case allows us to ask important, paradigmatic questions.

The question I want to raise in my case study is how to deal with autobiography, or more precisely: How shall we deal with the work of an author whose writing does not call for an autobiographical reading? Cécile Wajsbrot, a contemporary French writer of novels, essays, features and radio-plays,[2] has always been very reluctant to accept the idea of her texts being read as autobiographical. This reluctance is crucial to our discussion, I think, because the first nearby grip we get on Jewish Literature as a paradigm of polyphonic writing beyond the national may very well be the writer's biography. What I want to do in this contribution is to sketch a picture of the author that – on the one hand – takes into account her reluctance. On the other hand, I want to show that at least one aspect of her work can be inserted into our paradigm of Jewish Literature; and that this is possible not only despite the difficulties she seems to have with the autobiographical, but because of them.

---

[1] The notion "extrême contemporain" was forged by Michel Chaillou (1987) and has been developed more recently by Viart and Vercier (2005).
[2] Cf. The bibliography of her oeuvre (Huesmann 2017, 539–550).

Two years ago, when Wajsbrot was admitted to the *Deutsche Akademie für Sprache und Dichtung*,[3] She chose an interesting key-concept for her introductory speech. She was referring to her family name and the difficulty for French people to pronounce it. When she was younger, she writes, she did not like to introduce herself to others, especially not on the telephone. Nevertheless, she did not want to change the sound of her name either, into something like "Wesbro" for example, like her mother used to, reducing the difficulty to the spelling by doing so. Of course, the misspelling of her name and the mispronouncing was only the symptom of something more essential. The real issue was about the question of belonging.

> Darf ich es bekennen? Das Problematische in meinem Namen war der Buchstabe J, also J wie *je*, wie ich, J wie jüdisch. Sollte ich einen Roman ohne J schreiben – wie Perec damals ohne E? In den Jahren, in denen ich meinen Namen nicht sagen konnte, hatte ich sicher den Blick der Gesellschaft auf meine Herkunft, auf die Geschichte der Zerstörung, verinnerlicht, und so erlebte ich den Widerspruch zwischen der Außenwelt und der Innenwelt, ohne eine Brücke schlagen zu können ... Wer war ich? Mit dem Stolpern über die Aussprache stolperte ich über die Identität. Und wer weiß, ob ich nicht zum Schreiben gekommen bin, weil ich meinen Namen lieber nur schreiben wollte, anstatt ihn auszusprechen. [...]
> Der erste Schritt ist, den eigenen Namen zu sagen – ihn anzunehmen. Sich zu definieren, sich von den anderen zu unterscheiden. Und dann kommt die Aufgabe – das Schweigen und seine Folgen zu heilen, mit dem Erzählen zu beginnen.[4] (Wajsbrot 2017)

This self-introduction of a French writer to a German academy of language and literature is quite interesting for our purposes: the *choice* Wajsbrot made to address the "problem" of her name. It seems to me that she takes the viewpoint of her reader into consideration. As if her "Frenchness" was once more debatable:

---

[3] Being admitted to this academy is remarkable, and she shares this honour with French writers like Jean Cocteau or writers in French like Paul Nizan, Philippe Jaccottet or Claude Vigée. Since 2019 she is also a member of the renowned *Akademie der Künste* at Berlin.

[4] The "Vorstellungsrede" can be found on the website of the academy: https://www.deutscheakademie.de/de/akademie/mitglieder/cecile-wajsbrot/selbstvorstellung. (24 September 2019)

[My translation: May I admit it? The problem within my name was the letter J, that is J as in 'je', 'I', or as in 'jewish'. Should I write a novel without 'J' – just like Perec did once without 'E'? All those years when I could not say my name, I surely had internalized the gaze of society looking at my provenance, at the history of destruction, and so I experienced the contradiction between the outer and the inner world, not being able to bridge it. ... Who was I? By stumbling over the pronunciation, I stumbled over the identity. And who knows if I hadn't become a writer because I preferred to write my name instead of saying it. [...] The first step is to say your own name – to accept it. To define yourself, to be different. And then comes the task – to mend the silence and what comes after, to start narrating.]

If for French eyes and ears, she was not "one of us", especially in the seventies and still in the eighties, for German eyes and ears in 2017, she was, on the contrary, immediately recognizable as a writer who is dealing with the darkest part of "our" history.

It is not that I want to argue that Cécile Wajsbrot claims to be "French". However, I am not so sure that she claims to be "Jewish" either. What I see in this text is a certain ambivalence when it comes to claim any identity. You cannot be a writer without the acceptance of who you are, without the acceptance of your name. Does this mean that your writing has to be in the name of your identity, that it has to be in the name of your "name"? The last paragraph of the quotation has an interesting structure: First, you have to learn how to say your own name. Then you can concentrate on your task. This task obviously raises the question of belonging. But it also raises the question of how to get there. Alternatively, let me put it like this: The task of narration goes far beyond the autobiographical writing; it is not contained in a name, at least not in *one* name.

Considering the key aspect of this book, and in order to exemplify how the autobiographical issue emerges from her actual work, I would like to focus on a nonfictional part of Wajsbrot's writing. A recent example is *Une autobiographie allemande*, published in 2016 by Christian Bourgois Editeur. The small book is written *à quatre main*, because Cécile Wajsbrot wrote it together with Hélène Cixous.[5] It is a dialogue from the distance, an exchange of letters between the two writers, stretched over a rather long period (the idea of writing to each other goes back to 2012, when Wajsbrot interviewed Cixous for the revue *Sinn und Form*).[6] The title *Une autobiographie allemande* refers to Hélène Cixous in the first place. More precisely, it begins with referring to her mother's life, Eve ¬Cixous, who was born in Osnabrück in 1910 and who died in 1999, leaving a large void in the life of her daughter. In a very sensitive way Cécile Wajsbrot asks Hélène Cixous to write about this void, to write about her mother and the members of her German family, whose surviving members are spread all over the world. Not all of them survived though and photographs in the book remember those who were deported to Theresienstadt and murdered in Auschwitz.

I would like to compare Wajsbrot's gesture, at least in this part of the book, to the persona of a midwife. The careful way she approaches Hélène Cixous, the way she really "cares" for what is about to be remembered. Obviously – at least in those moments – she is not the one doing the labour of remembering, she is not the autobiographical centre of the book. However, she probably could not

---

5 Cf. Zepp 2017.
6 Cf. Hélène Cixous and Cécile Wajsbrot 2016, 10–11.

have exercised this maieutic function if it was not for her own biography. Her grandfather was murdered in Auschwitz and her mother hardly escaped the Vel' d'Hiv' Roundup. So finally, the title of the book "Une autobiographie allemande" refers to a common set of experience. It is what both writers share to elucidate the still prevailing voids of twentieth century history.[7] However, it seems to me that Cécile Wajsbrot needs the polyphonic structure of this text to go to the autobiographical heart of this experience. In order to commit to this task, to put her name on a book called "autobiography", she has to create a situation of "belonging", she has to be more than one.

Confronted with the dilemma whether to teach a class on a contemporary instead of a classical writer or how to integrate Jewish literature into our respective disciplines, we need questions rather than answers. When my students heard that Wajsbrot was a member of the German academy of language and literature (*Deutsche Akademie für Sprache und Dichtung*), they asked: But she is a French writer, isn't she? Does she have more German than French readers? Is the German perception of her work different from the French perception? Why might that be? These questions, some of which are still waiting to be answered, eventually pointed to the problem of biographical information and how to deal with it. They initiated discussions about identity politics, about the correlation of *témoignage* and literature, about the art of belonging,[8] allowing (not only) my students to exercise fundamental skills (not only) a literary scholar is supposed to have. Reading a novel written by Cécile Wajsbrot allowed all of us to engage with the purpose of literature beyond the national, the meaning of multilingualism within the realm of literature.

Bibliography

Bung, Stephanie. "'Vous trouverez ce livre…' – Cécile Wajsbrot and the Art of Belonging." *Passages of belonging. Interpreting Jewish Literatures*. Eds. Carola Hilfrich, Natasha Gordinsky and Susanne Zepp. Berlin and Boston: De Gruyter, 2019. 58–65.
Chaillou, Michel. "L'extrême-contemporain, journal d'une idée." *Po&sie* 41 (1987): 5–6.

---

[7] Cf. Cixous and Wajsbrot 2016, 16: "Il y eut, entre Cécile et moi, un pacte qui n'a jamais fait loi, suscité par l'amour de la littérature et ses corollaires: l'amour de l'autre, le goût vital de la mémoire et l'espoir." [My translation: There have been, between Cécile and me, a pact that was never forced upon us, provoked by the love of literature and its corollaries: the love of the other, the vital taste of memory and hope.]

[8] Cf. Stephanie Bung. "'Vous trouverez ce livre…' – Cécile Wajsbrot and the Art of Belonging." *Passages of belonging. Interpreting Jewish Literatures*. Eds. Carola Hilfrich, Natasha Gordinsky and Susanne Zepp. Berlin and Boston: De Gruyter, 2019. 58–65.

Cixous, Hélène, and Cécile Wajsbrot. *Une autobiographie allemande*. Paris: Christian Bourgois, 2016.
Huesmann, Hubert. *Das Erzählwerk Cécile Wajsbrots: eine literarische Suchbewegung*. Tübingen: Narr Francke Attempto, 2017.
Viart, Dominique, and Bruno Vercier. *La littérature française au présent. Héritage, modernité, mutations*. Paris: Bordas, 2005.
Wajsbrot, Cécile. "Vorstellungsrede." *Deutsche Akademie für Sprache und Dichtung* 2017. https://www.deutscheakademie.de/de/akademie/mitglieder/cecile-wajsbrot/selbstvorstellung, 2017 (24 September 2019).
Zepp, Susanne. "Geschichtserfahrung als hermeneutische Kategorie. Über Hélène Cixous' und Cécile Wajsbrots *Une autobiographie allemande*." *Literaturkritik.de* 2017. https://literaturkritik.de/public/rezension.php?rez_id=23726 (24 September 2019).

Nourit Melcer-Padon
Ways to integrate Jewish Literature into the Broader Context of Academic Teaching

The endeavour to integrate Jewish Literature in current curricula brought to mind a famous and successful writer whose factual life and literary works embody and exemplify many of the issues related to the subject at hand. I am referring to Shatan Bogat, aka Fosco Sinebaldi, aka Émile Ajar. Born in 1914 in Vilna to Russian parents who separated in his childhood, Roman Kassev, as he was called at birth, arrived in Nice at the age of 14, driven there by his fervently Francophile mother, who was convinced France was the only place that could promote her son's obvious talents. A somewhat nightmarishly archetypal Jewish mother, Mina Kassev destined her son to become a "Victor Hugo," a "D'Annunzio," a hero and a French ambassador. Happy to comply, Roman would seek a suitable pen name for his literary career, and ultimately change his name to Romain and then to Romain Gary, the most famous of his many pseudonyms. He would become a French consul to several countries, having been awarded the prestigious medal of the *Compagnons de la Liberation* by the hands of Charles de Gaulle himself for his bravery in battle as an RAF navigator in WWII, fighting as part of the free French, in the "Lorraine" squadron.

During the war, he would also start his formal career as a writer. In fact, he would become the only French writer to win the most lucrative Goncourt prize not once, as the prize regulations stipulate, but twice: as Romain Gary, for his novel *Les raciness du ciel*, published in 1956, and for the novel *La vie devant soi*, published in 1975, under the name of Émile Ajar. It is only after his suicide, on the 2nd of December 1980, that his literary confession was published, officially revealing the connection between Gary and Ajar, to the stupefaction of the great majority of his readers.

Despite his many achievements, Gary was a kind of underdog. A foreigner and a Jew to boot, he was hailed but also classified immediately upon the publication of his first novel, *L' education Européenne*, written during the war and first published in English in 1944. The novel depicts the struggle for survival of a Jewish child in WWII, amidst Polish partisans fighting the Nazis in the woods around Gary's native town. Gary's otherness was thus established. This distinction, purposefully underlined by Gary's ambiguous attitude towards his own Jewishness, constituted one more building block of his constructed self. On the one hand, he claimed (though this was not corroborated factually) that the Israeli listing of *Who's Who in World Jewry* refused him an entry since he

∂ OpenAccess. © 2020 Nourit Melcer-Padon, published by De Gruyter. This work is licensed under the Creative Commons Attribution-NonCommercial-NoDerivatives 4.0 License.
https://doi.org/10.1515/9783110619003-018

was not really considered a Jew, yet on the other hand he himself insisted that he was of Mongol origin on his father's side[1] (Gary 2007, 15–6). His commercial success certainly did not ingratiate him with the French intellectual aristocracy that snubbed Gary, disregarding his literary valour as well as his impeccable use – and inventive misuse – of the French language, especially in the novels signed Émile Ajar.

Gary's urge to reinvent his literary self was mainly driven by his conviction that he would never be allowed to step outside the category of the eternal foreigner whose narratives, however various, tiresomely centred on WWII and its repercussions, and on many protagonists who were Jews. For the French, Gary lamented, he would always be an "outsider writer"[2] (Gary 2007, 37). In order to peel off the label he felt was glued to the name 'Romain Gary' he started writing under a new name: Émile Ajar. Not only did he manage to produce a new style, and seemingly dealt with new themes and social issues in his writing, but he did it so well that only the few in the know could fathom that Gary was the original author. The first Ajar novel, *Gros Câlin* (1974) was quite a success, so much so that it was nominated for the Renaudot Prize, a list from which Gary felt duty-bound to withdraw the novel from, since this was not really his first novel. The second Ajar novel *La vie devant soi* (1975), became an even greater success, leading to the unforgettable performance of Simone Signoret as Madame Rosa in Moshé Mizrahi's 1977 film adaptation. Hence, Gary had been quite right in his argument that the name 'Romain Gary' on the cover of a novel could only elicit the same worn-out reaction from critics and public, while 'Émile Ajar' would receive a completely different welcome.

What Gary did not foresee was the extensive effect of this fresh literary triumph. He found himself compelled to concoct a false figure, complete with biographical details that were supposed to keep his real identity hidden. When the readers' pressure to find out who exactly the successful young new writer was grew, Gary convinced his cousin Paul Pavlowitch to pose as Émile Ajar and give interviews that Gary hoped would convince the public and distance the press from the real writer. Matters became complicated: the novel was nominated for the Goncourt prize, and several assiduous reporters found incongruities in

---

[1] In an interview, Gary claimed he had been refused an entry since his father was not Jewish. Supposedly, his 20$ fee was returned, and a letter from the biographical dictionary staff stated the Israeli law supported the decision of *Who's Who*. This in itself is a fantasy (if not a deception) on Gary's part, since the state of Israel considers anyone whose mother is Jewish as automatically eligible for citizenship, regardless of the father's creed (Gary, 2007, 15–6).

[2] Gary compared his literary reception and consideration in France to that of Joseph Conrad in England. (Gary 2007, 37).

the fabricated story that led to a series of near-discoveries. To dissuade further inquiry, Gary denied he had anything to do with Ajar in a written statement published on *Le Monde*. Yet what finally convinced the public that Émile Ajar was Paul Pavlowich's pen-name was nothing other than what Gary was masterful at: writing fiction. In a manner reminiscent of E. A. Poe's "Purloined Letter," Gary brilliantly exposed the truth in such a way that it became thoroughly buried under a multi-layered masquerade, composed of truthful statements and real facts. The novel *Pseudo* (1976), whose very title attests to its content, was construed as a lunatic's journal, supposedly Paul's autobiography, in which he admitted to being treated for schizophrenia in a clinic in Denmark. Many details taken from the long trail of lies accumulated since Émile Ajar came into existence were woven into the novel in a farcical, playfully absurd manner, and convinced the public that Paul Pavlowich was indeed the somewhat troubled but brilliant Émile Ajar. Gary thus admitted to the sham while at the same time tragically renouncing the possibility of publically enjoying the fruits of his labour, and particularly the recognition that his writing skill encompassed much wider possibilities than credited. Nonetheless, he did not give up on the opportunity to saturate *Pseudo* with the fundamental social, ethical and psychological precepts that can easily be traced in all his novels, regardless of the pseudonym used for each.

Gary's condition, albeit rather extreme, is typical of that of innumerable Jews over many centuries. One recalls the *Conversos* in Early Modern times, who had to negotiate different rulers, juggle between several identities and somehow reinvent themselves in a new location under precarious conditions, or Jews who later on considered themselves emancipated under the aegis of the age of Enlightenment, only to become disillusioned by the Dreyfus affair. Jews were often forced to adjust at best, or at worst flee for their lives, making their 'relocation' a vital necessity. Nevertheless, the ability to adapt to new circumstances and the versatility that allowed to survive changes while retaining a core identity, are capacities that are also required from displaced people and immigrants in other societies. Common to Italians in early years of the twentieth century in America, to present-day African immigrants' unwelcome arrival on European coasts, indeed to any other minority at any given historical time, are many of the 'Jewish' anxieties resulting from dangers and hardships they must tackle when seeking a safe haven. Gary was very much aware of the universality emphasized by the Jewish condition in his writing. Quoting Arthur Koestler, he claimed Jews were an extreme case of Man, adding that his entire oeuvre was geared at a search of the fundamentally, essentially human (Gary 2007, 25). He viewed his incapacity to lose hope and determination to vindicate Man, as the defenceless creature put on earth to try to survive life's challenges as best he can, as the very reason for his creative endeavour.

Gary's flamboyant personality and multi-layered, concealed identities are not the only attributes that made me think of him in the context of the present volume. Rather, it is one of his most powerful novels. Its plot and its date of publication make it doubly interesting, since it was not only written ahead of its time but especially because it was published at the wrong timing. *La dance de Genghis Cohn* was vehemently opposed by French Jews, who condemned Gary of making fun of the Shoa during the tense days preceding the Seven Days' war between Israel and its neighbouring Arab countries. The book was published three days before the war broke out, and although it was later translated into English by Gary himself, it never received (to my mind at least) proper recognition.

The novel stages the revenge administered by the ghost of a minor Yiddish cabaret comedian, who continues to use his wry Jewish humour to haunt Schatz, the Nazi responsible for his death. It is almost 22 years that Schatz has been hiding a Jew, jokes Cohn, and he can no more rid himself of this ghost than Germany can rid itself of its past. An agent of poetic justice, Cohn proves that Jews are an integral part not only of German history and culture, but also more fundamentally of the German psyche. Similarly to his namesake, Genghis Khan, whose hordes invaded Europe, Cohn freely overtakes the German subconscious, and has no intention of leaving: "they have stuck me in their subconscious, I'm staying there. I cannot be uprooted."[3]

While readers laugh at Schatz' dismay when he finds himself suddenly made to talk in Yiddish or to eat chopped liver, other facets of Gary's literary revenge may be less easy to digest. Schatz receives a psychiatric drug, which nearly rids him of the spirit haunting him. Surprisingly, Schatz fights back, and when the effect of the drug wears off, he is not only happy to still be hosting Cohn, but thanks Cohn for having saved him. Flabbergasted, Cohn realizes that victim and culprit are bound forever. Cohn may be inhabiting Schatz' subconscious, but Schatz also inhabits Cohn's subconscious, to the point that Cohn does not know anymore who haunts whom. What's more, they both find themselves knee-deep in a quagmire, a greater subconscious, one that evidently tries to rid itself of both of them. Cohn reflects, and concludes it could be the subconscious of the Messiah, who has come to liberate humans of their individual subconscious and lead them to the light, or it could be God's subconscious, who is trying to relieve himself of humans in order to have some peace and quiet. Clear-

---

[3] "Ils m'ont foutu dans leur sub-conscient, j'y reste. Indéracinable." (Gary 1967, 34).

ly, the stinking swamp they are both in belongs not only to the writer, who has inserted them there, but also to a sort of collective subconscious.

Cohn realizes to his horror the ramifications of being considered equal to Schatz: once Jews become part of normative society rather than remaining on its margins, they will also be morally implicated in the collective responsibility for the crimes perpetrated by humans, including their own extermination. Cohn rebels against the very idea that the victim could possibly have anything to do with the crime. He promptly decides fraternity with others is not for him, since the minute he accepts to be part of the human race he would have the blood of the victims of Hiroshima and of the Blacks in America on his hands.

According to Gary, the surviving victim must acknowledge Nazi conduct as part of the possible scope of human depravity, rather than the deeds of insane or inhuman people. The reintegration of the Jew into his rightful place within the rank of the human race compels one at the same time to take a renewed look at the Nazis, the French and all the other people who lived through the horrific times of WWII. The responsibility for the actions carried out by nations is laid not only at the door of their leaders, but also on the private thresholds of each individual citizen. "Pinochet and Amin Dada, are you and me," claims the main protagonist of Gary's novel *Pseudo*. As Gary said in an interview, he considered the entire Humanity to be the "I" of *Genghis Cohn*, its main protagonist and its main subject (Gary 2007, 34). The only way to avoid responsibility is by not being human at all, and the protagonist yells: "Fuck off! I don't know what I've done next, I don't read newspapers, but it wasn't me. I'm not the sort to. I am a disgusting reptile. I am nothing human. I am not responsible."[4] (Gary 2010, 11, 16).

Inspired by Gary, we can move forward and think of ways to combine organically into a working program his vision, his iconoclastic and irreverent stances, taken from Jewish traditions, which are undoubtedly relevant to Israeli literature, though mostly still unknown to European students. Gary's use of Yiddish humour, of jokes about the Shoa, of absurdity and dystopia, does not stand

---

4 In French: Ajar 1976, 20, 25: " Pinochet et Amin Dada, c'est vous et moi ... Foutez-moi la paix. Je ne sais pas ce que j'ai encore fait, je ne lis pas les journeaux, mais c'est pas moi. C'est pas mon genre. Je suis un reptile répugnant. Je n'ai rien d'humain. Je suis pas responsible." *Gros Calin*, Gary's first novel as Émile Ajar, is about a man who keeps a python as his pet, and ultimately becomes the python, rolling his coils and eating mice, having relinquished his frenetic pursuit of human affection. In *Kites*, the French cook and the German general cook together: "Nous sommes tous dans le sang et dans la merde et deux natures d'élite communient au-dessus de la barbarie ... Ces deux-là sont en train de préparer l'avenir. Bordel, j'aimerais voir ça." (Gary 1980, 285).

alone but indeed fits quite naturally in a continuum very much alive today as well. From Itzik Manger and Y. L. Peretz' Yiddish humour, to Orly Castel-Bloom's, Amos Kenan's and Benjamin Tamuz' dystopian novels, to Hanoch Levin's satirical Shoa plays, the legacy of Jewish history and literature that impregnated Gary's writing is kept alive in present day Israeli fiction. Such a combination of texts can also serve as an example to my modest suggestion of how to integrate Jewish literature and specifically modern Israeli fiction into European academic studies.

There are several problematic aspects when envisaging the integration of Jewish Literature in broader academic teaching. First, what is "Jewish Literature"?[5] How can it be defined – and should there be a conclusive definition? Would such a category include only literature written in Hebrew and in languages of the Jews, and/or literature written by Jews (and we can't fail to observe that there is no agreed upon answer to the age-old question "Who is a Jew?")? Should there be a differentiation between literature written in the land of Israel (from Biblical times to post-1948) and in the diaspora? Would there be a reference to the period in which this literature was written? In addition, can one consider certain texts as canonical texts, and if so what is the criteria for this category? Finally, the language in which Jewish texts were written, and the language into which they were translated play a major part of the possibility to include them in any program. For example, a text written in Yiddish and only translated into Hebrew, or a text that was translated from Hebrew but only into English, could be problematic for target readers in French or Italian universities.

I suggest producing modular study units, and the texts I have just mentioned with relation to Gary and his style could become one such module about the use of humour in literature. These modules could be taught separately or one after the other, depending on the needs of the target university. Integrating the study of Jewish texts into existing programs could rely on the professors presently teaching them and would therefore not necessitate the establishment of a special department or a chair for Jewish studies. Each module would be conceived in a manner that provides the suggested titles and an accompanying bibliography, as well as several relevant critical texts.

The full sequence of the modules could create an historical continuum, a time line along which the various texts would be discussed, according to their time of writing and/or publication. Such an approach would also provide the historical and social context in which each work was conceived and would constitute a full-length course on the subject of Jewish literature. Alternatively, each

---

[5] For a discussion of this issue, see: Salah 2003, 95–120.

of the modules could be studied separately, and fit into an existing curriculum, according to period and/or to geographical location studied at the target university.[6] Another option would be for teachers of Jewish literature to provide online courses that would be added to current course requirements. One such course presently exists in France, at the Lorraine University.

A clear constraint to this suggestion is the fact that any lists of existing Jewish works that have already been translated would necessarily contain diverse texts for various target countries. There are great differences between texts chosen to be translated into German, French or Italian, and translations into English would provide a different list altogether. Moreover, even a cursory examination of trends in publishing of translations of Hebrew literature reflects the underlying political reality: the tendency to publish such translations is very much in correlation with the current political atmosphere created in Europe and elsewhere at any given time. For example, the 1967 War or the signing of the Oslo Agreements (1992): both occurrences resulted in a positive political attitude towards Israel at the time, and produced a significant increase in the publication of literary translations from Hebrew in Europe and the United States.[7] Authors of the Israeli left, such Amos Oz or David Grossman, are more often than not invit-

---

6 Examples for possible units:
    A. a unit based on Gary's texts could be divided into three parts: 1. 'Beginnings': *La Promesse de l'aube* as well as Yoel Hofmann's *curriculum vitae* [no capital letters in the original] and Amos Oz's *A Tale of Love and Darkness;* 2. 'Birth of the Author': *Pour Sganarelle*, and *Pseudo*, as well as Hélène Cixous' "Coming to Writing"; 3. 'The Multiple 'I': reading Gary's texts against the background of Luigi Pirandello's *Six Characters in Search of an Author* and *One, a Million and No One* and Fernando Pessoa's *The Book of Disquiet*.

    B. a comparative approach: in a French course that centers on Marcel Proust's *Du Côté de chez Swann*, one could add a discussion of S. Yizhar's *The Days of Ziklag* [*Yemey Ziklag*]; in a course that includes Georges Perec's *W ou le Souvenir d'enfance*, one could read Yoel Hofmann's *Katschen and The Book of Joseph*; in a course that discusses Claude Simon's *La Route des Flandres*, one could add Yizhak Averbuch's The *Young Man* [*Haelem*].

In an Italian course focusing the subject of "War and its aftermath," that would include texts such as Umberto Eco's *La fiamma della regina Loanna*, one could consider adding a discussion of Israeli texts such as Yehudit Hendel's *The Mountain of Losses* or David Grossman's *To the End of the Land*.

    C. a themed approach comprising only of Jewish literature:
aside for the abovementioned course on "Humour", one could present a course entitled "The Auto portrait", that would include the following texts: H. N. Bialik's *Safiakh*; Tchernichovsky's autobiographical idylls, S.Y. Agnon's "Agunot"; Lea Goldberg's *And this is the Light* [*Vehu Haor*]; Yoel Hofmann's *The Book of Josheph*; Dan Tsalka's *Portrait of the Artist at the Age of 27*; Anton Shammas' *Arabesques*. In addition, one could envisage adding texts that would probably be known to the students: Amos Oz's *Black Box*, and A. B. Yehoshua's *Mr. Mani*.

7 For the political influence on literary reception in Italy and France, see: Carandina 2014.

ed to voice their political views at interviews and lectures and op-ed pieces, rather than contribute their literary input. To the politics of translation, one must add the local politics of editors and distributors in Europe and the US. In such a reality, the integration of Hebrew/Jewish literature in the future, from a cultural and academic point of view, should not be held hostage to the mood of the moment.

Indeed, an important way to promote the reading, propagation and eventual integration of Jewish literature in academic studies, lies in further promotion of translation.[8] Many Israeli authors are compelled to translate their work at their private expense, an effort that is not necessarily rewarded with publishing, similarly to the Israeli government's effort to sponsor translations by setting up a special fund, which often resulted in disappointment. In an ideal world, one could fathom the appointment of lectors who could compile lists of relevant texts and engage translators into various target languages. Until such time arrives, one could envisage using existing English translations, especially since these often appear before translations into other languages.[9] The National Library of Israel could assist the project by producing a list of all books that have been translated to date, according to language into which the books were translated and the time of translation, with added information regarding publishers, translators and more, all readily available in its databases.

It would be advisable to take Jewish literature out of its expected, "comfort zone," or habitual niche it has been classified under. In other words, while offering modules on Shoa literature, or famous and commercially well-known modern authors such as David Shahar in France or A.B. Yehoshua in Italy, not to be merely guided or restricted to these denominators, but rather to embrace a broader outlook and comparative approach. Such an approach would wrest the subject from the hands of commercial interests, alien to academic work and offer a no-nonsense, clear-eyed look at the material we wish to integrate, thus enabling us to expose its riches and possibilities. Jewish texts present a plethora of thematic foci, of stylistic features, of writing styles and of artistic approaches, especially since they are part of a living classical culture, with a continuous existence of over 3000 years.

---

[8] The site of the Institute for Translation of Hebrew Literature provides a comprehensive list of translated Hebrew books that have been translated into 82 languages. See: http://www.ithl.org.il/. (14 June 2019).

Specifically for translations of Jewish texts into Italian, see: https://www.israele.net/letteratura-ebraica-contemporanea-pubblicata-in-italiano. (14 June 2019).

[9] Regarding translations into French that customarily appear after English ones, see: Sapiro 2002, 84.

Writers like Romain Gary, whose tools, apparent in all his works, are humour, absurdity, slapstick, ridicule, and breaking of taboos, all used to put an uncomfortable mirror in front of society, thereby undermining exceptionalism – should be considered as beacons to such a project. Particularly if one is willing to adopt Gary's reflection regarding Jews, a mere twenty-five years after Auschwitz: while admitting to the short time that had passed, he considered that the extreme situations Man now had to face no longer belonged to the Jews, in terms of suffering (Gary 2007, 26). Far from forgetting Auschwitz or minimizing its unprecedented horror, Gary believed it was time to consider other sufferings as well, since even Auschwitz did not put a stop to man's capacity to inflict them upon other fellow men.

Bibliography

Ajar, Émile. *Pseudo*. Paris: Mercure de France, 1976.
Carandina, Elisa. "Per un canone esterno della nuova letteratura ebraica." *Griselda online* 2014. https://site.unibo.it/griseldaonline/it/letterature-del-mondo/elisa-carandina-canone-esterno-nuova-letteratura-ebraica (24 September 2019).
Gary, Romain. *Hocus Bogus*. Trans. David Bellos. Pennsylvania: Margellos World Republic of Letters, 2010.
Gary, Romain. *Le judaïsme n'est pas une question de sang*. Paris : L'Herne, 2007.
Gary, Romain. *Les cerfs volants*. Paris: Gallimard, 1980.
Gary, Romain. *Genghis Cohn*. Paris: Gallimard, 1967.
Salah, Asher N. "Y a-t-il eu un roman hébraïque? Roman et romanesque dans la littérature juive en Europe occidentale du XVIe au XVIIIe siècle." *Rhétoriques méditerranéennes* 7 (2003): 95–120.
Sapiro, Gisele. "L'importation de la Litterature Hebraique en France: entre Communautarisme et Universalisme." *Actes de la recherche en science sociales* 144.4 (Septembre 2002): 80–98.

Iulia Dondorici
Redefining and Integrating Jewish Writers into the Study of Historical Avant-Garde(s)

I will address the central question of this volume – how to integrate modern Jewish literatures into all areas of literary studies – by referring to the participation of Jewish writers in the Romanian and French avant-garde movements Dada and Surrealism in the first half of the twentieth century. After a short overview on the state of this research, I will offer a case study concerning Jewish writers of Romanian origins who emigrated to France, and more particularly Ilarie Voronca (1903–1946).

1 State of research on the Jewish dimensions of the historical avant-garde movements

In a recent study entitled *Jewish Aspects in Avant-Garde. Between Rebellion and Revelation*, the editors Mark Gelber and Sami Sjöberg conclude that, for all the important research from the last few decades, "no serious attempt has been made to understand the Jewish dimension of the avant-garde", the phenomenon as such remaining "largely uncharted". (Gelber and Sjöberg 2017, 1). Seeking a rather comprehensive answer to the question "how Jewish studies and avant-garde studies may benefit reciprocally from each other as interdisciplinary fields that complement each other's methodological repertoire" (Gelber and Sjöberg 2017, 12), both editors emphasize the necessity of a comparative approach which goes beyond micro-history, noting that "a method to clarify how one can approach both the avant-garde and Jewishness together on a more general level is still lacking". (Gelber and Sjöberg 2017, 12)[1]

As Steven E. Aschheim acknowledges, most of the attempts that have been made to explain the prominent Jewish participation in the avant-garde(s) are

---

[1] However, the complex and sometimes contradictory relationships between Jews and the avant-garde have generated important research in recent decades. Thus, in the above mentioned volume, Steven E. Aschheim identifies five major topics of study in this field: the role of writers and artists with a Jewish background within the various avant-garde movements, the role of Jewish cultures in the avant-garde(s), explicitly "Jewish" avant-garde projects, specific avant-garde attitudes to Jews, as well as anti-Semitic representations of Jews, particularly related to their participation in the avant-garde movements. (Aschheim 2017, 253)

OpenAccess. © 2020 Iulia Dondorici, published by De Gruyter. This work is licensed under the Creative Commons Attribution-NonCommercial-NoDerivatives 4.0 License.
https://doi.org/10.1515/9783110619003-019

"rather problematic". (Aschheim 2017, 253) The most frequent approach tend to see the anti-nationalism of the avant-garde as "particularly inviting" for Jewish artists and writers. (Gelber and Sjöberg 2017, 3) While this argument might be pertinent up to a point, Aschheim rightly points out that "the Jewish relationship to both 'official' and avant-garde culture and politics was generally tied to the complex dynamics, the possibilities and limitations of integration and assimilation". (Aschheim 2017, 258)

This last point seems particularly pertinent with respect to the Romanian and Francophone avant-garde movements. Given the Jewish belonging of an overwhelming majority of writers and artists constituting these avant-garde groups, most scholars feel that an explication is needed for this phenomenon. Thus, the wide Jewish participation is considered to be the effect of the national(ist) ideology which, in the first half of the twentieth century, did indeed dominate all spheres of public life in Romania.[2] In this context, Vasile Morar among others points to a more structural exclusion of Jewish writers from the definition of Romanian national literature and consequently from its literary canon and literary histories.[3] He even goes so far as to consider the Jewish appeal for avant-garde literature and for modernity at large as an intrinsic feature of Jewish literatures in Romania.[4]

Nationalism and antisemitism in the Romanian society serve also to explain an overwhelming majority of Jewish-Romanian avant-garde writers chose to emigrate to Paris in the 1920s and 1930s.[5] Beginning to write in French, so the argument continues, they successfully integrated themselves in the French avant-

---

[2] S. Morar 2018, 178 and Stern 2017, 35–49.

[3] This is particularly striking in the first two histories of Romanian literature that appeared in the first half of the twentieth century: Eugen Lovinescu: *Istoria literaturii române contemporane* (3rd vol., 1927) and George Călinescu: *Istoria literaturii române de la origini până în prezent* (1941). The canon that Lovinescu and Călinescu have established has been reproduced with little change in all subsequent literary histories, including the most recent one, published by the influential critic Nicolae Manolescu. S. Nicolae Manolescu: *Istoria critică a literaturii române*. Pitești 2008: Editura Paralela 45.

[4] S. Morar 2006, 14–15. One of the unintended effects of this kind of argument is the complete marginalization of a large number of Jewish writers who did not (or not substantially) join the avant-gardes, like Mihail Sebastian, Isac Peltz or Sergiu Dan, just to mention a few.

[5] In fact, we are often confronted with a non-linear migratory movement, as many avant-garde participants used to go back and forth between Bucharest and Paris in the 1920s and the 1930s. Moreover, during World War Two, they had to leave Paris either to find a refuge in the Southern of France (Ilarie Voronca, Claude Sernet, Benjamin Fondane, Tristan Tzara) or to leave Europe for North and South America. Others, like Céline Arnauld, had an errant, nomadic life in their childhood and youth and settled down in Paris, only to be obliged to flee in the face of the Shoah.

garde movements, so far as to act as leaders of those movements: Tristan Tzara for the Dada movement and Isidore Isou for the *lettrisme* stand as paradigmatic examples of this phenomenon. Morar considers that the emigré Jewish writers from Romania have received in France – "the quintessentially cosmopolitan home of avant-gardism" – "wide recognition as major figures of modern poetry and art" (Morar 2018, 181). Sjöberg goes even further, stating that "on account of their linguistic abilities and aesthetic sensibility, Romanian Jewish writers were not as a rule to be found on the margins of such French avant-gardes as Dada, Surrealism or Lettrism" but, quite the contrary, "these figures were at the very core of the French avant-garde canon from the late 1910s to the early 1950s." (Sjöberg 2019)

If these arguments doubtless contain a grain of truth, they are nonetheless problematic in their presuppositions. Thus, Jewish participation is considered to be the result of the somehow 'evident' anti-national(ist) character of the avant-gardes, though it would be more correct to acknowledge that it was on the account of the wide Jewish participation in the Bucharest avant-gardes that these movements movements acquired their strong anti-national(ist) character. Moreover, the implicit oppositions of transnationalism versus nationalism, and of (nationalist) Romania and (cosmopolitan) France are false. Indeed, transnationalism / internationalism and nationalism have coexisted in a majority of European avant-garde movements and groups, including those in Paris.[6] Instead, it would be more accurate to affirm that the undeniably wide Jewish participation in the Romanian and Francophone avant-garde during the first half of the twentieth century happened in spite of avant-garde nationalism and even antisemitism, and adapted to it in different ways in Bucharest and Paris.

But, what is perhaps even more urgent to question here is the very need to account for the wide Jewish participation in the Bucharest-based avant-garde movements. This need presumes the often unconscious, but widespread idea that only "Romanian" (basically in the sense of ethnic belonging) writers are supposed to be the main (if not the single) agents of literary activities developing within the borders of a national territory.

I will finish this part of my article by pointing to a more nuanced argument in the context of Jewishness and avant-gardes coming from the sociology of literature, and more particularly from the theory of literary field by the French so-

---

6 As far as phenomena of antisemitism and nationalism are concerned, one should avoid the risk of a too clearcut opposition between Romania and France, as the French literary field as well, including the avant-gardes, was marked by antisemitic and national(ist) attitudes. As Thomas Hunkeler recently showed, a wide range of European avant-garde, including the Paris-based movements, were clearly marked by nationalist tendencies and attitudes. (Hunkeler 2018)

ciologist Pierre Bourdieu. Thus, Bourdieu states that in nineteenth-century France, in the forefront of the literary field there are "bourgeois dévoyés ou déclassés qui possèdent toutes les propriétés des dominants moins une, parents pauvres des grandes dynasties bourgeoises, aristocrates ruinés ou en déclin, étrangers ou membres de minorités stigmatisées comme les juifs". (Bourdieu 1992, 88) The sociological research of Anna Boschetti and Norbert Bandier confirm a similar composition of the literary avant-garde at the beginning of the twentieth century.[7] Thus, Anna Boschetti notes that in the Paris-based avant-garde groups there is "un grand nombre d'étrangers: Apollinaire lui-même, Cendrars, Beaudin, Guilbeaux, les futuristes. Apollinaire, Cendrars, Marinetti, Salomon et Carco ont mené, dans leur enfance ou dans leur jeunesse, une vie errante et cosmopolite. Max Jacob est juif." (Boschetti 2001, 35) In this respect, Jewishness is no exclusive or singular attribute of the avant-garde agents, but migration and foreignness at large are significant factors as well.

2 Jewish writers, Romanian and French literary histories

Ilarie Voronca can be considered one of the most original and prolific avant-garde writers in either Romanian or French. In Bucharest he was co-founder of two of the most significant avant-garde magazines, *75HP* (1924) and *Integral* (1925–1928). Later on, he was a steady contributor to the main Surrealist revue *unu* (1928–1932). After making his debut in 1922 in the most prestigious literary circle of the time, *Sburătorul,* with its eponymous magazine – both led by the influential literary critic and historian Eugen Lovinescu – Voronca published an impressive number of volumes not only with different small avant-garde publishers in Bucharest, but also with more prestigious publishers such as "Vremea" and "Cultura Națională". Voronca thus had a well-established reputation in the Romanian literary field at the moment of his emigration to France. After moving back and forth between Bucharest and Paris from 1925 to 1932, Voronca and his wife, Colomba Voronca, finally settled down in Paris in 1933.

A similar development involves two other Jewish avant-garde poets, Benjamin Fundoianu/Benjamin Fondane (1898–1944) and Mihail Cosma/Claude Ser-

---

[7] S. Boschetti 2001, 33–35; Bandier 1999, 271–336. As for the Surrealist group around Breton, its core members were French, most of them even Parisian.

net (1902–1968).⁸ Both were members of the group "Integral" and steady contributors to its review. Although they emigrated to France much earlier in their careers, they created a bilingual literary work and participated equally in avant-garde endeavors in Bucharest and Paris. All three worked as literary translators (from Romanian to French and vice versa) and acted as cultural mediators. As Sernet left Bucharest for Padova already as an undergraduate student and moved from there to Paris in 1925, his literary work in Romanian is much less significant than his writing in French. Fondane left for Paris as a young poet, in 1923, after an extensive engagement with avant-garde theater in Bucharest – he had co-founded the avant-garde theater group "Insula" with the stage director Armand Pascal. His first book of literary essays, *Imagini şi cărţi din Franţa* (1921), published with the prestigious house "Cultura Naţională", generated a heated debate and made his author known in literary circles overnight. From Paris, Fondane contributed to influential Romanian avant-garde reviews like *Contimporanul* (1923–1933), *Integral* and *unu*.⁹

These itineraries clearly show that all three poets – Ilarie Voronca, Benjamin Fundoianu/Fondane und Mihail Cosma/Claude Sernet – were in different degrees deeply integrated in the Romanian literary field of their time. At the so-called "pôle restraint" of this field, where the literary avant-gardes must be situated according to Bourdieu, these poets definitely were main actors. Thus, they co-founded the most significant avant-garde groups and reviews in Bucharest in the 1920s and 1930s: *75HP*, *Punct*, *Integral* and contributed to other main reviews: *Contimporanul* and *unu*. Emigration to Paris did not interrupt their literary and artistic engagement in Bucharest. In the Romanian capital, they seem to have had good publication opportunities, at specific avant-garde publishers as well as at big, well-established publishing houses. They were part of a large network of artists and writers, and disposed of valuable contacts and connections in the literary and artistic field – in a word, of high social and cultural capital – such as they could founf groups and reviews that remained active for many years.

Thus, it seems that the widely spread antisemitic and nationalist attitudes in the Romanian artistic and literary world, instead of inhibiting avant-garde activities in general and the engagement of Jewish writers in them in particular, acted as a kind of catalyst for them. These avant-gardes groups instead seem to have developed into an inclusive, protective space for aesthetic (and implicitly polit-

---

8 Both changed their pen names after emigration. At the beginning of their careers in Bucharest Fondane signed Benjamin Fundoianu and Sernet, Mihail Cosma.
9 In 1930, "Cultura naţională" published a volume with Fondane's Romanian poems from 1917 to 1923 under the title *Privelişti. Poeme 1917–1923*.

ical) activities, an experimental space for otherwise marginalized Jewish writers. In this context, reviews like *Contimporanul* and *Integral* openly denounced the antisemitic and nationalist attitudes in Romania and fought against them. If the response of the literary and artistic establishment was not enthusiastic, this is part of a general rejection and even aggressive attitude towards avant-garde movements throughout Europe. However, as far as individual writers are concerned, a wide positive reception was possible in Romania. This was the case for Ilarie Voronca at the end of the 1920s and the beginning of the 1930s, before and about the time of his emigration to Paris.[10]

This analysis leads us to the conclusion that, in addition to the widespread nationalism and antisemitism of Romanian society, some other possible reasons for the emigration of avant-garde Jewish writers from Romania to France in the 1920s and 1930s should be taken into consideration.[11] One further reason might have been their legitimate desire to gain recognition in a country that was (and still is) perceived as the very center of an international and transnational literary and artistic avant-garde. The emigration option was clearly facilitated by the multilingualism of the writers as well as by a large network of relationships they had successfully established all over Europe and even beyond. Indeed, through the group Integral and the eponymous review, as well as the international exhibitions previously organized in Bucharest, Voronca, Fondane and Sernet were well aware of contemporary avant-gardes throughout Europe, being even able to offer a platform of expression to numerous fellow writers and artists.[12]

Voronca's publications shortly after his settlement in Paris as well as the collaborative work in which he was constantly engaged clearly support this statement. Thus, the poet had almost all his volumes illustrated by artists like Sonia and Robert Delaunay, Victor Brauner, Marc Chagall and Constantin Brâncuși. Voronca translated into French and published two of his last Romanian vol-

---

10 Thus, Voronca's last volumes in Romanian had numerous reviews, written by young as well as by established literary critics (Eugen Ionescu, Emil Gulian, Pompiliu Constantinescu, Perpessicius) in influential literary magazines like *Romania literară*, *Vremea* or *Viața românească*.
11 This is not to downplay the important role of antisemitic and nationalist attitudes in this context. However,Voronca's emigration to Paris clearly took place in the context of a deep existential crisis, probably reinforced by the fact that from 1932 the Romanian avant-garde scene was also in a transitory stage, with hardly any magazines and organized groups.
12 Among the international contributors to *Integral* there were Sonia und Robert Delaunay, Alice Halicka, Georges Ribemont-Dessaignes, Joseph Delteil, Max Jacob, Roger Vitrac, Tristan Tzara, Marcel Raval, Céline Arnauld, Paul Dermée, Pierre Reverdy, Michel Seuphor, to mention just a few.

umes: *Peter Schlemihl* (1932) and *Patmos* (1933).¹³ In 1933, his volume *Ulise* – perhaps the volume which received most positive reception during his life as well as posthumously – was translated into French by the avant-garde poet Roger Vailland, one of the core members of the Surrealist group "Grand Jeu" and prefaced by Georges Ribemont-Dessaignes, well-known for his Dadaist and more generally avant-garde activities.¹⁴ After these translations, the volume *Permis de séjour* (1935) was Voronca's first volume written directly in French. While *Ulysse dans la cité* appeared with La Sagittaire – the Surrealist publisher in Paris *par excellence* – all the other three volumes mentioned were published either "en compte d'auteur" or in small magazine collections like "Les Cahiers du *Journal des poètes*", the latter based in Brussels. The same is true for all of Voronca's subsequent publications.¹⁵ Similarly, his literary works have only been re-published sporadically after his death in 1946.¹⁶

As for Fondane and Sernet, their situation was not much different. Fondane was able to publish his first book only five years after emigrating, in the collection of the avant-garde magazine *Documents internationaux de l'Esprit Nouveau* (1927); his following two volumes of poetry appeared in the collection of the Brussels-based "Les Cahiers du *Journal des Poètes*". Three years after arriving in Paris, Sernet co-founded the group and the magazine *Discontinuité* (1928). The fact that *Discontinuité* had only one issue, and that afterwards Sernet needed nine further years to be able to publish his next volume, signify his poor social and cultural capital in Paris.¹⁷

If it is true that Voronca as well as Fondane and Sernet were able to integrate themselves in the French avant-garde field – basically because of their adopting French as the language of their further literary creation as well as their participation in a large artistic network in the Parisian field – they nonetheless participated exclusively in marginal groups. Thus, they were at all times excluded from the main avant-garde group, the Surrealist group around Breton, which from the beginning of the 1920s dominated the avant-garde field in Paris. Neither Voronca

---

13 Both appeared in French in 1934, the first as *Poèmes parmi les hommes* and the second under the same title.
14 Voronca himself co-translated this volume.
15 Sagittaire will publish one more book by Voronca, *La beauté de ce monde*, in 1940.
16 A new edition of *La poésie commune* appeared in 1979 (Paris: Plasma), *Journal inédit suivi de Beauté de ce monde* appeared in 2018 (Paris: Les Hommes sans Épaules éditions), *Petit Manuel du parfait bonheur* and *Ulysse dans la cité* were republished in 2019 (Paris: Cambourakis and Paris: Non Lieu respectively).
17 *Commémorations* (1937) and *Un jour et une nuit* (1938) were published by Tschad and Sagesse respectively, two small Paris-based publishers.

nor Sernet or Fondane were part of it or established close relationships with any of its influential members. Whereas the group that was best anchored and most powerful in the Parisian literary field at the time was evidently close to non-French migrant writers, the three Jewish poets approached rather marginal Parisian and Belgian Francophone avant-garde groups and reviews like the Surrealist *Le Phare de Neuilly* (1933), the group *Discontinuité* (1928), most of whose members were non-French migrant writers and artists, the group *Le Grand Jeu* (1925– 1928) or *Le Journal des Poètes,* a Francophone journal more generally committed to modernist aesthetics without committing itself to a specific avant-garde affiliation.

While scholars keep mentioning the success they enjoyed in France, the position of Voronca, Fondane and Sernet in the French literary field in the 1930s and 1940s as described here, as well as their hardly existent place in the French literary history until today, might well cast serious doubts on this statement. So, as far as their positions in the literary field are concerned, emigration hardly constituted an improvement – as can be seen with respect to the kind of publishing houses they are able to place their volumes, the magazines to which they contribute as well as their engagement in avant-garde groups.

In this respect, not even Tristan Tzara is a genuine exception. Thomas Hunkeler, in the above mentioned study on the nationalism of the European avant-garde, clearly shows Tzara's marginalization in the French literary field of the 1920s and 1930s. Largely concerted by "Breton et ses amis", this marginalization even seems to have been part of Breton's and Aragon's strategy of presenting Paris Dada as a genuinely French movement and thus gaining more acceptance for the avant-garde in general and for the emerging Surrealist movement in particular. (Hunkeler 2018, 231–237) If Tristan Tzara has indeed an important place in the memory of the French avant-garde today, this is rather due to his later approach to the Surrealist group around Breton as well as to the enormous cultural and social capital he had managed to acquire in the Zurich Dada. The huge Dada archive he possessed in Paris and the intense (auto)promotion work he was able to do worldwide after WW II was also decisive in this unique recuperation process, so that Tzara can now be largely perceived as the "chef de file" of the Dadaist movement in Paris.

The fact that Tzara wrote almost his entire literary work in French also facilitated his perception as a Francophone, if not French, poet. This is also true for Sernet and Fondane, so that they could be re-published and studied in the context of the French avant-garde, though as marginal actors. This is much less the case for Voronca, who wrote as much of his poetry in Romanian as in French, and is rather perceived as a bilingual writer, belonging to the Romanian and to the French literature as well. Given that literary history is still mostly written in a national framework, this double bind, linked to migration and multilingualism, proved rather a disadvantage. Thus, the research on Romanian avant-gardes retains mainly Voronca's activities in Bucharest and his literature in Romanian, while the little research in French on him focuses on his poetry in this language. As the translations are still missing, his entire literary work is available neither in Romanian nor in French. However, as far as the histories and more general research work on the Bucharest-based avant-gardes are concerned, Voronca and, to a lesser degree, Sernet and Fondane are perceived as main actors of these movements. Their central positions in the Romanian avant-garde histories are reinforced by their (real or alleged) success in Paris – their emigration into a more prestigious, "Western" literary field was and still is a source of literary and cultural capital in the context of a 'small', 'peripheral' literature such as the Romanian.

3 Migrant perspectives on Paris in Voronca's avant-garde poetry

Voronca's emigration to Paris meant a turning point in his life, and this significance was thoroughly documented in his poetry. As his enthusiastic engagement in such various avant-garde projects as *75HP*, *Punct*, *Integral* and *unu* shows, Voronca was not the kind of poet committed to a single movement or to a unique aesthetic. On the contrary, he experimented with various avant-garde poetics and directions, including Dada, Constructivism, Surrealism, as well as Integralism.[18] As was the case for Surrealist poets around André Breton, the city of Paris exerted a constant fascination on Voronca, who dealt with it in at least two of his major poems, *Ulysse dans la cité* (1933) and *Permis de séjour* (1935). The first was published in Romanian in 1928; the latter is Voronca's first poem written and published in French after establishing himself in Paris. As for his view on the French metropole, the two poems – separated by the experience of emigration – could not be more different, as I will show in a short comparative reading.[19]

---

[18] For the development of Voronca's poetry and his avant-garde activities in Romania, s. Pop 2015.
[19] Pop also states a radical difference between Voronca's poetry before and after 1931 and the subsequent emigration, but in order to claim that the latter does not any longer belongs to the avant-garde: "Ilarie Voronca as militant avant-garde poet existed only in the Romanian cultural context, during a period in his life when he was enthusiastically engaged with experiments in 'extreme' modernity, fighting against all 'conventions', whether stereotypes in poetic language or the conformism of the 'bourgeois' spirit" (Pop 2015, 15).

As contemporary critics noticed, *Ulysse dans la cité* is a modern reworking of the ancient myth and a literary documentation of the poet's life as a traveller – a traveller between Bucharest and Paris and a wanderer through these both cities. Inspired by Apollinaire's *Zone* as well as by Reverdy's conception of the poetical image, Voronca's poem shows an enchanted wanderer, whose zigzag movement encompasses various spaces. He explores small provincial towns as well as the metropole, countryside and an urban space depicted with its large central boulevards as well as with its peripheral spaces. Paris becomes an explosion of colors and sounds. The urban space embeds all of nature and extends to the universe, whereas the different, often disparate elements engage in a sensual, erotic relationship.

This modern Ulysses accomplishes his journey by arriving in Paris, a city that he recognizes and that calls forth memories and images from other journeys and past stays here. These last lines of the poem depict Paris as the quintessence of the modern metropole:[20]

> paris oraș ca o volută ca o amintire
> cum îți cunosc mansardele barurile cinematografele [...]
> piața concordiei ca un pântec se rotunjește se ridică
> bulevardele sună panoplia cuvintelor în luceferi
> desigur cerul sărută acoperișul bisericilor cazărmilor
> și turnul eiffel își întinde gâtul
> sângele acensoarelor circulă în marile hoteluri [...]
> paris ulei sfânt pentru încheietura gândului
> oscilează pe harta apusului ca un transatlantic
> te stingi ca o mătase pe buzele toamnei (Voronca 2003, 40–41)

> paris a city like a volute like a memory
> how well do I know your attics bars cinemas [...]
> place concorde round like a belly standing up
> the boulevards jingle the panoply of words in the stars
> of course the sky kisses the roofs of the churches of the barracks
> the eiffel tower stretches its neck
> the blood of the lifts circulates through the grand hotels [...]
> paris holy oil for the accomplishment of thoughts
> oscillates on the sunset's map like a transatlantic ship
> you set like silk on autumn's lips[21]

---

[20] Ion Pop points out the "overflow of images" in Voronca's poem. He writes: "The topos of the magical city with its illuminated billboards and colorful streets and crowds returns again and again in Voronca's verses, which suggest a particularly urban type of dynamism, rich with bold images." (Pop 2015, 10)

[21] Working translation mine.

Permis de séjour signifies a radical change of perspective on Paris, with the theme of migration as the focus of the poem. The metropole is now depicted in its nameless, poor, peripheral places. While in the previous volume the welcoming, embracing metropolitan space was populated by the poet's friends (sometimes mentioned with their real names) and by inhabitants participating in the urban daily life, solitude and fear now take hold of a disenchanted, cold space, that no longer resonates with the narrator's feelings and his experiences as a migrant:

> Dans ce monde nouveau, j'avais peur, je marchais doucement.
> Je ne savais pas comment il fallait me tenir, comment
> Il fallait respirer? Et mes mains? Que devais-je en faire?
> Ballantes, elles se heurtaient aux murs, aux réverbères,
> De grand morceau de ciel empêchaient mes mouvements,
> Il fallait tout recommencer. Tout réapprendre. [...] (Voronca 1935, 15)

And:

> On pourrait très bien monsieur, vous engager,
> Mais notre maison ne prend plus d'étrangers,
> Ni de poètes... J'avais faim. Un brouillard montait vers la cité.
> Loin ou près, les étoiles faisaient leur publicité. (Voronca 1935, 25–26)

The travelling and wandering poet from *Ulysse dans la cité* has now become the wandering Jew and the poems in *Permis de séjour* are conceived around the figure of the poet as a perpetual stranger, the stranger par excellence. A poet-narrator obsessed by the impossibility of making his words heard, dominated by the fear of disappearing without leaving any tracks of his passage.[22]

The urban space is divided into rich and poor quarters, and he, like the other *étrangers* clearly belong to the latter. The French word "étranger" (engl. "stranger", "foreigner") designates the status of the narrator in a double way: he is a foreigner, a migrant and a person who, as a poet, incorporates strangeness and remains strange to this city. The emigration is by no means the beginning of a new life, the streets of Paris rather recall death, as they resemble cemeteries. Thus, the narrator is continually in search of a refuge from the new world he has arrived in, while the rain is falling and the wind keeps blowing:

---

22 "Ici, comme partout ailleurs, ma voix est étrangère, / Partout je suis l'errant. Je ne serai nulle part / Celui qu'on attend. Il faut que je pense au départ" (Voronca 1935, 26).

> [...] Je n'avais moi-même nul abri. L'eau,
> La même eau, tombait triste, noirâtre comme dans la ville
> Lointaine et pauvre d'où je venais. Nulle île
> Pour fuir cette pluie... Il faisait froid. (Voronca 1935, 16)

The new home is not much different from the old one that he left behind, and is actually no home at all. Both cities are thus infused by an imaginary third space, a kind of paradise or a social utopia – the island and the sea:

> Nulle part un toit hospitalier, une mer bien heureuse
> Caressant doucement les joues des rives lumineuses. [...]
> Des gens très doux, très polis seraient descendus vers les plages,
> Et moi parmi eux tous, emmêlant nos visages,
> Planant entre les vitres claires, hautes des maisons,
> Frères tous, nous tenant par la main, si lumineux, si bons.
> Mais non, ici comme là-bas cette rivière morne,
> Ces souffles citadins, ces tristesses sans bornes,
> Cette ville de boue et de brume dont le nom
> Qu'importe? fût-il Paris, Londres ou Capetown.
> Ici comme ailleurs, ces maisons qui s'écroulent
> Et ces ponts sous lesquels un jour laiteux s'écoule. (Voronca 1935, 24–25)

The social utopia depicted here as an imaginary space immersed into light, a welcoming space where people behave like "brothers", announces a new phase in Voronca's poetry, inaugurated by his next volume, *La poésie commune*. There, his preoccupation for the life of ordinary people leads to a radical reworking of his poetics, so that Voronca's subsequent avant-garde poetry is meant to be accessible to ordinary people and to liberate them. At the same time, it announces a future time of happiness and brotherhood. Through a series of bright images, this utopia is clearly opposed to the darkness and coldness of the real city. It is not the Paris at night full of fascination and wonders (*le merveilleux*) praised by the Surrealists and by Voronca's Ulysses, but a darkness signifying loneliness, sadness, fear and material misery. The metropole has lost not only all its magic, but also its identity, and it is not the desired arrival point anymore, but seems to be interchangeable with any other metropolis like London or Capetown. The last verse recalls the refrain of Apollinaire's poem *Le Pont Mirabeau*, but in a "milky" daylight, the landscape has lost all its beauty and melancholy.

The distance that separate Ulysses from the wandering Jew – both mythical figures that the poet embodies – is clearer than ever in the following verses:

> Je ne vous imposerai pas des villes, des rues,
> Je ne tracerais pas la route d'autres migrations,
> Je ne fonderai nulle famille, nulle nation [...] (Voronca 1935, 33)

And:

> Je sais que cette argile n'est pas à moi. Non pas.
> Mais elle n'est à personne. La trace de ce pas
> N'est-elle pas plus libre que le pied qui l'a faite? (Voronca 1935, 41–42)

If, as David Pindar claims, the Surrealist movement is concerned with "resisting nationalistic and imperialist geographical imaginations" (Pindar 2009, 88), then Voronca's imagery of the modern metropole from the perspective of the stranger, or the migrant, errant poet is to be subsumed as an integral part of the Surrealist and more generally avant-garde imaginary and its thematic reservoir.

4 Conclusions: Jewish writers as integral part of the transnational avant-garde(s)

The 'problematic' state of research on Jewish writers in the Romanian and French avant-garde(s) reflects more general theoretical and methodological shortcomings of existing scholarship on the avant-garde movements. Firstly, as more and more scholars point out, the avant-garde movements continue to be studied within different national philologies and/or in a comparatist framework, thus being unable to account for their transnational, global character. It thus comes as no surprise that the question of Jews and/in the avant-garde(s) has hardly been explored in general or overview studies on the avant-gardes, nor can we find it in theoretical studies.

I will conclude by claiming that only a transnational and global framework for the study of the avant-gardes can account for the Jewish dimensions of these movements. Moreover, this transnational framework of (historical and theoretical) analysis of the avant-garde(s) must integrate the following two phenomena as its constitutive elements: migration as a global process, constitutive for the avant-garde phenomenon as well as the multi- and translingualism of the avant-garde(s).

As shown here, writers and artists with a Jewish historical experience stand for a specific form of diasporic and migrant belonging which is crucial for the emergence and the development of avant-garde movements. Avant-garde movements in Bucharest and in Paris are multilingual avant-garde(s). Whereas monolingualism is rather an exception, basically characteristic for those Paris based groups which had hardly migrants in their rows, in concepts of the avant-garde it is still regarded as the norm. The multilingualism of Jewish writers integrates itself into avant-garde aesthetics and practices, and a transnational framework would allow to account for a variety of forms of multilingualism more specific for Jewish writers in a wide range of local contexts.

Bibliography

Aschheim, Steven E. "The Avant-Garde and the Jews." *Jewish Aspects in Avant-Garde. Between Rebellion and Revelation.* Eds. Mark H. Gelber and Sami Sjöberg. Berlin: De Gruyter, 2017. 253–273.
Bandier, Pierre. *Sociologie du surréalisme*. Paris: La Dispute, 1999.
Boschetti, Anna. *La poésie partout. Apollinaire, homme époque (1898–1918)*. Paris: Seuil, 2001.
Bourdieu, Pierre. *Les règles de l'art. Genèse et structure du champ littéraire*. Paris: Seuil, 1992.
Gelber, Mark H. and Sami Sjöberg. "Introduction." *Jewish Aspects in Avant-Garde. Between Rebellion and Revelation.* Eds. Mark H. Gelber and Sami Sjöberg. Berlin: DeGruyter, 2017. 1–21.
Hunkeler, Thomas. *Paris et le nationalisme des avant-gardes (1909–1924)*. Paris: Hermann, 2018.
Lascu, Mădălina (ed.). *Epistolar avangardist*. Bucharest: Tracus Arte, 2012.
Morar, Ovidiu. *Scriitori evrei din România*. Bucharest: Ideea Europeană, 2006.
Morar, Ovidiu. "Cosmopolites, Deracinated, *étranjuifs:* Romanian Jews in the International Avant- Garde." *Romanian Literature as World Literature*. Eds. Mircea Martin and Andrei Terian. New York: Bloomsbury Academic, 2018. 175–195
Pindar, David. "Surrealism. Surrealist Geographies." *International Encyclopedia of Human Geography*. Volume 11. Eds. Rob Kitchin and Nigel Thrift. Amsterdam: Elsevier, 2009. 87–94.
Pop, Ion. "Ilarie Voronca and the Romanian Literary Avant-Garde." *Dada/Surrealism* 20 (2015). https://doi.org/10.17077/0084–9537.1297 (26 November 2019). 1–16.
Sjöberg, Sami. "An Other Transnationalism. Romanian Jewish Emigrants in Francophone Avant-Garde Literature." *French Studies*. 73.1 (2019): 33–49.
Stern, Radu. "Jews and the Avant-Garde: The Case of Romania." *Jewish Aspects in Avant-Garde. Between Rebellion and Revelation.* Eds. Mark H. Gelber and Sami Sjöberg. Berlin: De Gruyter, 2017. 35–51.
Voronca, Ilarie. *Ulise. Brățara nopților*. Cluj-Napoca: Dacia, 2003 [1928].
Voronca, Ilarie. *Permis de séjour*. Paris: Éditions R.– A. Corrêa, 1935.

Uri S. Cohen
Primo Levi: Between Literature and the World

While teaching at Columbia University in the first decade of the new millennium, I always concluded the introductory course on literature and the humanities with Primo Levi's masterpiece *If This Is a Man* (1947). I felt it was proper to end such a course in Auschwitz, indicating a form of a trajectory as well as the beginning of a new world, beyond a hallowed but hollow tradition.

While there are many reasons to admire Primo Levi, one of them is that his writings stand, like Fascism itself with the kind of education designed by Giovanni Gentile, at the end of the humanistic tradition as the Great Books course conceives it (Sani 2008; Isnenghi 1979). He also stands at the beginning of the new era that comes after Auschwitz not as a Jewish or a European event, but as a world event. Growing up under Fascism, Levi, like other Italian Jews, moved from an assimilated perspective where Judaism was a trivial matter to one where it was all that mattered. In this sense, his formation is bound to the classic tradition, which sees the heart of Europe (and hence the world) growing out of Italy twice, with the Roman Empire and the Renaissance. Man in the humanistic tradition is therefore at the very heart of what is no more after Auschwitz, along with the inevitability of both Europe and the world. Staggering out the gate when the Russians arrive, Levi is a bearer of ill news, a *mala novella*. Witness to what the idea of Man has done to Man, he inquires if this is a Man simultaneously about perpetrators and victims, masters and slaves, the drowned and the saved, Odysseus and his perished companions.

Canonical literary texts encompass multiple perspectives and present challenges to readers of many generations. In this sense, no one can deny that the tradition that invented Man and filled him with purpose, liberties and mental spaces, also came with him to Auschwitz.[1] Indeed, at least in some sense oppressors and oppressed shared both a literary heritage and a religious tradition, a literary Gray Zone. Ironically enough, Levi only became aware of his Jewishness as a textual tradition when faced with the racial laws of 1938, when Levi and a group of friends read for the first time texts from the tradition that came to define them (Levi 1984). I would argue that *If this is a Man* engages, not without irony, with both traditions as they end up with him at Auschwitz.

---

[1] For a discussion that repositions Fanon as a radical humanist see Gilroy 2010.

Levi stands at the end of this tradition as a prisoner. The classic tradition is employed to tell his tale of enslavement as a story of the world, giving both form to narrative and intelligibility to experience. Booted from a train after an unimaginable journey, a quote from Dante becomes the first mediator of the drastic experience. The direct references are present in such a manner that even as minor informants cross his path, Dante's writings continue as the frame for the representation of the experience, so that when the protagonist enters the gate, the gates of the Inferno are already invoked:

> The journey did not last more than twenty minutes. Then the truck stopped, and we saw a large gate and, above it, a sign, brightly illuminated (the memory still jolts me in my dreams): *Arbeit Macht Frei*, Work makes us free. [...] This is hell [*Inferno*]. Today, in our time, hell must be like this. A huge, empty room: we are tired, standing on our feet, and there is a tap that drips and the water cannot be drunk, and we wait for something that will certainly be terrible, and nothing happens and nothing continues to happen. (Levi 2015, 1:18)

In contrast to the scene in Dante's "Nel mezzo del cammin di nostra vita" [In the middle of the journey of our life] (Dante 1996, 26–27) in the first canto of the Inferno, Levi's protagonist reads a disheartening message that fills him with a chill that returns to jolt him in his sleep of the returned. It would seem that Levi the author has returned home, to find the camp returning to him. In Canto 3, Dante can see justice, where Levi sees nothing but an empty room where there is no why, as he is soon told. Dante the author remained in exile and never returned to Florence, but Dante the protagonist of the *Divina Commedia* experiences the horrors as intelligible, an expression of God's justice and love for the world:

> Through me the way into the suffering city,
> through me the way to the eternal pain,
> through me the way that runs among the lost.
> Justice urged on my high artificer;
> my maker was divine authority,
> the highest wisdom, and the primal love.
> Before me nothing but eternal things
> were made, and i endure eternally.
> Abandon every hope, who enter here. (Dante 1996, 55)

The words of the *Divina Commedia* oscillate between the old and the new. God is not to be found. Instead, there is a system devised by Man to enslave his fellow Man; work whose scope is death. Yes, the city is suffering but one, unfortunately, cannot abandon hope and the rest just falls away into cynicism. In Levi's seminal book, the sound of Dante's gate collapsing under the weight of a new infernal machination is represented in a manner that is not easily accessible to all readers. In November 1959, in one of his first public interventions after *If this is a Man* was republished by Enaudi in 1958, Levi addressed the matter. Speaking to a public of ex-deportees, like himself, he elaborated on the cynical motto "Arbeit Macht Frei":

> As everybody knows, these words could be read above the entrance gate of the Lager at Auschwitz. Their literal meaning is "Work makes you free." Their true meaning is much less clear; it cannot but leave us puzzled, and it lends itself to a number of observations. (Levi 2015, 2: 1134)

Levi begins with the literal translation, identical to the one he had used in his book in the passage quoted above, but something more needs to be said. The urgency is apparent, this being arguably the first matter Levi addresses as an Author – with the authority that came with the recognition following the republication of his book. The essay spells out in plain words what was implied in the literary text through its interaction with Dante:

> [...W]e must assume that that sentence—in the mind of whoever dictated it—was not intended to be understood in its basic sense, in other words in its obvious meaning as a proverb-moral. It is more likely that the sentence had an ironic meaning, that it arose from that heavy, arrogant, grim vein of humor to which Germans hold the secret, and that only in German has a name. Translated into explicit language, the sentence, it seems, would sound something like this:
> "Work is humiliation and suffering, and it is not suitable for us, Herrenvolk, a nation of gentlemen and heroes, but it is for you, enemies of the Third Reich. The freedom that awaits you is death." (Levi 2015, 2: 1134)

Levi is unusually quick to characterize the sentence "Arbeit Macht Frei" as deeply and perhaps exclusively characteristic of the Germans, underlining that it expresses and is an expression of Germans as he had come to know them. The words are not even a lie but chilly irony, the essence of the "Lager" and in turn the essence of Fascism: the final exposure of every lie Fascism ever told:

> So the camps were, in substance, "pilot plants," harbingers of the future assigned to Europe in the Nazi plans. In light of these considerations, sentences like "Work makes you free" at Auschwitz, or like "To each his own" at Buchenwald, take on a precise and sinister meaning. They are portents of the new Tablets of the Law, dictated by the master to the slave, and true only for the latter. (Levi 2015, 2: 1135)

The way Levi approaches the subject of work and its dignity is breathtaking as it treads on the margins of leftist political language (Tesio 1995). Instead of sliding into rhetoric, he stresses the systematic and all-encompassing nature of the "Lager", the inevitable product of politics of the lie. Lurking within the frame is a dystopian vision of a Fascist future, built on "Lager" and such verbiage, with new Ten Commandments, a formulation heavy with irony. The invocation of the Hebrew tradition has to do with the biblical presence in the book, a tradition that cannot be renewed thorough the "Lager" (Lang 1999). For Levi, the failure of religion is already implied in the failure of any tradition to prevent the "Lager," as God and all systems dependent on him have been transcended in the attempt to transcend humanity (Gilroy 2010).[2]

The "Lager," we must not forget, was a space that produced an unprecedented transnational gathering, mostly but not only of Jews. Levi speaks of Europe, but he too was a product of Fascist schooling and had no other "World." Levi ties colonialism to Fascism and Nazism through their common designation of work, real work, to the enslaved. The shared core of Fascism is found for Levi in this disparaging view of work, its "denigration." I believe it is fair to say that Levi is making a poignant socialist point at a time in which he was probably already working on *The Truce* (1963), the story of his liberation by the Russians and his subsequent Odyssey homecoming.[3]

To engage with the classics as a prisoner was to engage with them through memory, under duress. Levi is not a literary scholar and thus what he does is not a result of learned inquiry. The classics reached him mainly through the nationalist high school education he was also trying to resist (Genovesi 2009, 79).[4] This is how he stands at the end of a tradition, replacing the erudite discussion with a more immediate one, broken and incorrect, mixed with cabbage and soup. Levi recalls the tradition, repositioning it in the Inferno of the slaves, where there is no use for scholarship. Nowhere is this more present than the celebrated chapter "The Canto of Ulysses" (Cohen 2012). Levi goes to fetch soup with Pikolo (Jean Samuel), a French inmate and attempts to teach him some Italian by reciting from memory the last *terza rima* of Dante's magnificent Canto 26 (Samuel 2007). The chapter is a stunning human and artistic engagement with the classics as form that radically challenges and morphs their core meaning.

---

[2] Notably, Gilroy's discussion originates in the Futurist core of Fascism.
[3] It seems the first two chapters of *The Truce* were written in the wake of the first publication of *If this is a Man* in 1947. There is also evidence that Levi began working on a version in the mid-fifties, while he was preparing the second edition of *If this is a Man* for Einaudi.
[4] Nemo Villeggia writes: "At the same time the rhetoric of fascism leaned heavily on a historical political idea in which the concept of *romanitas* and all its correlatives where 'renewed' in the fascist regime. The classical high school, more than any other kind of educational institute, represented a sort of conservatorium of that *romanitas*." (Villeggia 2007, 19)

While writing this chapter in 1946, Levi is at home, or rather at the factory, writing during his lunch break by the end of which a draft of the chapter will be complete (Thomson 2002, 217). He can reach for a copy of Dante, and perhaps he does, but his writing is a drama of omission, the text in tatters, traces of an order that is no more. Yet he conceives of his situation in terms of world literature, with Dante and Shakespeare being main sources of reference. Ulysses is a central figure for Levi and the Odyssey is always within reach, figuring in many key moments of the text. Remembering, in this case is also dismembering, Odysseus turned Ulysses, can turn no more, the slave cannot not be saved by inhabiting the figure, even if it tells a story it is in a disrupted fashion, almost by omission:

> I would give today's soup to be able to connect "the highest I had ever seen" to the last lines. I try to reconstruct it through the rhymes, I close my eyes, I bite my fingers—but it's no use, the rest is silence. Other lines dance in my head: "The tearful earth gave forth a wind," no, it's something else. (Levi 2015, 1: 109)

Levi is impeded by the sight of Mount Purgatory, the highest mountain Ulysses had ever seen, but the lofty mountain, the wind coming from it, its message if you will, cannot be connected in the end to drowning, leading to the silence of Hamlet's dying words. This is no prince of Denmark, no revenge need be feared (Cohen 2012). What he would give his daily bread for, life itself, is about connecting the wind that came from that mountain; it is about meaning. Purgatory and its mountain partake in a necessary structure of punishment that makes pain intelligible, offering at least the possibility of redemption.[5] However, not for the Jews in the "Lager" for them and many others, there is no innocent advancement, only corruption and collaboration within a gray zone of participation in a crime committed against oneself. Again, this is a novelty that is not without that grim irony that Levi finds typically German. It is an insight so dark, Dante has to speak it for him by way of omission. Perhaps this is also an essence of testimony, the way what is lost speaks from it very loss. Ulysses, summoned by Dante and interpreted by Virgil, recounts his last voyage beyond the Pillars of Hercules. Promising his companions virtue and knowledge, they arrive within sight of Mount Purgatory as the lines Levi desires to remember tell us: "Noi ci allegrammo, e tosto tornò in pianto, ché de la nova terra un turbo nacque

---

[5] Levi makes this difference painfully clear in *If this is a Man:* "In fact, for them the Lager is a punishment, and if they do not die of exhaustion or illness they can expect to return among men; [...] For us, on the contrary, the Lager is not a punishment; for us, no end is foreseen and the Lager is nothing but the kind of existence that has been allotted to us, without time limits, within the German social organism." (Levi 2015, 1: 78)

e percosse del legno il primo canto" [We rejoiced, but it quickly turned to weeping; for from the new land a whirlwind was born and struck the forequarter of the ship] (Dante 1996, 404–405).

The lines Levi tells of not being able to recall speak of what awaits the survivor, even if he is to escape hell, even if he is to return home. What drowns Ulysses is a wind that comes from Purgatory, a future darkness. For Levi and Ulysses alike, there is no entrance. Levi will return, but he will not take revenge as Odysseus did; he will not cleanse a home. The figure of Ulysses breaks down, his ship's forequarter, *il primo canto* in Italian, is struck. Levi and the reader are immediately referred to the *primo* [first] canto of the *commedia*. Dante, lost in the middle of his life, finds Virgil sent by Beatrice's love to guide him. It is a parody not without comic genius. Virgil leading Dante past the beasts impeding his path while Levi and Pikolo dawdle towards the soup:

> It's late, it's late, we've reached the kitchen, I have to finish:
>
> *Three times it turned her round with all the waters;*
> *and at the fourth, it lifted up the stern*
> *so that our prow plunged deep, as pleased an Other.*
>
> I hold Pikolo back, it is vitally necessary and urgent that he listen, that he understand this "as pleased an Other" before it's too late; tomorrow he or I might be dead, or we might never see each other again, I must tell him, I must explain to him about the Middle Ages, about the so human and so necessary and yet unexpected anachronism, and something else, something gigantic that I myself have only just seen, in a flash of intuition, perhaps the reason for our fate, for our being here today... (Levi 2015, 1: 109)

The will of God being done in drowning, Ulysses leads Levi to something incredible, gigantic, a flash of intuition that says everything. Levi does not explain, perhaps having no name for it himself, perhaps feigning to tell us. Indeed, Ulysses is not the figure of the survivor; Levi's tale is no Odyssey even if he has returned. If anything, this intuition has to do with Ulysses as a way of thinking, the will of God superimposed on the urge to explore, an economic system formed by colonialism. A way of thinking that always found it just that there should be slaves, Levi and Pikolo the unnamed slaves rowing the ships of the Herrenvolk brave explorers of what Man can make of Man. The uneasy breaking away of reason from fate, united by Dante, leaves the world prey to the assertion of brute force and its dark consequences:

> We are now in the soup line, among the sordid, ragged crowd of soup-carriers from other Kommandos. Those who have just arrived press against our backs. "*Kraut und Rüben?*" "*Kraut und Rüben.*" The official announcement is made that the soup today is cabbage and turnips: "*Choux et navets.*" "*Kaposzta és répak.*"

Until the sea again closed—over us. (Levi 2015, 1: 109)

Dante and Ulysses mean nothing in the camp, and yet they allow Levi to structure his experience in relation to the frame provided by the *Divina Commedia*. What was perhaps imagined as a universal – the classic tradition – is uncommunicable. It might have imagined a world, but when the world meets the camp, Dante is buried under the weight of soup. The soup and its contents are repeated four times: as a question, as information and in two other languages. Dante's voice is muffled under the stark realism of cabbage and turnips, disrupted by the multilingual reality of a globalized prison.[6] Perhaps the multiplicity of languages is there to remind us of what remains unsaid, the "why" of their imprisonment.

Ulysses is seeking knowledge of the world, to experience what is behind the sun in the world without "*gente*". Perhaps the reason is one that is relevant to many, the Jews having ventured out of the walls of separation to begin with. Jews and Gentiles alike ventured beyond the walls and the very notion that allowed them to do so, the nation, now imprisoned them. They are indeed experiencing what is behind the sun, a world not without bio-people, but without God to uphold their humanity in the face of overwhelming force. It is therefore incomplete, the voyage undertaken without foundation without blessing, and is doomed to drown. What lifted Man from dust, from animal to Human being, depended on faith that separated humans amicably, compared to the new order willed by Fascism. War is certainly no novelty, as is slavery, but the value of created life has never been done away with it. The novelty, the innovation that escapes the camps, is that it works. Man can turn Man into a beast of burden, into infestation to be exterminated and it would work. Arguably, this is what leads Levi to the following stark realization:

> It becomes clear that we will not return. We traveled here in sealed freight cars; we saw our women and our children depart toward nothingness; we, made slaves, have marched countless times to and from our silent labor, dead in spirit long before our anonymous death. No one must leave here who might carry to the world, together with the mark stamped in his flesh, the evil tidings of what man's audacity made of man in Auschwitz. (Levi 2015, 1: 52)

---

6 This is the stark, endless realism under which intellect collapses in Jean Amery's view (Amery 1986, 15).

And in Italian:

> Nessuno deve uscire di qui, che potrebbe portare al mondo, insieme col segno impresso nella carne, la mala novella di quanto, ad Auschwitz, è bastato animo all'uomo di fare dell'uomo. (Levi 2016, 1: 178)

I cite the Italian to remember what is inevitably lost in translation; what the "world" will never know and can never know. No one is "*nessuno*" in Italian, literally no one and the name Odysseus gives himself in the Cyclops' cave. Polyphemos the Cyclops laughs at the Gods and eats his guests, reserving for *Nessuno*\Odysseus\Nobody the privilege of the survivor to be eaten last. The survivor realizes all of this as a novelty of Auschwitz and perhaps this is why no one *must* ("deve") return. The mark stamped in the flesh refers both to the scar of Ulysses as well as the number inked in the flesh. The evil tidings – *la mala novella* – is that Man has devised a fate worse than death for Man (the "Muselman") and a world where some would be masters, others slaves and others yet, something to be disposed of (Agamben 1998, 59–104). The survivor, the one saved for last, is condemned to witness the fate of his companions, as it becomes the story that will mark the rest of his life. It is not only a tale of suffering but a fracture in the world, in the shape of things, a new kind of evil: "L'Univers concentrationnaire" – The Universe of Concentration Camps – an industrialized complex based on unprecedented control over the body in slavery, serving its own annihilation (Rousset 1946).[7]

The humanism engendered by Homer, Dante and the image of Man collapses, emptied of meaning or function. The writing on the gate is to that tradition what Primo Levi the prisoner is to the idea of Man – a trace. When the Red Army tears down the gates of the concentration camp, he is ashamed, standing at ground zero, where an entire tradition, Europe and its universal idea of a world order based in white male superiority, has come to undo itself. Standing at this end allows Levi a long gaze into a symbolic system emptied of meaning, but not of art. Auschwitz as a world event is the end of Man as an idea and the threshold of a terrifying new world. The survivor is the first citizen, *princeps*, of a future republic built off the body in pain, the protection of it and its perils.[8] The message *Nessuno* carries in the flesh is exactly that the mark of humanity is failed by all the forms of thought and being that sought to elevate him above

---

[7] Within such terms we must agree with Rousset that the differences within that universe, such as the kind of relative improvements in prisoner life expectancy and quality afforded by Buna are only a matter of degree within a self-same system.

[8] There are many, most visible these days as the Coronavirus plays out. See Farneti 2011.

of his flesh. What the survivor survived is precisely that; being a servant to other's claim to mastery, the absolute devolution of Man to biological function and matter (Ignatieff 2001, 14–17).

Levi's conditional in the title of *If this is a Man* means in part: there cannot be Man without oppression, not in the sense intended by the classic tradition. The poem opening Levi's book is very clear on the kind of consideration we should give the matter:

> You who live safe
> In your heated houses
> You who come home at night to find
> Hot food and friendly faces:
>
> Consider if this is a man,
> Who toils in the mud
> Who knows no peace
> Who fights for half a loaf
> Who dies by a yes or a no.
> Consider if this is a woman,
> With no hair and no name
> With no more strength to remember
> With empty eyes and a womb as cold
> As a frog in winter.
>
> Ponder that this happened:
> I consign these words to you.
> Carve them into your hearts
> At home or on the street,
> Going to bed or rising:
> Tell them to your children.
> Or may your house fall down,
> May illness make you helpless,
> And your children turn their eyes from you. (Levi 2015, 1: 8)

Levi has seen what is coming for all of us and if we do not listen, if we do not consider his tale, we, or our progeny, will end up there, even if Auschwitz takes on a new face. This is no longer a matter of the West, no longer a question for and of men, but of people ("*gente*") in the world. The national perspective, Levi's message for Italy, is not necessarily the core of the matter, even though there is beauty and art in Levi that is only available in the Italian. The death of the tradition carried by the classics as the cultural foundation of a social and political order is no novelty and yet it does not diminish art. The art that remains enclosed in language, in particular contexts, many layers of beauty deep, somewhat justifies philology (Pollock 2009). As "The Canto of Ulysses" demonstrates, a broken violin can still make wondrous music. It can say something about the limits of Man and what lies beyond them, what he has seen and why we must never again explore those shores; as well as how we will inevitably end up doing just so.

Not unlike Levi, something of the tradition survives, something we can perhaps call with Celan "art as a problem" (Celan 2003, 37–55) Reading Levi remembering Dante and Homer is both the end and the beginning, a radical reading of the classic tradition from its end point, considering both the hero and his rowers are not figures of the survivor but are part of his tale (Horkheimer and Adorno 2002, 27–28). Levi is no Ulysses, nor is he a slave ennobled by an Odyssey. He is the one carrying in the flesh a terrible message, that if he is a Man then, he is now us.

We the refugees. We the survivors.

Bibliography:

Agamben, Giorgio. *Quel che resta di Auschwitz: l'archivio e il testimone: homo sacer 3.* Torino: Bollati Boringhieri, 1998.
Améry, Jean. *At the Mind's Limits: Contemplations by a Survivor on Auschwitz and Its Realities.* Bloomington: Indiana University Press, 1980.
Celan, Paul. *Selected Prose.* Transl. by Rosemary Waldrop. New York: Routledge, 2003.
Cohen, Uri S. "Consider If This Is a Man: Primo Levi and the Figure of Ulysses." *Jewish Social Studies* 18.2 (2012): 40–69.
Cross, Timothy P. *An Oasis of Order: The Core Curriculum at Columbia College.* https://www.college.columbia.edu/core/oasis. New York: Office of the Dean, Columbia College: 1995 (10 March 2020).
Dante Alighieri. *The Divine Comedy of Dante Alighieri, Volume 1: Inferno.* Transl. by Robert M. Durling. Oxford: Oxford University Press, 1996.
Farneti, Roberto. "The Immunitary Turn in Current Talk on Biopolitics: On Roberto Esposito's Bíos." *Philosophy & Social Criticism* 37.8 (2011): 955–962.
Genovesi, Piergiovanni. *Il manuale di storia in Italia: dal fascismo alla Repubblica.* Milano: FrancoAngeli, 2009.
Gilroy, Paul. "Fanon and Améry." *Theory, Culture & Society* 27.7–8 (2010): 16–32.
Horkheimer, Max, and Theodor W. Adorno. *Dialectic of Enlightenment.* Transl. by Edmund Jephcott. Palo Alto: Stanford University Press, 2002.
Ignatieff, Michael. *Human Rights as Politics and Idolatry.* Princeton: Princeton University Press, 2001.
Isnenghi, Mario. *L'educazione Dell'italliano: il fascismo l'organizzazione della cultura.* Bologna: Cappelli, 1979.
Lacy, Tim. "Dreams of a Democratic Culture: Revising the Origins of the Great Books Idea, 1869–1921." *The Journal of the Gilded Age and Progressive Era* 7.4 (2008): 397–441.
Lang, Ariella. "Reason as Revenge: Primo Levi and Writing the Holocaust." *Symposium: A Quarterly Journal in Modern Literatures* 52.4 (1999): 255–268.
Levi, Primo. "Beyond Survival." Transl. by Gail Soffer. *Prooftexts* 4.1 (1984): 9–21.

Levi, Primo. *Opere complete*. Torino: Giulio Einaudi, 2016. 3 vols.
Levi, Primo. *The Complete Works of Primo Levi*. Ed. Ann Goldstein. New York: Liveright Publishing Corporation, 2015. 3 vols.
Pollock, Sheldon. "Future Philology? The Fate of a Soft Science in a Hard World." *Critical Inquiry* 35.4 (2009): 931–961.
Rousset, David. *L'univers concentrationnaire*. Paris: Éditions du Pavois, 1946.
Samuel, Jean and Jean-Marc Dreyfus. *Il m'appelait Pikolo : Un compagnon de Primo Levi raconte*. Paris: Éditions Robert Laffont, 2007
Sani, Roberto. "The 'Fascist Reclamation' of Textbooks from the Gentile Reform to the School Charter of Bottai". *History of Education & Children's Literature* 3.2 (2008): 305–335.
Tesio, Giovanni. "Libertino faussone in cerca del suo lettore ideale." *Primo Levi: la dignità dell'uomo*. Eds. R. Brambilla, and G. Cacciatore. Assisi: Cittadella Editrice, 1995. 129–141.
Villeggia, Nemo. *La scuola per la classe dirigente : vita quotidiana e prassi educative nei licei durante il fascismo*. Milano: Unicopli, 2007.

V **Case Studies Latin American Literatures**

Verena Dolle
A Case Study in Latin American Literature: Ilan Stavans' *On Borrowed Words*

1 Introductory remarks

As mentioned in the editors' prologue, this project seeks to integrate paradigmatic Jewish literary texts, selected passages and issues into a modern syllabus of philological studies. They (i.e., the studies) often comprise a very reduced proportion of modules in literature and, furthermore, still tend to stick to outdated concepts of "national" literature, despite transnational and globalized movements, or rather, new *media-* and *ethnoscapes*, as Appadurai calls them, that challenge these concepts. To achieve such an outcome, texts must be paradigmatic and exemplary across a variety of disciplines. Additionally, they must offer a certain degree of accessibility and amenability to undergraduate students so they can be easily incorporated into an academic syllabus (in Germany and/or other countries).

This volume offers a broad thematic spectrum, which, in essence, deals with two fundamental questions: 1) How is Jewish historical experience represented through literature?; 2) How is Jewish diversity conceptualized in literature? My contribution to this reflection draws on diversity. To illustrate my point, I suggest reading an extract from the autobiographical text of Jewish Mexican-American author, Ilan Stavans, entitled *On Borrowed Words*, published in 2001 with the sub-title "A Memoir of Language" and translated into Spanish with a new appendix, *Palabras prestadas* in 2013. With the Jewish Ashkenazim linguistic heritage and (forced) migration experience as point of departure and base, the text, starting right from its title, puts to the fore questions of (linguistic) appropriation, belonging, possession or non-possession in addition to challenging the notion of traditional national/ethnic and even linguistic compartmentalization. Moreover, it deals with the relationship between (appropriated) language and an individual's identity. Further, it possesses paradigmatic traits for human existence in twenty-first century globalized, multilingual and mobile society/ies, despite being a personal reflection on the nineteenth and twentieth century Jewish experience.

2 On the author

Ilan Stavans is a prolific author, active in different genres, whose intellectual biography defies (simple) ethnic, national, and linguistic classifications and categories. Stavans was born in 1961 in Mexico-City as Ilan Stavchansky and son of Ashkenazim parents born in Mexico in 1933 and 1941. Facing pogroms and persecution, his grandparents from maternal and paternal sides migrated to Mexico from Eastern Europe, forming part of Ashkenazim migration to Mexico in the first decades of the twentieth century (cf. Hamui 2007; Dolle 2020). After sojourning in Europe and Israel, Ilan Stavans migrated to the USA in the 1980s and obtained US-American citizenship in 1994. Despite writing most of his works in English, a "foreign language" (Stavans 2002, 184) to him, in addition to migrating to the US and becoming a US citizen, Stavans is still an established author in the canon of Mexican Jewish writers. This is evidenced, e. g., by the article Angelina Muñiz Huberman dedicates to him in the special issue on Jewish Mexican Literature edited by Lockhart in 2013, a crucial anthology taking stock of contemporary Jewish authors.

3 On the text

On Borrowed Words is no work of fiction, but presents itself as a "memoir of language", in line with the 2001 subtitle, and as an "autobiografía" in the Spanish version (2013). Therefore, it belongs to the factual genre of life-writing containing autobiographical elements of a person retrospectively narrating episodes from his/her life, accentuating the history of his/her personality (such is Lejeune's classical definition of autobiography, cf. 1975, 14). These elements imply an identity between the narrator and protagonist inside the text using the personal pronoun "I" and the author's name placed on the cover (Lejeune 1975, 14 f.), thus evoking an "autobiographical pact". According to Lejeune, this represents a "guarantee" given to the reader that the narrator tells *the*, or better, *his/her* "truth", as certain experiences, feelings and states of mind are recollected. However, this is not and cannot be an absolute "truth", as neuroscience research has proven that human memory is, in general, defective and not only adapted to the individual's present situation, but also that memories and gaps therein are quite often marked and over-formed by imagination (cf. Welzer 2017, 19 f.). Therefore, it is not astonishing that all too often, the borders between factual and fictional writing are blurred, creating a hybrid genre in-between.

In Stavans' text, the I-narrator himself is aware of this point, as he writes, "[...] how much of what we are, what we know about ourselves, is really *true?* We are merely a sum of viewpoints, and human memory is treacherous and inconsistent" (Stavans 2002, 88).

On Borrowed Words is a reflection on the effects of multilingualism on individuals and their identity when passing through and/or living in different cultures. It relates to the Ashkenazi historical experience in the nineteenth and twentieth centuries, characterized by pogroms, persecution, escape, the pinnacle of violence and murder during the Holocaust and, for the survivors, the process of adapting to a new country, which in Stavans' case was Mexico.

Both title and subtitle pinpoint language as a crucial issue, which in a way becomes the focus of the entire book. The preposition "On" makes reference to the metatextual element of language (a nuance that was lost in the Spanish title, *Palabras prestadas,* where the corresponding preposition "acerca" or "sobre" is missing). Over six chapters, arranged in a more or less chronological order, the first-person narrator ponders upon his own linguistic and intellectual development and aims "to write a memoir about my own upbringing in Mexico and my emigration to America" (Stavans 2002, 87). The narration starts with his childhood in a Yiddish neighbourhood in Mexico-City and moves on to his academic career in Mexico, his trips abroad, his studies in the USA and his US-American nationalization in 1994. The final chapter recounts an encounter with Richard Rodríguez, a *latino* author who, too, had immigrated to the United States. Rodríguez was one of the first to publish an autobiographical text on the social and linguistic reality of Latin American immigrants in *Hunger of memory* and thus, conferring visibility to them (1982), an important text for Stavans himself ("the un-self-righteous coming-of-age chronicle of a mestizo Mexican American [...] I have read many times."; Stavans 2002, 247).[1]

Stavans' point of departure for his reflection on "borrowed" words, words that are obviously not his own, is the experience of (forced) migration of his Ashkenazim grandparents and their approach to, and use of language(s). His grandmother, Bela, wrote a diary addressed to him in Spanish, not in her mother tongue Yiddish, because she wanted to leave behind as a legacy a text that not only her grandson could read, but also her great-grandchildren (cf. Stavans 2002, 51). This circumstance impels him to reflect on her feelings regarding the

---

[1] At the time, Rodríguez made a strong case for monolingualism, the use of English only, because he held that this enables immigrants to (linguistically) assimilate to the new surrounding the greatest extent possible, with Spanish being an obstacle to social rise. This topic is not discussed in Stavans' text, but the intertextual reference can serve to measure the changes in mindset and maybe social standing of a certain language Stavans offensively represents.

Yiddish language and the role it has been playing for her and other Ashkenazim in Mexico:

> The Eastern European settlers, secular in their manner, understood language to be the conduit of tradition. They refused to give it up at the speed of their siblings north of the Rio Grande [...]. Their offspring, to remain Jewish, needed to be raised in the same verbal tradition. And so language was a tool of continuity, the mechanism through which Bela and her peers managed, magically, to go on living, as it were, in Eastern Europe. (2002, 77)

Yiddish, so to say, serves in this context as a heterotopy in Foucaultian sense, "her portable ghetto" (Stavans 2002, 87): "(it) was the umbilical cord with Europe, and was never finally cut" (Stavans 2002, 79). Moreover, with a whole chapter on "The Rise and Fall of Yiddish" (Stavans 2002, 45–90), *On Borrowed Words* is a de facto homage to Yiddish, the language threatened by extinction, with several Yiddish poems weaving their way through the text. At the same time, his grandmother's text causes him to ponder the (in)adequacy of her Spanish expressions, or a different tone as he notes that

> [...] her words have been modified – or shall I say –betrayed–have they not? [...] Her Spanish is pidgin all right–broken, ungrammatical– but it is hers all the same: it has style, it has pathos, it has power. It is the tongue of an immigrant–embryonic, wobbly, in constant mutation. (Stavans 2002, 51f.)

This leads to another key concept that preoccupies Stavans in his "memoir" – the "inauthenticity" of the Spanish expressions encountered in his grandmother's text, as Spanish is a language with which she lacked familiarity and that maybe is amending the past: "As I read and reread Bela's *diario* [...], the word 'inauthentic' comes back to me. I try to imagine how Bela would have written to me in her *true* tongue: Yiddish". (Stavans 2002, 88) But, that "inauthenticity" that has to do with a switch in language, with a historical decalage ("In seeking words absent from her childhood [...], has she amended her own past?", the I-narrator asks [Stavans 2002, 88]), is not perceived as something negative, but rather an inalienable element of Jewish Ashkenazim linguistic reality following the destruction of their life and culture in Eastern Europe and its insertion into, and existence in a new surrounding (cf. Stavans 2002, 52). Following his grandmother's example, he inscribes himself in this family genealogy, and tries to find, in his own text, an adequate expression for this inauthenticity. This is illustrated by the following quote where the I-narrator presents his linguistic (and poetic) reality to the reader:

> I'm aware that crafting my memoir in English will, in and of itself, be a form of treason. For shouldn't it be written in at least three if not four languages (Yiddish, Spanish, Hebrew, and English), the four tongues in which– and through which–I've experienced life? But no publisher in his right mind would endorse such an endeavor. [...] My aim, nonetheless, is to convey not my nationality but my *translationality*. To succeed, the original ought to read (sic) as if written already *in* translation–a translation without an original. I think of the segments in Anglicized Yiddish in Henry Roth's *Call It Sleep*, and those in "transliterated slang" in Richard Wright's *Native Son*; they appeal to me because they are bastardized forms of language, polluted, compromised. And an illegitimate language is exactly what I seek. (Stavans 2002, 88)

The I-narrator chooses "translationality", a neologism, over "nationality", the latter being a concept that often connects national classification/belonging to a specific official language. Moreover, writers are normally (with exceptions to the rule, of course) expected to write (and often do so) in their native tongue, the language they (are supposed to) know best in its aesthetic, stylistic and connotational facets. The original objective Stavans pursued was to write the autobiographical text in the four languages corresponding to the different phases of his life and acquired in different contexts. He writes, "Yiddish, for me, was truly the mother tongue, whereas Spanish, the street language, the one I most often used, was the father tongue" (Stavans 2002, 83). "Translationality", or "a translation without an original" (see quote above) is not limited to theoretical concepts, such as Derridean deconstructivism, where language and concepts are orbiting a void and permanently deferred, or where the real and true referent (such as truth/God/the Absolute) is and remains absent. Rather, for Stavans, it serves as a metaphor for his human (migrant) condition and, vis-à-vis an increasing global mobility, the rise of transnational groups, communities beyond national concrete territorial borders. Personally, this seems to me not only to be an expression of Jewish, but also modern existence in the twenty-first century.

The benefit of Stavans' text, obvious in the short extracts presented here, is, in my opinion, its provocative approach to national and linguistic affiliation, to the idea that mother tongue(s) are often held to be "pure" and to the high value attributed to perfect linguistic skills (only attainable for native speakers). Furthermore, with his intertextual references, Stavans inserts himself and his concept into US-American literary models dealing with the "translation" of voices (i.e. the "Anglicized Yiddish" of Henry Roth), which attempt to transfer orality into written form. The key notion I'd like to highlight here are the terms "polluted", "bastardized" or, to use another theoretical expression that has become *en vogue* in the last decades, "hybrid",[2] i.e. containing different traits of various origins that do not

---

[2] Hybridity according to Nestor Canclini's ground-breaking book *Culturas híbridas* (1990) differs

merge, but rather exist side by side to form something completely new. The adjective "illegitimate" is a counter-project to official, standardized language, or perhaps to academies prescribing or following the ideal of linguistic purity.[3]

Ilan Stavans has experienced a (transgenerational) migration. He is multilingual and uses an aesthetic distance to foreign languages to reflect on his life, career, belonging and multi-rootedness. The distance to his mother tongue(s), (the) language(s) one was brought up with, is experienced as fructiferous and vivifying. As stated by the author himself in the newly added appendix in *Palabras prestadas*, English is the first language he explicitly chose, whereas the others were "accidental":

> [...] quería escribir una memoria políglota, es decir, la primera parte de mi vida idish (la escuela y mi relación con la generación emigrante de la comunidad judía) sería redactada directamente en la lengua de Sholem Aleichem; la porción vivida en español (la vida de la calle y mi descubrimiento de México) sería en la lengua de Cervantes [...]; después el hebreo (la lengua del sionismo y de Israel, en donde pasé mis años formativos) [...]. Las memorias terminarían con una parte escrita en inglés, la lengua que he adoptado desde que me mudé a los Estados Unidos. [...] Necesitaba escoger un solo idioma. O, mejor dicho, una lengua necesitaba escogerme a mí. Nunca hubo duda de que fuese el inglés: es el único idioma que he escogido libremente, mi relación con los otros tres fue meramente accidental (Stavans 2013, 281).

4 Concluding remarks

To take up my introductory remarks, syllabi are not only valuable and extremely important for academic education and, especially, teacher training, but also for high school and all forms of secondary school (not only in the respective German federal *Länder*). It is widely known and has been proven by research that first and decisive mind sets regarding societal values are formed at school. This is why the importance of syllabi and school books should not be underestimated.[4] This is also why Jewish literature concerning diversity and historical experience should not only be disseminated at university, but also during the formative years at school.

---

by far from that of Mexican intellectual Vasconcelos' notion of a "raza cósmica" (1925), considered as a melting pot, where all differences merge into a harmonic equal new form.

3 In my option it is therefore only logical that Ilan Stavans is a fervent proponent for other forms of hybrid languages, such as Spanglish, which – according to him – correspond(s) to the real life of a considerable number of Latinos in the US.

4 Cf., e.g., Constantin Schreiber's recent study on school books in Muslim countries, *Die Kinder des Koran*. Düsseldorf: Econ 2019, with the conclusion that the analyzed corpus contains an extremely stereotyped representation of Jewish people and distorted historical events.

In this context, I'd like to offer another and final comment on issues surrounding school politics. Secondary/high schools shape the demand and supply of philological study programmes (in Germany and, I assume, in other countries as well). Despite the current official EU-based, foreign-language friendly policies in place (i.e. not only the promotion of English), the concrete situation at schools in several *Länder* has shown that there is not only a strong competition between the second and third foreign modern language offered at secondary/high schools over the last few years, but also that options and possibilities to pursue two Romance languages are restricted more and more[5]. In reality, this restriction in diversity has already shown consequences in the form of a declining number of students taking up Romance (philological) studies at university. Even if this is not the only reason for the decline in demand for studies in philology, one should be aware of this challenge in order to able to better disseminate Jewish literature in the forthcoming decades.

Bibliography

Bär, Marcus. "Französisch, Spanisch, Italienisch – Zur Stellung der romanischen Schulsprachen im deutschen Bildungssystem". *FLuL* 46.1 (2017). 86–99.

Dolle, Verena. "Intercultural memory and violence in Jewish literature." *The Cambridge Handbook of Intercultural Communication*. Eds. Guido Rings and Sebastian Rasinger. Cambridge: UP, 2020. 302–318.

Hamui, Liz. "Mexico." *Encyclopedia Judaica*, vol. 14. Eds. Michael Berenbaum and Fred Skolnik. Detroit: Macmillan Reference, (^{2}2007). 137–146. https://jwa.org/encyclopedia/article/mexico (October 17, 2019).

Lejeune, Philippe. *On Autobiography*. Minneapolis: Univ. of Minnesota Press 1989 (1975).

Muñiz Huberman, Angelina. "Ilán Stavans: la memoria en juego." *Critical Approaches to Jewish-Mexican Literature*. Ed. Darrell Lockhart (= *Chasqui. Revista de literatura latinoamericana*. Special Issue No. 4). 219–230.

Rodriguez, Richard. *Hunger of memory: the education of Richard Rodriguez, an autobiography*. New York, NY: Dial Press, 2005 (1982).

Schreiber, Constantin. *Die Kinder des Koran*. Düsseldorf: Econ, 2019.

Stavans, Ilan. *On Borrowed Words. A Memoir of Language*. New York: Penguin, 2002 (^{1}2001).

Stavans, Ilan. *Palabras prestadas. Autobiografía*. Traducción de Lety Barrera. México D.F.: FCE, 2013.

Welzer, Harald. *Das kommunikative Gedächtnis. Eine Theorie der Erinnerung*. München: Beck, 2017 (2002).

---

[5] Cf. Marcus Bär's, differentiated consideration of the standing of Romance languages in German educational system, especially his concluding remarks (2017, 96 f.).

Amalia Ran
Jewish Latin American Literary Studies: Between Old Challenges and New Paradigms

The growing interest in Jewish Latin American literature in recent decades led researchers and academic institutions to focus on the multiple expressions of Jewish identity and Jewishness in the hemisphere, on immigration, dislocation, and personal and collective affiliations, while often emphasizing the numerous conjunctions between history and the narrative act, as indicated in the large number of scholarly works and of courses on the subject.[1]

At the same time, particularly since the turn of the twenty-first century, emerges the demand to revise old paradigms in order to face new political, socio-economic, cultural and epistemological challenges in Latin America, within the Jewish world, and around the globe. In this framework, I seek to explore new pathways for researching and studying Jewish Latin American literature by reviewing the challenges with which we face at present in our profession and by suggesting alternative strategies for teaching and learning the subject.

The academic world underwent significant transformations related to the digital revolution, the changing nature of learning, and the omnipresence of knowledge and increasing number of data of various forms (Daniel, 2015; Scheffel et al., 2014; Pardo and Siemens, 2014; Becker et al., 2017). In the Humanities, the declining number of students and shrinking resources produced a new crisis, visible also in departments of Jewish studies around the world. How do these predicaments affect Jewish literary studies? Which academic practices should be promoted in order to face the decline in the number of students in courses such as Judeo-Latin American fiction or Sephardic literature, for example? Moreover, as technology and digital pedagogy reshape our field and set new norms for teaching and learning, our concerns relate also to methodological and theoretical aspects: Is it still possible to conduct a pure aesthetic relationship with the literary text in a world infiltrated by digital hypertexts and instant messages? In the following pages, I wish to highlight several challenges which we face today as scholars of Jewish literary studies. I should stress that these challenges are not unique to our field; yet, by confronting them, we may envision new para-

---

[1] See for example the list of syllabi at LAJSA website: http://www.lajsa.org/resources/syllabi-and-course-descriptions/ (24 September 2019).

OpenAccess. © 2020 Amalia Ran, published by De Gruyter. This work is licensed under the Creative Commons Attribution-NonCommercial-NoDerivatives 4.0 License.
https://doi.org/10.1515/9783110619003-022

digms for teaching, researching and learning Jewish literature on its various hemispheric expressions.

1 Challenge I: Decline in the Number of Students

In his 2015 survey for the AJS (American Jewish Studies Association), Michael Cohen (2015) underlined the retraction in tenure-track job opportunities in the field of Jewish studies, in public and private funding, and in course enrollments due to the financial crisis of 2008 in the United States, which presented new challenges for Jewish Studies, as well as for other academic fields in the Humanities, the arts and in sciences. Cohen reported the correlation between the decline in student enrollment and between the dwindling job market for new professors of literature and of other humanistic subjects. Nonetheless, his survey still found that amongst the most widely taught subjects were courses on Jewish literature (20%). Approximately 13% of the respondents in Cohen's survey specialized in modern Jewish history in Europe/Asia/Israel/ and other communities; only 1.8% of the participants in this survey reported being employed in Departments of Romance Languages, and 2.3% in Department of Comparative Literature (Cohen, 2015).

A census on behalf of the Modern Languages Association (MLA), which was conducted in 2013, supported these findings by reporting that overall enrollments of students in literary studies and linguistics in the United States were falling by 6.7% from the previous year. The MLA census did not specify whether the drop represented an anomaly in the growth of enrollments that had continued uninterrupted since 1998 or was the beginning of a sustained downward trend; something that had not happened since the 1970s. However, as indicated three years afterwards by the 2016 MLA census, enrollments in languages other than English fell in 9.2% in colleges and universities around the United States; thus, confirming a global trend in the Humanities (Looney and Lusin, 2018). In Israel, a similar process is reported as well. Most recently, Professor Eyal Ziser, Vice Rector of Tel Aviv University, emphasized the decline in the number of students in the Humanities in a panel on innovation and technology in institutions of higher education (2018): only 8–9% of the students choose to study a degree in the Humanities, claiming that it is unpractical, too academic, and does not prepare them for the job market. Nonetheless, insisted Ziser, leaders in the financial and business sectors are still seeking employees who are not only technocrats (with degrees for instance in computer sciences and engineering alone) but who have wide knowledge and critical skills attained by completing programs in humanistic disciplines.

Overall, the decline in student enrollment characterizes most of the fields in the Humanities, including Jewish studies and literary studies, and any future proposal for increasing student enrollments in these fields should address the question of how to appeal to new candidates, how to become relevant again for students at the twenty-first century, and how to use innovative technology and new learning pedagogies in order to attract future scholars into the research of Jewish literary studies on its multiple regional expressions.

2 Challenge II: Traditional Disciplinary Divisions

Academic institutions were and still are traditionally divided into spheres of knowledge based upon an imagined disciplinary line, resisting the growing demands for emphasis on interdisciplinary and multi-disciplinary connectivity and collaborations in the academia and beyond its walls. I should note that in a sense Jewish studies have always defied this rigid structure, since the field encompassed multiple scholarly disciplines (history, literature, languages, and religion among others). Within the particular sub-field of Jewish Latin American literary studies, its multiple roots in Latin American studies, in Jewish studies, as well as in literary studies, obfuscated any attempt for clear, hermetic, disciplinary categorization, which eventually led also to the creation of two independent academic associations as professional frameworks dedicated specifically to the subject.

AMILAT (*Asociación Israelí de Investigadores del Judaísmo Latinoamericano*) and LAJSA (Latin American Jewish Studies Association) were created exactly because of these multi-disciplinary affinities: Both organizations sought to constitute local scholarly communities to debate theoretical and practical concerns within the field of Jewish Latin America and beyond its multiple disciplinary borders. In a sense, both organizations, created in the late 1970s and 1980s respectively, deliberately or not, created a hybrid field of studies comprising scholars from different research fields, various hemispheres (Latin America, North America, Israel and Europe), and languages (English, Spanish, Portuguese, Hebrew, Yiddish and Ladino) who happened to share their expertise, including in philology and literary studies (Laikin Elkin, 2016).

At present, the need to revise traditional disciplinary structures is as urgent as ever before; what should we learn from the example of Jewish Latin American literary studies? Courses on Jewish Latin American fiction appeal to a wide audience of students from literary studies, Jewish studies, Spanish and Latin American literature, ethnic studies, and diasporic studies; should we use this sub-field as a model for successful hybrid and multi-disciplinary scholarly environment for promoting Jewish literary studies?

3 Challenge III: Teaching and Learning Jewish Latin American Literature and "Generation Z" Students

Most of our current students are "Generation Z" representatives also known as "iGeneration" natives (Montana and Petit 2008; Rosen 2011). This fact demands a shift in our teaching methodologies and in how we facilitate students' access to knowledge in our field. Much has been said about our current audience of learners: their alleged incapability of expressing themselves orally and by writing; their difficulties of analyzing a text into depth; their attention deficits and the effect of these shortages on learning; Moreover, their access to unlimited amount of data and information through the Web challenges professors' traditional role as single sources of knowledge. This generation of students is much more exposed to knowledge than their precursors (and much more globally oriented and open to embrace new trends and paradigms, I should add). It seems that in face of these circumstances, our third challenge is also our most urgent one: How to teach these students? How to enhance their knowledge and get them involved and interested in our field? In short, how to make Jewish literary studies relevant again for this new generation of students?

3.1 Old and New Paradigms

According to the *NMC Horizon Report: 2017 Higher Education Edition in Teaching and Learning* (Becker et al., 2017), to implement change in the academia implies endorsing a cultural transformation by:
1. Promoting the exchange of fresh ideas and advancing progressive learning approaches;
2. Relating to real-world skills in view of future employability;
3. Creating collaborations with learning communities and multidisciplinary approaches;
4. Shifting to digital humanities (for example, by using Blogs to foster deeper student learning, or by using blended learning designs such as a combination of traditional, face-to-face teaching with modes of technology-facilitat-

ed instruction like the flipped-classroom model, rearranging time spent in the classroom to promote more active learning and collaboration);
5. Promoting authentic and ubiquitous learning.

Consequently, it appears that a redefinition of the relationship between learners, knowledge and faculty is required. Instead of thinking of knowledge as something static, which passes from professors to students, knowledge should be perceived as something fluent, that is constantly created and revised; at the same time, as radical as it may sound, we ought to recognize our students' ability to contribute to the body of knowledge in our field by reconstructing our pedagogical and theoretical concepts of teaching and learning (DeRosa and Robinson, 2017). Yet, how should we implement these drastic changes in Jewish literary studies?

In the field of Jewish Latin American literature, we need to break free from discussing Jewish experience as an *a priori*, exceptional category of analysis, which ignores factors such as generational gaps, similar experiences of dislocation and marginality experienced by other minority groups in Latin America, the diminishing place Zionism and Israel occupies in the lives of Jews around the world at present, or the role of diaspora as a defining element in migrant identities. These new considerations should guide our way upon instigating a new curriculum.

Within the realm of Jewish Latin American literary studies, one should wonder how to classify new works published by Jewish Latin American authors who currently reside in Europe, Israel or in the United States such as Eduardo Halfon – a Jewish Guatemalan author who grew up in the United States – or the Jewish Argentine writer Eduardo Lázaro Covadlo who lives in Spain. Their works force us to rethink of old academic paradigms and consider new polemic proposals raised by the public of readers, by the academic and editorial world, and by the literary text itself, as they represent a unrooted, transnational and multilingual echoes that transcend their Jewishness and hemispheric affiliations. At the same time, as emphasized by a number of scholars in recent years, the exceptionality of Jewish protagonists as minor, marginal and excluded entities in many local contexts (for example: in Argentina, Mexico, Brazil) disappears in favor of new representations of urban, middle-class (often masculine) prototypes who accidently (or not) happen to be Jewish as well. They no longer represent only the marginal character who suffers from the "double-identity" crises due to dual loyalties and affiliations. Instead, they "float" between various imaginary and tangible territories without any apologetic tone or unique characteristics that single them out. Hence, these new considerations ought to be taken into account once remodeling the curriculum of Jewish Latin American literary studies.

Perhaps it is also the adequate moment to employ a new "academic language" and to constitute another kind of relationship with students and scholars in order to enhance Jewish literary studies. The field of Jewish studies originated from the millenary tradition of reading and interpreting the Book. Jewish literary studies in particular nourished from the polemic tradition of the sages and the Kabbalistic prism of multilayer inferences. However, this tradition is losing its primacy in Jewish literary studies at the digital era. By rethinking our relationship with the literary text, with our students and with the profession itself we may reach a new form for communicating and transferring knowledge. Following Roman Jacobson's model of communication (1960), this alternative "academic" language should offer a new channel for transmitting messages and discussing them while embracing new types of *senders* and *receivers*; and while accepting the changing contextual framework, as well as the channel of transmission and the codes.

The following example may illustrate in which way the adoption of new communication channels in our field led to the improvement of students' outcomes and involvement in the subject matter, by implementing an innovative curriculum and including the students in the research of the field: In his course entitled "Murder, Madness and Mayhem: Latin American Literature in Translation," Jon Beasley-Murray, a professor from the University of British Columbia in Canada, decided to incorporate an assignment that replaced a more traditional research paper, which was based on an initiative on behalf of the Wiki Education Foundation. He requested from his students to write or improve a Wikipedia article on Latin American literature. According to Beasley-Murray, this task consisted of "teaching the students research skills and writing skills in what [was] very much a real world environment." (De Rosa and Robinson 2017, 119). Hence, throughout the semester, the students researched in groups, wrote and edited an article, which was later evaluated not only by their classmates and by the professor, but also by the public of readers on the digital domain. Consequently, the amount of articles on Wikipedia that focused on Latin American literature increased, and although the question of their scholarly quality remains open, the public evaluation mechanism enabled their improvement and positive rating over time. This example demonstrates how by using alternative learning and teaching modes, Beasley-Murray engaged his students in research, triggering their curiosity and interest in the course, and conduced them to deepen their knowledge in the field.

Alternative channels of communication may be established also by incorporating Open Education Resources in the curriculum. Beyond their financial and social benefits for students, Open Education Resources could be critical essays, narrative texts, textbooks, video conferences, or any other educational material that are free of use (under certain limitations of privacy and copyrights) for academic purposes. This way, a tentative course on Jewish Latin American literature based upon OER may incorporate Halfon's[2] and Covadlo's[3] blogs for example. Both Jewish authors, mentioned previously, publish some of their stories online (as well as press interviews, personal statements and short biographies). Why not incorporating these narrative texts into the classroom? Students may also share their analysis and commentaries on the narrative text on a digital class blog. The literary text still reigns at the center of our attention but the methodological and pedagogical pathways to analyze and study it reflect an alternative attitude for learning, teaching and researching, referred previously as a new "academic language."

Lastly, certain traditional Jewish themes such as the wandering experience, migration, life in translation, solitude and alienation appear to be universal concerns at the twenty-first century. We no longer speak in terms of one single history to narrate, one single nationality, or a single identity to define oneself; many literary works emphasize this change at present. Hence, we should reflect it also in our profession: By addressing the needs of our new audience of learners, by thinking of alternative teaching and learning venues, and by fostering new themes and literary representations, and alternative research and pedagogical methodologies.

Bibliography

Becker, Samantha Adams, M. Cummins, A. Davis, A. Freeman, C. Glesinger Hall, and V. Ananthanarayanan. *NMC Horizon Report: 2017 Higher Education Edition.* Austin, Texas: The New Media Consortium, 2017.

Cohen, Steven M. *Profiling the Jewish Studies Profession in North America Highlights form the Survey of AJS Members.* The 2015 Association for Jewish Studies Membership Survey, 2015.

Daniel, Ben. "Big Data and analytics in higher education: Opportunities and challenges." *British Journal of Educational Technology* 46.5 (2015): 904–920.

DeRosa, Robin, and Scott Robison. "From OER to Open Pedagogy: Harnessing the Power of Open." In *Open: The Philosophy and Practices that are Revolutionizing Education and Science,* edited by Rojiv Jhangiani, and Robert Biswas-Diener, 115–124. London: Ubiquity Press, 2017. Retrieved from: DOI: https://doi.org/10.5334/bbc.i. License: CC-BY 4.0.

Jacobson, Roman. "Linguistics and Poetics." *Style in Language.* Ed. T. Sebeok, 350–377. Cambridge, MA: M.I.T. Press, 1960.

---

2 https://www.wordswithoutborders.org/article/white-sand-black-stone (24 September 2019).
3 http://www.covadlo.com/textos/textos.htm (24 September 2019).

Laikin Elkin, Judith. *The Origins of the Latin American Jewish Studies Association: 1982–1995.* Ann Arbor, MI: 2016.
Looney, Dennis, and Natalia Lusin. *Enrollments in Languages Other Than English in United States Institutions of Higher Education, Summer 2016 and Fall 2016: Preliminary Report Web publication*, 2018. Retrieved from: https://www.mla.org/content/download/83540/2197676/2016-Enrollments-Short-Report.pdf
Montana, Patrick, and Francis Petit. "Motivating Generation X and Y on the Job and Preparing Z." *Global Journal of Business Research* 2.2 (2008): 139–148.
Pardo, Abelardo, and George Siemens. "Ethical and Privacy Principles for Learning Analytics." *British Journal of Educational Technology* 45.3 (2014): 438–450.
Rosen, Larry, D. "Teaching the iGeneration." *Educational Leadership: Journal of the Department of Supervision and Curriculum Development* 68.5 (2011): 10–15.
Scheffel, Maren, Hendrik Drachsler, Slavi Stoyanov, and Marcus Specht. "Quality Indicators for Learning Analytics." *Educational Technology & Society*, 17.4 (2014): 117–132.
Ziser, Eyal. "Presentation at Teldan Conference." Tel Aviv, 14 May, 2018.

Laura Rivas Gagliardi
An Historical Approach to Contemporary Brazilian Literature: The Example of Bernardo Kucinski

The purpose of this paper is to discuss Brazilian author Bernardo Kucinski's novel *K.* as a case study for integrating Jewish literature in the broader context of contemporary Brazilian literature. This paper explores how the novel reveals the entangled nature of historical experiences in different parts of the world and how it presents a strong case for teaching global history and literature beyond national frameworks.

Bernardo Kucinski's first novel *K.*[1] (2011) can be understood as a paradigmatic case study for teaching Jewish literature and Brazilian literature alongside each other as a way of challenging identitarian notions of belonging. Jewish literature and Brazilian literature can hardly be understood apart from their relations to a global context – regardless of the specificity of each. Kucinski's novel is representative of both literatures, making evident the author's complex historical perspective: the uniqueness of his protagonists' historical experience illuminates a collective experience. Kucinski is the son of the prominent Yiddish poet Majer Kucinski, who had to flee Poland to Brazil due to his participation in the Marxist-Zionistic party *Poal'ei Tzion* in the 1930s. Bernardo Kucinski's novel makes use of the factual story of the enforced disappearance[2] of his sister Ana Rosa Kucinski Silva and her husband Wilson Silva by agents of the civil-military

---

[1] A second edition was published in 2012 and appeared also in the shortlists of the greatest book awards of the Portuguese language: *Portugal Telecom* and *Prêmio São Paulo de Literatura*. A third edition was published by Cosac Naify in 2014 slightly altered and without the drawings by Brazilian artist Ênio Squeff. The title was also changed to *K. Relato de uma busca* ["Report of a search", in a literal translation]. Since 2016 the book has been published together with other works of the author by Companhia das Letras.
[2] The concept of enforced disappearance is defined in the International Convention for the Protection of Disappearances (United Nations Convention on Human Rights) as "the arrest, detention, abduction or any other form of deprivation of liberty by agents of the State or by persons or groups of persons acting with the authorization, support or acquiescence of the State, followed by a refusal to acknowledge the deprivation of liberty or by concealment of the fate or whereabouts of the disappeared person, which place such a person outside the protection of the law" (Part 1, Article 2). See https://www.ohchr.org/en/hrbodies/ced/pages/conventioned.aspx (3 December 2019).

OpenAccess. © 2020 Laura Rivas Gagliardi, published by De Gruyter. This work is licensed under the Creative Commons Attribution-NonCommercial-NoDerivatives 4.0 License.
https://doi.org/10.1515/9783110619003-023

dictatorship in Brazil (1964–1985) to reflect on the consequences of the rise of authoritarian regimes in Europe in the 1930s and Brazil in the 1970s.

For present-day students of Brazilian studies, the novel *K.* offers the opportunity to face not only one of the darkest chapters of Brazilian history but also the crimes perpetrated by the Nazi regime, allowing students to recognize similarities and differences between these histories and their own. The novel performs a complex and critical shift – perhaps even a dialectical one – from the autobiographical to the collective experience. It does what literature does so well: combining universal and particular standpoints, national and global issues, personal and public practices. The novel issues a clear warning about the importance of not forgetting the past, in the process demonstrating the critical role of literature as a form of social memory and conscience.

The aim of this paper is to contextualize the publication of the novel and problematize its one-sided reception. Secondly, the paper will analyze the literary techniques used to transform the experience of the author's father and sister into fiction, beyond the (auto)biographical. Finally, it will reflect on the integration of Jewish immigrants in Brazil's society and propose a sense of belonging that is multiple.

1 Publication and reception in Brazil and abroad

K. was published at a time when the Brazilian government and public were seeking to enlighten the violent acts committed by the Brazilian state during the military regime from 1964 until 1985. In November 2011, exactly a month before the release of the first edition of book, Brazil's Truth Commission was officially opened by President Dilma Rousseff (2011–2016) in a ceremony in Brasília.[3] The Commission emerged from various initiatives since the so-called *Redemocratização*. The slow transition to democracy in the 1980s was a strategy to avoid

---

[3] Brazil's Truth Commission, made up of seven members and fourteen assistants, aimed to investigate the systematic violations of human rights perpetrated by the Brazilian state between 1946 and 1988. Launched by President Luís Inácio Lula da Silva (2002–2010), the purpose and tasks of the commission changed dramatically until the beginning of the investigations. At first, the Law for the Establishment of a Truth Commission provided only for the investigation of the civil-military dictatorship in Brazil between 1964 and 1985. However, political pressure from the military led to the expansion of the timeframe to include other moments of Brazilian history. Originally the task of the Commission was to identify crimes and their perpetrators, and lead to a legal judgement. In the end, however, the Commission was only allowed to recommend how the government should deal with the outcome of the investigations.

conflict and keep secret the macabre dimensions of the crimes committed under the previous regime. Essential for the supposedly conflict-free transfer of power to the civil president was the amnesty law passed by the military regime in 1979 and upheld by Brazil's Supreme Court in 2010: it actually consists of a power of mercy, which absolved both opposition and military agents from criminal convictions, shielding military agents from being judged until today. The late reappraisal of the civil-military dictatorship, only 26 years later, is also a symptom of its aftermath in the Brazilian government.[4]

If *K.*'s reception in Brazil contributed to shaping the public debate on the recent history of the country, its international reception focused on the history of left-wing Jewish exiles in Brazil in the 1930s. The trajectory of Majer Kucinskis, the author's father, encouraged many international Jewish editors, translators and publishing houses to work together to spread the book.[5] From this perspective, Brazil's civil-military dictatorship was not the central issue. However, it is precisely the interrelation between the historical, political and literary contexts that is the key point of the novel. In the book, the character K., whose name gives the book its title, synthesizes this assortment of contexts through his memories and his incessant search for his daughter. He co-founded the Marxist-Zionist party *Poal'ei Tzion* in Warsaw in the 1930s, like the actual Majer Kucinski. His daughter A., like the real Ana Rosa Kucinski, was a member of the clandestine revolutionary organization ALN (Ação libertadora nacional) in Brazil in

---

4 Perry Anderson compares the amnesty laws in Brazil and those in other Latin American states to illustrate how the official discourse has varied since the impeachment of Dilma Rousseff in 2017: "[...] the South American tyrannies of the 1960s and 1970s made an amnesty for their crimes a condition of withdrawing to the barracks. In every other country these were partially or completely annulled once democracy was consolidated. Uniquely, not in Brazil. In every other country, within one to five years a Truth Commission was set up to examine the past. In Brazil it took 23 years for one to be approved by the Chamber of Deputies and no action was taken against the perpetrators it named. Indeed, in 2010 the Supreme Court declared the amnesty law nothing less than a 'foundation of Brazilian democracy'. Eight years later, in a speech commemorating the thirtieth anniversary of the constitution enacted after the generals had left, the president of the Supreme Court, Dias Toffoli [...] formally blessed their seizure of power, telling his audience: 'Today I no longer refer to a coup or a revolution. I refer to the movement of 1964'." Anderson (2019).

5 *K. relato de uma busca* was translated into eight languages: in 2013 by Sue Branford into English, by Sarita Brandt into German under the title *K. oder die verschwundene Tochter*, by Teresa Matarranz into Spanish under the title *Las três muertes de K.*, and by Pere Comellas into Catalan under the title *Les Tres morts de K.* The novel was shortlisted for the *International Literature Award* in 2014 and for the *Impac Dublin Award* in 2015. In 2015 the Japanese translation appeared, followed in 2016 by the French translation by Antoine Chareyre and the Italian translation by Vincenzo Barca under the title *K. o la figlia desaparecida*.

the 1970s. Understanding K.'s and A.'s experiences arising from political activism within an ongoing historical process is a necessary step to grasp one of the richest meanings of the novel: questions of belonging and identity are shaped differently as these characters were involved in a revolutionary struggle.

2 Memory beyond biography

In the literary construction of the novel, these intertwined experiences are likewise inseparable: on the one hand, the polyphony of the narrative voices provides an overview of all those involved in the disappearance of A. On the other hand, the portrayal of K., which is the core of the novel, involves recounting the crimes of the Nazi regime against Jewish population, telling stories of persecution, extermination, flight and immigration as a crucial moment in world history with which Brazilian students should be more closely familiarized. K.'s indefatigable search is the link between the 29 chapters narrated by several voices in the first person and third person, also integrating into the narrative other text forms, such as letters and reports. However, unlike other characters, K.'s story has a unity: it begins with the disappearance of his daughter, it develops in 14 of the 29 chapters, and concludes with the death of K. in the chapter "The meeting at the barracks". In the plot, while searching for his missing daughter A., K. gains different views of his own past and present: his life in Poland before exile, his arrival in São Paulo and his devotion to Yiddish and then to Hebrew are presented as turning points in the development of his character, binding not only the fragmentary chapters but also different layers of time and experience.

Finally, the form of the novel problematizes its classification as an "autobiographical" or "testimonial" narrative: the narrator did not live the trauma as K. or A., instead he understands himself as a survivor of the loss of K. and A. The book opens with a warning: "Everything in this book is invented, but almost everything has happened". Thus, the story unfolds in an interval marked by the subtle distinction between "everything" and "almost everything". The first edition does provide a longer introductory statement explaining how the novel was written. In the following Brazilian editions as well as in many translations, however, this statement was omitted. In the English translation it appears as a warning "To the reader" at the end of the book, signed by "Bernardo Kucinski" (Kucinski 2013, 169). He states that he "let recollections flow from my memory just as they came." "Story-telling techniques", "imagination" and "invention" are presented as literary processes to fill the gaps of what he forgot. In the Brazilian edition, one can read from "physical shock" in order to "exhume the remnants of his memory" (Kucinski 2013, 169). At the end, he explains that the figure K. combines the fragmentary whole into a unity, as it appears at the beginning and end of the narrative.

3 Individual and collective history

K. also challenges the way in which history has been told in Brazil and beyond, showing that beyond apparently isolate events the driving force of history is the struggle against oppression. Considering fascism and its manifestations from a wide-range point of view, the character K. establishes the link between his own prison in Poland and the enforced disappearance of his daughter as products of a continuously victory of regressive historical forces. A complex reflection on the enforced disappearance and the Holocaust can be considered a revealing moment about the inherent correlation between two seemingly different historical moments in which authoritarianism has triumphed. This central statement is repeated in different situations of the book, particularly in K.'s search for his missing daughter. Already in the first chapter, "The vortex", when K. visits the Institute of Legal Medicine, the narrator says: "Even the Nazis, who'd reduced their victims to ashes, had registered the dead [...] There hadn't been this agony of uncertainty. These had been mass executions, not people vanishing into thin air" (Kucinski 2013, 14).

The overlapping of these temporal levels toward past and future in K.'s story radically transforms his subjective experience in the present. K.'s growing despair is presented chronologically, but at the same time he dives into his memories. Only by looking into the past does the character understand the issues in his present. However, this explicit use of memory as a basis for fiction results in neither testimonial literature nor autobiography, as already mentioned. In the novel, memory has a powerful capacity to reveal a concealed truth. As in Marcel Proust's *Du côté de chez Swann*, in *K.* a single element of reality triggers the involuntary memory, although, unlike in Proust, it provides only a negative epiphany. K. cannot find peace in his remembrance. His memories sharpen the negative correspondences between past and present, as the narrator explains in the following dialogue between K. and a rabbi: "Avrum had admonished him for comparing what happened to his daughter to the Holocaust. Nothing compared with the Holocaust, he'd said. He'd been so angry he'd got up to go. There's only one Holocaust, it's unique, absolute evil. K. agreed with this but said that for him, his daughter's tragedy was a continuation of the Holocaust" (Kucinski 2013, 69).

4 Language and experience

K.'s description of his youth in Warsaw and his arrival in São Paulo, as well his guilty feelings about the enforced disappearance of his daughter, are associated with shifts between Yiddish, Hebrew and Portuguese. An example of this is K.'s conviction that his devotion to Yiddish literature seemed to be an obstacle to his devotion to his family, so that his daughter's militancy went unnoticed by him. A different interpretation of K.'s belief is to consider his connection with Yiddish not as a passion but as a political decision, even if unconsciously: to cultivate Yiddish in Brazil in the 1930s under the dictatorship of Getúlio Vargas was already a kind of resistance. In this sense, the political struggle of his youth had turned into a literary one. Similarly, in a meta-reflection about the sense of continuing to write literature in Yiddish, K. decides to abandon his task as a Yiddish writer and communicate in Hebrew with his grandchildren in Israel, telling them the story of his experience in Brazil, including his daughter's disappearance. Portuguese appears in this context as the language of daily life, a language that K. learned for surviving but also for hearing the inspiring stories which people tell him while he is working his first job as a door-to-door salesman. The unique combination of the very personal experiences that characterize K. is also an expression of a collective, shared history. Pursuing the topic of language in the whole book can be a useful strategy to address central issues relating to memory and politics.

These narrative strategies to smooth boundaries between fiction and reality build the bridge between the Jewish literature and the Brazilian literature and allow one to recognize the resonances in the experience of living under authoritarian regimes.

5 Multiples senses of belonging

The sense of a lack of belonging has radically marked Brazil since colonial times, and even the tentative attempt to shape some form of "Brazilianness" was controversial in the nineteenth and twentieth century. Maybe for this reason, the kind of challenges for the Jewish immigrants in Brazil was completely different in comparison to other places where the notion of belonging was a condition for participating in social life. The young, urban generation of 1960s Brazil, deeply involved in emancipatory movements, had its origin in different geographical and cultural backgrounds. As in other countries, its life was strongly influenced by the pressures of the Cold War, although with a perception of historical movements different from that of the youth of central European countries. Helping to shape a new vision of the land, the most progressive part of Brazilian youth was committed to modernizing the country in cultural, economic and social fields. The example of the Cuban Revolution (1959) played a central role: it confirmed that a radical change in existing social conditions was not impossible.

The military coup in Brazil in 1964 interrupted this emancipatory process. The political, economic and cultural constraints of the dictatorial regime should have ensured a modified form of dependency in favor of a pact between Brazilian and international elites, clearly evidenced by the prompt recognition of the coup by the US government, and revealing that other interests were involved beyond the widespread discourse of a "red threat of communism and defense of democracy".[6] An opposition to the military regime was then formed by students and workers organized in leftist groups, which were soon forced into illegality. Working against any kind of nationalist reductionism, the historian Beatriz Kushnir states that these persons, many of whom had a Jewish background like Ana Rosa Kucinski, "were involved in the premises of socialism, believing in internationalism. So they lived in diversity: they were Jews, they were Brazilians, they belonged to the world" (Kushnir 2015, 31).

This international approach to the fight for emancipation, which is the lesson the reader takes from K.'s story, is a consequence of the diversity of cultural and geographical backgrounds of the young fighters themselves. Their struggle was the reappearance of the many struggles their ancestors had to fight, as Walter Benjamin brilliantly describes in his essay "On the Concept of History". In the ninth section, for instance, Benjamin refers to the notion of an ongoing violation placed in a historical continuum: "Where a chain of events appears before *us, he* [the Angel of History] sees one single catastrophe, which keeps pilling wreckage upon wreckage and hurls it at his feet" (Benjamin 1942, 392). According to the philosopher Michael Löwy, Benjamin questions here Hegel's concept of history, according to which every historical collapse is an inevitable event in the progress of Reason. Löwy notes that Benjamin reverses Hegel's concept of history by not legitimizing and naturalizing oppression, but instead by denouncing what has happened as a "catastrophe". For Benjamin, "wreckage" are traces of destruction and an eternal repetition of the past. In the eighth section, Benjamin explains how these two contradictory concepts of history relate to fascism (Benjamin 1942, 392): to fight fascism, one has to understand it correctly. For Benjamin, this means writing from the perspective of the oppressed, positioning oneself in their tradition and contrasting the state of exception, which has become a

---

6 Headline in the newspaper *O Globo* on 1. April 1964, date of the military putsch.

normal state of oppression, with a real state of exception: the state in which such a form of domination no longer exists.

In this context, *K.* would represent not only a literary form of debating the exemplary history of two individuals, Majer Kuckinski and Ana Rosa Kucinski, but also the collective tragedy connecting generations through their common resistance strategies against torture, murder and impunity. Thus, the crimes of fascism and Brazilian civil-military dictatorship acquire a universal dimension: they resonate in the biography of every subject who was a victim of political persecution at different moments in world history.

To conclude, the novel *K.* allows a paradigmatic integration of Jewish literature and Brazilian literature especially because of its wide range of meanings of belonging and its appeal to emancipation struggles. Jewish writers and intellectuals like Anatol Rosenfeld, Boris Schneiderman, Clarice Lispector, Paul Singer, Michael Löwy, Berta Waldman, to mention only a few names, shaped Brazilian culture in a decisive way. Their importance in the Brazilian literary scene is not questioned, but their relations with Jewish literature and culture should be taught more explicitly.

Bibliography

Anderson, Perry. "Bolsonaro's Brazil." *London Review of Books* 41.3 (2019): https://www.lrb.co.uk/the-paper/v41/n03/perry-anderson/bolsonaro-s-brazil (31 January 2020).

Benjamin, Walter. "On the Concept of History." *Selected Writings*. Ed. Michael W. Jennings. Cambridge, Massachusetts, London: Harvard University Press, 2003 [1942].

"International Convention for the Protection of All Persons from Enforced Disappearance" https://www.ohchr.org/en/hrbodies/ced/pages/conventionced.aspx (3 December 2019).

Kucinski, Bernardo. *K.* São Paulo: Expressão popular, 2011.

Kucinski, Bernardo. *K.* Trans. Sue Branford. London: Latin American Bureau, 2013.

Kushnir, Beatriz. "Nem bandidos, nem heróis: os militantes judeus das esquerdas armadas mortos sob tortura no Brasil (1969–1975)." *História Política* 63 (2015): 1–32.

Löwy, Michael. *Fire Alarm: Reading Walter Benjamin's 'On the Concept of History.'* New York: Verso, 2012 [2005].

Saúl Sosnowski
On Integrating Jewish Literatures into Teaching and Research

The question that has been posed for us is both operational and strategic; beyond its immediacy, it goes to the core of how academic disciplines are organized and structured. Not too subtly, it also underlies a more substantive issue: how are those who produce such texts visualized and evaluated within a socio-political system that ultimately decides on their inclusion or exclusion.

The following are some of the questions that mandate consideration while pondering a strategy to integrate Jewish literatures in core programs. To begin with, what are "Jewish literatures": Those written by Jews and/or by anyone on a Jewish topic? Written in one of two specific Jewish languages, namely Yiddish and Judeo-español / Judezmo? Is Hebrew literature by definition Jewish literature?[1] While too broad a topic for this venue, I would like to share several points that, I believe, will motivate a discussion and lead to the requested strategy for including Jewish literatures in German academia. I draft these pages as an Argentine-Jew (a unified version of multiple identities), a faculty member in a U.S. public university who has been teaching undergraduate and graduate courses on Latin-American Jewish literature, and has included Latin American-Jewish texts in mainstream Latin American courses, as well as in seminars on Argentine literature. Such courses are not unusual in the U.S. academy, as a sample list of Latin American-Jewish courses taught by colleagues and listed on the LAJSA website illustrates.[2] They are part of established and sustained research interests that can also be seen in the broader context of multi-ethnic and diversity agendas. Courses, minors and majors in Hebrew literature, taught in Hebrew and in English, as well as multidisciplinary Jewish studies programs are a regular feature in the U.S. From this perspective, the anomaly is the absence of such offerings elsewhere.

In order to focus centrally on Jewish literatures, I shall leave out Hebrew literature, as it has been for decades a *national* literature, much as any other literature that folds territory and language into a definition of self and nation. Hebrew literature is a product of Israel, whether written in that language by Jews

---

[1] Cf. Hanna Wirth-Nesher's introduction ("Defining the Indefinable: What is Jewish Literature?") to her edited volume, *What is Jewish Literature?* Philadelphia/Jerusalem: The Jewish Publication Society, 1994. 3–12.
[2] http://www.lajsa.org/resources/syllabi-and-course-descriptions/ (24 November 2019).

or by non-Jews (Israeli literature encompasses other languages as well). For their part, Jewish literatures exist in any number of languages spoken by Jews. Moreover, Judaism / Jewishness / Jewish cultures are at the same time local and portable; they possess roots but these roots can be and oftentimes are taken on the road, whether due to persecutions, forced or desirable migrations, or less dramatic causes. The Jewish component – even when seen linked through tradition to Israel as the original site – is perennially in transit. Nevertheless, as history continues to demonstrate, being Jewish is integral to an individual and a community in search of place; it can and does anchor itself in varying landscapes, subject, as all newcomers are, to welcoming cultures, religious adscriptions and rulers that allow for its settlement, survival, and further development. A development that then acquires the very taste of that land without necessarily relinquishing what it brings forth from prior beliefs and cultural tenets, as well as from other sites. Life in a shifting diaspora leads to multi-layered textured experiences. Without in any way disregarding the negativity of expulsions, exile, and migration, we know that wondering across the earth's surface yields the benefits and richness of cross-pollination, of adaptation, and of varying degrees of acculturation that, in turn, leads to richer, nuanced, identities. 1492, for instance, transformed Spanish Jews into carriers of the culture from which they were expelled. Nuanced identities, rooted as they are in a borderless view of the world, call into question any platform that repulses difference while entrenching itself in its nationalist uniqueness. Literature and the arts are responsive to a similar dynamic process.

At first, Jewish literatures, when seen as a Diaspora by-product, are by their very nature, transnational. They may be read as such even after being incorporated into the respective national canons. What determines their place is, as always, who their readers are and how they are read. An ideological compass affixes their place in the literary system. What is transnational cannot be pigeonholed in a single category. Being multiple, and this is a defining feature of Jewish letters, is to cultivate difference and heterodoxy.

In the case at hand, let us remember that to be born Jewish in the Diaspora does not grant citizenship nor nationality – an attribute and a right given by the State. This in itself may be one of the stumbling blocks for those who crave to organize literature according to national boundaries. Jewish literatures are, in a sense, 'marginal': they are not part and parcel of a sole territory, nor do they possess a single language; they are integral to *all* national literatures. The key linguistic exception is, of course, Yiddish, a supra language-literature-culture that hovered over Eastern and Central Europe and whose origins go back to the time where elsewhere Spanish was emerging as a separate language. The continuity of Yiddish was decimated along with its speakers during World War II, and now finds a haven in small clusters and in academia, where Sholem Aleichem and Peretz are read along Isaac Bashevis Singer, notably a regular staple in American literature courses. Still, its tones, traditions and the cultures Yiddish intimately carries are recognizable among writers who possess a limited knowledge and fluency in the language: a cognate whose echoes are found in Kafka, for instance, in Woody Allen and Philip Roth, in Germán Rozenmacher and Mario Szichman. Though not spoken by German Jews, Yiddish, that in time developed its own linguistic peculiarities, tones, variations and personalities, was initially forged out of a high dosage of the German language – a fact that may serve to elicit curiosity within German academia. After all, in many ways, including its almost total demise, the Yiddish world is part of this region's history, and to generate curiosity about it is, in itself, a viable strategy to achieve what we now seek.

Thematically, Jewish literatures have a varying repertoire depending on when and where they are produced; on the patterns of integration and the threat of antisemitism; on how multiple identities could be publicly exercised or shunned. Jews, like any other minority, but at times more than others, are 'the other', those who need to shed identifiable markers (starting oftentimes with the names) in order to become acclimatized or learn to live as one who shares citizenship and nationality but is still quite-not-the-same as members of the dominant culture.

Jewish literatures, by virtue of their multiplicity, may embody a response to monolithic power. At the very least – and clearly this is *not* applicable to all such practices – they are (fortunately and appropriately) bothersome, irritating, probing, questioning, accusatory of a status quo (Kafka is probably the loftiest example, having written, moreover, in a language into which he was not born but out of a tradition that cut across his very utterance). To be an 'other' cognizant of difference does not mean not to be part of a nation, its traditions, history, lore and expectations; it means to be able to see, understand, and analyze things from across the same street we share with all others. From within, then, but from a different angle. As for the majority, it is up to it to learn how to live with the different, particularly in a century that, as expected, is defined by mass migrations. There is no purity in nations, no pure cultures, no essential, immutable identities. All are in perpetual transition and transformation, constantly subject to change. A singular national literature is an imposed fiction that obliterates preexisting difference, an ideological construct that defies and negates the composition of its parts. For those who focus exclusively on national literatures, the multilingual diversity of Jewish letters has to be made known and interest in alternate views of the world brought to the fore. Desire for the unknown and the unexplored has to trace a recognizable signature. Without equating literary phenomena but bearing in mind possible strategies to achieve recognition and acceptance, weren't 'the real marvelous' and 'magical realism', in their variations – beginning with Alejo Carpentier's *The Kingdom of this World* (1949) and incrementally through García Márquez's *One Hundred Years of Solitude* (1967) and beyond – responsible for the West's attention on Latin America? (Of course, couched also in addition to the Cuban revolution and other political developments).

Cultural diversity and plurality – as diverse as the sites where these letters are written – are some of the major aspects to which Jewish literatures call attention. Contrary to a literary melting pot that obliterates the richness of diversity, difference accentuates the ability to identify a culture's density, it enriches what is seen as a national culture. It also facilitates recognizing the constituent layers that forged it, a recognition that, in turn, promotes acceptance of texts and, more significantly, of those who find themselves in those texts.

A literary text worth its salt is disquieting as it also carries the inscribed memories of its mother tongue, of a personal history – a tongue and a history that may or may not be fully translatable into another language. It can be shared, nevertheless, as an ongoing gift that stems from Babel: a dialogue across millennia and through cultural differences.

As for those who insist on monolingual national literatures, it may be useful to recall that in order to reach such an organizational canonical state, it is necessary to identify that the point of arrival began elsewhere, that no one is ever in, or from, a single place. In addressing 'national literature,' that which does not fit that rarefied and censored category must be known and incorporated. Jewish literatures from across the globe offer such an access. They can be read as spokes of the wheel that we view as a literary system, a system whose center is everywhere.

To foster doubt and cultivate uncertainty is a healthy practice to confront authoritarian models – be they in academic circles or in world politics. So is mining the multiple and the diverse, as Jewish letters continue to practice. While the coast may be in sight – a common motif for the persecuted –, there is no guarantee that the landing is assured, nor is permanence in a new found land guaranteed. Settled and also in transit, inquisitive and forever questioning: a useful recipe to craft letters and learn from the ingredients that continue to shape Jewish literatures –the ingredients that constitute renewed and enriched versions of the *Literature* we call home; another name, perhaps, for the library that Borges called the Universe.

Bibliography

Wirth-Nesher, Hanna. "Defining the Indefinable: What is Jewish Literature?", *What is Jewish Literature?* Philadelphia/Jerusalem: The Jewish Publication Society, 1994. 3–12.

VI Case Studies Hebrew and Yiddish Literatures

Allison Schachter
Jewish Writing and Gender between the National and the Transnational

Hebrew and Yiddish literary relations pose an interesting case study for discussions of national and nonnational literary cultures. These modern literatures arose in the declining Russian, Hapsburg, and Ottoman empires in the nineteenth century and amidst the newly emerging nationalist movements of the same periods. In the nineteenth and early twentieth centuries neither Hebrew nor Yiddish could claim a national home or a single center, divided by crumbling empires and newly forming nation-states. Their representatives strove for various forms of national identities and international legitimacy. In Eastern Europe and among the literary diaspora, both Hebrew and Yiddish literatures shared overlapping authors, centers, and literary institutions. However, by the middle of the twentieth century both came to be identified with very different histories, intellectual traditions, and literary cultures.

The story of Hebrew and Yiddish literatures' connection with International PEN captures the evolving historical relations of these diasporic literatures to a changing international political landscape. PEN International was founded in 1921 as an international organization of writers along national lines, a "League of Nations for Men and Women of Letters." When Jewish-language writers sought to establish a bilingual Jewish PEN club in Warsaw in 1927, they posed a challenge to this post-World War I national model. Their petition prompted great confusion by PEN International London, whose representatives posed questions such as what country did well-known Jewish writers, like Sholem Asch, represent? The writers responded with a fifteen-page history of modern Hebrew and Yiddish literature defined in extraterritorial and diasporic terms. This diasporic multilingual model of Jewish literature rapidly frayed. Hebrew writers later petitioned from Palestine for a Hebrew PEN club. A few years later separate Hebrew and Yiddish centers would be formed.[1] At the 1936 PEN conference in Buenos Aries, H. Leyvik, the pre-eminent, Russian-born, New York Yiddish poet articulated the complex place of Yiddish in the world in his speech to fellow PEN delegates, proclaiming: "The essential problem of our literature in the present century consists in finding a way to synthesize national and universal values (*vi azoy gefinen a sintez fun nationaln and universaln*). The Jew and the Universe: here lies the main drama of our life and our literature." (Leyvik 1963, 124) In the 1920s

---

[1] See my discussion of this history in Schachter 2012, 3–5.

Jewish writers sought to imagine a multilingual and diasporic Jewish literature in Eastern Europe. By the 1930s the problem for Yiddish, according to Leyvik, is not how it might transcend its national particularity and speak to the universal, but conversely, how its idiosyncratic worldliness – a wordliness indicated both by its global reach and by its internationalist ethos – might speak to a world composed of territorial nationstates.

By the post-war era, the massive destruction of European Jewry and the rise of the new Israeli nation completely transformed Jewish literary life. Hebrew now had a national home and no longer justified itself in diasporic terms, erasing its multilingual diasporic origins. The emerging Israeli state enforced Hebrew as the national language, at the expense of Jewish multilingualisms. According to the new national narrative, Hebrew became a national literature when its writers emigrated to Palestine, transforming the transnational and diasporic Hebrew past into a monolingual Israeli literature. This nationalist Hebrew literary history obscured and erased the fertile intersections of both languages (as well as others including Arabic) in their shared diasporic contexts.

Much of the comparative work on Hebrew and Yiddish literature in the past two decades has sought to illuminate the rich intersections between Hebrew and Yiddish in post-statehood Israeli culture and to challenge the monolingual and national Hebrew literary historical narrative in the pre-statehood period, tracing for example the continued relations of these literatures, and locating their rich overlap and dialogue. Interesting questions remain: how to assimilate this broader multilingual and multinational history beyond Israeli literary studies? To what literary culture for example did the London-based Yosef Chaim Brenner's work belong? What of Dovid Bergelson's modernist stories written and set in Berlin? How might his literary work be integrated into the study of a multilingual German literary culture? How might Hebrew and Yiddish literary relations serve as a paradigm for a new Jewish literary studies, attentive to peripheral circuits, translingual encounters, and multiple forms of identification?

In recent years, I have collaborated with Lital Levy to theorize the multilingual relations of Jewish-language literatures across continents and cultural contexts. In our article for the PMLA entitled: "Jewish Literature / World Literature: Between the Local and the Transnational" we argued that Jewish literary studies needs to move beyond the parochial and national borders that divide its subjects (Levy and Schachter 2015, 92–109). Despite Jewish language literature's inherent multilingualism and transnationalism, until recently, scholarship has focused on single languages or regions. While at the same time, we argue scholarship on world and transnational literary cultures has largely focused on the languages of the metropolitan center. In our *PMLA* essay, we set out to theorize world and Jewish literary studies in relationship to each other and develop new methodologies for a transnational Jewish literary studies. We furthered this methodology in the special issue of *Prooftexts* on *Jewish Literature/World Literature* that we co-edited.

Arguing that world literary studies should focus its attention on non-metropolitan circuits and on minor languages, we contend that the study of Jewish-language literature provides a compelling case for the centrality of minor languages to discussions of transnational literary culture. Multilingual, transnational, and mobile, modern Jewish-language literatures – including the case of Hebrew and Yiddish – move lucidly between local and transnational contexts, negotiating literary influences from non- Jewish contexts while circulating texts among Jewish languages.

> As a network that traverses multiple geographic regions, political systems, and linguistic frameworks, modern Jewish writing exposes the limits of a model that subsumes the "minor" to the nation and that does not allow for the many linguistic and spatial dimensions of diasporic communities, as well as the many meanings of "the world". (Levy and Schachter 2017, 4)

The story of Eugene Sue's 1843 novel French novel *Les Mystères de Paris (The Mysteries of Paris)* offered an instructive case for rethinking Jewish language literary relations.[2]

The Hebrew version of the novel appeared in Vilna (1857–1860) and was one of the first works of European literature translated into Hebrew. It was published in Yiddish in New York 1865, where it was a work of popular fiction; then in Ladino in the Constantinople Journal *EL Tiempo* in 1891. The novel was also meant as popular literature but held its French prestige; and in Judeo-Arabic in Calcutta in 1893 as part of a Haskalah project. Although it is generally (if erroneously) thought that European Jews modernized before their non-European brethren, the *The Mysteries* served moderately different ends for Yiddish, Ladino, and Judeo-Arabic readers in similar historical circumstances, linking these reading communities to larger and overlapping forces of literary and cultural transformation. A reading of the reception of this novel, shows its global Jewish reach, and pushes us to conceptualize its centrality to Jewish cultural modernity in translational and multilingual terms.

As we look at these broader more flexible models of literary historical thinking, I want to raise another set of issues that haunts both the nationalist global models of literary studies: the unreflexive masculinist paradigms that so often guide literary study and the study of Jewish culture modernity. The predomi-

---

[2] We discuss this at length in our PMLA essay (Levy and Schachter 2015).

nance of a nationalist model of literary history not only marginalizes Jewish writers, but also separates the transnational work of women writers from each other and magnifies their marginalization. Men serve as paragons of national literature, and are internationally recognized as such in global literary frameworks. I posit that a world/transnational and transcultural model must look carefully at women writers, who contribute to the creation of world literary networks and challenge the national literary frameworks that have dominated. Without their contributions, we would have a fundamentally one-sided, flawed understanding of transnational and world literary cultures. In my current work on Hebrew and Yiddish modernism, I bridge these two traditions to locate a shared, but obscured, transnational and diasporic modernist aesthetic among women writers.[3] Whereas in Yiddish women have been written out of the prose canon, in Hebrew they have been marginalized or read as isolated exceptions. Separated by languages and national homes, these women's prose innovations have been largely invisible to literary scholars, and viewed as isolated developments in minor languages. Read together across languages in multiple territorial centers, New York, Moscow, Tel Aviv, and Poland, makes their internationalist, modernist aesthetic visible.

Very briefly, I want to outline the connections among two of these writers in their surprising shared dialogue with Flaubert's *Madame Bovary*. Fradel Shtok and Dvora Baron were born within one year of each other, Shtok in Skala at the border with the Russian empire, and Baron in Uzda just outside of Minsk. The former educated in German classics, and the latter in Jewish tradition, one emigrated to the US and the other to Palestine. Both women retired from public view early in the careers: Baron continued to write after she retreated into her home, whereas Shtok went largely silent. Both have been mythologized for their retreat. According to the received narrative, Shtok was angered at Leyeles' negative review of her 1919 collection of short stories, and stormed into the offices of *Der tog*, slapped him across the face, and then dramatically broke off ties with Yiddish (Pratt 2008, 67–68).[4] The *Lexikon fun der yiddisher literature* describes her end in the 1930s, "Over time she became melancholic and died in a sanitarium for the mentally ill."[5] News of her death was premature. She wrote a Yiddish play in the 1920s, that can be found in the library of con-

---

[3] This is the subject of my current book manuscript, *Experiments in Prose: Women Writing Jewish Modernity*.

[4] Jacob Glatstein offers an extended account of Shtok's life, though he refers to her under a pseudonym. See: Jacob Glatstein, "Tsu der biografye fun a dikhterin," *Tog-morgn zhurnal*. September 19, 1965, p. 7.

[5] "Fradel Shtok," *Leksikon fun der yidisher literatur*, vol. 8 (607).

gress. Moreover, in a letter dated October 20, 1942, Shtok wrote to Abe Cahan, editor of the New York Yiddish daily, *Foverts*, sending along a story that Cahan published in November of that year (Neugroschel 2002, 463). My recent archival search has uncovered additional information about her life, including the tragic fact that she died in 1990 at Rockland State Hospital, where she was institutionalized in the 1960s.

Dvora Baron, immigrated to Palestine in 1910 and married Yosef Aharonovich, the editor of *Ha-Poel Ha-Tsair*. In 1922 she and her husband resigned from their editorial positions, and she famously secluded herself in her home. It was not until 1927 that she succeeded in publishing a collection of her short fiction in Hebrew. This was a source of enormous frustration for Baron, whose husband had twice raised the funds for the project and then chose to use them otherwise.[6]

In 1932, five years after the publication of her first collection of stories, her translation of Flaubert's *Madame Bovary* appeared in print. Baron was not the only female, socialist translator of the novel, Eleanor Marx, a socialist, feminist political activist, and Karl Marx's daughter, undertook her translation in 1885–1886, the same period that she put on the first performance of Ibsen's *A Doll House* in London, and published one of the most important documents of socialist feminism: "The Woman Question: From a Socialist Point of View."[7] Baron, Shtok, and Marx all found in Flaubert's work a sharp critique of capitalism and a feminist promise, even if one that was never realized in his novel.

Baron and Shtok's prose engage in a rich dialogue with Flaubert's novel, including his investment with breaking down the divide between art and life, and his innovative prose techniques, particularly *style indirecte libre*, while also critiquing his demonization of women's desires. Baron's story "Ketanot" or "Trifles" describes the fulfillment of a woman's aesthetic desires, while also critiquing the violence that limits those desires. Shtok's story, "Friedrich Schiller," mobilizes her female protagonist's material desires to disrupt the normative aesthetic hierarchies of European high culture. Separated by language and national home, these women's prose innovations have been largely invisible to literary scholars. However, when we examine their shared aesthetic practices we see two women writers united by an investment in the subversive artisitc potential of women's desires. Shtok envisions the desiring woman as an artist, endowing her with the aesthetic authority to transgress the boundaries between art and life, and be-

---

[6] According to Nurith Govrin's account, he raised the needed funds for the endeavor, but ultimately decided to use the money for "public good," writing to Brenner in 1911 that "he received the credit but used it to publish 'Ha-aretz ve-ha-avoda'" (Govrin 1988, 233).
[7] Rachel Holmes, *Eleanor Marx: A Life* (London: Bloomsbury, 2016) 249.

tween Jewish and Gentile culture. Through her dialogue with Flaubert, Baron theorizes the writer as aesthetic laborer who narrates women's engagement with material objects as both exploited producers and desirous consumers and transforms their creation of value into the substance of art. Viewed from this comparative perspective Baron no longer remains an outlier in Hebrew literary history who wrote modernist stories set in the restricted world of the shtetl, and Shtok enters Yiddish literary history as a compelling modernist writer of Jewish modernity. They are part of a larger transnational, modernist, and feminist critique of Jewish literary modernity.

These comparative and transnational approaches to literary studies are promising avenues for expanding the canon and moving past restrictive doxa that have limited women from our purview. Of course, institutions of higher education are driven by forces that promote national language and literatures tirelessly. We cannot escape these institutions, but in our teaching and scholarship we can promote the teaching of a rich body of literary works from a comparative angle. A comparative Jewish literary model, built on the tools of world literary studies could be a very useful paradigm for such a project.

Bibliography

"Fradel Shtok", *Leksikon fun der yidisher literatur* 8. 608 (1981): 39–45. Glatstein, Jacob.
  "Tsu der biografye fun a dikhterin." *Tog-morgn zhurnal.* (Septemeber 19, 1965): 7.
Govrin, Nurith. *Ha-Maḥatsit ha-ri'shonah: Dvora Baron.* Mosad Bialik: Jerusalem, 1988.
Holmes, Rachel. *Eleanor Marx: A Life.* London: Bloomsbury, 2016.
Levy, Lital and Allison Schachter. "Jewish Literature / World Literature: Between the Local and the Transnational." *PMLA* 130.1 (2015): 92–109.
Levy, Lital and Allison Schachter. "A Non-Universal Global: On Jewish Writing and World Literature." *Prooftexts: A Journal of Jewish Literary History* 36:1–2 (2017): 1–26.
Leyvik, H. [Leivick Halpern]. "Di heylkeyt fun mentshlekhn lebn (rede gehaltn afn pen-kongres in Buenos Aries)." *Esayen un redes.* Ed. Y. Zilberberg. New York: Alveltlekhn kultur kongres, 1963.
Neugroschel, Joachim (ed.). *No Star Too Beautiful: An Anthology of Yiddish Stories from 1382 to the Present.* New York: W. W. Norton & Company, 2002.
Novershtern, Avraham. "Ha-kolot ve-ha-makhela: shirat nashim be-yidish ben shtei milchamot ha-'olam." *Bikoret u-farshanut* 40 (2008): 67–8.
Pratt, Norma Fain. "Culture and Radical Politics: Yiddish Women Writers, 1890–1940." *American Jewish History* 70.1 (1980): 68–90.
Schachter, Allison. *Diasporic Modernisms: Hebrew and Yiddish Literatures in the Twentieth Century.* New York: Oxford University Press, 2012.

Hannah Pollin-Galay
Producing Radical Presence: Yiddish Literature in Twenty-first Century Israel

Should literature be taught as space of imagination or as a tool for building social conscience? This is a question heard and asked often these days. Given the current challenges facing the humanities – declining enrollment, profit-based measures of educational success, technological incursions on learning practices, and public leaders who proudly assert that they do not read – many scholars seek new ways to articulate the value of their profession, to defend literature in the public sphere. Martha Nussbaum has famously argued that the humanities are crucial for creating and maintaining a "people-sensitive democracy" (Nussbaum 2010, 25). Not all are pleased with this line of thinking. Nussbaum's detractors complain that, in arguing for the ultimate "use" of the humanities, she echoes the instrumentalism of those who want to destroy these same fields. Ben Saunders puts it this way: "We value money instrumentally, because it allows us to consume other things that we value intrinsically. Art and culture, I suggest, are such goods: worth spending money on because we value them in themselves, rather than regarding them as investments expected to produce some further benefit, either economic or political" (Saunders 2013, 250).

I would like to move away from the dichotomy between instrumental outcomes (strengthening democracy) versus intrinsic value (aesthetic or experiential pleasure) by thinking instead about the capacity of literature to *produce presence* – a notion that has been richly developed by the critic Hans Ulrich Gumbrecht. Gumbrecht defines presence as "a spatial relationship to the world and its objects. Something that is 'present' is supposed to be tangible for human hands, which implies that, conversely, it can have an immediate impact on human bodies." (Gumbrecht 2004, xiii). Perhaps counterintuitively, since literature is often considered an art of words rather than objects, Gumbrecht argues that certain texts have the ability to create presence, both by making readers more alive to the sensations of the moment that they are currently living, more attentive to the other human faces before them and also by *re*-presenting moments of the past, calling them up into the physical space of here and now (Gumbrecht 2003).

I believe that Yiddish literature has an especially valuable presence to produce today, particularly when taught in contemporary Israel. I first arrived at this proposition in the spring of 2018, my first teaching at Tel Aviv University. As part of an introductory course on Yiddish literature, I taught the classic fiction, *Di*

∂ OpenAccess. © 2020 Hannah Pollin-Galay, published by De Gruyter. This work is licensed under the Creative Commons Attribution-NonCommercial-NoDerivatives 4.0 License.
https://doi.org/10.1515/9783110619003-026

kliatshe [*The Mare*] by Mendele Moykher-Sforim (Sholem Yankev Abramovitsh)[1] (1873). *Di kliatshe* tells the story of a model student of modernity who meets a talking horse. The protagonist is a young man named Isroelik who lives alone with his mother in a *shtetl* in the Pale of Settlement. Despite the implications of his given name (literally "Little Israel"), Isroelik is determined to transcend the spatial and practical littleness of his Jewish life – by means of attaining a university education. He wants to become a doctor, a profession that would grant him the right to live in the Russian interior, beyond the Pale of Settlement. This relocation would allow him to dress like everyone else, act like everyone else, and even fall in love like everyone else. As Mendele puts it, "Isroelik wants to become a *mentsh* – a person." (Abramovitsh 1873, 9). Committed to social acceptance by means of rational self-improvement, Isroelik studies day and night for the university entrance exams. In the midst of his preparations, he hallucinates an encounter with an old, beaten-down female horse. In what should have been Isroelik's first warning sign that the world is perhaps less rational than he had hoped, the horse speaks Yiddish (in addition to her native *ferdish*-horsish). The mare, who actually houses the soul of a centuries-old Jewish prince, gives Isroelik a lesson in Jewish history, the main point of which is that rationality has never prevented cruelty. In depicting professors who were transmogrified into dogs, as one example, the mare asserts, "They had minds like people, but the hearts and mouths of dogs." (Abramovitsh 1873, 23). Posthallucination, Isroelik's mother echoes the horse's message. She urges Isroelik to lay off the books and explains that bribes, not intelligence, typically offer Jews access to the gentile metropolis.

Disregarding the warnings of both his mother and his new horse companion, Isroelik heads to the big city, presumably Kiev, to take his exams. Despite his capacities in mathematics, foreign languages and science, Isroelik is given an exam that he cannot pass:

> Di lerer zaynen gesezn ongebotn in mundirn mit meshene knep un gekukt azoy shtreng, azoy glaykh vi ikh hob geganvet oder gekoylet a mentshn, zey hobn gekukt azoy vi yene tsaytn a stanavoy, vos dos ershte borukh-hobe iz ba im geven: 'Iskudeva? Ya tebi!...Pasport mayesh?! [...]

> Es fartsheyt zikh, az fun zeyer barukh-hobe, hob ikh bald farloren dem kurasz un shoyn nisht gevust vos mit mir tut zikh. Oyb dos take meynt der posek, hobn di lerer derlangt zeyer vuntsh, vos derlangen heyst...Bald deruf hot zikh gevendet tsu mir a lerer...[mit] aza mine hot er tsu mir zikh gevendet un mikh mekhabed geven mit a posuk fun danen, fun dortn, biz me iz aruf af a mayse, akurat af der bobe yaga! Ikh hob mikh fardreyt,

---

[1] Sh. Y. Abramovitch, 1835–1917.

farplontert, farkhrokhn keyn Boyberik. Di lerer hobn mir ongeton koved, mikh geshenkt a gelekhterl, shoyn mit a freylekher mine un dermit iz gevorn eyn ek fun mayn gantzer mi, eyn ek a sof fun ale mayne hofenungen! (Moykher-Sforim 1873, 8)

[The teachers sat there, dressed in uniforms with brass buttons. They looked at me, as harshly as if I had robbed or killed someone. They looked at me like a policeman from those days, whose first words of welcome were: "*'Iskudeva? Ya tebi!...Pasport mayesh?!* [*In a combination of Russian and Ukrainian:* 'Where ya from! I'll give you...Got a passport?!'] [...] Of course, their welcome made me lose all my courage and my bearings. If that was their aim [*posek*], then they fulfilled it as well as anyone can fulfill anything....A teacher soon turned to me...He turned to me with such a face and honored me by spitting out one question after another, a verse [*posek*] from here, a verse [*posek*] from there, until we came to a fairytale about none other than Baba Yaga! My head began to spin, my mind ran adrift and crawled back to Boyberik. The teachers did me the honor of laughing at me, this time with happy faces and that brought an end to my exam, an end to my efforts; it ended, shut down all my hopes!][2]

Famously, this passage deals a brutal blow to the Jewish Enlightenment program, dramatizing the impotence of its promise (Wisse 2000, 330–336; Pines 2018, 24–47).

Even if Jews were to turn themselves into more universalist, rational beings, that would still not erase the particularist loyalties, the irrationality and the prejudice of non-Jewish society. Mendele echoes this narrative message on multiple formal levels. For one, he represents the examiner's voice in its aural original, as Yisroelik would have heard it, a combination of Russian and Ukrainian. Inserting this Slavic quote in the midst of the Yiddish text, Mendele refutes the existence of a translingual, transcultural space in which Jews and Slavs can meet as equals; They can only encounter one another with difference, each through their own tongue and their own lens.

While the brass buttons and militaristic look of the examiners intimidate Yisroelik, it is ultimately literature that obstructs Yisroelik's entrance into the enlightened world. He is drilled on Baba Yaga, a Slavic folk character that any non-Jewish applicant would easily recognize from bedtime stories and elementary school recitations. Professors of Slavic heritage, the dominant culture in this setting, seek to valorize their non-rational, non-materialistic cultural legacy by incorporating it into the required university curriculum. In the abstract, I doubt that anyone in the humanities today would object to such a goal. Adding complexity, the Ukrainian culture and language, which appears in the text from time to time, has historically undergone its own subordination to Russian lan-

---

[2] In translating this passage, I consulted Moykher-Sforim 1991, 335.

guage and culture. Nonetheless, in this moment, the formal study of literature and folklore becomes a tool for excluding cultural outsiders, in this case Jews.

Mendele wrote *Di kliatshe* in 1873. In 1881, the assassination of Tsar Alexander II lead to a wave of violent pogroms and further legal restrictions on Jews in Russia. In 1897 the first Zionist Congress took place in Basel. Isroelik's exam scene brings us into this specific historical moment in all of its emotional repercussions. Emancipation had failed the Jews of Eastern Europe and, in light of this brutal disappointment, Jews sought new solutions to poverty and exclusion, national sovereignty among them. Teaching this passage in contemporary Israel, this historical moment is actually not as accessible as one would think. So thoroughly exposed to slogans about the necessity of Jewish self-reliance, some of my students seemed to lack opportunities to pause on sensations of Jewish powerlessness. Faced with a nearly constant demand to *correct* for history, they seemed ill at ease with stepping *inside* history. On its simplest level, the scene asks us to be empathic witnesses to Jewish history, especially moments in which the dynamics of power differed substantially from those today.

Were it only for this memory of rejection and exclusion, rendered as a mood rather than an action plan, the text might be worth teaching. But, in my case, this scene from *Di kliatshe* produced an additional, riskier effect as well. When I first taught this text in an introductory course, the class included students of various Jewish backgrounds and one Palestinian woman. In studying this passage together as a group, there was no hiding the fact that we were in danger of reenacting the very narrative on the page. Yiddish – in an Israeli context, and at its reductive worst – could become a folkloric code of the ethnic group in power. Baba Yaga could easily be turned into Bobe Yente, the rich and challenging tones of the Yiddish corpus turned into comforting nostalgia. And all this could be activated in class as a way to convey to this Palestinian student among us that, if she would like to excel in the place where she lives, she had best internalize "our" cultural narratives. Literature has physical powers within Mendele's scene: It is the force that blocks Isroelik's entry into the more comfortable, universalizing zone of the metropolis. Beyond the text, in our classroom, the text had a different physical power – it required us to see the people who were right before us. The act of looking is in fact key to the passage. "Looking," "face" and "turning toward" are words that appear repeatedly: Under the right circumstances, this narrative passage can give the reader stage directions.

Dan Miron offers a way of reading *Di kliatshe* comparatively in a way that further enriches the presence produced by this scene. He describes the voice of Mendele, both the author and the character, as "Caliban language," in reference to the monster-slave character in Shakespeare's *The Tempest* (Miron 1973, 34–66). Caliban learns to speak from Prospero, the man who enslaved him:

"You taught me language; and my profit on't/ Is, I know how to curse. The red plague rid you/ For learning me your language!" Caliban stumbles, his sentences have awkward interruptions. He has internalized the tongue of power, but adapted it into his own monster-jargon. To the ears of the other characters in the play, Caliban's voice is supposed to be ugly. But, as delivered to us through Shakespeare's pen, it is full of art and dignity. According to Miron, Modern Yiddish literature was in part born of the desire to find such an ugly-dignified voice for East European Jews – to cultivate a creative presence within that voice, rather than to emancipate or reform it.

In my Yiddish Literature class, we watched clips of Caliban monologues as performed by different actors in various productions. We noted that this ugly-elegant voice is incredibly hard to create. We observed how easy it was for actors to fall either into the trap of self-mockery, which parallels the satirized Yiddish of some works of the Haskalah (think of the embarrassing too-Jewish blabber in Shlomo Etinger's 1873 *Serkele*)[3], or false tones of self-confidence (which one could compare perhaps to some works of Soviet Yiddish poetry).[4] We gained a new appreciation for how Mendele crafts elevated lowliness in his writing. For example, in the passage in question, Mendele repeats many words over and over: not just "looked," and "turned to," but also "verse," and "welcome," "end." He dramatizes a limited vocabulary, and thus a low register, but sets this basic lexicon into inverted and playful musical arrangements. For example, this happens in the sentence: "*hobn di lerer derlangt zeyer vuntsh, vos delangen heyst.*/Lit: The teachers fulfilled their wish, as fulfilling could mean." There is also a graceful rocking between self-irony and earnest expressions of pain. The last sentence, for instance, begins with protective sarcasm, "The teachers did me the honor…", but ends in earnest, "an end to all of my hopes." It is this candid emotional swinging that allows him to stage his complaint.

In addition to shining new light onto Mendele's Yiddish style, one of the clips that we watched created another, surprising opportunity for producing presence. The Caliban rendering that caught our attention was a student production of *The Tempest* from Georgia Southwestern State University in 2008.[5] The clip was not of high production value and the acting and directing appeared rough around the edges. But, something about this performance struck a chord. Notably, since the play was performed in the American deep south, the role of Caliban was played by a black student, while a white student played

---

[3] Printed in Ettinger 1935. The different registers of speech in this play are discussed in Roskies 2014.
[4] E.g. Peretz Markish. "Dem yidishn shlakhtman." *Far folk un heymland*. Moscow, 1943. 3–7.
[5] https://www.youtube.com/watch?v=FGcDBKIcIeU&t=92s (18 June 2019).

the role of the master, Prospero. While some would dismiss this production for typecasting, my students and I were captivated by the emotional charge between the actors on stage. It was a daring reenactment. The student performers re-presented their own pasts, perhaps even their own family histories, and we, their internet viewers thousands of miles away, became their witnesses. The production of presence revealed contagious potential, with one act of self-witnessing through literature engendering another.

This chance encounter, between Mendele, me, my students, Shakespeare, Dan Miron and the actors in Georgia, was one that performed the singularity of literature; the singularity not just of text but of reading. Beyond this chance encounter, I propose that Yiddish literature possesses a broader potential to create new types of presence in contemporary Israel and perhaps elsewhere. Because Yiddish is a Jewish language – but not the one that most students know and speak – it is both familiar and foreign. It thus calls Jewish history in the classroom, but with a space for seeing things differently, outside of set patterns. Perhaps Yiddish literature sounds to my students like Isroelik hears history from the voice of a horse: awkward yet comprehensible, uncanny. As in Isroelik's exam scene, the Yiddish corpus often explores what it means to be in a position of weakness vis-à-vis the majority culture around you. This then forms the platform for a new literary community, a space of writing and reading together with all the various accents and our dialects of today. This here-ness and with-ness is created through aesthetic as well as narrative means, so that it can be sensed rather than merely told or contemplated. In sum, such a reading experience upends the assumption that, while going about our daily business, we are living in a concrete reality, whereas literature releases us into an alternate dimension. In this case, it seems that all of Mendele's imaginative genius – the talking horse included – are what enabled us to actually notice our own here and now.

Bibliography

Ettinger, Shloyme. *Geklibene verk.* Ed. Max Erik. Kiev: Farlag fun der Ukraynisher visnshaft-akademye, 1935.
Gumbrecht, Hans Ulrich. *The Production of Presence: What Meaning Cannot Convey.* Stanford, California: Stanford University Press, 2004.
Gumbrecht, Hans Ulrich. *The Powers of Philology: Dynamics of Textual Scholarship.* University of Illinois Press, 2003.
Markish, Peretz. "Dem yidishn shlakhtman." *Far folk un heymland.* Moscow, 1943. Aufnahme der Produktion von The Tempest durch die Georgia Southwestern State University von William Shakespeare. Letzter Zugriff 17. 7. 2020
https://www.youtube.com/watch?v=FGcDBKIcIeU&t=92s (18 June 2019)

Miron, Dan. *A Traveler Disguised: A Study in the Rise of Modern Yiddish Fiction in the Nineteenth Century.* New York: Schocken Books, 1973.
Moykher-Sforim, Mendele (Sh. Y. Abramovith). *Selected Works of Mendele Moykher-Sforim.* Eds. Marvin Zuckerman, Gerald Stillman, and Marion Herbs. Malibu: Pangloss Press, 1991.
Moykher-Sforim, Mendele (Sh. Y. Abramovith). *Di kliatshe oder tsar bale-khayim.* Vilna, 1873.
Nussbaum, Martha Craven. *Not for profit: Why democracy needs the humanities.* Princeton, NJ: Princeton University Press, 2010.
Pines, Noam. "A Radical Advocacy: Suffering Jews and Animals in SY Abramovitsh's *Di Kliatshe.*" *Jewish Social Studies* 23.2 (2018): 24–47.
Roskies, David G. "Call It Jewspeak: On the Evolution of Speech in Modern Yiddish Writing." *Poetics Today* 35.3 (2014): 225–301.
Saunders, Ben. "Education for Democracy or for Itself: A Critical Note on Martha C. Nussbuam's *Not for Profit: Why Democracy Needs the Humanities*" *Representation* 49.2 (2013): 241–251.
Wisse, Ruth. *The Modern Jewish Canon: A Journey through Language and Culture.* New York: Free Press, 2000.

Iris Milner
The Unhomely In/Of Hebrew Literature

A symposium dedicated to research and teaching of Modern Hebrew literature within the framework of a wide, interdisciplinary literary context, provides us with a precious opportunity to reflect upon our work in the field. For me, one course such reflection may take is a renewed consideration of literature's embedded tendency to dismantle predominant narratives, among them monolithic national narratives which literature in general, and Modern Hebrew literature in particular, is often assumed to support and fortify.

This is particularly relevant to my present research and teaching; My readings of the literature of some of the prominent authors of Hebrew literature of the past 100 years focus on their attempts at transgressing confined borders, by way of constantly searching for "decentered-ness" and exposing a fundamental yearning for otherness. These readings indeed expose literature's embedded resistance to the canonization of a national narrative, founded on prescribed conventions of identity, place and time. I believe an emphasis on these subversive aspects of Modern Hebrew literature provides a ground for studying and teaching it in the context of such recently flourishing interdisciplinary discourses as Diasporic Studies, Exile Studies, Migration and Immigration Studies, Minority Studies, Trauma Studies and Post-Colonial studies in general.[1]

An outstanding example of a consistent resistance to a national narrative is the oeuvre of a unique and highly appreciated woman author of Hebrew prose, Yehudit Hendel. Hendel, a 2003 *Israel Prize* laureate, was a rather prolific writer until her death in 2014. Born in Warsaw in 1921 to "Bundist" parents who opposed Zionist ideology and refused to join their Hassidic family that had immigrated to Palestine, but later changed their mind, she arrived in Haifa at the age of 9.[2] She began publishing short stories at a very young age, and in 1949, after a

---

[1] See, among others, my essays on nomadism in literary works by Aharon Appelfeld: Milner 2011; 2013.
[2] The "Bund" (short for "The General Jewish Labor Bund for Lithuania, Poland and Russia"), founded in Vilnius in 1897 under the inspiration of the "General German Workers Association", strongly opposed the Zionist movement. Historian Yosef Gorny defines the two parties as "two different – clashing and rival – versions of the idea of Jewish national revival in modern society (Gorny 2006, 1), indicating that "[...] both were extreme negators of exile at the level of ethical values – one liquidating the Diaspora by leaving it, the other liquidating it by staying there, or, in the telling expression of post-Holocaust Bund leader Emanuel Szerer, 'to live in exile without the exile soul.'" (Ibid, 5).

ə OpenAccess. © 2020 Iris Milner, published by De Gruyter. [CC BY-NC-ND] This work is licensed under the Creative Commons Attribution-NonCommercial-NoDerivatives 4.0 License.
https://doi.org/10.1515/9783110619003-027

short period of service in the armed forces, was assigned with the mission of collecting and editing a "compact" anthology of literary texts, to be distributed among Israeli soldiers, titled *Lamagen* – "for the defender" (Hendel 1949). This positioned her at the center of the political and cultural Israeli hegemony of the time, and affirmed her successful metamorphosis from a diaspora-born into an "Israeli born", the so-called "Sabra". It was taken for granted that she upheld and supported the national narrative of nation and state building.

However, Hendel's literature eventually took subversive directions and never fully embraced the idea of the Israeli home as a haven, and as a yearned-for redemption from exilic existence. On the contrary, in her novels and short stories the Israeli home is often the scene of an unhomely experience, of *Das Unheimliche*, in Freudian terminology.[3] Her works perform in their style, and express thematically, extreme and sometimes devastating fissures and breaches in the figure of the "home" – and an accompanying sentiment of detachment, of a wish to flee from anything that is too strictly restraining. It is very often haunted homes that she describes, haunted, among other things, by the memory of homes abandoned in Europe, and of mother-tongues, Polish and Yiddish, forced to be forgotten in order to create an exclusive status for Modern Hebrew as the language of revival. A drive to flee, however, never leads the protagonists anywhere, and they find themselves in a restless motion in-between places, never attaining a true feeling of being-at-home. Such is the case in one of Hendel's early novels, *Hachatser shel Momo Hagdola* (Big Momo's Courtyard) (Hendel 1969). Its protagonist, a Holocaust survivor in his thirties, wanders throughout the 17 years that have elapsed since he emigrated to Israel after the war, from one small and unwelcoming rented room to another, carrying with him his only belonging: a small suitcase that contains his childhood diary, written in Polish, a language he does not remember and can no longer read:

> His possessions, on the shelf, were disordered, and the suitcase of the small, torn books, whose covers rolled on the floor, was still open. He picked them up, searching for the small notebook from the days of his childhood, and opened it, leafing through it, standing up, without knowing how to read a word, continuing to stand up, staring at the strange letters of his childhood handwriting, which he had forgotten. The faded pages, non-equal, were torn at the edges, held by a pin, and he put them together, spreading them in the palm of his hand, snuffling them, as if their smell gave him back their language, but in no way could he remember, and the strange, childish handwriting, his own, escaped him again. (Ibid 65, translation from Hebrew mine).

---

[3] On the Unhomely (the Uncanny, in the traditional translation of *Das Unheimliche* to English) in Hendel's literature, see my article "Zarim Babait: Haalbeiti Beyetsirata shel Yehudit Hendel" (Strangers at Home: The Unhomely in Yehudit Hendel's Oeuvre), (Milner 2016).

Hendel thus portrays a literary figure of a young man who is not only alienated from the concrete spaces he resides in, but also, and even more so, estranged from his core being as it was invested in his presently indecipherable childhood text. He is thus, as are other figures in Hendel's oeuvre, profoundly detached, and is ceaselessly on the move, never actually knowing what his destination might be, let alone succeeding in arriving at it: "The long summer day is fading, and he wanders along the allies, as if he knew them, and his being homeless again filled his heart with a strange sweetness." (Ibid 13, translation from Hebrew mine). This literary hero is as far removed as can be imagined from the hero of the national narrative, and he demonstrates the futility, for him, of the national project.

Indeed, Hendel's poetics is far removed from that of Hebrew literature of her time also in terms of her unique usage of language. Her sentences are long and associative, and at the same time missing and fractured. They often echo distinctly personal spoken words that are immersed in Yiddish tempo, syntax and figures of speech. Her texts break traditional literary modes (in a manner typical, to a certain extent, to women's writing – "écriture feminine"), and their awkward changes of modes, and above all their repetitiveness, manifest their restlessness, their constant transition and search for meaning and resolution.

In 1987 Hendel published a small book in which, under the title *Leyad Kfarim Shketim, 12 Yamim BePolin* (Near Quiet Villages – 12 Days in Poland) she assembled transcriptions of five radio talks, describing her visit to Poland a year earlier. It had been a trip initiated by The Israeli Broadcasting Authority, one of the very first official visits of Israelis to Poland in the post-Communist Era. The literary report of this trip, one of the first literary travelogues describing voyages to Poland that later became very popular, was, in a way, a "return of the repressed" as it exposed previously denied longings, an insatiable "Heimweh" ("home-pains") experienced, paradoxically, at home:

> [...] and suddenly I was in the midst of a turbulence of uncanniness and longings, and of a desire to forget and of hatred and streets and number of streets, and shall I go to Lodz, and shall I go to Lublin, and will I be in Częstochowa, in Częstochowa, and maybe you go to the cemetery in Lublin, maybe you find my father, and maybe you go the cemetery in Krakow, maybe you find my mother, and heavy sacks that each and every one carries on the back, and big stories and little stories, a thousand stones emitted at ones from this volcano which extinguished and died a long time ago and was not buried." (Hendel 1987, 16, translation from Hebrew mine).

Hendel does not mention in *Near Quiet Villages* the fact that she is travelling to her country of birth. Or rather, she does so only metonymically, in a description of her intended, but never carried out journey to the hometowns of three of her dearest ones: her mother, her husband (the prominent Israeli painter, Zvi Meirovich) and her friend, the acclaimed Modern Israeli poet, Avot Yeshurun (Yehiel Perlmutter). Titled "The Towns to Which I Did Not Go" (Ibid, 47–64) the chapter dedicated to this planned part of her journey, is, once more, a story about wandering around, approaching but never arriving, a story of avoidance and distance. This is how Hendel explains her decision to finally not to go to her mother's hometown, Kalushin: An old man, originally from Kalushin, said to her on the phone, before she left Israel, first in Hebrew (translated here to English), then in Yiddish: "מה יש לך לנסוע לקלושין"; "What have you to go to Kalushin? Even the cemetery is not there, the cemetery is a potato field: ".דער ביסעוילם איז אויך נישטו דער ביסעוילם איז א פעלד וואס ואקסן דורט קארטאפלן." (Ibid, 14–15).

Near Quiet Villages closes with an anecdote of a postcard Hendel sent her family in Tel Aviv while still in Poland, in which she praises the experience of homecoming. The postcard arrives at its destination when Hendel is already back in Israel. Thus she becomes the recipient of her own message, sent from afar. She reads (and writes) what the postcard says: "When this postcard arrives I will already be home and that will be fantastic." (Ibid, 102). Although "home" seems to refer specifically to her apartment in Tel Aviv, homecoming, as well as late arrival, are obviously rather ambiguous concepts here: they are, in fact, the essence of both journeys: *to* and *from* Warsaw, *from* and *to* Tel Aviv. Thus, the concept of home is decentered and loses its firm foundation, and the desire for home turns upon itself and collapses into a wasteland.

Merging geographical itineraries and back-and-forth movement are, then, the core of the written text – both the postcard and the entire travelogue that it synecdochally represents. Motion then seemingly finds its place of stability and rests only in the text. However, the text itself does not rest: it, too, as I have already mentioned, is in constant transition. Not only through the post (the postcard that "travels" from Warsaw to Tel Aviv, as does the childhood diary in the novel *Big Momo's Courtyard*), and not only among landscapes and longings, but also among languages (Hebrew, Yiddish, Polish, and English all appear in the text) and among styles (refined and eloquent Hebrew changes rapidly into idiosyncratic tropes and idioms). This is magnificent and at the same time menacing and hard to traverse. The restlessness of the text, in other words, is often a manifestation of the *Unheimlich* it represents.

In these terms, Hendel echoes the poetics of distinguished Hebrew writers from the beginning of the twentieth century onward, such as Russian born Y. H. Brenner and Polish-Galician born S. Y. Agnon. In the height of an era of what was conceptualized as a redemptive return to the Holy Land, of waves of idealistic immigration to the Land of Israel, their works were profoundly suspicious of the intended metamorphosis Zionism aspired to, the imagined transition of the Jewish subjects from a "nation of the book" (in Hebrew: "am hasefer") to a "nation of the land" ("am haaretz"), ironically, the latter being in fact a traditional offensive label for the illiterate. Brenner's and Agnon's works do not readily endorse such a transition and the relinquishing of Diasporic terms of existence it entails. Rather, they hesitatingly contemplate the possibility of nomadic, decentered being, as a cultural and ethical ideal. This is in line with thinkers such as Jonathan Boyarin and Daniel Boyarin (1994), George Steiner (1985) and others who have elaborated on Franz Rosenzweig's notion of nomadism as inherent to Jewish existence and as representing Judaism's singular contribution to Western Culture.

The protagonists of two of Brenner's central novels – *Mikan Umikan* (From Here and There, 1911), and *Shechol Vekishalon* (Breakdown and Bereavement, 1920)[4] – are psychologically disturbed men, traveling in small, shattered boats that leave the shores of Palestine, heading West. Both are so sick that eventually they are taken off board. Both leave behind, on deck, their orphaned scripts that contain the stories of their attempted, and obviously failed, Zionist endeavor. These are stories of long voyages through Europe, England and the United States, of a number of trips to Palestine, and of repeated movement – by train, by carriage or by foot – to and from Jaffa, a kibbutz in the Galilee, Jerusalem, Petach-Tikva and Jaffa again. The fragmented, haunted scripts (haunted by their authors who no longer have authority on them), are eventually published with the help of their alleged "discoverer" (also a fictional figure), a co-traveler on the boat leaving Palestine, himself a wanderer. They are published almost un-edited (in *From Here and There* more so than in *Breakdown and Bereavement*), chaotic as they were written and as they were found. The novels thus take the form of assemblages. They combine various practices and mediums of writing (letters, postcards, notebooks, journal articles, newspaper items, a diary); various levels of Hebrew (biblical, ritual, Talmudic, as well as the then newly invented Modern Hebrew); various traditional Jewish texts (primarily ancient songs of lamentation); various other languages (Aramaic, Yiddish, Russian, English, Arabic) as well as various non-verbal vocal communications, such as sighs, murmurs, cries and silences. This self-aware textual nomadism is a central aspect of Brenner's genius, constituting his main contribution to the emergence of Modernity in Hebrew literature. Abandoning the protagonists in a non-place, in the middle of a journey which they are unable to complete, after their having failed to find a home in the

---

[4] The novel was translated to English and published under the title *Breakdown and Bereavement* (Brenner 1971).

Place that was to be their ultimate Home, and leaving a legacy of a restless nomadic text, exemplifies Brenner's resistance of an oversimplified national narrative.[5]

Agnon in turn takes the protagonist of his 1939 novel "Ore'ach Nata Lalun" (translated into German in 1964 as "Nur wie ein Gast zur Nacht") for a long trip from Palestine to his hometown in Eastern Europe, only to find out that a concrete and straightforward return to a primal scene is, of course, impossible. The so-called guest holds a key to the old, deserted Beit-Midrash that he hopes to bring to life, but loses it. The key – to the Jewish house of scholars which is the "Beit-Midrash", and to its neglected library of Jewish texts – is finally found in the traveler's bag upon his return to Eretz-Israel. This is of course another version of a belated appearance of a "leftover", a relic, which is inherently destabilizing, as it offers an option of a textual rather than a material being.

For Agnon specifically, this is an almost overt literary manifesto, proposing that in his view, Modern Hebrew literature, written in Israel, is a continuous voyage toward, and the key to, Jewish multilayered textuality. This literature, Agnon thus states, is never of its time and of its place,[6] never "settled": it is inherently, and willingly, wandering. Indeed, almost none of Agnon's protagonists are sincerely comfortable in a concrete, earthly "home"; many of them yearn for the text as their homeland (to paraphrase George Steiner's "Our Homeland, the Text"). Agnon famously chose for himself, upon his immigration to Palestine, a family name that he had initially used as a pseudonym with which he signed one of his first published short stories, "Agunot" (Agnon 1908) – plural of the Hebrew word Aguna, originating from the Hebrew word Ogen – an anchor). Though this Halachic term, which pronounces a deserted woman being chained to her marriage, it has come to symbolize also an unsuccessful attempt to break away, a life in a limbo and in in-between-ness. Phonetically related to the word "Aguna", the name Agnon expresses this leading Hebrew author's profound identification with such terms of existence, which his entire oeuvre expresses and performs.

Many Israeli poets and prose authors, among them Avot Yeshurun, S. Yizhar, Yehoshua Kenaz and Yoel Hoffman, as well as women writers such as Dvorah Baron, Amalia Kahana-Carmon and Ruth Almog (who also write about gendered aspects of the "Un-homely") offer various versions of homes as haunted sites of das *Unheimlich:* haunted by the voices of previous homes and of previous, expelled, owners, haunted by the "refusal" of the mythical landscape to metamor-

---

[5] See a further discussion of these works by Brenner in my essay "Yosef Haim Brenner's 'Mikan Umikan': The Telling of Trauma" (Milner 2012).
[6] To paraphrase on the title of a novel by Yehuda Amichai, *Lo Meachshav Lo Mikan* (Not From Now, Not From Here), (Amichai 1968).

phose into a mundane homeland, haunted by an aspiration to transcend physical borders. It is in light of these aspects of restlessness, movement and transition, which is of course shared by both Jewish and non-Jewish Modern literary corpora, that I believe Hebrew literature can and should be integrated into the broader context of academic research and teaching. As such, it offers a unique view of the universal saga of the human project of settling: in a language, in a place called "home" and in an identity.

Bibliography

Agnon, Shmuel Yosef. "Agunot." *Haomer,* 2:1, (1908): 53–65.
Agnon, Shmuel Yosef. *Ore'ach Nata Lalun* (A Guest for The Night). Tel Aviv: Schocken, 1971 [1939].
Amichai, Yehuda. *Not of this Time, Not of this Place.* Translated from Hebrew by Shlomo Katz. New York: Harper & Row, 1968 [1963].
Boyarin, Daniel and Boyarin, Yonatan. "Ein Moledet Leisrael – Al Hamakom shel Hayehudim" (No Homeland to Israel – On the Place of the Jews), *Teoria Ubikoret* (theory and criticism) 5 (1994): 27–73.
Brenner, Yosef Ḥaim. "Mikan Umikan". *Kol Kitvey Y. Ḥ. Brenner.* Ramat Gan: Ha-kibbutz Ha-me'uchad, (1955 [1911]): 321–374.
Brenner, Yosef Haim. *Breakdown and Bereavement.* Translated from the Hebrew by Hillel Halkin, Philadelphia: Jewish Publication Society, 1971 [1920].
Gorny, Yosef. *Converging Alternatives: The Bund and The Zionist Movement, 1897–1985.* Albany: State University Press, 2006.
Hendel, Yehudit, Ed. *Lamagen.* Tel Aviv: The Israeli Workers Union's Information Department, 1949.
Hendel, Yehudit. 1969, *Hachatser shel Momo Hagdola* (Big Momo's Courtyard). Tel Aviv: Am Oved, 1969.
Hendel, Yehudit. *Leyad Kfarim Shketim, 12 Yamim BePolin* (Near Quiet Villages – 12 Days in Poland). Ramat Gan: Ha-kibbutz Ha-me'uchad, 1987.
Milner, Iris. "Beikvot 'Hasafa Sheba Medabrim Im Elohim' Politika shel Merchav Unedudim Basipur 'Bashemesh Hadromit'" (Following "the Language in which one speaks to God": Politics of Space and Nomadism in the Story "In the Southern Sun") *Esrim Vearba Kriot Chadashot* Bechitvei Aharon Appelfeld (Twenty four new Readings in the works of Aharon Appelfeld). Eds Avidov Lipsker and Avi Sagie. Ramat Gan and Jerusalem: Bar Ilan University Press and Shalom Hartman Institution, 2011. 467–488.
Milner, Iris. "Yosef Ḥayyim Brenner's Mikan Umikan: The Telling of Trauma.", *Prooftexts* 32.1 (2012): 33–62.
Milner, Iris. "Life in the Cafe: On Diasporism in Aharon Appelfeld's *All Whom I Have Loved* and *A Table for One.*" *The Jewish Quarterly Review*, 103.4 (2013): 459–468.
Milner, Iris. "Zarim Babait: Haalbeiti Beyetsirata shel Yehudit Hendel" (Strangers at Home: The Unhomely in Yehudit Hendel's Oeuvre). *Mikan* 16 (2016): 55–85.
Steiner, George. "Our Homeland, the Text", *Salmagundi; a Quarterly of the Humanities and Social Sciences* 66 (1985): 4–25.

David Stromberg
The Yiddish Roots of Modern Jewish Writing in Europe and America

Jewish literatures in Europe underwent tremendous tensions and pressures within the specific contexts of modernity. My case study focuses on Rabbi Nahman's tales, which were told orally by him in Yiddish and subsequently written down by his disciples. The stories were published ten years after his death in a bilingual edition featuring both Yiddish and Hebrew (Mi'Breslev 1815).[1] This inherent bilingualilty, I argue, characterizes the various traditions of Jewish literatures that emanated from Europe. As David Roskies has noted, even Y. L. "Peretz himself recognized [that] all roads led back to Nahman of Bratslav whom he hailed as the harbinger of modern Yiddish culture" (Roskies 1985, 69).

Such an understanding of the history of modern Jewish literatures involves a paradigm shift that would be comparable to teaching a survey of Western literature starting with Aesop's fables rather than Homer's *Iliad* or *Odyssey*. In the modern Jewish context, it involves being conscious, even as we teach secular texts, of the roots of this literature in religious mysticism and Hasidism – in a tension between geographical provinciality, spiritual searching, and political marginality. It also means recalling the demands of creating and maintaining communality, religious adherence, and national perseverance – all of which drove, in part, the stories that would later serve as both conscious and unconscious models for Jewish writing in Europe and, later, in the Americas.

In this essay, I hope to propose a framework in which late nineteenth- and early twentieth-century Yiddish and Hebrew literatures are considered in relation to each other. I will broach these topics in general terms and broad strokes in order to present my vision for teaching and studying European Jewish literatures – and the literatures it has influenced. My position, it should be noted, is less connected to canon-building – I am not interested in outlining specific works to be studied – and more in an inclusion of perspectives on religious Jewish life-worlds and their texts.

Rabbi Nahman (1772–1810) was known as the great-grandson of the Baal-Shem Tov, the spiritual leader credited with establishing, along with his disciples, the religious movement of Hasidism and a tradition of community building around a *Rebbe* – a kind of a *tsadik* (righteous man) who leads a group of fol-

---

[1] See Arthur Green's entry, "Naḥman of Bratslav," in *The YIVO Encyclopedia of Jews in Europe* (Green 2010).

∂ OpenAccess. © 2020 David Stromberg, published by De Gruyter. This work is licensed under the Creative Commons Attribution-NonCommercial-NoDerivatives 4.0 License.
https://doi.org/10.1515/9783110619003-028

lowers. Rabbi Nahman was a special case because, while he had disciples and offspring, he left no surviving sons or other successors. Rabbi Nahman faced antagonism from within the Hasidic movement, more antagonism from the *Misnagdim* who opposed Hasidism, and even more antagonistic pressures on religious life from early forms of *Haskalah*, or Jewish Enlightenment, which from an orthodox perspective could be seen as a kind of semi-assimilation. Rabbi Nahman also suffered from tuberculosis and has been posthumously diagnosed with emotional challenges described as bipolarity or manic-depression (Green 1979; Beale 1996). His disciples, the most prominent of whom was Rabbi Natan, wrote down and published his stories and his teachings, and also created a community that followed the oral teachings of this lost sage. Other figures, like Joseph Pearl, parodied Nahman's tales as part of an Enlightenment critical critique, bringing a different kind of renown to these Yiddish tales, yet still placing them within modern cultural discourse (Dauber 2004).

Perhaps the most interesting circumstance for our consideration is the fact, mentioned above, that the first publication of Rabbi Nahman tales in 1815 was itself a bilingual edition which included Rabbi Natan's renditions of Nahman's Yiddish originals underneath Hebrew translations of the same text (Dauber 2004, 229). This bilingual method has complex literary, religious, and social implications, as, within the religious community in which these languages developed ahead of modernity, Yiddish books were generally printed for women, while Hebrew books consisted mostly of commentaries on holy writings, intended for men. Yet this book was printed within the religious community in both the Jewish vernacular *and* in the holy tongue – featuring strange, symbolic tales drawing on imagery from traditions religious and secular, Jewish and non-Jewish, and, to boot, published under the name of a religious leader who never wrote down anything of what he said and who left behind no dynasty.

One of the roots of modern Jewish literatures in Europe, then, is characterized by the linguistic tensions between Yiddish and Hebrew, by religious tensions and secular pressures of the period, as well as by spiritual, psychological, and stylistic elements that make up the subject of literature. The stories reflect European courtly and folklore storytelling traditions, with kings, princesses, and viceroys, as well as magical forests, mountains, and creatures. Yet they also incorporate Zoharic traditions of Kabbalistic thought and symbolism, including their Persian and Arabic influences.[2] The language of their composition is Yiddish, which did not, when Rabbi Nahman's tales were published, yet have valence as a modern language with literary properties. Even the collection's title,

---

2 For an example of Arabic influences on early Kabbalah, see Ebstein and Weiss 2015.

Sipurei Mayses, combines Hebrew proper with Yiddishized Hebrew language: *sipur* means "story" in Hebrew, yet *mayse* has both Hebrew and Yiddish usages, both of them meaning "tale," but used slightly differently. A Yiddish *mayse* is a tale or story, but a *ma'aseh* in Hebrew is an action or occurrence – a word used by rabbinical sages when describing a series of events centered on certain actions. Rabbi Nahman's book is often called *The Tales of Rabbi Nahman*, but it should really be called Rabbi Nahman's *Stories of Tales*, in the sense that he not only told tales, but also already embedded in his work a self-conscious form of telling that is usually associated with late high Modernism or early Postmodernism.[3] He was not telling tales, he was telling *stories about telling tales*, he was making listeners – and later readers – aware of the value of the *telling* no less than the *told*. And this was done in *both* Yiddish and Hebrew.

Comprehending these influences – and certainly teaching them in a literature class – involves interdisciplinarity, which I believe is better seen as *integrative*. This kind of integrative approach is rooted less in the desire to bring methods and concepts from different areas of study into a pluralistic approach, and more, like the Yiddish language, in an attempt to synthesize all of the different influences that flowed into the singular case of Yiddish storytelling. Without understanding some Zohar and Kabbalah, some European vernacular and chivalric literature, some of the history of Hasidism and its influence, some notion of the political and historical trajectories of the period[4] – and without also having a sense of the Jewish life-worlds addressed by the tales themselves – it becomes difficult to fully understand the importance of Rabbi Nahman's tales and their far-reaching influence on modern Jewish literatures in Europe. At issue are complex influences from the earliest writers in Yiddish and Hebrew to the rest of Jewish traditions that extended from the nineteenth- to the twenty-first-centuries.

With Rabbi Nahman's texts, we focus an important chapter of Jewish writing in Europe around the beginning of the nineteenth century.[5] The next step would be to consider some of the trends in Jewish writing in the second half of the nineteenth century – which means, undoubtedly, a look at S. Y. Abramovitsh, also known as Mendele Moykher-Sforim, or Mendele the Bookpeddler. Abramovitsh's role as a founder of modern literary writing in Hebrew and Yiddish is nearly-un-

---

[3] For a discussion of Rabbi Nahman as storyteller, see Roskies (1996, 20–55).
[4] This aspect of Rabbi Nahman's life and work is only now being properly explored by Ofer Dynes of the Hebrew University.
[5] The fact that one of the earliest Maskil or Enlightened Yiddish writers of the time, Yisroel Aksenfeld, was a former Bratslav Hasid only strengthens the case for beginning such a class with Rabbi Nahman, as does the fact that yet another early Maskilic Yiddish writer, Solomon Ettinger, wrote in both Hebrew and Yiddish, strengthening the bilingual focus of this approach.

disputed,[6] but it may be worth noting that he continues an important structural node in the network of Jewish writing in Europe – in which Yiddish plays a prominent role without existing in isolation from other movements, trajectories, or languages of Jewish life.

Abramovitch's vacillation between Yiddish and Hebrew introduces an ideological view different from Rabbi Nahman's tales. While Rabbi Nahman attempted to integrate the secular and the sacred in a newly deployed from of spiritual storytelling, Abramovich presented a modern, forward-looking, non-religious vision of the Hebrew language as a Maskilic subject and tool. This presents one of the Haskalah's central problematics – its attempt to help Jews move *out* of an insular culture by modernizing an ancient language and using it with new methods of studying religious, philosophical, and scientific topics – a paradoxical issue that should be explored in a class on Jewish literatures in Europe. Yet setting aside these inherent contradictions, a renewed interest in the vitality of Hebrew also generated an interest in subjects that had not yet been incorporated into traditional Jewish life. This coincided with changes in the political, social, and economical status of Jews, secular or cultural perspectives on Jewish tradition, nationalistic ambitions, as well as on literary forms of storytelling that had not existed before. All this was accomplished in a literary mode that was, at least in part, influenced by the translatability that existed between Hebrew and Yiddish – and which has already been embedded into Rabbi Nahman's tales.

This trajectory from Rabbi Nahman's to Abramovitch's bilinguality traces an important shift in the relation of Yiddish and Hebrew– a shift, interestingly, which preserved the idea of Hebrew having a higher status than Yiddish. Either way, the translatability between Hebrew and Yiddish literature at the outset of modernity also exposes the underlying links, however tense, that existed between different sectors of Jewish society, whether religious, secular, nationalistic, reformist, or, a little later, socialist and communist. One powerful model for how to explore and teach the two literary strands together can be found in research on the role of women in Jewish literatures, especially since it often addresses the early Yiddish context *together* with creative production in the later modern period in both Yiddish and Hebrew.[7] In thinking about approaches to teaching Jewish literature beyond Europe, I propose keeping in mind the degree to which the founders of modern Hebrew literature – like Abramovitch, H. N. Bialik, Ahad Ha-Am, Leah Goldberg, S. G. Tchernichovsky, Y. H. Brener, and S. Y. Agnon – enacted

---

[6] For a recent discussion of his work, see Miriam Udel's introduction to her monograph, *Never Better!: The Modern Jewish Picaresque* (Udel 2016, 2–7).

[7] See Seideman (1997), Parush (2004), Schachter (2012), Weiman-Kelman, (2012) and Brinn (2019).

a translation, more conscious at some times than at others, of Yiddish language and literature in their work. A similar effect, I would argue, can be traced in major-language Jewish authors writing in both Europe and the Americas, before and after the World Wars. And at the core of my approach is an attempt to delineate not only historical and literary influences, but also mystical and spiritual points of inspiration from within the Jewish tradition and the Yiddish language – which, I believe, entered into and enriched the parallel development of Yiddish and Hebrew literature within secular contexts.

Bibliography

Beale, David. "Between Melancholy and a Broken Heart: A Note on Rabbi Nahman of Bratslav's Depression." *Graven Images* 3 (1996): 107–111.

Brinn, Ayelet. *Miss Amerike: The Yiddish Press's Encounter With The United States, 1885–1924*. Dissertation, University of Pennsylvania, 2019.

Dauber, Jeremy. *Antonio's Devils: Writers of the Jewish Enlightenment and the Birth of Modern Hebrew and Yiddish Literature*. Stanford: Stanford University Press, 2004.

Ebstein, Michael, and Tzahi Weiss. "A Drama in Heaven: 'Emanation on the Left' in Kabbalah and a Parallel Cosmogonic Myth in Ismāʿīlī Literature." *History of Religions* 55.2 (2015): 148–171.

Green, Arthur. *Tormented Master: The Life and Spiritual Quest of Rabbi Nahman of Bratslav*. Tuscaloosa: University of Alabama Press, 1979.

Green, Arthur. "Naḥman of Bratslav." *YIVO Encyclopedia of Jews in Eastern Europe*, 2010. https://yivoencyclopedia.org/article.aspx/Nahman_of_Bratslav (27 March 2020).

Mi'Breslev, Nakhman. *Sipurei ma'asiyot ha'menukad*. Hotsa'at keren r' Israel Dov Uster zts'l, Yerushalayim, no date specified, first edition published 1815.

Parush, Ilana. *Reading Jewish Women: Marginality and Modernization in Nineteenth-Century Eastern European Jewish Society*. Waltham: Brandeis University, 2004.

Roskies, David G. "The Story's the Thing." *Prooftexts* 5 (1985): 67–74.

Roskies, David G. *A Bridge of Longing: The Lost Art of Yiddish Storytelling*. Cambridge: Harvard University Press, 1996.

Schachter, Allison. *Diasporic Modernisms: Hebrew and Yiddish Literature in the Twentieth Century*. Oxford: Oxford University Press, 2012.

Seideman, Naomi. *A Marriage Made in Heaven: The Sexual Politics of Hebrew and Yiddish*. Berkeley: University of California Press, 1997.

Udel, Miriam. *Never Better!: The Modern Jewish Picaresque*. Ann Arbor: University of Michigan Press, 2016.

Weiman-Kelman, Zohar. *"So the Kids Won't Understand": Inherited Futures of Jewish Women Writers*. Dissertation, UC Berkeley, 2012.

Adriana X. Jacobs
The Place of Hebrew: Maya Arad's *Another Place, a Foreign City*

In 1995, the Israeli writer Maya Arad was completing a Ph.D. in Linguistics at University College London, when she picked up a copy of *The Golden Gate*, the debut novel of the Indian author Vikram Seth. Published in 1986, Seth's novel about academic life in the San Francisco Bay Area consisted entirely of Pushkin sonnets, a variation on the sonnet form developed by the nineteenth century Russian poet Aleksandr Pushkin for his narrative poem *Yevgeny Onegin* (Seth 1986). Seth's novel inspired Arad to revisit Pushkin's *Onegin* in the Russian original, and it was this rereading that prompted Arad to take a closer look at Avraham Shlonsky's highly lauded 1937 Hebrew translation of *Onegin* (Shlonsky 1937), which she has described as, "the best translation ever written for the most perfect masterpiece of world literature" (Arad 2008).[1] These three texts – Pushkin's Russian classic, Shlonsky's Hebrew translation and Seth's contemporary English-language novel – persuaded Arad to write a Hebrew novel-in-verse on contemporary Israeli identity from an expatriate perspective. By the time she completed the first draft of her novel, Arad herself was living in California, where she has been a writer-in-residence at Stanford University for many years – and also where Seth had resided during the writing of *The Golden Gate*. Published in 2003, Arad's *Makom acher ve-'ir zara* (Another Place, a Foreign City) was an immediate bestseller in Israel, where it won numerous literary prizes and was later made into a stage musical that ran at the Cameri Theater in Tel Aviv for a year, starring the Palestinian Israeli actress Mira Awad.

In the Israeli press, appraisals of *Another Place, a Foreign City* focused on its linguistic virtuosity and its complex portrayal of Israeli identity vis-à-vis immigration (Lev-Ari 2005; Melamed 2003; Melcer 2003). Describing the novel's rich language, Liam Azoulay-Yagev wrote, "for lovers of Hebrew, this rhyming book is the equivalent of a mound of ice cream with syrup, whipped cream, and a cherry on top" (Azoulay-Yagev 2004). In fact, the writer and linguistic Ruvik Rosenthal was even moved to compose his own review in Pushkin sonnets (Rosenthal 2004). In addition to the themes of identity that Arad explores, the novel also brought together her interests in translation, intertextuality, classic poetic forms, and the continued influence of the Russian literary tradition on

---

1 All translations from the Hebrew are mine unless otherwise noted.

modern Hebrew writing.² The Israeli scholar Aminadav Dyckman, in a blurb on the book's back cover, observed that by using a Russian text as her inspiration, Arad had created a framework for writing that allowed her to explore Israeli identity and belonging in new, and, in his word, "refreshing," ways (Arad 2003).

Arad herself left Israel in 1994, a year after the signing of the Oslo I Accord, and as a Hebrew writer who no longer lives in Israel, her work has entered discussions on the future coordinates of Israeli literature and the status of Hebrew diasporic literature in Israel. As Yaron Peleg notes, the fact that contemporary Hebrew diasporic writing exists is not on the face of it remarkable, indeed, as he puts it, "the concentration of Hebrew in one geographic location is a relatively recent phenomenon" (Peleg 2015, 323). Nonetheless, he argues that writers like Arad create works "written outside of Israel only in relationship to the sovereign Hebrew state" (Peleg 2015, 324) and discerns in such works an "ambivalent" expression of the author's own immigration. Rachel Harris, on the other hand, sees a different trend at work, one that reflects the increasingly "transcultural identity" of Israeli literature represented by writers who, in her words, "are comfortable exploring other cultures and other places, while simultaneously re-exploring their homeland and notions of home" (Harris 2015, 3). In his work on Hebrew writing in the United States, Michael Weingrad also considers how writing in the digital age problematizes characterizations of this literature as diasporic and transnational. Citing Arad's visibility and success in the Israeli literary market, Weingrad argues that "technology and new media make separate, geographically identified linguistic subcultures less distinct if they exist at all" (Weingrad 2015, 295). As a work composed in the United Kingdom and the United States, Arad's novel calls attention to the transnational routes by which Hebrew literary texts may continue to circulate in the twenty-first century, but as a Hebrew writer in the United States who writes for a readership that resides primarily in Israel, Arad's work is also, as Weingrad describes it, "an extension of Israeli literature" (Weingrad 2015, 295).³ Indeed, how far Israeli literature may extend has been a point of contention in Israeli cultural discourse, touching on anxieties concerning the relation between territory and language in formulations of contemporary Israeli literature, anxieties that Arad's novel addresses.⁴

---

2 Since its debut issue, Arad has been affiliated with the journal *Ho!* which positioned itself at the forefront of a neoformalist turn in early twenty-first century Hebrew writing. For a discussion on contemporary Hebrew neoformalism, see Jacobs (2017).
3 See Pinsker (2010) and Shachter (2011) for rich discussions on the transnational routes of Hebrew and Yiddish literatures in the nineteenth and early twentieth centuries.
4 The latter became a point of contention when Ruby Namdar, who lives in New York City, won the prestigious Sapir Prize in 2014 for his novel *Ha-bayit asher nechrav* (The Ruined House), the

The backdrop of Arad's novel is Tel Aviv in the early 1990s, when the dissolution of the Soviet Union precipitated a major wave of immigration to Israeli, resulting in radical and rapid demographic shifts in Israeli society. In the first section or canto of the novel, we are introduced to its protagonists, Orit and Jason "Jay" Rifkin. Orit is less than a year away from completing her military service, and in addition to writing a manual on Israeli identity, she has been asked to mentor Jay, a recent immigrant from Canada. Jay is fulfilling his army service in the Education Corps – the division in which Arad completed her own army service – and when the novel opens, he is still struggling with his Hebrew language skills. Orit is captivated by, and even infatuated with, the new immigrant. Jay, on the other hand, appreciates the access to Israeli culture that Orit's presence in his life provides, but, for the most part, remains oblivious to her desire for a romantic connection. When the novel's narrator turns her attention to Jay, he's often sitting alone in a cafe or wandering aimlessly through Tel Aviv (Arad 2003, 34). "To improve his language skills" he reads Hebrew literature or peruses Israeli newspapers, but most of his every day interactions with Israelis can be summarized by the occasional "shalom" that he exchanges with his neighbors (Arad 2003, 40).

Jay's – and Orit's – anxious and ambivalent sense of belonging intensifies in a pivotal episode in Canto III, when Orit invites Jay to join her on a short excursion to Jerusalem, where she has arranged an interview with Professor Yehuda Haim Ets, a venerated Israeli scholar of international repute. Jay instantly recognizes the name – he recalls that he attended a lecture the Professor gave on "Theology and the Holocaust" in Toronto. Ets was born somewhere in Europe before World War II but intentionally keeps the details of his biography as a "riddle" for his supporters and detractors to solve (Arad 2003, 49). Regardless, the peripatetic Ets, who divides his time between academic posts in Geneva, Germany, Los Angeles and Jerusalem, is considered a major ambassador of Israeli scholarship abroad. He is bemused and fascinated by Orit's question "What is Israeli Identity?" and in a response that spans several sonnets (Arad 2003, 60–65), Ets meditates on the distinction between cultural and religious Judaism and how it has shaped Israel-Diaspora relations, but to Orit's exasperation, he refuses to give her question a straight answer and is openly troubled by her insistence on a separation between cultural and religious Judaism. In Sonnet #31, he offers a passionate assessment of the legacy of biblical Hebrew and the debt that modern Hebrew literature owes to it:

---

first time the award went to an expatriate writer. Due to the subsequent backlash, the prize guidelines now stipulate that residency in Israel is required.

"מַה כָּל כֹּחָהּ שֶׁל סִפְרוּתֵנוּ,
כְּבוֹדָהּ בִּמְקוֹמוֹ מֻנָּח,
לְלֹא עֲטֶרֶת כּוֹתַרְתֵּנוּ,
הֲלֹא הוּא סֵפֶר הַתָּנָ״ךְ?!
הֵן הָעִבְרִית הַחֲדָשָׁה הִיא
טִפָּה שֶׁל קֶצֶף עַל הַמַּיִם,
דִּמְעַת-עֳנִי, רְסִיס גַּלְמוּד,
מוּל מְצוּלוֹת יָם הַתַּלְמוּד!
אוֹצְרוֹת שְׁלֹמֹה!״ יְסַפֵּק כַּפַּיִם.
״אֵין גְּבוּל לָעֹשֶׁר בְּחֻבָּם:
שִׁירַת סְפָרַד, וְהָרַמְבַּ״ם,
פְּרִי בִּכּוּרֵי שָׁנִים אֲלָפַיִם,
דּוֹרֵי דּוֹרוֹת שֶׁל יְצִירָה:
לֹא דָת! תַּרְבּוּת! זוֹ הַצָּרָה!״

"What is our literature (*sifrutenu*) worth
in the end, with all due respect,
without its crowning jewel:
the Bible, the crème de la crème?
In truth modern Hebrew is but
a poor tear, a solitary fragment,
a bit of foam on the surface
of the Talmud's ocean depths!
King Solomon's treasure!" He cheers.
"A wealth of debt: Maimonides,
the poetry of Andalus,
the fruits of two thousand years,
generations of creative acclaim:
Not religion! Culture, you say! Shame!" (Arad 2003, 63)

Ets defends the place of religion in cultural Judaism and, by tying it to Hebrew literature, in Israeli culture as well, but his characterization of modern Hebrew literature as "a solitary fragment" vis-à-vis the Hebrew Bible invokes the continuum model of Hebrew literary history. References to the Talmud and the poetry of al-Andalus recall the long diasporic history of Hebrew literature, but his characterization of Hebrew literature as "sifrutenu" – our literature – is notable here. In his work on Jewish literature, Dan Miron has addressed the psychological valence this term carried in the pre-Statehood period where it "conveyed a sense of intimacy, of belonging" that later became outmoded, replaced by an interest in Hebrew literature as both a "general literature" and a national one (Miron 2010, 10 – 11). Ets's understanding of "sifrutenu" is also explicitly monolingual; what is conspicuously missing here is Hebrew literature's longstanding, dynamic relation to other languages, like Yiddish and Arabic.

It is during this interview with the great scholar that Jay, who until then had been struggling with his Hebrew, finds his voice. Arad captures the moment when Jay summons the will to speak in highly charged, dramatic language. The right words literally "rise from the deep," breaking from the restraints of Jay's limited and insecure vocabulary (Arad 2003, 66). What makes this moment remarkable is that throughout the novel Jay's language constantly marks him as a non-native Hebrew speaker. Often, he'll slip into English, particularly when he is overcome with emotion, but also when he calls his family, conversations that appear in the novel in English. In an early scene, Orit even traces his initials, J. R., with Roman letters, on the misted glass of her bedroom window (Arad 2003, 44). Arad renders these moments without disrupting the prosody of the Hebrew text. Hebrew finds a way of accommodating English, of working with it to keep the conventions of the Pushkin sonnet intact. But it isn't English alone that marks Jay as a new immigrant. His Hebrew also contains "ketsat mivta," a slight accent, which even years later Jay is unable to shake off (Arad 2003, 42).

When Jay finishes his speech – a passionate proclamation that Israel-Diaspora relations can be reconciled only through immigration – Ets turns to Orit and asks her where she is from. To which Orit indignantly replies "Me? From here! From Israel!" Without skipping a beat, Ets confesses that he had assumed Orit was the immigrant (Arad 2003, 67). The irony is not lost on Orit – that she has been assigned the role of native informant to acclimate Jay to native Israeli culture. And yet, it is she, the "sabra," as Ets calls her, who is struggling to complete her manual on Israeli identity. (Later, we learn that Orit has completed a highly praised guide on Israeli identity though the narrator never reveals its contents.) Throughout the novel, it is Orit, even more so than Jay, who feels restless, unsettled, grappling with the feeling of not feeling quite at home. Jay, who was raised in Montréal, has been part of a religious and cultural minority most of his life. Indeed, the fact that he speaks English with his parents and not French is consistent with his affiliation with Montréal's primarily Anglophone Jewish community. For Jay, living in Israel allows him to be part of a majority culture for the first time. His attempts to acquire the trappings of Israeliness – the Hebrew language, army service – give him a sense of footing and purpose in Israel. However, Orit's slippery hold on her own Israeliness suggests that the relation between territory, language and identity has been destabilized, precisely when Jay is most relying on its durability. For Orit, Jay's presence in her life brings a different horizon into view, the possibility of a life in a "makom acher."

Canto I of *Makom acher ve-'ir zarah* opens with an epigraph from A.B. Yehoshua's 1989 book of essays *Ha-kir ve-ha-har* (The Wall and the Mountain): "The typology of Hebrew literature has become slightly monotonous in its maturity [...] perhaps one could attempt to expand this typology through Jewish ideas from outside of Israel" (Yehoshua 1989, 98; Arad 2003, 7). Arad's turn towards older, canonical texts allows her to interweave a wide range of literary texts from various languages, cultures and historical periods. In so doing, Arad expands the perceived borders of Israeli writing to let new and different voices bear on familiar and long-standing debates and questions concerning Israeli identity, reflecting on the recent past of the twentieth century from the vantage point of the twenty-first. The very language of Arad's novel explores the continued presence of "outside ideas" on late twentieth century Israeli writing in Hebrew though she does not restrict her sources to Jewish ideas, as Yehoshua recommends. In fact, by using Pushkin's *Onegin* as a framework for a novel set in Israel, which she began in London and finished in Stanford, Arad advances the possibility of "narrating the nation," in Homi Bhabha's words (Bhabha 1990, 1), within or through non-Israeli, and even non-Jewish, frameworks. But at the same time, through her rereading and citation of Shlonsky's translation, Arad calls attention to the ways in which Hebrew writers throughout the twentieth century have explored, and even contested, the Israeli "inside." In this respect, Arad positions her own writing as both a continuation and an intervention.

On the one hand, globalization has resulted in cultural, linguistic and national affiliations that are increasingly shifting and in flux, but on the other, the technologies of communication and commerce that shape global communities have also allowed authors to continue to work and participate remotely within national frames. Teaching and discussing this novel in the United States and in the United Kingdom affords an opportunity to consider these concerns in contexts where the relation between nation and language is also highly contested and to contemplate what happens when we bring Arad into the orbit of "literature in the United States" and "Jewish American literature." But these moves often require that I rely on my own partial and selective English translation (Jacobs 2007), which introduces the additional complication of translation into English, the dominant language of the global literary market.[5] Translation can radically reconfigure literary canons by introducing, but also making visible, what Johannes Göransson terms the "transgressive circulation" of texts and authors (Göransson 2018), while running the risk—particularly in the case of Anglophone translation—of reinforcing hegemonic monolingualism. At the same time, teaching Arad in English translation brings her work into relation with what Melissa Weininger terms "Hebrew literature in English." Written in English by Israeli

---

[5] Arad's novels have not appeared in full English translations, though excerpts from *Oman ha-sipur ha-katsar* (2009, Master of the Short Story) and *Ha-'alma mi-kazan* (2015, Our Lady of Kazan), both translated by Jessica Cohen, are available in print issues of *World Literature Today* and *Paper Brigade* respectively. Cohen's translation of the short story "Omsk" is available online: https://www.jewishfiction.net/index.php/publisher/articleview/frmArticleID/244 (1 June 2020).

writers, these works, Weininger argues, "reverse the process of territorialization Hebrew underwent through the establishment of the State of Israel by deconstructing the relationship between language and nation, and nation and place" (Weininger 2015, 18). In these works, English may be the primary language of these texts, but Hebrew is nonetheless "inflected" throughout (Weininger 2015, 22). Such inflections are present in Arad's novel as well, not only in its references to Jay's accented Hebrew, but also in the very language of the novel—a Hebrew drawn from a Russian text (Pushkin) and its various translations and reworkings in Hebrew (Shlonsky) and English (Seth).

In a conversation that Arad and I conducted in the pages of *Sh'ma, A Journal of Jewish Responsibility*, I asked her to reflect on the relevance and importance of translators and translation, and the prominent place both occupy in her work, which prompted the following, personal reflection:

> Why this emphasis? We care about translation because we care about history. We need translation because we need the ironic distance it provides. Israeli culture tends to be too "literal," too "direct," and too obsessed with its own present state of being. It was against this background that my generation rebelled. You are right that my work addresses identity – Israeli, Jewish; these are my themes. But bear in mind the irony in all of that, the sense that there is also something faintly absurd in all those Israeli obsessions. Identities are always clichés (they are, after all, what is supposed to make things *identical*)...I am distant from Israel, in several ways. (Arad and Jacobs 2010, 13)

Translation and identity (or a resistance to defining it) go hand in hand for Arad. In its broadest formulation, translation is about bringing that which is distant closer – a work in a language someone doesn't know is made accessible through translation – but for Arad it also provides in her words "an ironic distance" that her work retransmits into the Israeli local.

By creating a literary text that so explicitly engages translation, multilingualism, and intertextuality, Arad acknowledges the heterogeneity of Israeli literature, the continued presence of "outside ideas" and marginalized "inside ideas" at work in Israeli culture, and the transnational and diasporic future of Hebrew literature. To the extent that Arad's work addresses these questions, it also interrogates the very notion of a "national canon" in a world where authors and texts circulate in – and are translated into – increasingly global and transnational networks. Indeed, in the second sonnet of Canto Eight, her narrator proclaims "lo tov heyot adam cavul," It is not good for a man to be tied down – a line that echoes Genesis 2:18, "lo tov heyot ha-adam levado," It is not good for the man to be alone (Arad 2003, 167).⁶ In *Makom acher, ve-'ir zara*, Orit ultimately abandons her romantic attachment to Jay, but Arad's radical revision of the biblical text foreshadows the other ties from which she'll disengage.

Several years later, Orit and Jay run into each other in Tel Aviv, an event that Arad's narrator relates in Canto 8, the final canto of the novel. Jay is now 34 and pursuing a course of study at the Hebrew University under the supervision of Professor Ets. He is proud to show Orit that in Ets's most recent book he is acknowledged for his translation assistance. Still single and, despite his long stay in Israel, restless, Jay now he sees Orit in a different light, as a missed opportunity to feel more settled in his new home. He wonders if there is a chance still for the two of them, but Orit is disillusioned by the encounter. The narrator remarks, alluding to Numbers 13:32, "in his youth he greedily ate up the land– / and now she eats him up" (Arad 2003, 172). All that remains of the young man she once loved is "oto mivta, oto chiyukh," the same accent, the same smile (Arad 2003, 176). When he offers to stay in touch, she informs him that she lives "somewhat far away," in Vancouver. Jay receives this news with surprise because there is nothing about Orit that suggests that she no longer lives in Israel.

On the flight back to Vancouver, Orit is roused by the morning light – and for a moment, in that state between sleep and waking, she is somewhere between Vancouver's sunrise and Tel Aviv's sunset:

וְלִימִינָהּ מִיָּד נוֹפֶלֶת
(שָׁם מוּכָנָה לָהּ כְּבָר כָּתֵף).
עוֹד רַב הַלַּיְלָה וְאָפֵל הוּא,
מִכָּל הָעֲבָרִים עוֹטֵף.
כְּשֶׁשֶּׁמֶשׁ בַּשָּׁמַיִם אוֹרָה
גַּם הִיא מִזְּהָרָהּ נְעוֹרָה,
עֵינֶיהָ נִפְקָחוֹת לְאַט:
הִנֵּה עוֹד רֶגַע, עוֹד מְעַט,
תָּשׁוּב הַבַּיְתָה, שָׁם עוֹד אֶמֶשׁ...
וּמֵאָחוֹר, בְּתֵל אָבִיב,
הַיּוֹם נוֹטֶה לְהַעֲרִיב,
אוֹרוֹ כָּלֶה: רְאֵה, הַשֶּׁמֶשׁ,
כְּבֵדָה, שׁוֹקַעַת עַל הָעִיר.
אֶצְלָהּ הַשַּׁחַר אַךְ הֵאִיר.

She immediately falls to her right
(a ready shoulder awaits her there)
another long and dark night
envelopes her from all sides.

---

6 This line from Genesis 2 also appears in a poem by Natan Zach that has been set to music and performed by a number of notable Israeli musicians including Matti Caspi and Yehudit Ravitz.

> When the sun brightens in the sky
> she's roused again by its glow,
> her eyes begin to open slowly:
> In just a moment, a little bit,
> she'll be back home, there it's still the night before....
> Behind her, in Tel Aviv,
> the day stretches into evening,
> its light extinguished: See, the sun,
> heavy, setting over the city.
> But where she's sitting the day is breaking (Sonnet #48, Arad 2003, 190).

This parting image of Orit suspended mentally between the two cities recalls Leah Goldberg's 1955 poem "Oren" (Pine), which contains the iconic lines "ulai tsiporei masa yodot/ke-she-hen tluyot beyn erets ve-shamayim/et ze ha ke'ev shel shtei ha-moladot" (Goldberg 173, 143). Perhaps traveling birds know/ as they hover between earth and sky/ this pain of the two homelands. Arad's closing scene suggests, as in Goldberg's poem, the possibility of being in two places at once, in a state of translation. "I am there, in Israel," writes Arad, "but not quite" (Arad and Jacobs 2010, 13). And as Orit crosses the horizon, for a moment, it's almost like she has never left.

Bibliography

Arad, Maya. *Makom acher ve-'ir zara* [Another Place, a Foreign City]. Tel Aviv: Xargol Books, 2003.

Arad, Maya. "Hine kakh hu ha-mefuzar: Masa 'al 'Ha-mefuzar mi-kfar azar" ve-'al mekoro ha-rusi" [On "The Scatterbrain from the Village Azar" and its Russian Source]. *Ho!* 1 (January 2005): 145–160.

Arad, Maya. "Ve-kan ha-pele ha-gadol" [And here, the great wonder]. *Haaretz* (7 January 2008). https://www.haaretz.co.il/literature/poetry/1.1299327 (1 June 2020).

Arad, Maya and Jacobs, Adriana X. "Another Voice: Letters on the Art of Translation." *Sh'ma: A Journal of Jewish Responsibility* (December 2010): 12–13.

Azoulay-Yagev, Liam. "Kulam sho'alim ma ze sabudi/ beyn ha-tohim gam Balsar Dudi." *Nana* (5 January 2004).

Bhabha, Homi K. "Introduction." *Nation and Narration*. Ed. Homi K. Bhabha. London: Routledge, 1990.

Goldberg, Leah. *Shirim* (Poems), vol. 2. Ed. Tuvia Ruebner. Tel Aviv: Sifriyat po'alim, 1973.

Göransson, Johannes. *Transgressive Circulation: Essays on Translation*. Blacksburg, VA: Noemi Press, 2018.

Harris, Rachel S. "Israeli Literature in the 21st Century: The Transcultural Generation: An Introduction." *Shofar* 33.4 (2015): 1–14.

Jacobs, Adriana X. "Another Place, a Foreign City – An Excerpt." *Zeek: A Jewish Journal of Thought and Culture* (December 2007): http://www.zeek.net/712fiction/ (20 November 2019).

Jacobs, Adriana X. "*Ho!* and the Transnational Turn in Contemporary Israeli Poetry." *Prooftexts* 36.1–2 (2017): 137–166.

Lev-Ari, Shiri. "A View from Abroad." *Haaretz* (22 September 2005). https://www.haaretz.com/israel-news/culture/1.4875285/ (1 June 2020).

Melamed, Ariana. "Zan nadir" [A Rare Species]. *Ynet.co.il* (11 November 2003). https://www.ynet.co.il/articles/1,7340,L-2812746,00.html (1 June 2020).

Melcer, Ioram. "Mifgash mi-sug acher" [A Different Kind of Encounter]. *NRG Maariv* (11 December 2003). https://www.makorrishon.co.il/nrg/online/archive/ART/606/107.html (1 June 2020).

Miron, Dan. *From Continuity to Contiguity: Toward a New Jewish Literary Thinking*. Redwoods City, CA: Stanford University Press, 2010.

Peleg, Yaron. "A New Hebrew Literary Diaspora? Israeli Literature Abroad." *Studia Judaica* 18.2 (2015): 321–338.

Pinsker, Shachar. *Literary Passports: The Making of Modernist Hebrew Fiction in Europe*. Redwoods City, CA: Stanford University Press, 2010.

Rosenthal, Ruvik. "Sod ha-nikayon" [The Secret of Cleaning]. *NRG Maariv* (13 February 2004). https://www.makorrishon.co.il/nrg/online/archive/ART/647/726.html (1 June 2020).

Schachter, Allison. *Diasporic Modernisms: Hebrew and Yiddish Literature in the Twentieth Century*. Oxford: Oxford University Press, 2011.

Seth, Vikram. *The Golden Gate: A Novel in Verse*. New York: Random House, 1986.

Shlonsky, Avraham. trans. *Yevgeny Onigin (roman be-charuzim)* [Evgeny Onegin: A Novel in Verse] by Aleksandr Pushkin. Tel Aviv: Va'ad Ha-yovel, 1937.

Weingrad, Michael. "Hebrew in America." *The Cambridge History of Jewish American Literature*. Ed. Hana Wirth-Nesher. Cambridge: Cambridge University Press, 2015. 281–296.

Weininger, Melissa. "Hebrew in English: The New Transnational Hebrew Literature." *Shofar* 33.4 (2015): 15–35.

Yehoshua, A. B. "Likhtov proza: reya'on" [Writing Prose: An Interview]. *Ha-kir ve-ha-har* [The Wall and the Mountain]. Tel Aviv: Zmora-Bitan, 1989.

VII **Case Studies Russian, Eastern European and Hungarian Literatures**

Lilla Balint
Traces, Memories: On Péter Nádas

In Péter Nádas' recently published memoir, *Világló Részletek* (2017; 'Illuminated Details')¹, the word "kosher" makes an early appearance. Scarcely a bare few pages into the autobiographical narrator's childhood reminiscences, he recounts a day when

> [m]y grandmother came to pick me up, my mother's mother, Cecília Nussbaum, who was on her way to the market hall on Klauzál square. Why there, I don't know, as I don't know exactly why at that very moment; especially since she usually frequented the market at Garay square. She had her marketeer there. And her kosher butcher too.² (Nádas 2017, 12–13)

It is a single word, mentioned almost in passing; an additional detail of quotidian life that constitutes the fine web of memories. And yet, "kosher" sticks out. Instead of melting into its narrative environment, as one more snippet of memory, it is noticeable (in part) because it carries a lot of weight. For it is with this single word that the first-person narrator establishes that on the maternal side he was born into a Jewish family that may not have observed kosher dietary laws anymore but certainly frequented Jewish merchants. How much work the word "kosher" performs becomes more evident if we consider the tempo with which the narrative moves. Relying on the narrative possibilities granted by memoirs, the narrative maneuvers skillfully between a maternal grandmother whose habits and speech resonate with the history and experience of the Orthodox Eastern European Jewry—and paternal grandparents who are assimilated, liberal Jews. From there, it transitions seamlessly to communist parents who fight in the Hungarian underground resistance movement during World War II, but for whom Christmas is nonetheless important enough to acquire a Christmas tree amidst the siege of Budapest by the Soviet Red Army: "[…] we lit a candle in an apart-

---

1 *Világló Részletek* has not been translated into English yet. For the sake of simplicity, I will use my translation of the Hungarian title in English throughout my essay in reference to the text. All translations from the Hungarian original are mine. Bibliographic references following the quotations in translation refer to the Hungarian edition. The original text in Hungarian will be supplied in the footnotes.
2 "A nagymama jött értem, anyám édesanyja, Nussbaum Cecília, aki innen a félig romos Klauzál téri vásárcsarnokba ment, nem tudom miért, nem tudom miért éppen akkor, ha egyszer ö a Garay téri piacra járt. Ott volt a kofája. Ott volt a kóser hentese."

ment on the third floor of the intact half of the house in Damjanich Street, which was bombed into two" (Nádas 2017, 53).[3]

For those familiar with Nádas' oeuvre, the bold strokes with which two generations are quickly traversed and sweeping ideological changes are painted is a technique that is reminiscent of his two most celebrated and widely translated novels *A Book of Memories* (1997; *Emlékiratok könyve*, 1986) and *Parallel Stories* (2011; *Párhuzamos történetek*, 2005). What unites these three magnum opuses (Nádas can, in fact, boast with three of those) is their complex narrative tapestry, in which different narrative threads are woven together, be it through the exploration of memory as both a literary technique and a technique of the self – to echo Michel Foucault – as in *A Book of Memories* and in 'Illuminated Details,' or through the intricate forms of historical narration, as in *Parallel Stories*. Yet from the perspective that is most relevant for the volume at hand, these three main prose works are marked by significant differences regarding the ways in which they engage with questions such as Jewish origin, tradition, belonging, and history. More precisely, what shifts over the forty-year course of Nádas' oeuvre, from the publication of *The End of a Family Story* in 1977 to the most recent, 'Illuminated Details,' in 2017, is how central a place these concerns are assigned within the texts, be that readily visible or not. What this essay aims to trace is thus a change in intensity in his oeuvre —a grappling with Jewish belonging that becomes more pronounced as we move toward the present.

While Nádas is today one of the most well-known and celebrated contemporary authors in his native Hungary,[4] recipient of many literary prizes both at home and abroad,[5] in the 1970s he was banned from publishing in his own coun-

---

[3] "[...] mi a kettészelt Damjanich utcai ház épen maradt felében gyertyát gyújtottunk a karácsony-fán a harmadik emeleti lakásban."

[4] Outside of his native Hungary, Nádas started to gain popularity through the translation of his works into the major metropolitan languages. The exact timeline of his reception varies from one linguistic context to the next. In the German-speaking world, he was introduced by Suhrkamp almost immediately after the Hungarian publication of *The End of a Family Story* in 1979, followed by a translation of most of Nádas's works. In the English-speaking context, the first translation that appeared was *A Book of Memories* in 1997, followed by *The End of a Family Story* a year later. In France, Nádas was first translated in the 1990s, with his plays, after which *The End of a Family Story* appeared. *A Book of Memories*, moreover, won the Prize for the Best Foreign Book (Prix du Meilleur Livre Étranger) in 1998. The first Russian translation of Nádas's works appeared as late as 2015, with the *A Book of Memories*.

[5] His prizes and awards include the Austrian State Prize for European Literature (1991), the Hungarian Kossuth Prize (1992), the Leipzig Book Award for European Understanding (1995), the French Prize for the Best Foreign Book (1998), the Franz Kafka Prize (2003), and the Brücke Berlin Prize (2012), among many others.

try. Born into a Jewish family in 1942, then baptized, his parents were committed communists. Nádas' mother passed away from illness early in his life: his father, a highranking political functionary in Hungary's communist regime after World War II, committed suicide after the Soviet intervention in the Hungarian Revolution of 1956. In the majority of accounts, Nádas' Jewish origin warrants not more than a fleeting mention, which is to highlight that revisiting his oeuvre from the vantage point of its relations to Jewish references is a far from obvious undertaking. His first longer work of fiction, *The End of a Family Novel* (1988; *Egy családregény vége*) appeared in 1977, after several years of censorship during which Nádas was limited to publishing theater critiques in one of Hungary's Catholic journals (*Vigília*).[6]

Set in Budapest in the 1950s, *The End of a Family Story* revolves around the first decade of communism in Hungary under Mátyás Rákosi, and at the same time in the world of Jewish stories, invoking the tradition of storytelling as such. The child protagonist Péter Simon's grandfather relates tales from both the Bible and the Talmud—which are interwoven with the newly emerging world of communism and call upon literary imagination for it to persist despite the Rákosi regime. Yet the novel remains true to its title insofar as it narrates an ending. It is a Jewish family history cut short, which translates into the actual brevity of the novel. *The End of a Family Story* begs to be read against the tradition of grand family sagas, which presuppose a sense of continuity—even as they narrate historical turmoil—against the backdrop of which generations can reproduce, necessitating the genre's habitually substantial length.[7] Brevity, however, suggests the severing of ties, identities, and histories—a theme foreshadowed in this early novel that plays out in different forms in Nádas' novelistic enterprise.[8]

While still barred from publishing, Nádas embarked upon writing his magisterial *A Book of Memories*, a novel that brings together three distinct temporal dimensions: one thread revolves around, once again, the 1950s in Hungary but interweaves the childhood memories of the first-person narrator with the story of his ménage à trois with an actress called Thea and the writer Melchior in East-Berlin of the 1970s. The third thread goes back all the way to the fin de siècle

---

6 See Gábor Csordás, *Párhuzamos olvasókönyv*, 101. There is also a German translation of this compendium to *Parallel Stories*, which comprises different documents such as Nádas' letters, emails, notes, articles, and essays about the novel. See Graf, *Péter Nádas lesen*. (2012)
7 For a brief trajectory of the Hungarian Jewish family novel, see the essay "A magyar zsidó családregény" by Károly Alexa.
8 While Nádas' text itself does not refer to Hassidic storytelling, what may reverberate here as well is the prominent role that the end of storytelling plays in the Hassidic tradition. (I would like to thank Natasha Gordinsky for drawing my attention to this connection.)

in Heiligendamm at the Baltic Sea. Whereas the Proustian theme of remembrance of the past reverberates throughout, the book's Jewish allusions and references are less foregrounded. Despite their tacit nature, they are significant for *A Book of Memories*, as Ivan Sanders has argued convincingly.[9] Sanders, astute reading has revealed the web of Jewish references throughout the text, most notably the fact that the main female figures of the novel, Thea Sandstuhl and Hédi Szán—the first-person narrator's childhood sweetheart—are both Jewish; through their characters, the novel renders an entire milieu and a set of sensibilities. On whether *A Book of Memories* should be read as a "Jewish novel," Sanders remains ambivalent, noting that due to its inexhaustible richness the text lends itself to many different readings. Sanders is undoubtedly right, for what is most notable about *A Book of Memories* are the ways in which it takes up memory as both a subject of literary inquiry and its principal technique, playing deliberately with high modernist themes and forms. In doing so, the novel not only examines the legacy of modernism but employs it very deliberately in this belated fashion, if we will, to engage with the problem of bourgeois individuality—under socialism. While the novel itself thus grapples with the quiddity of self and selfhood, *A Book of Memories* also raises the theoretical question of what it means to invoke the literary canon of memory under the political conditions of socialism— tacitly calling upon figures such as Marcel Proust, Rainer Maria Rilke, and Walter Benjamin, to name just the most obvious representatives—, which has fundamentally shaped the (undoubtedly male) bourgeois subject.

For the purposes of this essay, however, individual works are less significant than the arc that appears once the focus widens to Nádas' oeuvre as a whole. Put differently: the point is not to determine if any single piece could be qualified as a "Jewish text," to echo Sanders, but to determine the trajectory that may become visible over time. Thus far, Nádas' two longer works of fiction have taken us from biblical references and Jewish tradition (and family story cut short), to characters of Jewish origin and allusions to the Holocaust and Jewish lifeworlds in Hungary after World War II. Once we arrive at Nádas' most recent and highly acclaimed novel, *Parallel Stories* (2012; *Párhuzamos történetek*, 2005) not much appears to have changed at first sight. Nádas's ambitious text —woven, once again, from multiple narrative strands that run in parallel fashion, as the title suggests, but also crisscross several times—tells a history of Central Europe in the "short twentieth century," as the historian Eric Hobsbawm

---

9 See Ivan Sanders, article "Metakommunikáció haladóknak: Nádas Péter Emlékiratok könyvének zsidó olvasata."

called the years between 1914 and 1989.¹⁰ The text switches back and forth in time, between Berlin and Budapest and multiple other locations, juxtaposing and conjoining different eras, intimating historical continuities beyond the temporal markers of 1918, 1945, and 1989.

Experimenting with the form of the historical novel, *Parallel Stories* is perhaps one of the few ones to have been written in the modernist mode.¹¹ Composed of a tantalizing number of scenes, which *peu à peu* emerge as narrative threads, *Parallel Stories* aims at painting a picture of Central Europe's twentieth century, while steering clear of employing a totalizing narrative structure. If we consider that Nádas, by and large, also does away with the established distinction between main and minor characters so that most narrative threads gain equal importance and are shown in their interrelatedness, a pressing question emerges: What, in fact, holds the complex narrative architecture of *Parallel Stories* together? How does the novel not disintegrate into an array of loosely connected episodes? The intense close-ups in the text, to borrow from a term from film analysis, often rendered in form of a stream of consciousness or extended interior monologues are both motivated and held together by the question: how could the atrocities of twentieth century have occurred? More specifically, the Holocaust. For the moderately attentive reader, this may not be apparent, as barely any direct representation of the death camps makes it into the novel, nor do they play any significant role at the level of plot. Circumventing the much-debated question of representational adequacy and attendant ethical quandaries, the Holocaust is transmuted into what Nádas calls the "silent poetic structure" of *Parallel Stories:* "For the last ten years [written in 2003], I have mostly been reading only about the Shoah, or the Holocaust. The Shoah or Holocaust, call it what you will, barely makes it into any scene at the level of plot, but both the Holocaust and its consequences determine the 'innermost structure' of the book."¹² What this means exactly, cannot be recapitulated here in detail—

---

10 See the title of Hobsbawm's book *The Age of Extremes: The Short Twentieth Century* (1996).
11 See Perry Anderson's article "From Progress to Catastrophe" (2011), in which Anderson draws on Fredric Jameson to argue that "modernism proper, because of its commitment to the primacy of immediate perception, appears to have been constitutively incapable of generating the totalising retrospect that defines a true historical novel."
12 "Seit etwa zehn Jahren gilt meine Lektüre wieder fast ausschließlich der Shoah oder dem Holocaust, nenne man, wie man will, werden in die Handlung meines Buches szenisch kaum eingehen, sie und ihre Folgen bestimmen aber die innere Struktur" (Graf 2012, 96; translation mine). I am quoting here from the German edition of the compendium to *Parallel Stories* because this text was originally composed in German as a report for the Institute of Advanced Study in Berlin (*Wissenschaftskolleg zu Berlin*), which supported Nádas' work with a fellowship. Nádas also uses slightly divergent terms, as Gábor Németh pointed out in his interview with Nádas.

suffice it to say that the novel's emphatically close look and sustained gaze at the twentieth century is animated by the urge to not only understand motives and actions but also to trace how these give rise to the century's atrocities.

This leave us to ask how we can make sense of the trajectory that starts with stories from the Bible and the Talmud, invokes the tradition of Jewish stories and storytelling, and leads to the all-encompassing question of the Holocaust that suffuses the poetic structure of *Parallel Stories* without necessarily being foregrounded at the level of plot; from there it shifts to the grappling with Jewish belonging and intellectual legacy in 'Illuminated Details.' It is at once accurate and inaccurate and not to describe the trajectory that I have just sketched as one in which Jewish references, allusions, and themes become more pronounced over time. The ambivalence occurs because the question can be taken in the absolute or relative sense, by taking political circumstances into consideration or leaving them aside. It is difficult to ascertain how references to the Old Testament and the Talmud in *The End of a Family Novel* in communist Hungary of the late 1970s relate to the mention of the halachic practices of the grandparents in 'Illuminated Details,' published in 2017. The conditions of what can be said have shifted. Was it because of the interweaving of Jewish religious texts—invoking the tradition of storytelling not only *in* but also *in spite of* the early communist years of the 1940s— that this early text of Nádas' had to wait several years for its publication? Perhaps, the censorship was more concerned with the ways in which those initial years of communism were portrayed? Or did Nádas' modernist aesthetics in *The End of a Family Novel*, its fragmentation into different narrative threads, raise objections?

Read side by side, the word "kosher" in 'Illuminated Details' certainly appears more overt, gesturing towards a milieu. Particularly in conjunction with "butcher," it is suggestive of an entire world of daily habits and customs that regulated life, from the quotidian to the feast days, for a part of the population who were was numerous enough to sustain a Jewish meat merchant. Perhaps the invocation of biblical stories, related by Péter Simon's grandfather in *The End of a Family Novel*, was read as just as direct a gesture in the historical present of 1977 as is the mention of the word "kosher" in 2017. *Direct* less in the sense of literary technique—as the stories are thoroughly woven into the text, which is precisely what makes their insertion less apparent—and more in the sense of its immediate legibility, as an act of deliberate marking. From the vantage

---

While in the report cited above Nádas speaks of "the innermost structure," in an article for the Hungarian literary weekly *Élet és Irodalom*, he also calls it "silent poetic structure" (see also Graf 2012, 111).

point of the contemporary moment, their potentially provocative nature has been rendered illegible, not only by the forty years that have since passed, but also by the change in the political circumstances that co-determined the conditions of not only what could be said and published in socialist Hungary at the end of the 1970s, but also how things were read.

Is the early appearance of the word "kosher," signifying the fact that Nádas' autobiographical narrator was born into a Jewish family, an answer to the intensifying antisemitic political and public discourse in Hungary at the dawn of the twenty-first century? The way in which 'Illuminated Details' unfolds—to which I turn shortly—also allows for a more nuanced reading thereof:

> A long time, a really long time, perhaps even half a century or more had passed in my life before I grasped that my Hungarian patriotism was utterly futile. [...] I could have lived my life a lot more comfortably had I been able to align myself either with the big family of Hungarian nationalists or that of Jewish nationalists. Because of the hefty weight of my intellectual legacy, I find both repulsive.[13] (Nádas 2017, 117)

These are the words of the narrator, and as if to lend the already powerful statement further emphasis, a few lines later he reiterates that "I should have contended the failure of the Hungarian Jewish tradition of patriotism, roughly fifty years later. But I did not do that either" (Nádas 2017, 118–19).[14] In what follows, I zero in on a few select moments in 'Illuminated Details' that allow us to give contours to the ways in which Nádas' memoir engages with the questions of Jewish origin, tradition, and belonging.

If I started this essay by noting the near-immediate appearance of the word "kosher" in Nádas' memoir 'Illuminated Details,' it was precisely to highlight the unusual nature of this occurrence within his oeuvre, echoed perhaps only by a scene in his 'Autobiographical Sketch' (*Életrajzi vázlat*, 1994), in which the first-person narrator relates the moments before his birth in the following way:

> It is with the elemental happiness of my verbosity that I let you know that I was born into this world on October 14, 1942; it was such a warm summery day, according to my mother, that she was wrapped in a light silk dress only when she took the tram to the Jewish hos-

---

13 "Sokáig, nagyon sokáig, tán fél évszázad eltelt az életemből, és még mindig nem láttam át, hogy magyar patriotizmusommal a levegőbe beszélek. [...] Jóval kényelmesebben zajlott volna az életem, ha a magyar nacionalisták vagy a zsidó nacionalisták nagy családjának valamelyikébe sikerült volna befarolnom. Tudati örökségem mozdíthatatlan tömege miatt mindkettő taszít."
14 "A magyar zsidó patrióta hagyomány csődjének minden tanulságát, mintegy fél évszázados késéssel, nekem kellett volna belátnom. De én sem láttam be."

pital after her first contractions set it, so much so that it did not even cross her mind to take any warm clothes with her.[15] (Nádas 1994, 16)

What connects the mention of the Jewish hospital in which the mother gives birth and the grandparents' grandmother's kosher butcher—perhaps a sign for the grandparent's adherence to kosher law— is not only their factual nature but also that they are referred to in passing, as seemingly incidental.[16] Put differently: while they could become markers of the narrators' Jewish identity, they fail to do so. For their function is not to signify continuity but rather to mark a rift, which is underscored by the way in which they are presented in the narrative; that is as isolated facts. Thus, in a peculiar way, they remain unactualized, in the sense that there is no thick story of belonging or family tradition that ensues from them and into which they, conversely, would be embedded—this hearkens back to the end that is referenced in the title, *The End of a Family Story*.

I have singled out these two details from Nádas' autobiographical texts because they are indicative of the vexed status of a Jewish origin and/or belonging for their respective narrators. To give this reading further nuance, these instances should be read in juxtaposition with the very first mention of the word "Jew" in 'Illuminated Details,' which appears in a very different form and context. Though "kosher" remains an isolated fact to which the narrator has no apparent personal connection anymore, it is nonetheless employed as a self-description by him when relating his childhood memories. In contrast, the word "Jew" enters the narrative in the form of a semi-quotation from an official decree published in the bulletin of Budapest called *Fővárosi Közlöny*[17]:

> It had to happen this way, because on June 16, 1944, the *Fővárosi Közlöny* ['Bulletin of the Capital'] published the decree that Jews had to move into houses marked by a yellow star, and the house on Pozsonyi út 12 was declared a yellow star house. According to the decree,

---

15 "Közlékenységem elemi örömével tudatom veled, hogy 1942. október 14-én jöttem e világra, anyám beszámolója szerint egy olyan nyáriasan meleg napon, hogy amikor megjöttek első fájásai, egyetlen szál selyemruhában villamosozott be a Zsidó Kórházba, s eszébe se jutott valami meleg holmit vinni magával" (translation mine).

16 What remains unmentioned is that the Jewish Hospital in Budapest still existed in 1942. In fact, it operated throughout World War II also treating also members of the SS, Hungary's Arrow Cross Movement, and Hungarian soldiers. After Hungary's occupation by the German force on 19 March 1944, the hospital was forced to relocate from Szabolcs utca to Wesselényi utca.

17 The literal translation would be "Bulletin of the Capital."

every Jewish family was allowed one room, so our apartment ceased to be our apartment.[18] (Nádas 2017, 47)

Even though quotation marks are not employed, the word "Jew" makes its way into the text as an external ascription by way of the narrator, who relays the official language of the decree that orders Budapest's Jewish population to relocate into one of the "Yellow Star Houses" by June 21, 1944. By filtering the official language through his idiom, modulating it with his own words, rather than incorporating it as a quotation proper, the narrator appears to try on the label "Jew," the designation that official political discourse has attached to him. Read together with the word "kosher" from the very beginning of 'Illuminated Details,' they delineate the space within which Nádas' autobiographical narrator moves between, on the one hand, the kosher laws and Jewish traditions that have become dead facts of the past for him, and, on the other hand, there is the seemingly inescapable labeling as Jewish by official political discourse. However, we may also extend this to public discourse. This position is nothing new when it comes to the assimilated Hungarian Jewry, and it resonates with Mary Gluck's assertion that for Hungarian intellectuals of the time, their "Jewishness was fundamentally irrelevant" (Gluck 2016, xi).

What is new however, is the way in which Nádas' narrator confronts this position in 'Illuminated Details.' What is left between the abandoned Jewish tradition of his grandparents' generation and the label "Jew" that is ascribed to him? To answer this question, we have to turn to a moment in the text that receives extensive narrative attention, unfolding as it does over long stretches in the first volume of Nádas' memoir. It revolves around the publicist and politician Ernő Mezey, the younger brother of the narrator's great-grandfather Mór Mezey. Nádas grants Mezey a formidable entry into the text by way of Mezey's epistolary exchange with Theodor Herzl. It is, in fact, more accurate to say that Nádas introduces Mezey via his dispute with Herzl, a dispute that concerns precisely the patriotism of Hungarian Jews. That the text becomes bilingual here, as Herzl and Mezey's epistolary exchange is translated by the narrator within the text, if we will, interlacing the original German and Hungarian translations within sentences, is a striking linguistic strategy that can only be mentioned but not unraveled here. Herzl's words, and the gist of their disagreement—also

---

[18] "Már csak azért is ekkor és így kellett megtörténnie, mert 1944. Június 16-én jelent meg a *Fővárosi Közlöny* 30. Számában a rendelet, amely kötelezővé tette a zsidóknak, hogy sárga csillaggal megjelölt házakba költözzenek, a Pozsonyi út 12. számú házat pedig csillagos házzá nyilvánították. A rendelet szerint egy zsidó családnak egy szobára lehetett igénye, s ezzel a lakásunk meg is szünt a mi lakásunk lenni."

rendered without explicit quotation and integrated directly into the narration—read as follows: "The antisemitism will hit the Hungarian Jews brutally as well, es wird auch über die ungarischen Juden kommen, and the later, the harder, je später um so härter [...] There is no escape. Davor gibt es keine Rettung"[19] (Nádas 2017, 115–16). Nádas' autobiographical narrator—addressing us at the dawn of the twenty-first century—agrees with Herzl, and yet rejects of the political position that both conditions and follows from Herzl's statement.

Instead, 'Illuminated Details' embarks upon a detailed recapitulation of Ernő Mezey's political work. More specifically, his speech given to the Hungarian Parliament on the occasion of the ritual murder trial of Tiszaeszlár—a case that, at the end of the nineteenth century, not only made it onto the front page of Hungarian newspapers but garnered much attention across the European press. In short: after the disappearance of a Christian girl called Eszter Solymosi in April 1882, thirteen Jewish defendants from a small village called Tiszaeszlár, located in northeastern Hungary, were arrested and charged with ritual murder. As a member of the Hungarian Parliament for the Independence Party, Ernő Mezey weighed in. Addressing the Secretary of State for Justice, he charged the justice system with procedural errors, the state secretary himself with negligence in handling the investigations, and the country with sliding into the state of lawlessness. Not only in Mezey's talk recapitulated in painstaking detail in 'Illuminated Details,' but what also makes its way into the narrative are the reactions of the members of parliament. Channeling the official minutes of the parliamentary sessions, two entwined stories unfold: that of Ernő Mezey and his appeal to reason and justice, on the one hand; and on the other, that of rampant anti-Jewish sentiment manifesting in disruptive comments, sarcastic laughter, and demands directed at Mezey to "Stop that right now. Immediately."[20] (Nádas 2017, 153). Rendered not as quotations from the official protocol but incorporated into the narration sans quotation marks, these passages are also interspersed with the narrator's comments, not only highlighting the emotionally gripping nature of the session, but also actualizing it in and for the present.

Mezey thus plays an important role in the first volume of 'Illuminated Details' on at least two different accounts: his figure is certainly crucial for historical reasons, as it is through him that Nádas recapitulates—*pars pro toto*, so to speak—the political atmosphere of late nineteenth-century Hungary and its pal-

---

[19] "Az antiszemitizmus azonban brutálisan le fog sújtani a magyar zsidókra is, es wird auch über die ungarischen Juden kommen, s minél később, annál keményebben, je später um so härter, annál vadabbul, minél hatalmasabbak lesznek addig, umso wilder je mächtiger sie bis dahin werden. Nincs menekvés. Davor gibt es keine Rettung."
[20] "Hagyja abba. Álljon el."

pably growing political antisemitism and antisemitic public discourse. Moreover, and perhaps more importantly, Mezey also carries personal importance, as it is through him that it becomes clear what the "hefty intellectual legacy" that made Nádas oppose both Hungarian and Jewish nationalism might mean. For Nádas' autobiographical narrator, Mezey represents an attempt to fill the space that opens up between the Jewish tradition of the grandparents and "Jewish" as a label employed by political discourse. Through the figure of Mezey, the Hungarian Jewish tradition becomes an intellectual one. More specifically, he is a representative of the "futile Hungarian Jewish patriotism," as the narrator calls it— the futility of which he himself should have long since come to terms with, as he states ("I should have contended the failure of the Hungarian Jewish tradition of patriotism;" Nádas 2017, 119). Futile, because as Herzl predicted, belief in the principles of liberalism and free thinking did not save Hungarian Jews from antisemitism and persecution (Nádas 2017, 115–16). And yet there is an undoubtedly recuperative aspect to this textual politics of 'Illuminated Details:' while the figure of Ernő Mezey, along with his speech, may have become lost in the annals of history, in Nádas' memoir, they are granted ample narrative space to stand in for a tradition that has proven neither politically opportune, nor successful.

What to do with this legacy, 'Illuminated Details' seems to ask. It poses this question with reference to not only the late nineteenth and twentieth centuries; indeed the urgency of the inquiry that shines through in Nádas' memoir appears to be motivated in equal measure by the political realities of early twenty-first century Hungary: its dwindling democracy, increasingly authoritarian political structures, and the preponderance of both anti-European and xenophobic political and public discourse.

Bibliography

Alexa, Károly. "A magyar zsidó családregény" (The Hungarian-Jewish Family Novel), *Kortárs Online*, http://www.kortarsonline.hu/2003/08/a-magyar-zsido-csaladregeny/8002. Accessed 15 March 2020.
Anderson, Perry. "From Progress to Catastrophe." *The London Review of Books*, https://www.lrb.co.uk/the-paper/v33/n15/perry-anderson/from-progress-to-catastrophe. Accessed 20 March 2020.
Csordás, Gábor, editor. *Nádas Péter: Párhuzamos olvasókönyv*. Pécs: Jelenkor, 2012.
Gluck, Mary. *The Invisible Jewish Budapest*. Madison: The Univ. of Wisconsin Press, 2016.
Graf, Daniel and Delf Schmidt, editors. *Péter Nádas lesen: Bilder und Texte zu den Parallelgeschichten*. Reinbek bei Hamburg: Rowohlt, 2012.
Hobsbawm, Eric. *The Age of Extremes: The Short Twentieth Century*. New York: Vintage, 1996.
Nádas, Péter. *A Book of Memories*. London: Vintage, 1997.

Nádas, Péter. *Egy családregény vége*. Pécs: Jelenkor, 1993.
Nádas, Péter. *Emlékiratok könyve*. Pécs: Jelenkor, 1986.
Nádas, Péter. *The End of a Family Story*. New York: Farrar, Straus and Giroux, 1998.
Nádas, Péter. "Életrajzi vázlat" (Autobiographical Sketch), *Nádas Péter bibliográfia 1961–1994*. Eds. György Baranyai and Gabriella Pécsi. Pécs: Jelenkor, 1994. 16–28.
Nádas, Péter. *Parallel Stories*. New York: Farrar, Straus and Giroux, 2011.
Nádas, Péter. *Párhuzamos Történetek*. Pécs: Jelenkor, 2005.
Nádas, Péter. *Világló Részletek*. Budapest: Jelenkor, 2017.
Sanders, Ivan. "Metakommunikáció haladóknak: Nádas Péter Emlékiratok könyvének zsidó olvasata" (Advanced Metacommunication: A Jewish Reading of Péter Nádas' *A Book of Memories*), *Szombat*, http://www.szombat.org/archivum/metakommunikacio-haladoknak. Accessed 27 March 2020.

Natasha Gordinsky
Osip Mandelstam's Postmultilingual Condition

Over the past decade the field of Russian-Jewish literature, a subject which had previously been overlooked in German scholarship, has finally received attention in the work of Klavdia Smola and Olaf Terpitz. This important trend will, hopefully, continue to grow in the coming years.[1] This paper suggests approaching Jewish literature as part of the Russian canon by examining the question of linguistic belonging. Osip Mandelstam (1891–1938) reflected on this very idea in his poetry, by including the trope of a "mother tongue" in his writing. Mandelstam was one of the major poets of the twentieth century, and although he was not a Soviet poet, his life corresponded, chronologically, with the Soviet era.[2] His poetry, I would like to argue, problematizes the trope of belonging by integrating the multilingual dimension of language, or its heteroglossia, within a monolingual poetic project.

The publication of Jacques Derrida's seminal essay *Monolingualism of the Other or the Prosthesis of Origin* brought to light the political implications underlying the concept of a mother tongue. Subsequently, literary critics have begun to reevaluate the mechanisms of inclusion and exclusion inherent in the concept. Derrida reminds us that speaking and writing in your first language, and perceiving it within the logic of its origins as a mother tongue, can create an epistemic blind spot that prevents us from reflecting on the otherness of our first language. Thus, the metaphor of the mother tongue is rooted in the history of national states and their imagined communities. It is a concept that should be historically and politically contextualized and only then be analyzed within the poetic context. Focusing on the historical and political conditions in which the concept emerged proves particularly productive for understanding Russian-Jewish literature, for the issue of a first language already manifests itself in describing these writers as *Russian-Jewish*.[3]

Russian gradually became a language spoken by Jews in the late period of the Russian Empire, and this process was inseparable from the longstanding political transformations of Jewish life-worlds in the Pale of Settlement as well as

---

[1] See: Smola 2019, Terpitz 2008.
[2] For Mandelstam's poetic biography see: Freidin 1987.
[3] On the terminology of Russian-Jewish Literature versus Jewish-Russian literature see: Shrayer 2018, xxi–1.

OpenAccess. © 2020 Natasha Gordinsky, published by De Gruyter. This work is licensed under the Creative Commons Attribution-NonCommercial-NoDerivatives 4.0 License.
https://doi.org/10.1515/9783110619003-031

those that took place within Russian society itself.⁴ It was in the middle of the nineteenth century when Jews in Tsarist Russia started referring to themselves, as, or, rather began aspiring to be, "Russian Jews,". In order to do so they had to master a language that would eventually become the native tongue of the Russian Jewish intelligentsia. This interwoven relationship finds poignant expression in a letter written by Emanuel Levin, a close associate of Baron Ginsburg and one of the first members of the Society for the Promotion of Culture among the Jews of Russia. In this letter, he raises a striking question – "Is there, in the actual areas where the Jews are granted permanent residence…a language of the fatherland, a *Muttersprache?* The bureaucrats speak and write, though poorly, in Russian, the nobility in Polish, and the middle estate does not know how to write at all, and speaks in the Ukrainian, Lithuanian or Zhmud dialect" (Nathans 2002, 53).

The process of defining and shaping Russian as both the mother tongue and the national language of the Jewish population living in the Russian Empire that took place in the early decades of the nineteenth century marked a gradual but dramatic loss of what the historian Israel Bartal coined Eastern European Jewish diglossia (Bartal 1993, 141). The question of a mother tongue includes the complex relationship between the different political and cultural identities within the Jewish community and no less importantly, beyond it. Yasmin Yildiz analyzed the changes in the perception of European linguistic identities that have taken place since the eighteenth century from a political and cultural perspective. She characterizes these changes as a monolingual paradigm, in which individuals and social formations are imagined to possess one "true" language, a "mother tongue," and through this possession they organically belong to an exclusive, clearly demarcated ethnicity, culture, and nation (Yeldiz 2012, 2).

The emergence of Osip Mandelstam and Isaak Babel[5] on the literary arena represents the dramatic transition from multilingualism to monolingualism that took place in Jewish, and also Russian, literature written during the rise of the Russian Empire. It is through studying this shift that Russian-Jewish literature can be integrated into the teaching curriculum of Russian Literature. Mandelstam's understanding of a native language can be divided into two simultaneous strategies. At first glance they might appear to be mutually exclusive, but they can be integrated by turning to Derrida's paradoxical statement on the possession of language, "I have but one language – yet that language is not mine." On the one hand, Mandelstam emphasizes both the singularity of his mother

---

4 For the cultural and political history of Russian Jewry see: Nathans 2002.
5 On Babel's Cultural Biography see: Sicher 2012.

tongue and his ownership of the language, but on the other hand he develops an understanding of the otherness within language, which leads him to a new understanding of language in general, and of poetic language in particular, which he articulates in non-biological terms in his essay "Conversation on Dante."

Born in 1891, Osip Mandelstam was the first male member of his family to speak Russian as his first language. In his case Russian was, in fact, a tongue that his mother spoke, and he experienced it as his native language. It was his father, though, who enabled his son to enter Russian culture. His profession as a glovemaker enabled him to obtain a merchant's certificate of the first guild and to bring his family to St. Petersburg, where, at the turn of the century, Osip started studying in the prestigious Tenishev School. Whereas Mandelstam's predecessors followed the classical rules of the genre of the autobiography and presented their mainly Jewish audience with a detailed account of their life written in Russian, Mandelstam's fragmentary modernist texts resisted the conventions of the genre. Instead, he explored the possibility of creating a non-individual autobiography, a text that registers the changes in time and of the times through poetic language, thus creating a poetic self, conditioned by its historical existence in language. Unlike his bilingual or even trilingual contemporaries, such as Shmuel Joseph Agnon or David Hofstein, Mandelstam did not have to choose the language in which he would write, since he was raised monolingual. His "post-multilingual" condition influenced his perspective on the question of a mother tongue both from a historical and a poetic point of view. Mandelstam offers his readers a genealogical, and at that same time geological, understanding of a native tongue in *The Noise of Time*. It is in this experimental autobiographical text that he reveals the different layers of cultures, the traditional Jewish, and the secular Russian and German, which influenced the formation of his Russian, which he, in a Derridean sense, does not view as his own language:

> In my childhood I absolutely never heard Yiddish; only later did I hear an abundance of that melodious, always surprised and disappointed, interrogative language with its sharp accents on the weakly stressed syllables. The speech of the father and the speech of the mother – does not our language feed throughout all its long life on the confidence of these two, do they not compose its character? The speech of my mother was clear and sonorous without the least foreign admixture, with rather wide and too open vowels – the literary Great Russian language. Her vocabulary was poor and restricted, the locutions were trite, but it was a language, it had roots and confidence. Mother loved to speak and took joy in the roots and sounds of her Great Russian speech, impoverished by intellectual clichés. Was she not the first one of her whole family to achieve pure and clear Russian sounds? My father had absolutely no language: his speech was tongue-toe and languagelessnes. The Russian speech of a Polish Jew? No. The speech of a German Jew? No again. Perhaps a special Courland accent? I never heard such. A completely abstract counterfeit language, the ornate and twisted speech of an autodidact, whose normal words are inter-

twined with the ancient philosophical terms of Herder, Leibniz, and Spinoza, the capricious syntax of a Talmudist, the artificial, not always finished sentence, it was anything in the world, but not a language, neither Russian nor German. (Mandelstam 2002, 85)

It is striking to note that despite the fact that the four languages that appear in the text – Yiddish, Russian, German, and Aramaic (which remains unmentioned) – constitute a multilingual place, Mandelstam negates its existence. Furthermore, it seems like Mandelstam's writing is an attempt to overcome this inherited multilingualism, or at least to overcome its oral, phonetic traces. For is the ability to speak pure Russian not what is at stake here?

In her critical reading of Derrida, Emanuel Berger summarizes one of his main arguments in the following way: "The language spoken by any mother is an other's language, prior to becoming the language of the self and an element of the 'identity' of the subject who inherits it; for 'my' mother who gives me 'my' language is first of all an other to me. The language of Derrida's monolingual, Jewish mother from colonized Algeria is a language of the other and by no means her own" (Berger 2012, 14). And so is the language of Mandelstam's mother, her Russian is the language of the Russian Empire in which she was born and to which she strove to belong, and the very fact that Mandelstam calls it "Great Russian" attests to this historical and social context, just like his description of his mother's limited Russian reveals his internalization of the imperial monolingual paradigm. How important is it for him to stress the fact that the speech of his mother was clear and "without the least foreign admixture?" Should Mandelstam's description of the origins of his language therefore be understood as an attempt to mask her accent, to get read of that foreign admixture? But that would be only a partial reading, for while viewing his father's Russian as non-language, Mandesltam at the same time also capitalizes on his father's idiosyncratic version of multilingualism. His father's languagelessness proves to be extremely creative, precisely because his Russian functions as a site of otherness that resists the logic of origin.

In her reading of Mandelstam's seminal essay "Conversation on Dante," which was dictated to his wife Nadezhda around 1934–1935, Wai Chee Dimock asserts that Mandelstam's denationalization of language began with his attempt to learn Italian in order to read *La Divina Comedia* (Dimock 2001, 176). But as the quoted passage shows, he began questioning Russian's role as a national language a decade earlier. In his description of Russian, the Jewish mother tongue exists as traces left by a series of concealed languages, among them Yiddish, Aramaic, and German. Herein lies the crucial difference between Mandelstam's and Derrida's versions of how monolingualism becomes visible. Whereas Derrida emphasizes his own ability to write without an accent, when he claims that no one would be able to detect his accent, unless he declared he was "French Algerian" (Derrida 1998, 46), Mandelstam seems to be interested in the contrary, namely, in incorporating the accent and non-language of his father into his accentless mother tongue. As a result, Mandelstam's poetic speech became a site of constant negotiation between the lingual and monolingual paradigm, in which the Great Russian of his mother is imbued with the accent of his father, creating an accented Russian.

Bibliography

Bartal, Israel. "From Traditional Bilingualism to National Monolingualism." *Hebrew in Ashkenaz: A Language in Exile*. Ed. Luis Glinert. New York: Oxford Univesity Press, 1993.141–150.
Berger, Anne Emmanuelle. "Politics of the Mother Tongue." *Parallax* 18.3 (2012): 9–26.
Derrida, Jacques. *Monolingualism of the Other or the Prosthesis of Origin*. Transl. Patrick Mensah. Stanford, CA: Stanford University Press, 1998.
Dimock, Wai Chee. "Literature for the Planet." *PMLA* 116.1. Special Topic: Globalizing Literary Studies (Jan. 2001): 173–188.
Freidin, Gregory. *A Coat of many colors. Osip Mandelstam and his mythologies of self-presentation*. Berkeley, CA: University of California Press, 1987.
Mandelstam, Osip. *The Noise of Time: Selected Prose*. Transl. Clarence Brown. Evanston, IL: Northwestern University Press, 2002.
Nathans, Benjamin. *Beyond the Pale: Jewish Encounter with late Imperial Russia*. Berkeley, CA: University of California Press, 2002.
Sicher, Efraim. *Babel in Context: A Study in Cultural Identity*. Boston, MA: Academic Studies Press, 2012.
Shrayer, Maxim D. (ed.). *Voices of Russian-Jewish Literature*. Boston, MA: Academic Studies Press, 2018.
Smola, Klavida. *Wiedererfindung der Tradition: Russisch-jüdische Literatur der Gegenwart*. Wien, Köln, Weimar: Böhlau-Verlag, 2019.
Terpitz, Olaf. *Die Rückkehr des Štetl: russisch-jüdische Literatur der späten Sowjetzeit*. Göttingen: Vandenhoeck & Ruprecht, 2008.
Yeldiz, Yasmin. *Beyond the Mother Tongue: The Postmonolingual Condition*. New York: Fordham University Press, 2012.

Klavdia Smola
About the Integration of Jewish Literatures into Slavonic Studies

1 Historical Traumas and Academia

Today, we witness an increased interest in European Jewish culture in general, and in East European Jewry in particular. This greater interest can be seen in different areas of public life, such as cultural events, art, media, but also in the human sciences. In Germany, we can observe an increased presence of Jewish culture in the academic community, particularly: studies of the Jewish diaspora becoming more often a part of philological disciplines such as German, English, Romance and Slavonic Studies.[1] However, we still have extraordinarily few academic chairs or established degree programs with a focus on research and teaching Jewish "hyphen-areas", especially beyond German-Jewish Studies. Yiddish Studies and Jewish studies are still perceived as two distinct disciplines, eschewing the contact with studies of other cultures, which in contrast with the very facts of European Jewish history.

Especially in Germany, but to some extent also in East European countries such as Poland, Ukraine and Russia, Jewish studies going beyond the boundaries of their Judaic academic agenda tend to focus on a limited set of subjects, ranging from the annihilation of Jews during the Shoah over antisemitism and the commemoration of Jewish sacrifice, to the topic of loss. The prevalence of these by all means significant subject matters, illustrating the permanent processing of collective historical tragedies, results in the *mechanization of Jewish memory* and stands in the way of a broader, more creative and balanced approach of Jewish history, culture and especially literature.

Popular interest in Judaism in Europe over the last decades (the so-called Jewish Revival following the historical reappraisal after the fall of the iron curtain) has promoted a rather superficial ethnographic form of acquaintance with Jewish, and especially with the heavily mythologized "Eastern Jewish" cul-

---

[1] A de-essentionalizing, multilingual concept of Jewish literature(s) has been intensely discussed and researched by the international academic community within the last several decades. In this respect, the volume of essays, edited by Hana Wirth-Nesher 1994 and authored by famous writers and scholars (Wirth-Nesher 1994), is particularly interesting.

ture.² This comes as no surprise after a long period of communist taboo and depression. Today, both historical traumas and nostalgia, especially in Germany and in post-communist East European countries, have an impact on the academic approach of Jewish culture. *Reconstruction, catastrophic memory, and revitalization* have become key concepts of Judaism. At present, conserving, *museumizing* strategies and procedures are dominant, also in literary discourse: a (cultural-)historical comment, the tendency towards similarity and reproduction, towards collection, explanation and canonization. It is not without reason that the Holocaust, the process of mourning, memory, and criticism directed at communist oppression are main issues in the works of Polish-Jewish authors such as Henryk Grynberg, Hanna Krall and Piotr Paziński. It is precisely for this reason that the understanding of Judaism in the academic world nowadays requires an unprecedented de-essentializing of the subject matter and an openness towards popular cultures. Meanwhile, in Slavic language "high literatures" too, ever more ironic-subversive and daring techniques and subjects that radically update and challenge memories of Shoah, emerge. In his novel *Noc żywych żydów (Night of the living Jews, 2012),* Igor Ostachowicz reflects the Shoah by means of multiple allusions to horror films and kitsch, to give but one example.Similarly, in Polish art the multilayered cultural medialisation of Shoah memory has become topicof significant, sometimes provocative works, as for example by Zbigniew Libera or Wilhelm Sasnal.³

2 Academic Institutions, Research and Teaching

As we can observe by looking at the academic chair of Slavonic-Jewish Studies that was established at Regensburg university some years ago⁴, a set of components is of central importance to the successful integration of Jewish culture and Judaism in the research agendas of other philological disciplines. First of all, there is the incorporation of Slavic-Jewish lectures and seminars in general study programs such as East European studies, study programs with a double degree (bachelor and master) or teacher training in Russian or Ukrainian studies. However, there is need for a study program specifically dedicated to Slavonic-Jewish Studies, that can be completed aside from other study programs within

---

2 See Ruth E. Gruber's groundbreaking study on this topic (Gruber 2002). About Jewish Revival in (post-) Communist Russia cf. Smola 2019.
3 Cf. Marszałek 2010.
4 https://www.uni-regensburg.de/sprache-literatur-kultur/slavistik/institut/slavisch-juedische-studien/index.html (3 December 2019).

the domain of Slavonic philology. In order for such study programs to guarantee a professional double competence for the future, a program of Jewish language courses (in the case of East Europe, Yiddish would even be more important than Hebrew) would be an indispensable part of this. Moreover, language courses within the interdisciplinary program of the respective philological disciplines and (formally) *independent of Jewish Studies institutes* would be necessary. The formation of Slavonic-Jewish Studies in Regensburg is a rare but already very successful beginning of this politics of scholarly and educational integration in Germany. Nonetheless, even this case did not give birth to an independant "hyphen-area" of education.

The integration of international research collaborations – in particular those involving Jewish diaspora studies in countries such as the US and Israel, where these studies have long left the narrow field of Jewish/Judaic studies and have found an interdisciplinary context at universities – should also be a part of the groundwork in both teaching and research. Conceivable are tandem-events, workshops, joint seminars and the participation of international partners at Slavonic postgraduate schools. Especially the integration of international Jewish studies in postgraduate programs – what has seen an increased institutional significance in recent years – could stimulate the linking of teaching and research in this field: Doctoral students would without a doubt benefit from such initiatives that would allow for an open view of the global Jewish scientific community. As was mentioned before, a pointed collaboration with Jewish institutes and chairs in Germany, aligned with the respective sub-disciplines such as Russian, Polish, Czech or Ukrainian Studies, would be necessary: This would allow for a more in-depth bicultural training, in which the thousand years old religious and cultural history of the Jews as well as Palestine Studies could be productively linked to regional Eastern European Studies.

3 Jewish Cultural Studies

Jewish literatures in non-Jewish languages are increasingly incorporated in a broader culture theoretical context. An example of such a context is the *spatial turn*. As a result of the spatial turn, semantic representations of concepts that are central to Jewish culture and history, such as home and exile, or the relation between the center (Palestine) and the periphery (diaspora), are now again questioned and theoretically substantiated. Recent research also draws upon historical events that have fundamentally altered the concept of Jewish space in East Europe in the twentieth century: the First World War and its subsequent migration waves, the Shoah, Communist regimes with their latent official anti-Semitism, Zionism and the founding of the state of Israel, the fall of East-European dictatorships and, finally, post-Communist migration flows. Following these developments, there has been a repositioning of Jewish traditional topoi: The Jewish perception of space and concepts such as Makom, Galut, Aliya and the gathering of the dispersed in the Promised Land are amongst others once again dealt with and redefined.[5]

In literary studies, linguistic and poetic interferences and contingencies are seen as the meeting ground where Yiddish, Hebrew and Slavonic writings and identities encounter. These interferences and contingencies draw attention to a desideratum that holds a considerable potential for Slavists. The spatial-topographical side of Jewish Studies today can be integrated with new methodic discussions on transculturality, post-colonialism and cultures of translation or cultural transfer. More traditional conceptions can be tried through the use of new theories.

These and other, similar theoretical shifts have brought about a new focus in the field of Jewish Studies. For instance, phenomena essential to the Jewish Diaspora, such as migration, biculturality and the concept of the border, are merged with postmodern, poststructuralist and postcolonial paradigms, which calls for considerations about categories such as displacement, mimicry, othering and cultural hegemony. As a result of this process, remarkable volumes has appeared, such as Goetschel/Quayson 2016 and Hesse 2016 among others.

4 Slavonic-Jewish Studies

The attempts to merge Jewish literatures in different languages into a whole has been described polemically by Dan Miron as "[t]he hunt for an imaginary lost unity of Jewish literature". Instead, he calls for the "acceptance of an inevitable fragmentation" and he postulates "looser, more fluid forms of contact" in a non-hierarchical cultural system" (Miron 2007: 159, 163–166).

As a matter of fact, the "Slavic" component merely refers to similarities concerning political, historical and cultural factors of influence (such as Communism, emigration and the post-dictatorial elimination of official taboos on Jewish interests), as well as the relative simultaneity of artistic reactions to historical deprivations and gaps such as the Holocaust, enforced silence, the call for a

---

[5] In the course of spatial turn and a new interest in Jewish topographies in 2000–2010s, several volumes have been published within the last 10–15 years, i.e. Kümper et al. 2007; Lipphardt et al. 2008, and Smola and Terpitz 2014.

Communist supra-nationalism and the revival of tradition in a post-Communist and postmodern context. At present, for example, these 'contextual analogies' can be analyzed as the symptoms of a posthuman and post-memory culture characterized by similar processes, a culture that largely unfolds in the absence of Jews.

The designation "Slav(on)ic-Jewish" therefore seems rather essentialist in comparison to "East European-Jewish". However, specific linguistic aspects of these literatures can indeed be regarded as essential. First of all, there is the bi- and multilingualism of Jewish authors writing in Ukrainian, Russian or Polish, who were born and socialized between 1910 and 1940, before the start of rigorous assimilation processes due to Sovietization. In many cases, these authors lived in multicultural (peripheral) regions (of which the region of Galicia – a historical region in West Ukraine and South Poland is probably the most well-known), in which Yiddish and the respective Slavic languages and dialects were mixed. For the Jewish authors, this was a variously weighted double orientation: towards the familiar and religious Jewish tradition on the one hand, and the predominantly Christian, partly Muslim or secular diaspora setting on the other hand. This circumstance affected the polyphony of literary works by such authors as Isaak Babel, Bruno Schulz, Leonid Pervomais'kyi, Ilya Erenburg and Adolf Rudnicki. The authors' double- or multiple rootedness in various languages resulted in the integration of distinct cultural traditions into their work. Precisely through the examples of such authors, forms of hybridity that cross over from the authors' real-life identities onto their unique poetics can be determined, something which has gained wide interest in research over the last years.[6] It is important to switch from the purely thematic orientation of literary studies, often resulting in some sort of historiographic or ethnographic analysis by means of the text, to the complex relations that constitute the phenomenon of so-called "hyphenated literatures".[7]

To provide a more prominent example, Isaac Babel's works not only belong to the Russian-Ukrainian-Jewish literature because of the fact that they deal with the Odessan Jews' life and fate, but rather also because they combine references to Hebrew holy writings and Yiddish classics with the Russian-Yiddish dialect and the narrative habitus of Russian "high literature" (most notable of Nikolai Gogol'). Babel's ironic, playful way with his readership's multilingualism, his purposeful juggling of subtexts and even the possibility of diverging cultural re-

---

[6] Cf. Koschmal 1997, Grübel 2002, or Sicher 2012.
[7] In this context, controversial discussions about the term "Russian-Jewish literature" could be mentioned (see Markish 1995 and Shrayer 2008).

ceptions (cf. the fitting expression of "double book-keeping" in Sicher 2012: 24) mark a cultural situation that was soon – already in the 1950s – to become unthinkable to Jewish authors in East Europe. Assimilated Jewish authors of the late communist era at best drew their knowledge of Judaism and Yiddish from by then disparate memories and from literature. Babel's subtle differentiation between his readers through connotations and various culturally determined layers of meaning (for example the equation of revolution and messianic redemption) gave way to the commemorating gesture of the idealizing, nostalgic unification of the Jewish world, the homogenizing view from a temporal and a cultural distance. If at all, acculturated authors with Russian, Ukrainian or Polish as their sole literary basis use Yiddish lexical items as an artificial, quoting technique of imitation in the absence of living native speakers.[8]

The example of Babel shows both researchers and students how prominent Jewish authors – in spite of their own literary monolingualism – will remain incomprehensible to a large extent, unless various languages and pretexts are studied. Precisely because of this reason, a collaboration between Jewish, Yiddish and Slavonic Studies would without a doubt be significant and fruitful. It would show that the contact between the disciplines is not a mere addition, but rather a necessary synthesis reflecting the nature of its subject matter.

5 East European-Jewish Studies

The boundaries of East European national philological disciplines have recently been pushed and also blurred by the emergence of Jewish literatures on different continents, written in the language of their "host countries" – in English, German, Modern Hebrew or in French. A literary multiculturality emerges, that is still very different from the abovementioned 'classic' Jewish double-rootedness. It is a form of transculturality that entails a post-confessional and highly medialized approach of Judaism – the result of a family history of assimilation or a secondary return to Judaism through readings and geographical reorientation.[9] There can be no question of a Jewish diaspora here any longer. Israel is an exception: a country in which immigrants from East Europe learn Jewish traditions such as Mishnah, Hasidism or Kabbalah anew. Here, intellectuals, artists and writers more likely discover religious and cultural impulses for their creative ac-

---

[8] In my book (Smola 2019), I analize the specifics of Jewish poetics in the late Soviet and post-Soviet prose.
[9] Arian Wanner's monograph was one of the first major studies on this kind of heterolingual Jewish literature (cf. Wanner 2011).

tivities. In other diasporic constellations, however, the Jewish part is hardly recognizable as an ethnic-religious (primordial) culture in and by itself. In texts by such authors as Gary Steyngart, Lena Gorelik and Vladimir Vertlib, Judaism is rather reflected in contemplations on antisemitism and stereotypes; in confessing to the increased dissolution of belonging, and in the attempt to align individual post-memory with the institutionalized cultural memory. These developments, too, bring about new conditions and contexts for both research and teaching. Jewish literary studies thus entail at least three distinct cultural components in this case (that of the country of birth, that of the host country and the Jewish).

Jewish literature of the twentieth and twenty-first century is a multilingual phenomenon *par excellence*. It will be a real challenge for scholars of today and tomorrow to obtain insight into this complex multicultural field: Comparative studies of Jewish literatures in East Europe are to a large extent still a *terra incognita* and demand a strong interdisciplinary competence.

Bibliography

Goetschel, Willi, and Ato Quayson. "Introduction: Jewish Studies and Postcolonialism—ERRATUM." *The Cambridge Journal of Postcolonial Literary Inquiry*, vol. 3, no. 1 (2016): 165–165., doi:10.1017/pli.2015.35.

Grübel, Rainer. "Ein literarischer Messias aus Odessa. Isaak Babel's Kontrafakturen des Chassidismus und der odessitischer Kontext jüdisch-russischer Kultur." *Jüdische Autoren Ostmitteleuropas im 20. Jahrhundert.* Ed. Hans H. Hahn and Jens Stüben. Bern: Peter Lang D, 2002. 429–481.

Gruber, Ruth E. *Virtually Jewish. Reinventing Jewish Culture in Europe.* Berkeley: University of California Press, 2002.

Hesse, Isabelle. *The Politics of Jewishness in Contemporary World Literature. The Holocaust, Zionism and Colonialism.* London: Bloomsbury Academic, 2016.

Koschmal, Walter. "Kulturbeschreibung aus der Peripherie: Babel's Odessa-Poetik." *Mein Russland. Literarische Konzeptualisierungen und kulturelle Projektionen. Beiträge der gleichnamigen Tagung von 4.–6. März 1996 in München.* Ed. Aage A. Hansen-Löve. Bern: Peter Lang D, 1997. 311–336.

Kümper, Michal, Barbara Rösch, Ulrike Schneider, and Helen Thein: *Makom. Orte und Räume im Judentum – Real – Abstrakt – Imaginär. Essays.* Hildesheim, Zürich, New York: Georg Olms, 2007.

Lipphardt, Anna, Julia Brauch, and Alexandra Nocke. *Jewish Topographies. Visions of Space, Traditions of Place.* Aldershot: Ashgate Publishing, 2008.

Markish, Shimon. "Russko-evreiskaia literatura: predmet, podkhody, otsenki." *Novoe literaturnoe obozrenie* 15 (1995): 217–250.

Marszałek, Magdalena. "Anamnesen: Explorationen des Gedächtnisses in der gegenwärtigen polnischen Literatur und Kunst (eine intermediale Perspektive)." *Nach dem Vergessen.*

Rekurse auf den Holocaust in Ostmitteleuropa nach 1989. Ed. Magdalena Marszałek and Alina Molisak. Berlin: Kadmos, 2010. 161–171.

Miron, Dan. *Verschränkungen. Über jüdische Literaturen*. Göttingen: Vandenhoeck & Ruprecht, 2007.

Shrayer, Maxim D. "In Search of Jewish-Russian Literature: A Historical Overview." *Wiener Slawistischer Almanach* 61 (2008): 5–30.

Sicher, Efraim. *Babel' in Context. A Study in Cultural Identity*. Boston: Academic Studies Press, 2012.

Smola, Klavdia. *Wiedererfindung der Tradition: Russisch-jüdische Literatur der Gegenwart*. Wien, Köln, Weimar: Böhlau-Verlag, 2019.

Smola, Klavdia, and Olaf Terpitz. *Jüdische Räume und Topographien in Ost(mittel)europa. Konstruktionen in Literatur und Kultur*. Wiesbaden: Harrassowitz, 2015.

Wanner, Adrian. *Out of Russia: Fictions of a New Translingual Diaspora*. Evanston, IL: Northwestern University Press, 2011.

Wirth-Nesher, Hana. *What is Jewish Literature?* Philadelphia, Jerusalem: Jewish Publication Society, 1994.

Agnieszka Hudzik
Polish Jewish Literature: A Brief History, Theoretical Framework, and a Teaching Example

"There is no Polish history without the Jews, and there is no Jewish history without Poland." Such are the words of the prominent historian Jacob Goldberg, who was born in Łódź, survived the Buchenwald concentration camp, and immigrated to Israel in 1968, where he became a professor at the Hebrew University of Jerusalem. Since the Middle Ages, a shared past and historical experience has linked Polish and Jewish literatures inextricably, as manifested in its Polish denomination "literatura polsko-żydowska". This term denotes, I would argue, Jewish literatures (in the plural) written in Hebrew, Yiddish, and Polish in the territories of Poland, including, but not limited to, those landscapes historically Polish.

This article consists of two major parts and a teaching example: the first part briefly outlines the history of Polish Jewish literatures, while the second part discusses two essays by Władysław Panas (1947–2005), a leading Polish literary scholar whose essays *The Writing and the Wound: On Polish-Jewish Literature* (1987) and *The Eye of the Tzaddik* (1999) reflect the methodological complexity inherent in thinking about Polish Jewish literatures. Finally, I present an exemplary program of a seminar course I have developed for students of the Master's degree program in "East European Cultural Studies" at Potsdam University in winter term 2016/2017, most of whom do not know the source languages.

1 History, definitions, and fields of study

The long history of Polish Jews began with the rule of the Piast dynasty in the tenth century. It started with the arrival of the first Jews travelling along trade routes leading eastwards and intensified during the time of the crusades, which resulted in large waves of emigration by Jewish people banished from Western Europe.

A look into the medieval legend describing the arrival of Jewish emigrants in Poland underlines the special role that this country plays in Jewish thought and history more broadly. One of its versions can be found in the beginning of *Das Buch von den polnischen Juden* (The Book of the Polish Jews), edited by S. Y. Agnon and Ahron Eliasberg and co-authored by Martin Buber, among others.

This extraordinary work was printed in Berlin (Jüdischer Verlag) in 1916 during the First World War at a time when the Polish state had not existed for more than 120 years following the Partitions of Poland, which began in 1772 and divided the country between the Habsburg Empire, the Kingdom of Prussia, and the Russian Empire. It was written in German in the tradition of the genre called 'Heimatbuch' (books about homelands, their history and regional traditions) by two authors who did not speak Polish with the aim of introducing the Polish Jewry to a German speaking audience.

In the medieval legend that Agnon retells at the beginning of this book, we read about banished Jews travelling from Western Europe eastwards who suddenly received a sign: a piece of paper fell from heaven, and on it were the words *Gehet nach Polen*, go to Poland! (1916, 3). On their way, they discovered a forest where a tractate of the Talmud was carved into every tree. This was the Kawczyn (now Kawęczyn) forest that led to Lublin (4). They decided to stay there also because they ascribed a special etymology to the name of the country. Poland, in Hebrew *Polin*, consists of two words *po – lin*, which means: rest here for the night (4).

The nature of the land is described as predestined for the Jews and filled with spirit, scripture, and languages. We can trace here the urge to charge a physical space with symbolic meaning: messianism played an important role in the thought of eastern European Jewry, and Poland became an important place in Judaism.

The long-lasting experience of a common history and shared space is certainly reflected in literary texts. There are many historical and literary studies that systematize this material (for example Żurek 2008, Ben-Zvi 2011, Prokop-Janiec/Żurek 2011, Kołodziejska/Antosik-Piela 2017, 2018). In order to outline this vast area of study, several milestones in research will be briefly discussed in what follows.

The development of Jewish literature on the territory of the Polish–Lithuanian Commonwealth is associated with the Haskalah – the Jewish Enlightenment. During the time of the partitions of Poland, there were several leading thinkers writing in Hebrew who lived in Galicia or Podolia – including, among others, Menachem Mendel Lefin (1749–1826) and Josua Höschel Schorr (1818–1895), called the "Voltaire of Galicia." In this region, Hebrew was the dominant language of Jewish writings in the nineteenth century. Many Hebrew journals began to be published, including the weekly magazine *Hacefira* in Warsaw and the literary monthly *Ha-Boker Or* in Lwów, as well as an emerging body of Hebrew secular literature. At the same time, literary writing in Yiddish became more popular. This was mainly due to the limitations presented by Hebrew literature, which was read primarily by the intellectual elite. As a result, many writers began to produce works in Yiddish (for example Isaac Leib Peretz), and some others (such as Joseph Perl) who had previously written in Hebrew, also switched to their native language.

The first works written in Polish by Jews stem from the turn of the eighteenth century and are connected with the Frankists, a Jewish religious movement, centered on the leadership of the Jewish Messiah claimant Jacob Frank (1726–1791) (Maciejko 2011). The development of a tendency towards acculturation in Poland in the nineteenth century fostered the beginning of Jewish journalism and Jewish literatures in Polish. The heyday of Jewish Polish literature came in the interwar decades (1918–1939), when it became a distinct artistic and cultural phenomenon (Prokop-Janiec 2003, Molisak/Dąbrowski 2006). Its rise was influenced by the acculturation of Jewish communities and their linguistic Polonization. The high circulation of material published by Jewish presses in Polish contributed significantly to these processes. These presses published literary manifestos as well as discussions on the role of the Polish language in Jewish life, the nature of Polish Jewish literary works, and their place in the changing Jewish culture. Especially notable is the Trade Union of Jewish Writers and Journalists, which was founded in 1916, with its seat in Warsaw. It was also called the Union of Men of Letters (Yiddish: *Literatn Farajn*) and had an important voice in the literary society in Poland. Its members were men of letters who wrote in either Yiddish or Hebrew, as well as bilingual authors writing in Polish-Yiddish and Polish-Hebrew (Segałowicz 2001).

Polish Jewish literatures are the result of two cultures and of their merging into a new dynamic cultural sphere. Its complexity consists, according to Polish literary scholar Jacek Leociak, in "the consistent adoption of the stigma of the Jewish fate of exiles and entry in the space of the drama of existence torn, thrown, between (at least) two cultures and two languages. The decision to choose a language meets head on with the act of national self-identification" (Leociak 1995, 145). For some authors (such as Julian Tuwim or Antoni Słonimski), this was a decision to strongly identify with Polish cultural belonging and for others (such as Maurycy Szymel or Roman Brandstaetter), a decision to create Jewish literature in Polish. Both of these literary developments were part of a dynamic cultural process. For these writers, Polish was no longer an assimilation tool; it became a cultural medium that functioned as a bridge between two communities.

Polish Jewish literature has a heterogeneous character and is part of both multi-lingual Jewish writing and also Polish culture: literary works created by writers of Jewish belonging and addressed to a Polish audience are part of Polish national literature. In addition to the authors mentioned above, this circle includes, for example, Bolesław Leśmian, Bruno Jasieński, Jan Brzechwa, Jan Lechoń, Janusz Korczak, Tadeusz Peiper, Józef Wittlin, Julian Stryjkowski (Hutchens 2019), Adam Ważyk, Aleksander Wat, or the contemporary writer Henryk Grynberg (Polonsky/Adamczyk-Garbowska 2001). There were also many Polish Jewish female authors: inter alia Malwina Meyersonowa, Maria Blumberg, Lena Bandówna, Salomea Perl, Czesława Endelmanowa, and Aniela Korngutówna (Prokop-Janiec 2013, 140–141). Literary scholars underscore that nineteenth-century Polish Jewish prose was "largely a domain of women" (ibid.). The female writers mentioned above chose prose genres more often than female authors writing in Yiddish and Hebrew, who tended to prefer poetry. Anita Norich explains this phenomenon as a result of the strong male story-telling tradition that was characteristic of these languages (Norich 1992, 12). In the beginning of the twentieth century, several Polish Jewish female poets became visible on the literary scene, such as Anda Eker and Debora Vogel, the latter one wrote in Polish and Yiddish.

The field of study generally called Polish Jewish literature addresses the major issues in defining this body of literature. In the following, I would like to highlight some of the problems and challenges its researchers have to deal with.

The first step is defining appropriate categories as a preliminary condition for the study of the complex phenomenon under discussion. It is difficult to specify exactly what Polish Jewish literature is. Jewish literature is defined in general as a phenomenon created in many languages in the context of different cultures of individual countries (Adamczyk-Garbowska 2004). Multilingualism is also its determinant in Poland (Prokop-Janiec 2002). Literary texts are written in Hebrew, Polish, and Yiddish, but also in Karaim, as is the case, for example, of the by Aleksander Mardkowicz.[1] The criterion for ethnical belonging attributed to their authors is not always sufficient: scholars are often guided by thematic or biographical determinants, often referring to autobiographical sources – the statements of the writers about themselves (Molisak/Kołodziejska 2011).

Secondly, and as a consequence of the preceding assumption, problems arise concerning translation and reception. The point is that such diverse criteria also allow for the inclusion of translations in the textual corpus of Polish Jewish literature: these demonstrate a literary exchange between Poles and Jews. However, we are dealing here with a certain asymmetry that gives rise to separate studies. Within Poland, non-Jewish Polish writers of the Romantic or Positivist periods were interested in Jewish topics and placed Jewish protagonists in their texts as subjects of description, even as there were very few translations into Polish of works by actual Jewish authors writing in other languages. This

---

[1] See Karaim Digital Archive https://jazyszlar.karaimi.org/ (1. August 2019).

means that while there was an interest in topics concerning Jewish themes among Polish authors (essentially a question of representation), texts by authors of Jewish belonging written in other languages were only rarely being translated into Polish and thus were not being read (a question of distribution, access, and impact). Inside and outside of Poland, Jewish writers translated many works of Polish literature into other languages (Löw 2000). For example, the political text *The Books of the Polish People and of the Polish Pilgrimage* (1832) by Polish national Romantic poet Adam Mickiewicz was translated into Hebrew immediately after it was published. Therefore, the phenomenon of Polish Jewish literature has to be extended to include the often asymmetrical aspect of translation and reception between multiple languages.

Thirdly, when studying Polish Jewish literature, we also have to focus on the metaphorical phenomenon, termed today as the forgotten continent: Polish Jewish literature should also be thought of in terms of its broader comparative context. Jewish communities played a key role in neighboring countries outside of Poland. Small towns with large Jewish populations called *shtetls* were located mainly in Poland, but also in Lithuania, Belarus, Ukraine, Slovakia, the Czech Republic, Romania, and Hungary. It was almost as if these lands formed another continent that completely vanished during the Second World War – a borderland between East and West, an eastern province of Europe that shaped a similar or comparable literary experience that reverberated in literatures of different languages.

Fourthly, there is the challenge of the geographical spaces where the literature in question was created: Polish Jewish literature does not necessarily have to be written in Poland or in the territories that historically belonged to it. For a long time, between 1795 and 1918, Poland did not exist as an independent state. Numerous Jewish authors migrated during that time, and especially after the Second World War, and later after March events in 1968. Among those who survived, some writers began to publish all over the world: in France, Israel, in the U.S. or in Latin America. For example, one of the most important places of Polish Jewish culture was Buenos Aires, where, for example, Mark Turkow, a famous actor of the Yiddish theatre and cinema in Warsaw in the 1920s, edited a book series *Dos pojlische jidntum* (The Polish Jewry). Between 1946 and 1966, he published over 175 books; this would not have been possible in communist Poland where the Polish Jewish past had been silenced and repressed for decades. Thus, when reflecting on Polish Jewish literature, we have to acknowledge a diversity of languages, literary genres, and places of writing and publishing – and, of course, the incredible void after 1945. Therefore, our research field should also include the literary and artistic narratives operating between different cultures and imaginaries that search for a new language to express this emptiness.

2 Research: the case of Władysław Panas

The best-known platform for the exchange of ideas in studies on Polish Jewry is the *POLIN* journal that has been published since 1986 under the general editorship of Professor Antony Polonsky of Brandeis University. Its establishment coincides with a certain general tendency: the trilingual Jewish culture of Poland was largely ignored until after the end of communism. One of the recent volumes (28/2016, eds. Adamczyk-Garbowska, Prokop-Janiec, Polonsky, Żurek) is devoted to Jewish writing in Poland. It is fitting that the more than five-hundred-page volume opens with Władysław Panas's essay *The Writing and the Wound* first published in 1987.

A well-known literary scholar and professor of the Catholic University of Lublin, Panas was one of the pioneers of research on Polish Jewish literature, authoring books on semiotics, modernist poetry and prose, and Jewish motifs in Polish literature, with a special focus on Bruno Schulz. His monograph *Księga Blasku: Traktat o kabale w prozie Brunona Schulza* (The Book of the Splendor: The Treatise about the Kabbalah in the Prose of Bruno Schulz, 1997) deals with the traces of Jewish mystical thought, especially of the Lurianic Kabbalah, in Schulz's writings and was seen as a breakthrough for *Schulzology*. Incidentally, the topic of Schulz, Judaism, and Jewish mysticism is intensely studied, even though Schulz never explicitly thematized Jewish issues. For example, synagogues are never mentioned in his short stories, but there are some allusions to more general Jewish imagery, traditions, and motifs. Recently, a little 'discovery' has electrified Schulz-specialists all over the world: a forgotten essay by Schulz for a newspaper in 1937 on the illustrator and printmaker Ephraim Moses Lilien has been found and reprinted. Reflecting on his own works in this essay, Schulz wrote about Lilien as a Jewish artist and used the word Zionism for the first time (Schulz 2015).

Panas's essay *The Writing and the Wound* tries to define Polish Jewish literature by beginning with the Polish word for the graphic sign known as a 'hyphen': *literatura polsko-żydowska*. He makes a phenomenological and deconstructivist interpretation of this sign, which is written but cannot be heard while speaking – it unites and separates at once. This ambivalence of presence and absence symbolizes for him the voiceless trace of the wound and opens "a field of archetypical, essential gestures and meanings which dramatically pose the problem of Identity and Difference, of the Same One and the Other, the Whole and the Part" (18).

Panas states that in the 1930s in Polish literature we can observe the birth or "a full literary articulation of Jewish subjectivity" (22). For a long period, Jewish protagonists could appear in literary discourse, for example in Julian Ursyn Niemcewicz's novel *Lejbe and Siora* (1821). There were some Polish authors of Jewish descent like Julian Klaczko or Wilhelm Feldman who wrote explicitly about Jewish issues, but in accordance with the dominant style of Polish literature – from the perspective of a Jew as an object described from outside. According to Panas, the situation changed in 1931 with the publication of Maurycy Szymel's poetic debut *Powrót do domu* (*Coming Back Home*, see Szymel 2013). Panas emphasizes that the Jewish lyrical subject speaks to its readers for the first time as a Jew in Szymel's poems; Panas further sees in this Jewish speaking subject an archetype of the figure of the Other and Otherness, a symbol of some elemental experiences that could be split between the categories of "Ours and the Alien, the Native and the Foreigner, Sameness and Otherness, Identity and Difference" (22).

Panas distinguishes among various ways that Polish Jewish poetry expresses this difference that repeatedly proves to be an open wound in the writers' poetical belonging. The first tendency is that a Jewish lyrical speaker appears as the Other. To illustrate this, he quotes a line from a poem by Maurycy Schlanger, where he refers to himself as "a Polish poet, in Hebrew mute" (23). In this case, Jewish lyrical speakers describe a situation of exile, perceiving themselves as orphans or abandoned persons whose place is elsewhere. In such imagery, we encounter many dichotomies such as "here/there" or "Polish/Hebrew" or even elegies about the Hebrew language. Jewish lyrical speakers increase their speechlessness by speaking in Polish and express their longing for an absent world that cannot be reached. Such lyrical utterances reveal the complex belonging of these subjects as a wound that can be healed only by writing and script. Panas finds this mode of expression in the poetry of Maurycy Schlanger and Maurycy Szymel. The second tendency distinguished by Panas can be summarized with a verse by Włodzimierz Słobodnik: "I'm a son of Masovia, a grandson of ancient Judea" (25). The Jewish lyrical speaker understood as the Other wants to proclaim its otherness, but from the inside and as part of a bigger community.

The editors of the above mentioned POLIN volume observe in the introduction that Panas presents "the concept of Polish Jewish literature as a separate world (*obieg*) and offers a reading which treats as its basic distinguishing characteristic the attempt to record the experience of Jewish otherness / difference / estrangement" (10). According to Panas, Polish Jewish literature has to be understood "as a means of communication between Polish-speaking Jews. The key role in its functioning is played by its Polish Jewish readers" (10), the majority of whom disappeared after the Holocaust. Therefore, in Panas's understanding, Polish Jewish literature is limited to the interwar years and connected with some poets, prose writers, essayists, translators, and critics, as well as titles of newspapers and magazines from this period (19–20).

In the context of Polish Jewish literature, the most interesting aspects are the case studies of particular writers and the question of how they imagine their belonging. Reflecting on this complex matter, Panas shows that the accompanying literary discourse should deal with ethics and politics, especially regarding relationships among strangers who live close by but nevertheless remain unintelligible to one another. Consequently, the language he uses to grasp these very fragile phenomena is inspired by the philosophy of Edmond Jabès, Emmanuel Levinas, and Jacques Derrida.

Panas extends this thought in his other essay *The Eye of the Tzaddik* (1999), where he demonstrates the process of creating a myth, a mythology of a place that was left empty and forgotten after the Holocaust – the Jewish district in Lublin, a town in the eastern part of Poland. Instead of repeating familiar historical patterns, Panas chooses a widely unknown figure and thoroughly and patiently develops a story of Lublin Hasid Jacob Isaac Horowitz also known as "the Seer of Lublin" (1745–1815), who was largely responsible for putting the city on the map of the Hasidic movement. Panas's essay can be read as a Kaddish for the destroyed Jewish district, its inhabitants, and their literature. He looks for the place where the house of the tzaddik could have stood and tries to reconstruct it according to symbolic traces found in maps, poems, and artifacts such as a matzevah. Panas reads them as self-referential cultural texts that can be projected into this space and are also able to shape and arrange it so that the space is no longer a subject of description but a form in the process of eternal becoming.

The essay, however, can also be read as a text neither about the tzaddik nor about Lublin. History and geography are rather literary constructions that the essay ironically plays with. The tzaddik and the city have only an exemplary function in the essay, providing an impulse to introduce broader topics on how to reflect and write about the Polish Jewish past. The essay consists of ten parts, named after the letters of the Hebrew alphabet, from Aleph to Jod, but the allusions to Jewish mysticism are not the only field of reference for Panas. Placing the essay in the context of urban and memory studies as well as the theory and criticism of humanities in the sense of the German term *Wissenschaftstheorie und -kritik* can shed new light on it and explain the diversity of theories and disciplines that Panas combines. He uses categories from various research fields including semiotics, hermeneutics, geopoetics, philosophy of history, and phenomenology. Implicit and explicit references to the writings by Martin Buber, Mircea Eliade, Carl Gustav Jung, Maurice Halbwachs, Emmanuel Levinas, Yuri Lotman, Maurice Merleau-Ponty, Pierre Nora, and Gershom Scholem appear throughout Panas's essay.

The Eye of the Tzaddik teems with intertextual allusions and can also be read as a literary piece: it resembles, for example, the short stories by Jorge Luis Borges. The intertextuality and metafictionality, autothematism and meta-commentaries, the interruption of narrative linearity initiated by the division of the essay according to the Hebrew alphabet, and the questioning of logical-rational reasoning constitute the special poetics of the text. Panas emphasizes how academic language and the language of theory is embedded in various discourses (religious, literary, philosophical, public) and points out that there is no axiologically 'neutral' way to reflect on historical facts. Therefore, he creates a complex narrative in which several languages from different registers flow together: poems, city maps, Hasidic stories, philosophical treatises, inscriptions on the matzevah, etc. Thus, the essay gets very close to the object of its description.

Panas seems to agree with Derrida that any language about a phenomenon "cannot be excluded from its object" (Derrida 1982, 90) and that the culture and text analysis requires the use of "the parodying heterogeneity of the style, the styles" (Derrida 1979, 99). It is only thanks to this diversity that the text avoids the reduction of the described phenomenon to an object of unambiguous definitions; leaves space free for undecidability and further interpretations; and distances itself from the hermeneutic project "which postulates a true sense of the text" (Derrida 1979, 107). The radical anarchy and heterogeneity of Panas's text, according to his writing style and methodology, can be understood as an ironic play with conventions and a theoretical proposal on how to reflect Polish Jewish history and literature.

The awareness in the essay of the relativity and constructability of history and its negotiable character go hand in hand with an emphasis on the power of storytelling. This is why Panas mentions the Hasidic story that he quotes after Scholem (Scholem 1993, 384), who in turn tells it after Agnon. The tale is about the Hasidim worrying how to face difficult tasks if their Master is gone and they do not have access to some parts of the ritual:

> "We can no longer light the fire, nor do we know the right prayer; we even don't know where the place in the forest is located, but we can always tell the story about how everything happened." And the *tzaddik*'s tale was just as effective as the deeds of those who came before him. (Panas 2015, 70).

A quotation in a quotation – a story in a story that says that when all is lost, the narrative about absence can work wonders. Again, a self-referential moment in the essay emphasizes that a narrative always postulates participation and interaction. The essay is not a closed product; the narrative functions only by retelling. Panas proposes a different view on the theory, which can be understood as a challenge to reality, as participation, taking action and intervening in the world inseparably connected with it or constituting its symbolic universes as well as a performative answer to it/them. This means a different approach to acting, located somewhere between theory and practice, underlying the immersion of the writer and researcher in the world or topic of research, and the readiness on both sides to transform each other.

This is an exemplary approach which shows how writing about Polish Jewish literature requires and fosters the invention of an extraordinary theoretical and self-critical language capable of reaching and grasping the complexity of this phenomenon. It would have to be creative and heterogeneous, engaging different conceptual frameworks that belong not only to literary theory, but also other disciplines in the humanities. Panas consistently crosses disciplinary borders and seeks new sources of inspiration in philosophy, aesthetics, cultural studies, theology, and Jewish mysticism. Transforming his programmatic principle into teaching, one could imagine including a variety of texts on the reading list: a diverse combination of primary and secondary literature, different genres from different epochs that on the one hand illustrate some of the challenges of teaching and thinking about Polish Jewish literature and, on the other hand, develop the student's theoretical capacities.

3 A teaching example

A syllabus for a seminar in Polish Jewish literatures has to offer a broad array of appropriate texts. In choosing the texts for my seminars, I emphasize the multilingual and multicultural dimensions of this literary phenomenon. A comparative perspective necessarily includes diverse literary genres and styles, as well as texts from different periods. Although the diachronic juxtaposition of oeuvres requires extra time to contextualize them, I see it as an opportunity to review key concepts of the history of literature and literary theory. I also tend to focus on a specific geographical context – on Lublin and the Lublin region, i.e. on texts that were written in or about this area. The aim here is to stress that Polish Jewish literatures should be associated with the area where they were produced rather than attributed to one language. This also enables me to introduce theoretical categories such as the spatial turn and geopoetics and to point to a region that is not as strongly present in literary and cultural studies as, for example, Bukovina, Galicia (Galizien), and the Hutsul region (Hutsulshchina).

The title of the seminar I taught in the winter term 2016/2017 at Potsdam University was: *Literary Topographies and Cultural Entanglements: The City of Lublin and the Lublin Area in Jewish and Non-Jewish Literatures*. The uniqueness of the region consists of the fact that the city was a melting pot – a cultural space that cannot be mapped in terms of nation states because it was historically multi-ethnic and multicultural, strongly influenced by its Jewish population. The area became prominent thanks to the works of Isaac Bashevis Singer, the 1978 Nobel Prize winner, the first and to date only Yiddish writer to receive this honor. In his novel *The Magician of Lublin*, the town of Lublin became the symbol of the lost pre-World War II world of Polish Jews. The global audience has also had the opportunity to get to know this region through Martin Buber's *Tales of the Hasidim*.

In class, we analyzed literary texts written before and after the Holocaust that depict the cultural and historical contexts of the region. We focused on aspects such as the Hasidic tradition of storytelling and its echoes in modern times; the literary avant-garde and the historical experiences of Eastern Europe; and representations of the Holocaust in poetry and prose.

We began the seminar with stories about the Jewish town of Lublin. We compared the reportage of his journey in Poland in the 1920s by German novelist Alfred Döblin (2016, 147–168) with two historical narratives: excerpts from *Die Judenstadt von Lublin* (1919), a monograph about this district which was written in German, published in Berlin, and authored by Majer Bałaban (often regarded as the founder of contemporary Jewish historiography in Poland); and a chapter from *Jewish Lublin: A Cultural Monograph* (2009) by contemporary Mexican scholar Adina Cimet (2009). We debated on how the narrator in Döblin's text – an assimilated, well-educated Jewish writer from the German metropolis – perceived Lublin and how he represented it. We compared the narrative perspective of his travel report with the metaphoric language used by historians to describe relationships between the Polish and Jewish parts of the town.

The next part of the seminar program was a discussion of the figure of the abovementioned Hasid Jacob Isaac Horowitz, the Seer of Lublin – a rabbi, tzaddik, and leader of the early Hasidic movement who lived in the Jewish district of the town in the late eighteenth and early nineteenth centuries. He is not only a historical but also a literary figure: there is much hagiographic literature in Yiddish about tzaddik Horowitz in addition to tales and legends about the miracles he performed.[2] He is also present in the stories by Martin Buber (1957, 7–10) and Jiří Langer (1976, 179–198).

---

[2] The collection of hagiographic texts about the Seer of Lublin was translated into Polish and published as *Księga cudów Widzącego* (Doktór et al. 2015).

In our course, the Seer of Lublin functioned as a bridge – a transition to the subject of Hasidism and the Hasidic tradition of storytelling in modern literature. Several classes were devoted to the works of Yiddish writers of different generations such as Isaac Leib Peretz and Isaac Bashevis Singer. Both are associated with this region and its *shtetls:* Peretz was born in Zamość, while Singer was connected with Biłgoraj through his mother's family (see Adamczyk-Garbowska/ Wróblewski 2005). The Lublin region was often an inspiration for Singer's works – not only Lublin itself, which is explicitly present in his two novels *Satan in Goray* (1935) and *The Magician of Lublin* (1960), but also the nearby cities of Chełm and Biała Podlaska, which appear in *The Fools of Chelm and Their History* (1973) and *The Family Moskat* (1950), respectively. We analyzed the representation of time and space in selected short stories by both authors and discussed common points among their styles, supplementing our knowledge by studying secondary literature on the topic (e.g. Roskies/Roskies 1975, Roskies 1995, Ronen/Molisak 2017).

An examination of Singer's works directed our attention to another Nobel Prize laureate: S. Y. Agnon, who in 1966 became the first Hebrew-speaking winner of this award. Although the plot of his posthumously published novel *In Mr. Lublin's Store* (1974) is set in Leipzig during the First World War, it nevertheless registers the significance of the subject of Polish Jewish migration.

After this, we turned to poetry: on the basis of selected poems by Arnold Słucki, we studied how the lyrical speaker addresses the theme of Polish Jewish belonging. Słucki, born in 1920 as Aron Kreiner in the town of Tyszowce in the province of Lublin, began his poetic career in Yiddish. After the war, he switched to Polish. After the anti-Semitic violence unleashed by the Polish government in 1968, he left Poland and died in West Berlin in 1972. After his death, the first extensive anthology in Polish edited by him, containing translations from Yiddish, including his own, was posthumously published under the title *Antologia poezji żydowskiej* (*Anthology of Jewish Poetry*). When analyzing the poems, we focused the motifs of dilemma, of seeking poetic language, and the loss of the world of *shtetls* and one's roots.

The theme of loss was also present when we discussed the poems by another poet, Józef Czechowicz, an important representative of the Polish poetic avant-garde in the interwar period. He was born in Lublin where he also died a tragic death during an air raid in the first days of the Second World War. He devoted many texts to his hometown, such as a volume of verse *Stare kamienie* (*Old Stones*) and the "Poemat o mieście Lublinie" ("A Poem About Lublin"), which is also available in English translation (2008, 5–18). Czechowicz is often termed a catastrophic poet – the feelings of a coming tragedy, uncertainty, and anxiety are strongly present in his poems. Some of them have been recently reedited by Iwona Chmielewska in form of a picture book that develops its own intermedial poetics of the loss (2016).

When we dealt with the Holocaust, we focused on Majdanek, a concentration camp named after the Lublin district of Majdan Tatarski. We used earlier testimonies about the camp: a piece of reportage by a camp survivor, Mordechai Strigler, writer and journalist writing in Yiddish (1947, German translation 2016), and compared it to the report of the Polish-Soviet "Extraordinary Commission to Investigate German Crimes Committed in the Majdanek Extermination Camp in Lublin" (Moscow 1944). We considered the differences in literary means and tropes, stylistic figures, and narrative constructions that exist among reportage, nonfiction, and testimony.

We discussed literary representations of the Holocaust both in poetry and in prose. We read the poems by Jacob Glatstein, a Yiddish-writing poet living in Lublin, who immigrated to New York in 1914. In his works, Lublin became a symbol of the destruction of the pre-war world of Polish Jews. We also discussed prose writings by Anna Langfus, Lublin-born writer. During the war, she stayed in the Lublin Ghetto; after the war, she settled in France, where she began her writing career in French. Her novels, such as *Le Sel et le Soufre* (1960, English translation *The Whole Land Brimstone*) and the prestigious Prix Goncourt-awarded *Les Bagages de sable* (1962, *The Lost Shore*), are some of the first to represent the Holocaust from the perspective of a woman's experience. To highlight Langfus's laconic and matter-of-fact style, we compared her texts with excerpts from the famous novel *La Disparition* (1969, *A Void*) by Georges Perec – French essayist, writer, and filmmaker, whose father and grandparents came from Lubartów near Lublin and who was born in Paris in 1936 after his family emigrated to France in the 1920s. We ended the seminar with a reflection on literature written after the Holocaust and on the phenomenon of postmemory. We also included non-Jewish writings dedicated to the memory of perpetrators. In this context, we analyzed Jonathan Littell's controversial bestseller *Les Bienveillantes* (2006, *The Kindly Ones*). More than one hundred pages of this novel – written from the perspective of an SS officer, a mass murder recounting his unscrupulous crimes – take place in Lublin and its surroundings.

As the language competencies varied within the student group, we relied mainly on translations, which was a separate subject we tried to critically discuss by referring to theories of translation. The reading list was compiled so as to make all literary texts available in English and/or German translations, with the originals available to those interested. Although the city of Lublin and its surroundings served only as a case study for becoming acquainted with broader issues of Polish Jewish literature, it was very important that the students should not only view these specific localities as literary fictions, but also have the opportunity to physically experience them. Thanks to the support provided by the German Academic Exchange Service (DAAD), I was able to organize a study visit to Lublin for the students.

I complemented the extensive collection of texts with multimedia presentations. The students were encouraged to study individually with material available on the Internet. Appended below is a list of several links to databases on Polish Jewish literature, which turned out to be useful in teaching:

- The "Grodzka Gate – NN Theatre" Centre and its Digital Library: http://teatrnn.pl/en/
- Project *Shtetl Routes* – A Travel through the Forgotten Continent by Shtetl Routes of the Polish, Belorussian and Ukrainian Borderland: http://shtetlroutes.eu/en/
- The Jewish Historical Institute in Warsaw and its library: http://www.jhi.pl/en/zasoby; https://cbj.jhi.pl/
- POLIN Museum of the History of Polish Jews: https://www.polin.pl/en/research-and-publications
- Journal *Polin: Studies in Polish Jewry*: https://www.liverpooluniversitypress.co.uk/series/series-12813/
- Encyclopedia Judaica: Polish Literature: https://www.jewishvirtuallibrary.org/polish-literature
- The YIVO Encyclopedia of Jews in Eastern Europe: http://www.yivoencyclopedia.org/article.aspx/Polish_Literature
- Collection of digitalized books in Yiddish: https://polona.pl/collections/institutions/1/literatura-jidysz,NDIOODQ1MDAyNzc3NDcyMzY2MA/?sort=score%20desc

The focus on geopoetics, on geographical territory as a binding point for heterogeneous texts, has proven productive in developing courses on Polish Jewish literatures. My wishes and expectations with regard to teaching in this field is to demonstrate that our object of study is a multilingual and multicultural phenomenon with a long history and continuity up to and including the present moment.

Bibliography

Adamczyk-Garbowska, Monika. *Odcienie tożsamości: literature żydowska jako zjawisko wielojęzyczne*. Lublin: UMCS, 2004.

Adamczyk-Garbowska, Monika and Bogusław Wróblewski (eds.). *Biłgoraj czyli Raj: rodzina Singerów i świat, którego już nie ma*. Lublin: UMCS, 2005.

Adamczyk-Garbowska, Monika and Eugenia Prokop-Janiec. "Introduction." *Polin: Studies in Polish Jewry* 28 (2016). Eds. Monika Adamczyk-Garbowska, Eugenia Prokop-Janiec, Antony Polonsky, Sławomir Jacek Żurek. 1–14.
Agnon, Shmuel Yosef. *In Mr. Lublin's Store*. Trans. Glenda Abramson. New York: Toby Press LLC, 2016.
Agnon, Shmuel Yosef and Ahron Eliasberg (eds.). *Das Buch von den polnischen Juden*. Berlin: Jüdischer Verlag, 1916. https://sammlungen.ub.uni-frankfurt.de/freimann/content/titleinfo/4666820 (1 August 2019).
Bałaban, Majer. *Die Judenstadt von Lublin*. Berlin: Jüdischer Verlag, 1919. https://sammlungen.ub.uni-frankfurt.de/freimann/content/search/729867?query=balaban (1 August 2019).
Ben-Zvi, Hava (ed.). *Portraits in Literature: The Jews of Poland. An Anthology*. London, Portland: Vallentine Mitchell, 2011.
Buber, Martin. *Gog und Magog: eine Chronik*. Frankfurt am Main: Fischer, 1957.
Cimet, Adina. *Jewish Lublin. A Cultural Monograph*. Lublin: UMCS, 2009.
Czechowicz, Józef (poems), Iwona Chmielewska (illustrations), and Abram Zylberberg (photographies). *Dopóki niebo nie płacze*. Lublin: "Ośrodek Brama Grodzka –Teatr NN," 2016.
Czechowicz, Józef. *A Poem about Lublin*. Trans. Małgorzata Sady and George Hyde, Lublin: "Ośrodek Brama Grodzka – Teatr NN", 2008. http://pretekstyliterackie.art.pl/historia/czechowicz%20angielski.pdf (1 August 2019).
Derrida, Jacques. "Of an Apocalyptic Tone Recently Adopted in Philosophy." Trans. John P. Leavey Jr. *Semeia* 23 (1982): 63–97.
Derrida, Jacques. *Spurs: Nietzsche's Styles*. Trans. Barbara Harlow. Chicago and London: University of Chicago Press, 1979.
Döblin, Alfred. *Reise in Polen*. Ed. Marion Brandt. Frankfurt am Main: Fischer, 2016.
Doktór, Jan, Agnieszka Żółkiewska, and Nirit Neeman (eds.). *Księga cudów Widzącego*. Trans. Agnieszka Żółkiewska. Lublin: Ośrodek "Brama Grodzka – Teatr NN," 2015.
Glatstein, Jakob. *I Keep Recalling: The Holocaust Poems of Jacob Glatstein*. Trans. Barnett Zumoff. Hoboken and New York: Ktav Publ. House, 1992.
Grözinger, Elvira. "Das verlorene Paradies. Zu Arnold Słuckis Dichtung." *Suche die Meinung. Karl Dedecius, dem Übersetzer und Mittler zum 65. Geburtstag*. Eds. Elvira Grözinger and Andreas Lawaty. Wiesbaden: Harrassowitz, 1986. 320–339.
Hutchens, Jack J. B. "Julian Stryjkowski: Polish, Jewish, queer." *Canadian Slavonic Papers / Revue Canadienne des Slavistes* 61.1 (2019): 57–80.
Kołodziejska, Zuzanna and Maria Antosik-Piela (eds.). *Literatura polsko-żydowska 1861–1918: studia i szkice*. Kraków: Wyd. UJ, 2018.
Kołodziejska, Zuzanna and Maria Antosik-Piela (eds.). *Literatura polsko-żydowska 1861–1918: antologia*. Kraków: Wyd. UJ, 2017.
Langer, Jiří. *Nine Gates to the Chassidic Mysteries*. Trans. Stephen Jolly. New York: Behrman House, 1976.
Langfus, Anna. *The Lost Shore*. Trans. Peter Wiles. New York: Pantheon Books, 1964.
Langfus, Anna. *The Whole Land Brimstone*. Trans. Peter Wiles. New York: Pantheon Books, 1962.
Leociak, Jacek. "Recenzja (Eugenia Prokop-Janiec, Józef Wróbel, Natan Gross)" *Pamiętnik Literacki* 3. 86 (1995): 144–153.

Littell, Jonathan. *The Kindly Ones*. Trans. Charlotte Mandell. New York: Harper, 2009.
Löw, Ryszard. "Literatura polska w przekładach hebrajskich" *Archiwum Emigracji: Studia, Szkice, Dokumenty* 3 (2000): 93–101.
Maciejko, Paweł. *The Mixed Multitude: Jacob Frank and the Frankist Movement, 1755–1816*. Philadelphia, PA: University of Pennsylvania Press, 2011.
Molisak, Alina and Mieczysław Dąbrowski (eds.). *Pisarze polsko-żydowscy XX wieku: przybliżenia*. Warszawa: Elipsa, 2006.
Molisak, Alina and Shoshana Ronen (eds.). *The Trilingual Literature of Polish Jews from Different Perspectives*. Cambridge: Cambridge Scholars Publishing, 2017.
Molisak, Alina and Zuzanna Kołodziejska (eds.). *Żydowski Polak, polski Żyd: problem tożsamości w literaturze polsko-żydowskiej*. Warszawa: Elipsa, 2011.
Norich, Anita. "Jewish Literatures and Feminist Criticism: An Introduction to Gender and Text." *Gender and Text in Modern Hebrew and Yiddish Literatures*. Eds. Naomi B. Sokoloff, Anne Lapidus Lerner, and Anita Norich. New York: Jewish Theological Seminary of America, distributed by Harvard University Press, 1992.
Panas, Władysław. "The Writing and the Wound: On Polish-Jewish Literature." Trans. Christopher Garbowski. *Polin: Studies in Polish Jewry* 28 (2016). Eds. Monika Adamczyk-Garbowska, Eugenia Prokop-Janiec, Antony Polonsky, Sławomir Jacek Żurek. 17–29.
Panas, Władysław. *Oko cadyka. The Eye of the Tzaddik*. Trans. Marcin Garbowski. Lublin: Warsztaty Kultury, 2015.
Panas, Władysław. *Pismo i rana: szkice o problematyce żydowskiej w literaturze polskiej*. Lublin: Dabar, 1996.
Perec, Georges. *A Void*. Trans. Gilbert Adair. Boston: D.R. Godine, 2005.
Polonsky, Antony and Monika Adamczyk-Garbowska (eds.). *Contemporary Jewish Writing in Poland: An Anthology*. Lincoln: University of Nebraska Press, 2001.
Prokop-Janiec, Eugenia, and Sławomir Jacek Żurek (eds.). *Literatura polsko-żydowska – studia i szkice*. Kraków: Księgarnia Akademicka, 2011.
Prokop-Janiec, Eugenia. *Living in Languages: Jewish Multilingualism as Reflected in the Polish and Polish-Jewish Literature of the 20th Century*. Kraków: Księgarnia Akademicka, 2002.
Prokop-Janiec, Eugenia. *Polish-Jewish Literature in the Interwar Years*. Trans. Abe Shenitzer. Syracuse, NY: Syracuse University Press, 2003.
Prokop-Janiec, Eugenia. *Pogranicze polsko-żydowskie. Topografie i teksty*. Kraków: Wydawnictwo UJ, 2013.
Roskies, David G. *A Bridge of Longing: The Lost Art of Yiddish Storytelling*. Cambridge, MA: Harvard University Press, 1995.
Roskies, Diane K. and David G. Roskies. *The Shtetl Book: An Introduction To East European Jewish Life And Lore*. New York: Ktav Publishing House, 1975.
Scholem, Gershom. *Die jüdische Mystik in ihren Hauptströmungen*. Frankfurt am Main: Suhrkamp, 1993.
Schulz, Bruno. "E. M. Lilien." *Schulz/Forum* 6 (2015): 82–96. https://terytoria.com.pl/modules/nxproduct/images/1101/fragment-schulz-forum-6-strony_1496392929.pdf (1 August 2019).

Segałowicz, Zusman. *Tłomackie 13: (z unicestwionej przeszłości): wspomnienia o Żydowskim Związku Literatów i Dziennikarzy w Polsce (1919–1939)*. Trans. Michał Friedman. Warszawa: Wydawnictwo Dolnośląskie, 2001.

Strigler, Mordecai. *Majdanek: verloschene Lichte. Ein früher Zeitzeugenbericht vom Todeslager*. Trans. Sigrid Beisel. Springe: zu Klampen, 2016.

Szymel, Maurycy (Mosze). *The Shy Hand of a Jew*. Trans. Aniela and Jerzy Gegorek. Merrick, NY: Cross-Cultural Communications, 2013.

Żurek, Sławomir Jacek. "As One Kabbalist to Another... On Arnold Słucki's Mystical Visions in the Poem 'Bruno Schulz'." *(Un)masking Bruno Schulz: New Combinations, Further Fragmentations, Ultimate Reintegrations*. Eds. Dieter de Bruyn and Kris Van Heuckelom. Amsterdam: Rodopi, 2009. 67–82.

Żurek, Sławomir Jacek. *From the Borderland: Essays on Polish-Jewish Literature*. Trans. Thomas Anessi. Lublin: KUL, 2008.

www.ingramcontent.com/pod-product-compliance
Lightning Source LLC
Chambersburg PA
CBHW020608300426
44113CB00007B/554